LUKE

HISTORIAN & THEOLOGIAN

I. Howard Marshall

InterVarsity Press
Downers Grove, Illinois

39033499

InterVarsity Press
P.O. Box 1400, Downers Grove, IL 60515
World Wide Web: www.ivpress.com
E-mail: mail@ivpress.com

©*1970 The Paternoster Press*
Paperback edition 1979. Third edition 1988.

Published in the United States of America by InterVarsity Press, Downers Grove, Illinois, with permission from Paternoster Publishing, Carlisle, U.K.

InterVarsity Press® *is the book-publishing division of InterVarsity Christian Fellowship/USA*®*, a student movement active on campus at hundreds of universities, colleges and schools of nursing in the United States of America, and a member movement of the International Fellowship of Evangelical Students. For information about local and regional activities, write Public Relations Dept., InterVarsity Christian Fellowship/USA, 6400 Schroeder Rd., P.O. Box 7895, Madison, WI 53707-7895.*

Cover illustration: Roberta Polfus
ISBN 0-8308-1513-9

Printed in the United States of America ∞

Library of Congress Cataloging-in-Publication Data

Marshall, I. Howard.
  Luke: historian & theologian/I. Howard Marshall.
    p.   cm.—(New Testament profiles)
  Originally published: Exeter: Paternoster Press, 1970.
  Includes bibliographical references and index.
  ISBN 0-8308-1513-9 (pbk.: alk. paper)
  1. Bible. N.T. Luke—Theology. 2. Bible. N.T. Acts—Theology.
3. Bible. N.T. Luke—History of Biblical events. 4. Bible. N.T.
Acts—History of Biblical events. 5. Bible. N.T. Luke—History of
contemporary events. 6. Bible. N.T. Acts—History of contemporary
events. 7. Salvation—Biblical teaching. I. Title. II. Series.
BS2589.M37   1998
226.4'06—dc21
                                    98-23480
                                         CIP

21	20	19	18	17	16	15	14	13	12	11	10	9	8	7	6	5	4	3	2	1
15	14	13	12	11	10	09	08	07	06	05	04	03	02	01	00	99	98			

TO JOYCE

CONTENTS

FOREWORD

Contemporary study of the Gospels is very much interested in the theology of the four Evangelists and attempts to express as clearly as possible the distinctive message of each Gospel. The purpose of the present book is to examine the writings of Luke – both his Gospel and the Acts of the Apostles – from this point of view. It has three main suggestions to make.

The first is that Luke's theology is closely related to that of his sources. One of the dangers of recent study of the Gospels is that it tends to accentuate the differences between the Evangelists and their sources. Luke's work, however, represents a development of ideas already present in the traditions which he used. Luke, it may be claimed, was a historian who wished to give a faithful portrayal of the ministry of Jesus and the life of the early church. He did not, therefore, write a work of creative imagination, but was very much controlled by his sources. He believed that the Christian faith rested upon the events associated with the work of Jesus and the apostles, and so he gave a historical (not a "historicizing") account of what had happened in order to confirm the faith of his readers.

A second suggestion is that the key concept in the theology of Luke is "salvation". This is a wide term. As employed by Luke, it refers to the content of the good news preached by Jesus, a message which brought men and women deliverance from their sin and the joy of the kingdom of God. In the preaching of the apostles it comprised the offer of forgiveness of sins and the gift of the Holy Spirit. Salvation was thus a present possession, whose reality was known by those who repented and believed in Jesus Christ, but at the same time it was a foretaste of the future blessings associated with His parousia.

This means that Luke was primarily an Evangelist or preacher, concerned to lead men to Christian belief on the basis of a reliable record of the historical facts. Development of this theme leads, thirdly, to a critical assessment of some contemporary trends in Lucan study. Luke's work, for example, should not be dismissed as typical of "early catholicism" with the implication that it is somehow inferior to that of Paul. On the contrary, there are grounds for believing that his grasp of the gospel is in essential harmony with that of Paul, even if he has his own individual understanding of it. Nor again is it the case that Luke has replaced the original eschatological understanding of the Christian faith by a carefully constructed scheme of "salvation-history" in three phases. With O. Cullmann I believe that the concept of salvation-history can be traced back to Jesus Himself and that it is not to be placed in contrast with so-called eschatological or existentialist forms of the Christian message. Luke, therefore, was not attempting to transform the content of the message but to set it out through the medium of a historical account for the benefit of Theophilus and all like him who want a reliable foundation for their faith.

The present work has grown out of an interest in the Gospel of Luke extending over several years. During my studies at Cambridge under the tuition of the Rev. W. F. Flemington the Gospel of Luke was a set text in the Theological Tripos; it was also the theme of lectures and seminars by Professor J. Jeremias at Göttingen in 1959–60. I look back with gratitude to the teaching which I received then, and appreciate the stimulus which it has given me to further study.

I must also express my warm thanks to Dr Graham Stanton, Lecturer in New Testament at King's College, London, for his careful reading of the manuscript and helpful suggestions, and to Mr B. Howard Mudditt of The Paternoster Press for his ready acceptance of this book and for the great efficiency with which he has undertaken its publication.

Some of the material in the book has appeared elsewhere in earlier forms, and I should particularly like to thank Dr C. Leslie Mitton, Editor of *The Expository Times* for his consent to my use of material from two articles on "Recent Study of the Gospel according to St Luke" and "Recent Study of the Acts of the Apostles" (Exp. T 80, 1968–9, pp. 4–8 and 292–6). It was very much due to his request for these articles that I felt spurred on to take the matter further in the present form. The invitation to contribute a section on the Gospel of Luke to *The New Bible Commentary: Revised* (1970) is also gratefully acknowledged as an encouragement to my study.

I am conscious of many gaps in my reading, and regret that, despite the efficient service of Aberdeen University Library, one or two books (notably those by H. W. Bartsch, P. Borgen and W. C. Robinson, Jr.) reached me too late to receive more than passing mention in the footnotes.

The publication of a limp cover edition of this book has given me the opportunity to correct a number of minor misprints, to incorporate additions to the bibliographical information, and to make a number of other, small alterations. I am grateful to the friends who have offered me suggestions for improvements and corrections.

Aberdeen, April, 1978   I. HOWARD MARSHALL

ABBREVIATIONS

AG W. F. Arndt and F. W. Gingrich, *A Greek–English Lexicon of the New Testament and Other Early Christian Literature*, Cambridge, 1957 (English translation of W. Bauer, *Griechisch-Deutsches Wörterbuch zu den Schriften des Neuen Testaments*, Berlin, 1952[4]).

AHG W. W. Gasque and R. P. Martin (ed.), *Apostolic History and the Gospel: Biblical and Historical essays presented to F. F. Bruce*, Exeter, 1970.

BC F. J. Foakes-Jackson and K. Lake, *The Beginnings of Christianity*, 1920–33.

Bib. *Biblica.*

BJRL *Bulletin of the John Rylands Library.*

BNTE W. D. Davies and D. Daube, *The Background of the New Testament and its Eschatology*, Cambridge, 1956.

CBQ *Catholic Biblical Quarterly.*

CHI W. R. Farmer, C. F. D. Moule and R. R. Niebuhr, *Christian History and Interpretation: Studies Presented to John Knox*, Cambridge, 1967.

EL F. Neirynck (ed.), *L'Évangile de Luc: Problèmes littéraires et théologiques*, Gembloux, 1973.

EQ *The Evangelical Quarterly.*

Ev.Th. *Evangelische Theologie.*

Exp. *The Expositor.*

Exp.T. *The Expository Times.*

GL I. H. Marshall, *The Gospel of Luke: A Commentary on the Greek Text*, Exeter, 1978.

JBL *Journal of Biblical Literature.*

JTS *Journal of Theological Studies.*

MM J. H. Moulton and G. Milligan, *The Vocabulary of the Greek New Testament Illustrated from the Papyri and other Non-literary Sources*, 1914–29.

NBD   J. D. Douglas (ed.), *The New Bible Dictionary*, 1962.
NIDNTT C. Brown (ed.), *The New International Dictionary of New Testament Theology*, Exeter, 1975–78.
Nov.T   *Novum Testamentum.*
NTS   *New Testament Studies.*
OCD   M. Cary *et al.* (ed.), *The Oxford Classical Dictionary*, Oxford, 1949.
SB   H. L. Strack and P. Billerbeck, *Kommentar zum Neuen Testament aus Talmud and Midrasch*, München, 1956³.
SE   F. L. Cross (ed.), *Studia Evangelica (Texte und Untersuchungen)*, Berlin.
SG   D. E. Nineham (ed.), *Studies in the Gospels. Essays in Memory of R. H. Lightfoot*, Oxford, 1955.
SJT   *Scottish Journal of Theology.*
SLA   L. E. Keck and J. L. Martyn (ed.), *Studies in Luke–Acts*, Nashville, 1966.
Th.R   *Theologische Rundschau.*
Tyn.B   *Tyndale Bulletin.*
TDNT   G. Kittel and G. Friedrich (ed.), *Theological Dictionary of the New Testament*, Grand Rapids, 1964–76.
ZG   E. Dinkler (ed.), *Zeit und Geschichte: Dankesgabe an Rudolf Bultmann*, Tübingen, 1964.
ZNW   *Zeitschrift für die Neutestamentliche Wissenschaft.*
ZTK   *Zeitschrift für Theologie und Kirche.*

Where the place of publication of a book is not mentioned, it can be assumed to be London.
Other abbreviations for versions of the Bible, etc., follow normal practice.

CHAPTER I

THE MODERN APPROACH TO LUKE–ACTS

THE WRITINGS OF LUKE HAVE BEEN DESCRIBED AS THE STORM CENTRE of modern New Testament study.[1] With his two-volume work spanning the ministry of Jesus and the development of the early church, Luke figures in most of the problems of contemporary New Testament science. What can we know of the ministry and teaching of Jesus? Can we reconstruct the preaching and life of the early church? How did the mission of the church develop? What is the real significance of Paul in the general growth of the church? What is Luke's own version of the Christian faith, and how does his understanding of it compare with that of other leading writers in the early church? And what is the historical place of Luke – is he the faithful reporter of early traditions or is he refashioning the story of Christian origins in order to justify the "early catholicism" thought to be typical of his own era in the sub-apostolic church?

Questions such as these crowd in upon the student of Luke, and indicate that solution of the Lucan problem would contribute greatly to answering the general question of Christian origins.

It is not surprising, therefore, that the volume of scholarly work on Luke–Acts has grown considerably in recent years.[2] The main impetus to contemporary studies is generally recognized as having been provided by H. Conzelmann in his important work, *Die Mitte der Zeit*.[3] This work set the direction for much recent study, for it was both pioneering in its application of new methods of study to Luke and at the same time representative of the use of such new methods in wider areas of biblical study.

---

[1] W. C. van Unnik, "Luke–Acts, A Storm Center in Contemporary Scholarship," SLA, pp. 15–32.

[2] For surveys see E. Grässer, "Die Apostelgeschichte in der Forschung der Gegenwart," Th.R n.f. 26, 1960, pp. 93–167; *id.*, "Acta-Forschung seit 1960," Th.R n.f. 41, 1976, pp.141–194, 259–290; 42, 1977, pp. 1–68: C. K. Barrett, *Luke the Historian in Recent Study*, 1961; D. Guthrie, "Recent Literature on the Acts of the Apostles," in R. P. Martin (ed.), *Vox Evangelica*, 1963 edition, pp. 33–49; J. Dupont, *Études sur les Actes des Apôtres*, Paris, 1967; W. W. Gasque, *A History of the Criticism of the Acts of the Apostles*, Tübingen/Grand Rapids, 1975; C. H. Talbert, "Shifting Sands: The Recent Study of the Gospel of Luke," *Interpretation* 30 1976, pp. 381–395; F. Bovon, *Luc le théologien: Vingt-cinq ans de recherches (1950–1975)*, Neuchâtel/Paris, 1978.

[3] H. Conzelmann, *Die Mitte der Zeit*, Tübingen, 1954. Quotations are given from the 5th edition (1964). Translations are normally taken from the English translation, *The Theology of St. Luke*, 1960, the English page reference being given in brackets. In a number of places the text of the later German edition is different and the rendering has been altered accordingly. For Conzelmann's views see also "Zur Lukas–Analyse," ZTK 49, 1952, pp. 16–33.

The new type of study received the name of *Redaktionsgeschichte*, the name, not too readily translatable into English, being an indication of the country of origin; "history of editing" is the nearest, but clumsy, English equivalent, but "redaction criticism" (on the analogy of "form criticism" for *Formgeschichte*) seems likely to become the corresponding English technical term.[1]

✳ Redaction criticism may be said to begin where form criticism left off, or perhaps to pick up one of the loose threads left by form criticism. As originally practised, form criticism accomplished two things. First, in the hands of K. L. Schmidt it was an instrument for dissecting the Gospels so that the connecting narrative framework was set on one side as being a secondary composition of no further interest to the student of the historical Jesus.[2] The real interest lay in the various items of tradition, narrative units and isolated sayings of Jesus, now prised loose from their secondary settings in the Gospels and capable of being studied on their own.

Second, the various narrative units and sayings were classified according to their literary and oral forms, and were then studied in order to discover in what circles in the church they were handed down (the question of their life-setting or *Sitz im Leben*)[3] and how they had been affected by this process of transmission.[4] Conservative practitioners of the art hoped that by this method it would be possible to remove the later accretions which had been received by the material in the course of transmission and thus to recover the primitive tradition about Jesus in a pure and reliable form. The work of J. Jeremias on the parables may be cited as an excellent example of such study by a scholar who has made his aim "nothing less than a return, as well grounded as possible, to the very words of Jesus himself," and who believes that such an aim can be fulfilled.[5] Other scholars, however, came to results of a different kind, generally termed

---

[1] J. Rohde, *Rediscovering the Teaching of the Evangelists*, 1968 (English translation of *Die redaktionsgeschichtliche Methode*, Hamburg, 1966); S. Smalley, "Redaction Criticism," in I. H. Marshall (ed.), *New Testament Interpretation*, Exeter, 1977, pp. 181–195.

[2] K. L. Schmidt, *Der Rahmen der Geschichte Jesu*, Berlin, 1919.

[3] The phrase *Sitz im Leben* refers to a typical situation in the life of a community. Scholars who hold that such a communal *Sitz im Leben* may be the locus of the transmission of a piece of tradition rather than the place where it was created sometimes use the same term "*Sitz im Leben*" to refer to the historical situation in the life of Jesus in which a particular saying originated. H. Schürmann, however, has insisted on the sociological meaning of the term, and argued that it is an inappropriate term to apply to a single historical situation ("Die vorösterlichen Anfänge der Logien-tradition," in H. Schürmann, *Traditionsgeschichtliche Untersuchungen*, Düsseldorf, 1968, pp. 47 f.).

[4] R. Bultmann, *Die Geschichte der Synoptischen Tradition*, Göttingen, 1921, 1958⁴ (English translation: *The History of the Synoptic Tradition*, Oxford, 1968²); M. Dibelius, *Die Formgeschichte des Evangeliums*, Tübingen, 1919, 1966⁵ (English translation: *From Tradition to Gospel*, 1934).

[5] J. Jeremias, *The Parables of Jesus*, 1963², p. 9 (English translation of *Die Gleichnisse Jesu*, Göttingen, 1962⁶).

"radical;" they asserted that almost nothing can be learned about the ministry and teaching of Jesus, so thoroughly has the tradition been altered in the course of transmission.[1] This rather extreme tendency, which almost despairs of finding any reliable tradition in the Gospels, has been considerably modified in the work of the last few years; those scholars who have been popularly but inaccurately described as following "A New Quest of the Historical Jesus"[2] have argued that historical information about Jesus is to be found in the Gospels, even if there is not a great deal of it.[3]

But before the rise of this so-called "New Quest" form criticism was already giving rise to two other types of study. On the one hand, fresh attention was being paid to the changes undergone by the Gospel material in the course of transmission. In the attempt to get back to the historical Jesus these changes had been regarded as complicating factors, and the aim was to dismiss them from the reckoning as quickly as possible. But now it was realized more fully that the alterations wrought in the tradition were themselves significant – for the study of the situations in which they were made. It was important to ask *why* the tradition had been shaped in particular ways, since the answer to this question could shed light on the situation and character of the church which had produced the alterations. Gospel study was thus linked up with the attempt to discover pre-Pauline material taken over and used in the Pauline Epistles, and other early liturgical, creedal and catechetical material preserved elsewhere in the New Testament writings. By comparison of such material it is possible to reconstruct the history of the development of theology in the early church in the period before our written sources.[4] This type of study, springing from form criticism, has been dubbed "tradition criticism" (*Traditionsgeschichte*); it will be clear that it overlaps to a considerable extent

---

[1] R. Bultmann's famous dictum, "I do indeed think that we can now know almost nothing concerning the life and personality of Jesus" (*Jesus and the Word*, 1935, p. 8 (English translation of *Jesus*, Berlin, 1934²)), applies strictly only to the personality of Jesus and the general story of His life; the book itself is evidence that Bultmann believed that something could be recovered of His teaching. However, R. H. Lightfoot's remark does not seem to have been limited in its scope: "It seems, then, that the form of the earthly no less than of the heavenly Christ is for the most part hidden from us. For all the inestimable value of the gospels, they yield us little more than a whisper of his voice; we trace in them but the outskirts of his ways" (*History and Interpretation in the Gospels*, 1935, p. 225). Later Lightfoot claimed that his statement had been misunderstood as more radical than it was intended to be (*The Gospel Message of St. Mark*, Oxford, 1950, p. 103), but he certainly left himself very open to misunderstanding.

[2] From the title of J. M. Robinson's survey, *A New Quest of the Historical Jesus*, 1959 (the German translation, *Kerygma und historischer Jesus*, Zürich, 1967², is considerably expanded and somewhat altered).

[3] The fruits may be seen in G. Bornkamm, *Jesus von Nazareth*, Stuttgart, 1956 (English translation: *Jesus of Nazareth*, 1960). See I. H. Marshall, *I believe in the Historical Jesus*, 1977.

[4] The method has been most thoroughly practised in the area of christology. See F. Hahn, *Christologische Hoheitstitel*, Göttingen, 1964² (English translation; *The Titles of Jesus in Christology*, 1969); R. H. Fuller, *The Foundations of New Testament Christology*, 1965.

with form criticism, but the new name is a more accurate indication of what is being done.[1]

On the other hand, scholarship has taken up the Gospel framework, which K. L. Schmidt had set aside, and discovered that this too has its value. It can shed light on the historical and theological conceptions of its originators, the Evangelists themselves. The fact that they arranged the Gospel material in the ways that they did and not in other ways is significant and may afford clues to their own theological outlook. Further, they did not take over the various units of tradition without imprinting them with the stamp of their own style and interests. Consequently, the Gospels can and must be studied from the point of view of redaction criticism; their contents will throw light on the Evangelists themselves and the communities for which and in which they wrote.

The application of this method has been its own justification: it has proved fruitful. Within a comparatively short time a large number of studies have appeared in which the individual Gospels, or themes in them, have been discussed for the light which they can shed on the final stage in their composition.[2] It has been claimed that the Evangelists must no longer be thought of as "scissors-and-paste" compilers, mechanically arranging their sources like a magazine editor struggling to fit his articles into the available space in a neat form; they are theologians in their own right, working with their own conceptions of the subject matter of a Gospel and freely adapting their sources to fit their intended pattern.

Redaction criticism thus has two uses. It is of interest for its own sake in shedding light upon the period of final composition of the Gospels; the Gospel writers are seen as creative theologians, worthy to rank beside Paul and the writer to the Hebrews, and thus the theological interest of the New Testament is widened. The contrast between the outlook of an earlier day and that of the present time may be seen by a comparison of the New Testament Theologies of R. Bultmann (1948) and H. Conzelmann (1967). The former not only – as is well known – reduced the teaching of Jesus to "a presupposition for the theology of the New Testament rather than a part of that theology itself," but also virtually ignored the Synoptic Evangelists as theological witnesses in their own right.[3] By con-

---

[1] Scholarship has thus come into line with T. W. Manson's suggestion that the term "form criticism" should "be reserved for the study of the various units of narrative and teaching, which go to make up the Gospels, in respect of their form, and that alone" ("The Life of Jesus: Some Tendencies in Present-day Research" BNTE, pp. 211–221; quotation from p. 212). It was with regard to form criticism as thus defined that Manson insisted that it was irrelevant to the historical value of the material classified.

[2] The field is well surveyed in J. Rohde, *op. cit.*

[3] R. Bultmann, *Theology of the New Testament*, 1952, I, p. 3; the Gospels as such are briefly treated in Vol. II (1955), pp. 123–127 (English translation of *Theologie des Neuen Testaments*, Tübingen, 1948–53).

trast the latter devoted the second main section of his book (after a section on the early church) to the Synoptic kerygma.[1] Here at last fuller justice is done to the distinctive importance of the Gospels.

The other use of redaction criticism is that it forms an important stage in working back to the earliest form of the tradition. The last stratum of alteration to the tradition must be the first to be removed in the process of working back through the successive levels to the bed-rock.

It was the work of H. Conzelmann on Luke which played such a large part in initiating this new phase of Gospel study and which has also helped to bring Luke into the forefront of New Testament study generally. Almost immediately afterwards, however, there appeared a massive commentary on Acts from E. Haenchen in which the principles of redaction criticism were applied systematically to that book, with results that upset a considerable number of generally accepted conclusions, especially as regards the historicity of Acts.[2]

It is understandable that redaction criticism should have attracted the attention of the more radical wing of New Testament scholarship. Indeed some of its results so far appear to have confirmed the general verdict of form criticism that the Gospels – and Acts – are extremely poor quarries for bed-rock tradition. The strata of original tradition are thin and inaccessible beneath considerable layers of other rock and much rubble. Further, if the metaphor may be pressed, they now consist of largely metamorphosed rocks whose original composition, shape and position must be a matter of uncertain conjecture. To put the matter like this may sound extreme, but it appears to be the position of some contemporary practitioners of redaction criticism. We may suspect that part of the contemporary attraction of this form of study is that it enables scholars who have come more or less to a dead end in study of the historical Jesus to continue to study the Gospels without raising the problem of historicity; they can thus make some progress in understanding of the Gospels while leaving aside this issue. The literature abounds with disclaimers of such a kind as: "Our primary concern in the following essay is with the soteriology of Mark . . . We are not interested in what Jesus Himself thought of the meaning and purpose of his life and death." The statement is admittedly qualified by a "primary," but its general direction is significant.[3]

The present study is devoted to a consideration of Luke–Acts from this

---

[1] H. Conzelmann, *Grundriss der Theologie des Neuen Testaments*, München, 1967, pp. 115–172 (English translation: *An Outline of the Theology of the New Testament*, 1969, pp. 97–152).

[2] E. Haenchen, *Die Apostelgeschichte*, Göttingen, 1956[10], 1961[13]; cf. H. Conzelmann, *Die Apostelgeschichte*, Tübingen, 1963.

[3] E. Best, *The Temptation and the Passion: The Markan Soteriology*, Cambridge, 1965, p. ix.; later Best does emphasize the importance of this kind of study for the quest of the historical Jesus (pp. xif.).

point of view of redaction criticism. It is concerned with the theology of Luke as a whole, and its purpose is to attempt to discover the central theological concern of Luke. It is consequently deeply indebted to the work of contemporary scholars, both to those who have explored the general theme of Lucan theology and to those who have examined particular aspects of his thought. At the same time it is critical of a number of the assumptions and conclusions of such study.

Any method of study can lead to a one-sided approach and to half-truths as its conclusions, especially in the first flush of enthusiasm for a new procedure. In our opinion this has to some extent happened in contemporary study of Luke. Today the stress is on Luke as a theologian, and the general trend of study is to explore his theological selfconsciousness and idiosyncrasies. Half a century ago the emphasis lay at the opposite extreme. The significance of Luke lay in his position as the historian of apostolic Christianity, and the great value of his work lay in the information which it offered on Christian origins. Sir William Ramsay could claim: "Luke is a historian of the first rank."[1] Whether or not the verdict be accepted, it indicates where the importance of Luke was seen to lie, namely in his work as a historian. Such an approach may have been one-sided, but it may be argued that the contemporary approach which regards Luke almost exclusively as a theologian is equally one-sided.

It is our contention that a proper balance needs to be achieved in study of Luke. Part of our thesis is that Luke is *both* historian *and* theologian, and that the best term to describe him is "evangelist," a term which, we believe, includes both of the others. E. Käsemann has stated of Luke: "We can only understand him as an historian, if we have first understood him as a theologian."[2] This is true, but we are in danger of forgetting that the converse is also true: Luke can be properly appreciated as a theologian only when it is recognized that he is also an historian.

The point that we are making is not that Luke's basic interest was in history, either in the sense that he was content simply to record facts from the past for their own sake or in the sense that he took the theological facts expressed in the preaching of the early church and proceeded to reformulate them in the guise of history. Neither of these positions is a correct statement of what Luke was doing. Rather we mean that as a theologian Luke was concerned that his message about Jesus and the early church should be based upon reliable history. His theology was based upon

[1] W. M. Ramsay, *The Bearing of Recent Discovery on the Trustworthiness of the New Testament*, 1915, p. 222.

[2] E. Käsemann, *Essays on New Testament Themes*, 1964 p. 148 (English translation of *Exegetische Versuche und Besinnungen*, Göttingen, 1960²). A better formulation is that of E. E. Ellis: "Luke is an historian, but he can be appreciated best when he is recognized also as a theologian and *littérateur*" (*The Gospel of Luke*, 1967, p. ix).

tradition which he evaluated to the best of his ability. He used his history in the service of his theology.

At the same time, Luke's purpose was not simply to write theology as such. The title of evangelist which we are suggesting for him is meant to indicate that his concern was to present the Christian message in such a way as to promote and confirm faith in Jesus Christ. His intention was evangelistic. And therefore his concern was not so much to express the faith in terms of what has been called "salvation-history" as rather to bear witness to the salvation revealed in Jesus Christ and proclaimed by the early church. Hence the common view today which sees Luke as the theologian of "salvation-history" needs some correction of emphasis. Luke certainly believed that salvation had been revealed in history, but his interest was not so much in recording the history for its own sake as in indicating its significance as the means of salvation.

It will be apparent that the position which will be advocated here differs at some points from that associated especially with the work of H. Conzelmann and E. Haenchen. First, a number of scholars might wish to reject our case at the outset by insisting that it is not possible to be both a theologian and a historian; or at least that in so far as he was a theologian Luke could not have been a good historian. Luke, it has been contended, has so misrepresented the facts in the interests of his theology that we can hardly expect to find a reliable historical basis in his work. We must therefore begin by examining this basic assumption with care: do history and theology stand in opposition to each other?

Second, our exposition of the main theme of Luke's theology constitutes a corrective of the thesis associated with Conzelmann. We shall argue that Luke's concern is with salvation as such rather than with salvation-history. This may seem to be simply exchanging one rather broad term for another. "Salvation" is a broad term, and Luke's use of the concept extends beyond his use of the specific word-group. But our point is that Luke's concern is basically with the salvation established by the work of Jesus as an experience available to men.

Third, we shall claim that in the essentials of his theological message Luke was building upon tradition and not creating his own new scheme. In this sense he was a conservative theologian rather than an innovator. Naturally he has his own distinctive ideas which come to expression from time to time, but basically he builds upon tradition and treats it faithfully. We shall, therefore, attempt to show throughout our study that Luke's theology is in fact based upon tradition.

It is arguable that the distinctive elements in Luke's theology should be sought in the places where he differs from tradition or is not dependent upon tradition instead of in the areas where he reproduces tradition with little or no change. But the fact that Luke took over tradition shows that he regarded it as important. The traditions which he took over from his sources should not be regarded as awkward intrusions into his work but rather as its basis. F. Schütz has rightly argued that the use of a tradition can still be a pointer to the theological outlook of the Evangelist even when he has not made any redactional modifications in it; for in such a case the tradition itself so clearly expressed his intention that there was no call for him to alter it.[1]

Fourth, if this analysis of Lucan theology is correct, it may be claimed that Luke's outlook was not so different from that of his predecessors as is sometimes implied. The view, for example, that his work represents an "early catholic" distortion of primitive Christianity is an exaggeration of the facts. He has his distinctive points of view, as we shall show, but his work does not constitute a basic alteration of the theology of the primitive church. On the contrary, he has performed a vital service in re-expressing it for his own contemporaries – and for us.

[1] F. Schütz, *Der leidende Christus: Die angefochtene Gemeinde und das Christuskerygma der lukanischen Schriften*, Stuttgart, 1969, p. 19.

CHAPTER II

HISTORY OR THEOLOGY

The Nature of History

THE TASK OF INTERPRETING THE RELATIONSHIP BETWEEN HISTORY AND theology is not made any easier by the variety of definitions of history which have been current among practitioners of the art, especially in contemporary discussion. Nevertheless, we may begin from certain fairly clear concepts and proceed to understand something of the work of the historian.

The word "history" itself may be used in two senses in English. It can refer to events which have actually happened; we may speak, for example, of the Battle of Bannockburn as "an event in history" and contrast it with the incident in which Martin Luther is supposed to have uttered the words "I can do no other! Here I stand," a statement whose position as an event in history is generally rejected.[1] In such a context the word "history" is used to denote the actual course of past events. The other use of the word is that found in a book title like *A History of Israel* where it means the *account* (written or otherwise) of past events. The historian thus studies history (in the former sense) and writes history (in the latter sense). We may use the word "historiography" to describe the study of what historians do, or to refer to "history writing" itself.

The interest of the historian is in past events, and this interest may be defined in three ways. First, it goes without saying that he is interested only in real events, things which actually happened. He separates fact from fiction, and a large part of his skill lies in his ability to discriminate between these two categories in previous records of the past. Second, the historian's choice of events is limited to those which were part of, or affected, the life of mankind. There are many past events in the physical world which are of no interest to the historian because they did not affect in any direct way the life and thought of mankind. On the other hand, an event such as the famous Lisbon earthquake of 1755 is of interest to the historian because (unlike other earthquakes on uninhabited islands in the Pacific Ocean) it not only had disastrous consequences for the people of Lisbon but also exerted a profound influence on the thought of the time as men wrestled

[1] J. Atkinson, *The Great Light: Luther and Reformation*, Exeter, 1968, p. 67 n.

with the problems of suffering and theodicy.[1] Clearly the line between events which interest the historian and those which do not is a fluid one, but it is nonetheless distinct. Clearly too it is a somewhat arbitrary one, but some division between the tasks of, say, historians, zoologists, geologists and physicists is necessary, and its value has been proved by experience.

The third point is that the historian selects out of the vast mass of events those which he considers significant. It is here, of course, that the problems begin. Significant from what point of view? What is the criterion? The answer may be one of definition. Many historians have concentrated their attention upon political events. The validity of their selection of events will then depend upon whether they have taken into account whatever may be regarded as affecting the politics of the period studied. It would be irrelevant, for example, to give details of what some king regularly had for breakfast, since this is hardly likely to have had much effect on his political life, but a historian would be bound to mention the morning when poison was inserted in his food and he died, thus precipitating a political catastrophe. If, however, the historian was interested in social and economic factors, then an account of what kings ate for breakfast might well be of real significance. And if, at a deeper level, it is contended that politics are moulded by social and economic forces, then the political historian who confined his attention to ostensibly political factors would be guilty of following an inadequate principle of selection.

But how does one decide which kind of history is ultimately significant? Political, social and economic histories each have their justification, but can any one of them, or any combination of them, be said to express truly the significance of the past? From the point of view of a Christian, the few brief lines in which Tacitus mentions casually who founded the sect of Christians whom Nero cruelly tortured touch on a theme far more significant than anything in the rest of his historical writings. Yet Tacitus was not in a position to see this in his own time. Nor would a Marxist attach the same absolute value to the events surrounding the birth of the Christian church as a Christian would, even although (unlike Tacitus) he would recognize that the events had had very significant consequences in the subsequent course of history. It is plain that we cannot talk of absolute significance attaching to any particular historical events or to any particular type of historical study without adopting a standpoint whose validity is incapable of historical proof.[2]

In general a historian does not have direct contact with the historical

[1] D. P. Fuller, *Easter Faith and History*, Grand Rapids, 1964, pp. 29 f.
[2] May there not, however, be some historical fact which forces us to accept some particular interpretation of history as a whole? For example, if the resurrection of Jesus were to be regarded as an indisputable historical event, then its significance would obviously have important and compelling implications for history as a whole.

events which he wishes to record. Even in the case of events in his own lifetime, his own observations will give at best only a one-sided, incomplete view of what happened. This means that the historian's contact with what happened is indirect. He is dependent upon historical *evidence* of various kinds such as contemporary documents, archaeological finds, and the writings of other historians. All this evidence must be sifted with care in order that a historical explanation may be framed which will make sense of all the available data. In doing this, the historian will make use of various generally accepted methods of inference and argument, and various technical skills which have been developed by historical study. The term "warrants" is sometimes used to designate the criteria used for evaluating historical data.[1]

On the basis of his data the historian composes his record of what he believes to have happened. Since, however, it is possible, and even probable, that a historian's reconstruction of the past may not correspond with what actually happened, some writers have found it useful to introduce a terminological complication at this point, and to make a distinction between "events" and "facts." According to this technical use, "the term *event* is used to denote something which has happened in the past, irrespective of anyone's apprehension of it. *Fact* is used to denote what the historian knows of something which has happened in the past."[2] If perfection were possible in historical study, then "events" and "facts" would completely correspond with each other. Since, however, evidence is often inadequate and historians are fallible in their reasoning, the "fact" may not be an entirely correct representation of the "event." We may perhaps compare the historian to a man looking through a telescope at a distant object. The object itself is definite and real, but the image to which it gives rise in the eye of the observer as the light rays pass through the telescope is not identical with it, nor is it a perfect replica of it. Irregularities in the lenses, the inability of the telescope to survey the object in its entirety, and the transition caused by the representation of a three-dimensional object in two dimensions – these all exert a distorting influence. It is so with the historian in his survey of the past. To be sure, the use in a technical sense of the words "event" and "fact" is unfortunate, since in common parlance "historical fact" is tantamount to "actual event," but, whatever terminology we use, the difference is a real one. The historian's reconstruction of the past cannot be identical with the past itself.

An important corollary of this description of historical activity must be noted before we take up our main theme. What has been said implies that in general one cannot claim absolute reliability for the results attained

[1] Van A. Harvey, *The Historian and the Believer*, 1966.
[2] J. F. Peter, *Finding the Historical Jesus*, 1965, p. 18.

by a historian. His conclusions are not like those of a mathematician who can proceed with perfect certainty from a set of premises to a conclusion. *All* historical reconstructions have an inherent element of uncertainty about them. Some new evidence may turn up, which completely alters an accepted picture. One may instance the way in which the discovery of an early papyrus fragment of the Gospel of John effectually put a stop to historical reconstructions of the authorship of the Gospel as a late second century document. Or a historian may produce a fresh, more coherent and intrinsically more convincing reconstruction on the basis of the existing data. Another historian may be able to show that the adoption of a particular set of presuppositions had inhibited earlier scholars from a proper appreciation of certain data. Absolute reliability is thus in principle unobtainable.

What must be emphasized, however, is that this does not mean that the historian is reduced to methodological doubt, with the result that he denies the possibility of historical *knowledge* and feels that he must qualify every historical pronouncement with a "probably" or even a "possibly" – rather like those church announcements which qualify every prophecy of the coming week's events with a pious "D.V." (James 4:15 is not meant to be taken so literally!) In reality many historical facts have been established beyond all reasonable doubt; the historian who says that "probably" or even "almost certainly" the Scots defeated the English at the Battle of Bannockburn is not doing justice to the quality of the historical evidence. Other facts may be arranged in a scale of relative probability because of the comparative scantiness of the evidence and the difficulty of interpreting it. To say, however, that history cannot produce reliable knowledge of the past is to be pedantic and unrealistic. There is perhaps a parallel to be found in the debate concerning the possibility of inductive reasoning regarding future events. It is impossible to prove in a logically conclusive manner from the experience of all the mornings up until today that the sun will rise tomorrow morning. Strictly speaking we should perhaps speak of the overwhelming probability that it will do so, but in point of fact we speak and act as if it is a complete certainty. Such probability is tantamount to certainty.[1] No doubt the prophecies of physics regarding future solar activity have a greater certainty about them than historical reconstructions of the past, but this does not mean that it is wrong to speak about the virtual certainty of innumerable historical facts.

In various spheres of contemporary study – physics, chemistry, geography and history, among others – the concept of the model has become a useful expression of basic method. The physicist, for example, does not

[1] See the discussion in P. Edwards, "Bertrand Russell's Doubts about Induction," in A. G. N. Flew, *Essays on Logic and Language* (First Series), Oxford, 1951, pp. 55–79.

observe his protons and electrons directly, but simply has access to a large quantity of experimental data from various sources. What he does is to construct a "model," in the sense of a postulated system analogous to observable phenomena which will account for his data; thus, for example, the data may be explicable on the hypothesis of an atomic nucleus with electrons revolving round it, like a set of balls revolving in grooves round an axis. The physicist has no proof that atoms look like this model – they are in principle inaccessible to his sight – and therefore he claims for his hypothesis no greater status than that of a model which in certain respects is like the atom (as a doll may resemble a baby in shape and outward appearance) but in other respects probably entirely fails to represent its characteristics (as the material of which a doll is made is no guide to the "stuff" of which a baby is made). To this extent, the model is an objective representation of reality.[1]

In the same way, we are suggesting that the historian produces a model of past events, and for this model he can claim a certain objective validity. Like the physicist, he may find that new evidence compels the alteration or even the abandonment of one model in favour of another; again, his vision is limited by the character of his instruments. Nevertheless, in both cases objectivity is the aim, and even if it is recognized that it is ultimately unattainable, neither science will give up its search for it.[2]

History and Objectivity

Implicit in the above remarks is the assumption that the task of the historian is to reconstruct the past, to give an account of events as they actually happened. A description of history in these terms clearly reflects the often quoted remark of L. von Ranke that the historian's task is to reconstruct the past "as it actually happened" ("wie es eigentlich gewesen").[3] Whatever be the precise significance of this phrase as originally used, it has come to be used as typical of a certain kind of history which has now fallen into disfavour. We must, therefore, look into this point more closely.

If Ranke's statement be taken to mean that the aim of the historian is rigid accuracy, then it must be claimed that this remains the aim of any contemporary historian worthy of the name of historian. His pursuit for truth must be quite rigorous, and he will not ignore awkward facts for his reconstructions nor falsify the evidence. The true historian obviously differs from the kind of person who is willing to manipulate the evidence in order to prove some pre-conceived theory. F. F. Bruce has quoted a

[1] C. Brown, *Philosophy and the Christian Faith*, 1969, p. 279.
[2] On the analogy between history and science see J. F. Peter, *op. cit.*, pp. 84–94.
[3] L. von Ranke, *Sämmtliche Werke*, Leipzig, 1874, Vol. 33, p. vii.

famous classroom story concerning Hegel. "Hegel was propounding his philosophy of history with reference to a particular series of events, when one of his hearers, a student of history, interposed with the protest, 'But, Herr Professor, the facts are otherwise.' 'So much the worse for the facts,' said Hegel."[1] The story may be apocryphal – for the sake of Hegel's reputation one hopes that it is – but it illustrates in exaggerated fashion a thoroughly unhistorical attitude. History, written to serve the interests of a particular theory and twisting the evidence accordingly, is not history.

From the same point of view, much ancient history must also be regarded as falling below the standard of modern history writing. Many of the Hellenistic historians were more concerned with the rhetorical qualities of their writings than their historical verisimilitude. They wrote to produce a literary effect, and were perfectly capable of adjusting the facts to suit their literary requirements. "The principal historians of the Hellenistic age, disregarding documentary evidence and technique of historical writing, aimed, as a general rule, not at being accurate and learned, but readable."[2]

Ranke's phrase stands guard against all such low ideas of history writing. From another angle, however, the ideal represented by nineteenth century scientific history has been itself criticized. In his influential monograph, *A New Quest of the Historical Jesus*, J. M. Robinson has written: "We have come to recognize that the objective factual level upon which the nineteenth century operated is only one dimension of history, and that a whole new dimension in the facts, a deeper and more central plane of meaning, had been largely bypassed. The nineteenth century saw the reality of 'historical facts' as consisting largely in names, places, dates, occurrences, sequences, causes, effects – things which fall far short of being the actuality of history, if one understands by history the distinctively human, creative, unique, purposeful, which distinguishes man from nature. The dimension in which man actually exists, his 'world,' the stance or outlook from which he acts, his understanding of his existence behind what he does, the way he meets his basic problems and the answer his life implies to the human dilemma, the significance he had as the environment of those who knew him, the continuing history his life produces, the possibility of existence which his life presents to me as an alternative – such matters as these have become central in an attempt to understand history."[3] In line with this change in interest Robinson claims that there has also been a change in method: "We have already noted how the positivistic understanding of

[1] F. F. Bruce, *The New Testament Documents* 1960.[3], p. 14 n. 4.
[2] P. Treves, "Historiography, Greek," OCD, p. 433. Cf. H. J. Cadbury, F. J. F. Jackson and K. Lake, "The Greek and Jewish Traditions of Writing History," BC II, pp. 7–29. This verdict, however, is certainly not true of all ancient historians; see below, pp. 54–57.
[3] J. M. Robinson, *A New Quest of the Historical Jesus*, pp. 28 f.

history as consisting of brute facts gave way to an understanding of history centring in the profound intentions, stances, and concepts of existence held by persons in the past, as the well-springs of their outward actions. Historical methodology shifted accordingly from a primary concern for recording the past 'wie es eigentlich gewesen,' i.e. cataloguing with objective detachment facts in sequence and with proper casual (*sic*) relationships. Instead, the historian's task was seen to consist in understanding those deep-lying intentions of the past, by involving one's selfhood in an encounter in which one's own intentions and views of existence are put in question, and perhaps altered or even radically reversed."[1]

There would appear to be a certain possibility of confusion in this statement. On the one hand, Robinson, following the lead given by such philosophers of history as R. G. Collingwood, has rightly perceived that history must not restrict its interest to the "outside" of events, but must also consider their "inside" quality.[2] This is surely a correct insight. On the other hand, however, Robinson may have given the impression that the procedure of the twentieth century historian is less objective than that of his nineteenth century predecessor. This impression is strengthened by Robinson's development of an existentialist approach to history in which the historian himself is involved. In itself such an approach may be sound enough, and, as we shall see, it is very relevant to the question of biblical history. What must be resisted, however, is any suggestion that thereby history becomes less a matter of enquiry into objective facts and more an expression of the subjective impressions of the historian. It may be much more difficult to enquire into the motives of some man of the past than to establish the date of a particular event in his life; it may also need much more human insight on the part of the historian to determine the former than the latter; and consequently a statement regarding the former will be much less precise and loaded with more qualifications than one regarding the latter; nevertheless both the man's motives and the date in question are brute facts ("events" in the technical sense), and the investigation of both must take place with the same scrupulous objectivity. J. F. Peter has already stressed sufficiently the givenness and objectivity of events, and rejected the claim that "there can take place qualitative changes in events after they have happened." He rightly points out that past events can have a continuing series of after-effects – particularly, we may say, in the minds of historians – but this does not affect the original givenness of the events themselves.[3]

We may claim, therefore, that modern history must be concerned at all

[1] *Ibid.*. p. 39.

[2] R. G. Collingwood, *The Idea of History*, Oxford, 1946, p. 213. Cf. J. F. Peter, *op. cit.*, pp. 78 f.

[3] J. F. Peter, *op. cit.*, pp. 101 f.

times with objectivity and accuracy. Yet this is not the end of the problem. For it may be asked whether the modern concept of history is not of such a kind that objectivity may be impossible. We have already observed how the significance of a particular event may appear differently to different historians. Each historian brings to his work his own particular presuppositions. This is something different from the tendentiousness mentioned above which is completely alien to the spirit of the objective historian. It is rather the fact that each historian is moulded unconsciously by the age in which he lives; he has his own understanding of truth and his own ideas of what is historically probable and improbable. An ancient historian, for example, may be ready to admit magical or demonic forces as historical explanations of events, where a modern historian believes that some other, "human" explanation must be possible, even if in individual cases he cannot always discover what it was. Just as presuppositionless exegesis of a text is impossible, so too presuppositionless historiography is ruled out.

We have, therefore, to allow that different historians, and especially historians from different cultures, will approach their work with differing presuppositions and that this will affect the character of their historical conclusions. But to deduce from this the conclusion that objective history is unattainable is to exaggerate the difficulty. The historian who is concerned to be objective will seek, as far as possible, to be conscious of his own presuppositions and to make due allowance for them. He will attempt to record and assess the evidence both for and against his own conclusions, so that his readers may test his conclusions for themselves. And, further, there must be a continual dialogue between historians of different outlooks so that they may be able to cross-check their conclusions and arrive, as far as is possible, at a common mind. Such considerations as these will not mitigate the effects of presuppositions altogether, but in our opinion they do mean that the goal of historical objectivity is not a ridiculous one.

Naturally, presuppositions have their uses. The scholar who studies religious history from a sociological point of view may well believe that sociological considerations are largely sufficient to explain it. He may be wrong in adopting such an absolute standpoint – a Christian believer would certainly want to claim this – but nevertheless the adoption of his standpoint will probably bring to light historical facts and explanations which would have eluded the historian who ignored the insights of sociology.

History and the Supernatural

The biggest question concerns the place of the "supernatural" (in the broadest sense) in the sort of historical events which lie behind the New

Testament. There would appear to be three main points of view on this problem.

First, there are scholars who declare categorically that supernatural events do not happen and did not happen. Any story in the Bible or elsewhere which contains a supernatural element must therefore be explained away, either as a misapprehension of what actually happened (e.g. when a "miraculous" cure was really wrought by psychological means) or as a legend with no factual basis.[1]

Second, there are scholars who allow that a man *qua* believer may accept the possibility of supernatural events, but he may not do so *qua* historian. Such events fall outside the field of the historian. By definition the historian's world is one in which phenomena take place in strict accordance with natural laws of cause and effect; miraculous events fall outside this frame of reference, and in this sense they are beyond history. They cannot, therefore, be included in a historical narrative. Thus a historian may refer to the event of the Easter faith of the disciples that Jesus had risen from the dead; there is nothing necessarily supernatural about this faith as such, and plenty of historians who have admitted its existence have offered natural explanations of it – such explanations being "allowed" in history. But, goes the argument, a historian may not refer to the event of the resurrection of Jesus as being the cause of the Easter faith, since this would be to call in a supernatural cause to explain a historical event and such causes lie outside the historian's frame of reference. To allow such causes would, it is said, make havoc of historical writing. The most that a historian who is a believer may do is to point to the inexplicable nature of the Easter faith. Thus G. E. Ladd writes: "The supernatural dimension of the Kingdom of God which has invaded history in the person of Jesus creates an insoluble problem for the historian as historian, for he knows nothing of supernatural events; he can deal only with purely natural occurrences. The evidence of the supernatural is inexplicable to the historian. That is why the person of Jesus presents a continuing problem to historical scholarship, for the essential fact of his person and mission transcends historical explanation."[2]

The Christian believer will naturally dispute the first of these attitudes as being inconsistent with his faith. It is true that there are some so-called Christians who would deny anything supernatural about the origins of Christianity; they cannot be called Christians according to the New Testament understanding of Christianity (which is surely the decisive

[1] E. and M.–L. Keller, *Miracles in Dispute: A Continuing Debate*, 1969 (English translation of *Der Streit um die Wunder*, Gütersloh, 1968).

[2] G. E. Ladd, *Jesus and the Kingdom: The Eschatology of Biblical Realism*,1966, p. 188 n. 53; cf. G. Bornkamm, *Jesus von Nazareth*, p. 165. Contrast F. F. Bruce, *The Dawn of Christianity*, 1950, Ch. 5 (= *The Spreading Flame*, 1958, Ch. 5).; *New Testament History*, 1969, p. 195.

criterion).[1] Since this is not a study in Christian apologetics, we shall not here discuss that point any further. But a Christian believer may well hesitate between the second attitude described above and a third possible attitude, according to which history may take account of supernatural events.

To the present writer the second attitude is surrounded by grave difficulties. It is at once open to suspicion because it attacks the integrity of the Christian historian. He is forced to make a sharp distinction between what he believes as a Christian and what he is allowed to state as a historian. He must not only recognize that acceptance of the Christian faith is a presupposition of his approach to reality, but he must also discard that presupposition when he undertakes historical study. But this is to introduce an impossible dichotomy into his mind. He is allowed to say one thing in the pulpit (if he is a frequenter of such a pedestal), but he must say something else in the classroom. Intellectual honesty surely forbids the erection of such a mental barrier. For if the Christian believes that the events of history cannot be exhaustively explained in naturalistic terms, then it is entirely unreasonable that he should be asked to reject the one explanation of reality that makes sense for him when he writes history.

Further, the argument often brought forward, that to introduce the possibility of the supernatural would be to make historical study impossible, since the search for rational causes and effects would then be continually threatened by the intrusion of arbitrariness into the field of historical interest, is without force. It has been taken up by D. Fuller who develops a point made by W. Pannenberg. He writes: "If the report of a unique event cannot be explained as a result of the witness's imagination, it must have happened. The historical method remains undisturbed by such irregularities, so long as we may assume that the witness has acted in a manner that corresponds with reality. The resurrection of Jesus took place in defiance of preceding causes in this world, but this was not the case with the report of the apostles. Their report was not brought about by imagination, for after the death of Jesus they wished only to disbelieve. Thus when the witnesses behave normally, we may accept their reports of miracles as true, provided that their reports can be explained only in this way."[2] And W. Pannenberg himself says: "As long as historiography does not begin dogmatically with a narrow concept of reality according to which 'dead men do not rise,' it is not clear why historiography should not in principle be able to speak about Jesus' resurrection as the explanation that is best established of such events as the disciples' experience of the

[1] Persons who deny anything "supernatural" in the ordinary sense of the term about Jesus may sometimes describe Him in terms of "transcendence"; to do so, however, is surely to admit the existence of the "supernatural" in some kind of sense.

[2] D. P. Fuller, *Easter Faith and History*, p. 251.

appearances and the discovery of the empty tomb."[1] To say this is not to accept every account of the supernatural at its face value; in every case historical criticism must be allowed its proper place.

It would appear, therefore, that there are serious objections to the second of our three attitudes, and that the Christian historian should adopt the third. We must, however, deal with an objection which is commonly brought against it. This is stated by W. Künneth who argues that to make, say, the resurrection into a historical event is to reduce it to the level of yet another relative fact in history. "It stands in continuity with a multitude of other known and unknown factors belonging to this world, is an element in historical existence and as such possesses no absolute validity but is subject to conditions and thus to the uncertainties and probabilities of all history. To insist upon the historic character of the resurrection has the result of objectifying it. The historic fact of the resurrection becomes a possible object of historical criticism and an object of rational analysis. That means, however, that the assertion of its historicality leads to an irresistible process of dissolution, which ominously threatens the reality of the resurrection itself."[2] The essence of this objection is that to make the resurrection into a historical event is to objectify it and thereby to expose it to risk. For this reason Künneth feels that the definition of the resurrection as a historical fact involves considerable dangers.

Now Künneth makes it quite plain that he does in fact believe in the reality of the resurrection event. His criticisms of its "historicality" do not therefore mean a denial of its reality. Nevertheless, his attempt to safeguard its reality at the cost of its historicality is both confused and misleading. If Künneth's view of the resurrection is correct, similar considerations must surely apply to the other events in the New Testament which are of a similar character; the whole ministry of Jesus and the experience of the Spirit in the early church surely belong in this category – unless one denies all supernatural features in the New Testament records. But, whereas the resurrection event itself can theoretically be distinguished and separated off from the events of the Easter faith of the disciples and the empty tomb, this sort of procedure is not possible with the other supernatural elements in the New Testament. The natural and supernatural are so inextricably bound up with each other that a simple differentiation is not possible. In other words, we may doubt in principle whether we can distinguish between those elements in the New Testament which can be allowed to form part of the historian's field and those which must lie

[1] W. Pannenberg, *Jesus – God and Man*, 1968, p. 109 (English translation of *Grundzüge der Christologie*, Gütersloh, 1964).

[2] W. Künneth, *The Theology of the Resurrection*, 1965, pp. 24f. (English translation of *Theologie der Auferstehung*, München, 1951).

outside or beyond it. Nor is it clear that the resurrection itself can be separated off in the way that Künneth would like. For the resurrection itself occupies a particular locus in time and space, "on the third day." As such it is open to historical or scientific investigation; it cannot be placed beyond their reach. We cannot work forwards via the crucifixion to the shutting of the tomb and say "No road"; nor can we work backwards via the appearances to the earliest point of human observation on Easter Sunday and then write "No road" at the other end. Historical study cannot rest content to remain out of the area delineated by the two "No road" signs; it has the right to ask what lies between.

Künneth's defence of the resurrection as a separate category of event, therefore, is not effective. Nor is it necessary. For to allow that the resurrection is a historical event is not to sum it up completely. It can also have the character of an event that transcends "natural" history. This is the point that Künneth wishes to safeguard, and he is quite correct to do so. What must be brought out with greater clarity is that it is not a case of "either .. or .." but rather of "both .. and ..." with the emphasis lying heavily on the "and .." Hence, in Künneth's own words, "No matter how important the historical relationships may be in detail, when the resurrection message is looked at in its essential character it does not exhaust itself in history but points decisively beyond the sphere of history."[1]

From all this we may conclude that there is no objection to the inclusion of "supernatural" elements in history from the Christian point of view. This necessarily entails the consequence that a Christian account of history may include elements which will not be universally acceptable to all historians, that is to historians who work within a naturalistic framework. This objection must be frankly admitted. The whole point of the Christian claim is that reality does not make sense apart from a Christian interpretation of it. The Christian is as justified in making his claim as is the Marxist who argues for his materialistic understanding of history.

Faith and History

In all that has been said so far, the justification for our interest in the nature of history has been that Christian faith is based on history.

If Christian faith were merely a matter of ideas, then the question would not arise. There are many issues in philosophy and mathematics which are purely in the realm of ideas and are entirely divorced from history. The truth of the theorem of Pythagoras is quite independent of whether the theorem was discovered by Pythagoras or by somebody else. Scientific

[1] *Ibid.*, p. 30.

statements too do not depend for their validity on the particular person who made them. Boyle's law would still be true even if some other chemist had discovered it. The study of the history of science or mathematics has little relevance to the truth or falsity of scientific hypotheses or mathematical ideas.

To some people the same is true of Christianity. Essentially it is regarded as a system of ideas or a philosophy of life. Consequently its "truth" does not depend upon any historical events. Just as the lesson conveyed by a parable remains true, regardless of whether the parable narrates fact or fiction, so the truth of Christianity is independent of any particular events. The teaching of Jesus would have been equally true if somebody else had given it. To be sure, value is attached to the kind of life which Jesus lived. The fact that He lived such a life is welcome proof that such a life can be lived, but if the historicity of His life were doubtful, this would not be a tremendous loss, since we would still have the ideal associated with the biblical picture of His life to set before us as a goal. And if one wished to assert the supreme value of the ideal displayed in the story of Jesus – even if one was an atheist – then it would be possible to make use of traditional language and speak of Jesus as divine or as God, using these terms purely as a means of expressing the fact that this concept of Jesus is one's ultimate concern.

It would appear to be as a result of this approach that G. E. Lessing formulated his famous dictum. He regarded the essence of Christianity as being a set of ideas, what he termed "necessary truths of reason." And his claim was that such truths cannot be proved on the basis of "accidental truths of history." A historical fact cannot be the proof of an idea.[1]

This theorem has often caused headaches for Christians who have felt that the validity of religious claims was being called in question by it. Attempts have been made to find a flaw in Lessing's logic. But the theorem appears to be sound enough, and the reply to it is to be framed rather in terms of its irrelevance. Biblical Christianity is not concerned to establish "necessary truths of reason," or at least not primarily; there is obviously a place for the Christian to engage in philosophy and to relate the truths discovered by reason to his general Christian world view. Biblical Christianity is basically concerned with the interpretation of historical facts and the communication of divine revelation. The proposition that "God" loves is not a necessary truth of reason; it could perhaps equally well be the case from a philosophical point of view that God was cruel. Rather the biblical claim that God loves is based on His activity in revealing Himself in this way; it may be based on reflection on the meaning of an event such as the

[1] H. Chadwick, *Lessing's Theological Writings*, Cambridge, 1956, pp. 51–56. See G. W. Bromiley, "History and Truth: A Study of the Axiom of Lessing," EQ 18, 1946, pp. 191–198.

cross – " the Son of God loved me and gave himself for me" (Gal. 2:20) – or it may be based on a revelation received by a prophet – "The Lord passed before him and proclaimed, 'The Lord, the Lord, a God merciful and gracious, slow to anger, and abounding in steadfast love and faithfulness'" (Exod. 34:6).

If, however, the "necessary truths of reason" concept is less popular today, there is another point of view which is equally untrue to the character of biblical religion. According to the exponents of this view, religion is not so much a matter of reason as of faith. To be a Christian is to make an act of existential commitment to Jesus. It cannot be justified in terms of reason, nor can it be justified in terms of history. This view is especially associated with the name of R. Bultmann. Bultmann draws his main evidence for it from the Gospel of John in which he finds that Jesus simply presents Himself as the Revealer of God and demands to be accepted as such without providing any proof whatsoever that He is what He claims to be. "Jesus as the Revealer of God *reveals nothing but that He is the Revealer*. And that amounts to saying that it is he for whom the world is waiting, he who brings in his own person that for which all the longing of man yearns: life and truth as the reality out of which man can exist, light as the complete transparency of existence in which questions and riddles are at an end. But how is he that and how does he bring it? In no other way than that he says that he is it and says that he brings it – he, a man with his human word, which, without legitimation, demands faith. John, that is, in his Gospel presents only the fact (*das Dass*) of the Revelation without describing its content (*ihr Was*)."[1]

The motive for this kind of statement is obvious enough. It is an attempt to preserve the true character of faith. Faith, if it is to be true faith, must not be dependent upon factual proofs. Once something has been proved either historically or by reason, it becomes a matter of knowledge and ceases to be a matter of faith. Furthermore, if faith were dependent upon historical facts, it would at once be deprived of its certainty and be put at risk, since there would always be the possibility that the facts might be disproved by historians. To make faith dependent upon history would be to destroy the character of faith as faith and to substitute fallible knowledge for it.

This approach is open to a variety of criticisms. Basically it does not do justice to the biblical idea of faith. Such faith is rooted in the historical. The Jews, for example, believed that God led their ancestors through the Red Sea into the promised land. Such a statement of belief has two sides. The Jews believed that their ancestors had come through the Red Sea, and they also believed that this crossing of the Sea was to be regarded as an act

[1] R. Bultmann, *Theology of the New Testament*, II, p. 66.

of God. Of these two elements in their faith, the first does not logically entail the second; it is possible to believe that Moses led the Israelites out of Egypt and through the Red Sea, whether or not this is interpreted as an act of God. But the second element, which is an interpretation of the first element, can be true or valid only if the first, factual element is historically true. The belief that God did something for the Israelites at the Red Sea would be completely discredited if it could be shown historically that the Israelites had never been near the Red Sea. (There is some dispute about whether it was the Red Sea or some other piece of water which the Israelites actually crossed, but this is a matter of secondary importance.) If the historical element is a fiction, then the interpretation of it in a case like this (where the claim is made that God acts in history) falls to the ground. On the other hand, if archaeological and historical science can produce some confirmation that the Israelites did make the crossing, then this makes it possible to go on to raise the question whether the event was an act of God. The presence of historical proof affords confirmation of the factual aspect of the belief, and thereby makes it reasonable to go on to ask about the validity of the interpretative aspect of the belief. Consequently, the question of historical proof cannot be set aside as easily as Bultmann wishes. If, for example, the Johannine evidence on which Bultmann bases his view of Jesus as the Revealer who reveals only that He is the Revealer were to be disputed from a historical point of view, then faith in that kind of Jesus would be impossible. Biblical faith is a compound of various elements, including knowledge, trust and commitment, and commitment is based on knowledge.

The point of view for which we are contending is stated sharply by H. von Campenhausen in his discussion of the resurrection. He vigorously rejects the viewpoint which regards the resurrection as being beyond historical study and says: "All that remains is simply the biblical witness as such, the kerygma, which demands faith, and to which, therefore, one has to submit in faith."[1] Rather, he says, "a theology of the resurrection must abandon the old and foolish attempt to restrict reason to such an extent that the only way out is, apparently, to believe."[2] History "belongs, in fact, of necessity to the witness, which, apart from it, would lose its meaning. Notwithstanding its actual, life-giving sense, the resurrection remains a real event of the historical past, and is the object of tradition, preaching and faith. Its preaching, therefore, cannot evade the historical problem, nor can it, by any means, be exempted from historical examination. Already

---

[1] H. F. von Campenhausen, "The Events of Easter and the Empty Tomb," in *Tradition and Life in the Church*, 1968, pp. 42–89; quotation from pp. 88 f. (English translation of *Tradition und Leben – Kräfte der Kirchengeschichte*, Tübingen, 1960).

[2] *Ibid.*, p. 89.

the Evangelists conducted themselves on these lines in their accounts of Easter. With all their *naïveté* and awkwardness they faced the 'critical' doubts which showed themselves and, as well as they could, refuted them 'historically.' Even Paul did so, though for him faith itself did not rest simply as an 'historical' basis."[1] Faith, therefore, would be irresponsible if it did not examine its own historical credentials. If it could be proved that Jesus did not appear alive to His disciples, and that His tomb was not found to be empty, then there would be no basis for faith in the resurrection. Once, however, these facts have been shown to be probable or even certain, then the question arises, "How is this to be explained? Is it an act of God?" At the same time, however, the ultimate question cannot be evaded: "How does this divine act affect my life? Do I commit my life to the God who raises the dead?"

Similarly, W. Pannenberg has claimed that "the essence of faith is destroyed where it appears as an unfounded risk. The ground of faith must be as certain as possible."[2] Pannenberg's reason for making this assertion is that faith has no means of access to the events of the past that is inaccessible to the historian. This point is open to challenge; it ignores the possibility of a divine revelation in which the meaning of past events may be directly disclosed to a man; biblical prophecy is concerned with the interpretation of what has already happened as well as with the prediction of what is to happen. Nevertheless, Pannenberg's basic contention remains inviolate: the contemporary believer must go back to history, even if it is biblical history, if he is to find the basis for his faith.

What, then, about the apparent removal of the element of risk in faith? Pannenberg explains that "the essence of faith is preserved by the eschatological tension of the 'not yet' in which the believer lives on the basis of the Christ event." There is still "an openness to the eschatological future, an openness into which the person is also drawn who enters into this event, and that is the element of truth in speaking about the character of faith as risk."[3] Here Pannenberg has clearly grasped one aspect of the risk involved in faith: the future remains a matter of faith and hope, whatever may be true of the past. But there is still an element of risk in faith with regard the past. On the one hand, the historical status of the facts on which faith builds may be questionable. As we have seen earlier, many historical facts must be qualified with a "probably." On the other hand, the interpretation of the facts may also be uncertain. The reason why Pannenberg himself fails to suggest this lies in his view of the relation of history to

[1] *Ibid.*, pp. 87f.
[2] W. Pannenberg, *Jesus – God and Man*, p. 110.
[3] *Ibid.*, p. 110.

revelation, according to which revelation is found in history itself without the need for any inspired interpretation from another source.[1] Faith, then, does contain an element of risk, despite Bultmann. But this does not mean that the believer lives in constant doubt. For faith is not dependent upon one fact but upon many, and the doubt that may attach to one fact does not necessarily attach to the others. Again, faith is closely linked with the personal experience of the believer, so that he finds that it is confirmed or jeopardized by experience itself. Nevertheless, the believer is interested in history, and is concerned that the historical foundations of his faith should be adequately investigated, so that he may distinguish solid rock from shifting sand. History is not irrelevant to faith, but historical statements form part of the substance of faith. The question now arises as to the attitude of Luke to this problem.

Luke and History: The Prologue

In the preceding discussion we have assumed that a particular point of view regarding the relation of faith to history, which commended itself to us as intrinsically reasonable, was in fact that of the Bible. Biblical faith is based upon history. But is this assumption justified? In particular, is it justified in the case of Luke with whom we are here principally concerned? What is his view of the relation between history and faith, and does he provide an adequate justification of his view?

We are fortunate in having Luke's own comment on his intentions at the beginning of his Gospel. Following the literary conventions of the time he commences his work with an exordium whose wording we may conveniently reproduce here: "Inasmuch as many have undertaken to compile a narrative of the things which have been accomplished among us, just as they were delivered to us by those who from the beginning were eyewitnesses and ministers of the word, it seemed good to me also, having followed all things closely for some time past, to write an orderly account for you, most excellent Theophilus, that you may know the truth concerning the things of which you have been informed" (Luke 1:1-4).[2]

Although this prologue, written as it is in good Hellenistic Greek and in marked contrast with the rather Hebraistic style of the immediately fol-

---

[1] D. P. Fuller, "A New German Theological Movement," SJT 19, 1966, pp. 160-175.

[2] See H. J. Cadbury, BC II, pp. 489-510; id., "'We' and 'I' Passages in Luke-Acts," NTS 3, 1957-58, pp. 128-132; N. B. Stonehouse, *The Witness of Luke to Christ*, 1951, pp. 24-25; id., *The Origins of the Synoptic Gospels*, 1964, pp. 115-128; G. Klein, "Lukas i. 1-4 als theologisches Programm," ZG, pp. 193-216; H. Schürmann, "Evangelienschrift und kirchliche Unterweisung. Die repräsentative Funktion der Schrift nach Lk 1, 1-4," in *Traditionsgeschichtliche Untersuchungen*, pp. 251-271; S. Schulz, *Die Stunde der Botschaft*, Hamburg, 1967, pp. 242-250 R. Glöckner, *Die Verkündigung des Heils beim Evangelisten Lukas*, Mainz, 1976, pp. 3-41; I. H. Marshall. GL, pp. 39-44.

lowing narrative, conforms in certain respects to the typical pattern of ancient literary prologues, the wording is not to be regarded as simply a piling up of conventional expressions with little or no regard being paid to their content. Luke has rather made use of the common literary pattern of his time to express his own particular sentiments. The point in the adoption of the conventional form is that Luke was claiming for his work a place in contemporary literature and thereby commending it to the attention of readers. He is confessedly writing a piece of literature, no doubt meant for a wider audience than would be found within the circle of the Christian church. In effect, therefore, he was affirming that his theme formed part of world history. How far his predecessors may have had similar thoughts is a moot point; the evidence of the surviving Christian literature of the time preserved in the New Testament suggests that their intended readership was more probably in the church.

Luke states that his aim was to write an orderly account of what had been happening and he uses a word (διήγησις) to describe his venture (and that of his predecessors) which means "a narrative." The aim, therefore, may certainly be characterized as the writing of history according to the standards of the time. We may note a number of characteristics of the way in which Luke conceived his task.

There is first of all a stress on the accuracy of what is to be presented. Theophilus, who is Luke's literary patron, is to be made aware of the truth concerning the things of which he had already been informed. The type of instruction which Theophilus had already received is uncertain: does the verb used (κατηχέω, "to inform") mean that he had picked up some knowledge of Christianity by hearsay or had he received a more formal training? Scholars who are inclined to reject the second alternative rightly point out that a developed system of catechetical training for Christian converts is not attested for this period, but it is surely not necessary to assume that Theophilus had undergone a formal Christian education in the sense of the later catechumenate in order to have a reasonable knowledge of the Christian faith. Since Luke is able to say that what Theophilus had already learned possessed "reliability" (ἀσφάλεια), it appears likely that he had had more than a hearsay acquaintance with Christianity;[1] the possibility too that as Luke's literary patron he would be expected to help in the publication of the book would suggest that he was in fact a Christian.[2]

What, therefore, Luke intended to do by his fresh exposition of Christian beginnings was to confirm for Theophilus the truth of the facts

---

[1] The more general sense is adopted by H. W. Beyer, TDNT III, pp. 638–640. For the meaning adopted here see especially H. Schürmann, op. cit., pp. 254 f.

[2] Cf. E. Haenchen, Die Apostelgeschichte, p. 105 n. 3; cf. n. 4.

which had already been transmitted to him. The provision of a new, orderly narrative would act as further confirmation of what was already known. Luke thus wished to stress the accuracy of the historical facts which formed part of early Christian teaching.

This view of Luke's intentions has been subjected to criticism by U. Luck.[1] He has argued that Luke's purpose was to give a guarantee for the content of the apostolic preaching by showing that the life of Jesus was a series of divine deeds worked by the same Spirit as was now operative in the church and testified to by the apostles who were chosen under the guidance of the Spirit. Luck therefore asserts that the ἀσφάλεια of which Theophilus had to be convinced was concerned not with a historically grounded certitude which rested only on the transmitted facts but rather with the recognition of the "things" (πράγματα) as acts of God. Luke's aim was to show that the life of Jesus was a series of divine acts rather than to affirm the factual certainty of those acts. This thesis may be regarded as correct in what it affirms, but wrong in what it denies. It ignores the use of such words as "eyewitnesses," "accurately," "in order" and (in Acts 1:3) "many proofs," all of which point to a writer for whom correct history was a matter of importance. It may well be that we are to trace here the existence of a gnostic or docetic form of teaching which minimized the importance of the historical Jesus and against which Luke thought it necessary to mount an attack.[2]

A second point which emerges in the prologue is concerned with Luke's own credentials for the task of writing. He describes himself as "having followed all things closely for some time now" (παρηκολουθη-κότι ἄνωθεν πᾶσιν ἀκριβῶς). The verb used means literally "to follow, accompany." In a number of places H. J. Cadbury has contended strongly for the view that the verb, as used here, can only mean "to observe," so that Luke is here claiming the authority of an eyewitness for his history.[3] Cadbury denies that the verb can have the meaning "to investigate": "The writer's information had (notice the perfect tense) come to him as the events took place; it was not the result of special reading and study."[4] In the opinion of later writers, however, Cadbury has circumscribed the meaning of the verb too narrowly. Since Luke expressly distinguishes himself from the eyewitnesses (verse 2), it is unlikely that he is here claiming to be an eyewitness in the full sense himself, and since, as Cadbury allows, the verb can be used of "following what is read or said," it seems better to allow a broader sense to the verb and not restrict it to

[1] U. Luck, "Kerygma, Tradition und Geschichte bei Lukas," ZTK 57, 1960, pp. 51–66.
[2] H. Schürmann, *op. cit.*, p. 254; cf. C. H. Talbert, *Luke and the Gnostics*, Nashville, 1966.
[3] H. J. Cadbury, as in p. 37 n. 2 above; "The Knowledge claimed in Luke's Preface," Exp. VIII, 24, 1922, pp. 401–420.
[4] H. J. Cadbury, in BC II, p. 502.

personal participation.[1] At the same time, however, it must be remembered that the prologue is probably meant to refer to both parts of the two-volume work.[2] If this is the case, then Luke may well be referring to his own participation in some of the events described in Acts as well as to his more general acquaintance with early church history.[3]

We should probably construe the adverb "accurately" ($\dot{\alpha}\kappa\rho\iota\beta\hat{\omega}s$) with the verb "to follow" ($\pi\alpha\rho\alpha\kappa o\lambda ov\theta\acute{\epsilon}\omega$) rather than with the following "to write" ($\gamma\rho\acute{\alpha}\psi\alpha\iota$).[4] If so, it indicates that Luke was careful in his investigations of the available material. The immediately following "orderly" ($\kappa\alpha\theta\epsilon\xi\hat{\eta}s$) will qualify $\gamma\rho\acute{\alpha}\psi\alpha\iota$ and describe the character of Luke's narrative. But the precise import of this word is uncertain. Most commentators take it simply to refer to orderly and lucid narrative, but it may imply in a fairly general manner that Luke is following chronological order in his narrative.[5] Whatever be the precise force of the adverbs, the main impression is plain. It is confirmed that Luke had certain standards in the composition of his work. He was prepared to characterize his work as being based on careful observation and incorporating an orderly narrative.

The third feature of the prologue is the way in which it refers to Luke's predecessors in his task. To be sure, the opening "many" ($\pi o\lambda\lambda o\acute{\iota}$) is not to be pressed, but is rather a literary convention; we may compare the "many years" of Felix's governorship in Acts 24:10, which is also formal. Again, while we know that Luke had predecessors in the composition of Gospel material, the existence of predecessors in writing about the early church is much less certain. What is important is that there were predecessors and that Luke obviously made use of their work. It has been alleged that the tone of Luke's reference to them is disparaging: they merely "attempted" ($\dot{\epsilon}\pi\epsilon\chi\epsilon\acute{\iota}\rho\eta\sigma\alpha\nu$) to compose their narratives, and the fact that Luke went on to compose a fresh one indicates that he found fault with their attempts.[6] But this is undoubtedly a false reading of what Luke says. In itself the verb $\dot{\epsilon}\pi\iota\chi\epsilon\iota\rho\acute{\epsilon}\omega$ does not imply the success or failure of an attempt.[7] Moreover, Luke appears to place himself alongside his predecessors ($\kappa\dot{\alpha}\mu o\acute{\iota}$) rather than over against them, and the way in

---

[1] N. B. Stonehouse, as in p. 37 n. 2 above.

[2] G. Klein, op. cit., p. 205. Contra: E. Haenchen, op. cit., p. 105 n. 3; G. Delling, TWNT VIII, pp. 32 f.

[3] E. Trocmé, Le "Livre des Actes" et l'histoire, Paris, 1957, pp. 125–127.

[4] H. J. Cadbury, BC II, pp. 504f., seems inclined to take it with $\gamma\rho\acute{\alpha}\psi\alpha\iota$.

[5] J. Jeremias in a seminar (1959–60) adopted the meaning "hereinafter" (suggested in H. J. Cadbury, BC II, p. 505). G. Klein, op. cit., pp. 210f., holds that it refers to the chronological linking of the story of Jesus and the time of the early Church.

[6] S. Schulz, Die Stunde der Botschaft, p. 244; G. Klein, op. cit., pp. 195f. Contra: W. G. Kümmel, Introduction to the New Testament, 1966, p. 91 (English translation of Einleitung in das Neue Testament, Heidelberg, 1965).

[7] MM, s.v.; N. B. Stonehouse, The Witness of Luke to Christ, pp. 31f.; H. Schürmann, op. cit., p. 259.

which he speaks of Theophilus receiving fresh confirmation of the accuracy of what he has already learned suggests that he had a high regard for his predecessors. The force of the sonorous opening conjunction "inasmuch as" (ἐπειδήπερ) should not be overlooked. It is causal rather than concessive, and the sense is that Luke is using the work of previous writers positively to justify his own further attempt rather than stating that he is writing *although* they have already written.

This view of things is confirmed strongly by the way in which Luke states that their work, like his, was based on information supplied by "those who from the beginning were eyewitnesses and ministers of the word." By his use of this phrase Luke differentiates himself from the class of early witnesses and places himself in the second or a subsequent generation of believers. The phrase which he uses indicates that one class of people, who were both eyewitnesses and servants of the word, is meant, and we are probably to see the apostles as being comprehended within the group. In this way Luke is claiming to reproduce early tradition concerning the ministry of Jesus, and the verb which he uses (παρέδοσαν) may perhaps be taken to indicate the official manner in which the tradition was handed down.[1]

The content of the tradition is described as "the things which have been accomplished among us" (τῶν πεπληροφορημένων ἐν ἡμῖν πραγμάτων). The use of this verb suggests that Luke is thinking of events which were promised and performed by God: it conveys the idea of fulfilment.[2] Thus the events recorded by Luke are seen as having a particular interpretation; they are not mere events, but form part of a series planned and carried into effect by God. The use of the perfect tense stresses this idea of completion and fulfilment. Whether, however, it should be pressed to mean that the series of past events forms a completed whole[3] is less certain.

We have now looked at the main features of Luke's prologue, and have seen that it indicates a concern to provide reliable history, confirming previous accounts and based on sound evidence. According to his own testimony Luke wished to be taken seriously as a historian. Whether his work measures up to the standards expected of an accurate historian is a question to be discussed in due course. In the meantime another point demands our attention.

Witness to the Resurrection

It would be inadequate to base an interpretation of Luke's activity as a historian solely on the evidence of the prologue. Is there confirmatory

---

[1] For this usage cf. 1 Cor. 11:2, 23; 15:3.
[2] G. Klein, *op. cit.*, pp. 196-200.
[3] So G. Klein, *ibid.*

evidence to be found elsewhere in his writings? Does Luke make it apparent in the course of his work that he attaches importance to the reliable recording of facts?

Evidence of Luke's attitude on this point is readily available if we turn to the Acts of the Apostles and notice there the way in which he develops his ideas concerning the resurrection. For Luke the resurrection is the crucial event in salvation-history, and consequently his treatment of it is of especial importance.

The typical argumentation of the early preachers before a Jewish audience in Acts is described in Luke's own words as "explaining and proving that it was necessary for the Christ to suffer and to rise from the dead, and saying, 'This Jesus, whom I proclaim to you is the Christ'" (Acts 17:3). The form of the argument is simple enough. First, on the basis of the Old Testament a case is developed by which one may recognize the Christ when He comes: Old Testament prophecy is said to show that the Christ will suffer and rise from the dead. Then, it is argued that a particular person, namely Jesus, fulfils these requirements. Therefore, the conclusion follows that Jesus is the Christ. Admittedly the middle step in the argument is not spelled out in the passage under consideration, but it is implicit in the statement. Elsewhere Luke indicates that the resurrection of Jesus was a matter of considerable dispute. Not only was it an object of scorn to the cultured critics of Paul at Athens (Acts 17:32), but also Jews, who accepted the doctrine of the final resurrection readily enough (Acts 23:8; 24:15) found it hard to believe that the final resurrection had already been anticipated in the case of Jesus (Acts 26:8).

It is not surprising, therefore, that the kingpin in the Christian case, as presented by Luke, lay in the provision of evidence for the resurrection; there was naturally no need to prove that Jesus had suffered and died. At the very beginning of Acts Luke informs us that Jesus "presented himself alive after his passion by many proofs" to the apostles (Acts 1:3). The language used ($\tau\epsilon\kappa\mu\eta\rho\iota o\nu$) suggests the convincing and decisive nature of the proof that was offered.[1] The fact that the apostles ate and drank with Jesus is regarded as evidence for the reality of His resurrection (Acts 10:41). Since, however, the appearances of Jesus did not take place to the people at large but only to those who were chosen by God to act as witnesses (Acts 10:41), it is not surprising that a particular stress falls upon the function of these witnesses. Luke in fact singles out the Twelve as the decisive witnesses to the fact of the resurrection. Already in Acts 1 the story of the choice of Matthias to replace Judas shows the importance which was attached to the Twelve; the Twelve had a special ministry to perform, described as being witnesses to the resurrection (Acts 1:22).

[1] AG s.v.

Luke has little to say about the function of the Twelve as leaders in the church; as witnesses to the resurrection and close associates of the earthly Jesus, they must undoubtedly have formed the leadership of the church in the earliest period, but in the narrative in Acts they very quickly disappear from view so far as this aspect of their work is concerned; after Acts 16:4 they do not reappear. It is their character as witnesses which is of significance, and the terminology of witness, which is comparatively rare in Paul, is greatly used by Luke in this connexion.

The main task of the witnesses was to affirm the reality of the resurrection (Acts 2:32; 3:15; 4:33; 5:32; 10:41; 13:31); this is in complete harmony with the view of Paul, according to whom an apostle is one who has seen the risen Lord and has received God's commission to preach (*i.e.*, in Lucan terminology, to witness) (1 Cor. 9:1f.; Gal. 1:15f.). But Luke differs from Paul in laying stress on the fact that the apostles had to be men who had been companions of Jesus from the time of His work in Galilee, and even from the baptism of John (Acts 1:21f.; 10:39; 13:31). This Lucan emphasis is no doubt to be explained by the necessity that those who bore testimony to the resurrection must be men who had already known Jesus and therefore were properly qualified to recognize that it was the same person who was risen from the dead. At the same time, however, the events of the earthly ministry of Jesus were important for Luke – otherwise he would not have composed a Gospel – and it was vital for him that there should be proper testimony to them. Thus what is said about the witnesses in Acts fits in with the important place which is assigned to them in Luke 1:1-4.[1]

The theme of witness is not prominent in the Gospel of Luke, except in the context of the resurrection (Luke 24:48) where the point developed in Acts is already adumbrated. Nevertheless, we may notice that the same stress on the factuality of the saving events is present. In Luke 7:18-23 there is the incident of John the Baptist sending his messengers to Jesus to enquire whether Jesus was the coming one or not. In Matthew's version of the incident (Matt. 11:2-6) Jesus merely tells the messengers to inform John of what they hear and see, but in Luke's version this command of Jesus is preceded by a description of various mighty works carried out in the presence of the messengers. It is a fair inference that Luke regarded the provision of visual evidence for the messengers as important. In the same way we may perhaps see significance in the promise of God to Simeon that he should see the Lord's Christ and in its fulfilment in the temple; Simeon praised God and confessed himself to be at peace "for mine eyes have seen thy salvation" (Luke 2:30).

[1] On the apostleship of Paul see my article "The Resurrection in the Acts of the Apostles," in AHG, pp. 92-107.

The evidence of specific statements in the Gospel is slight. But the general impression made by the Gospel and Acts is forceful. H. Conzelmann has claimed that Luke saw the life of Jesus as a piece of redemptive history, indeed the central part in the history of salvation, and that he wrote something resembling a biography of Jesus. Further, the way in which Luke articulated the life of Jesus and the apostolic age into one single piece of historical writing shows that he was conscious of acting as a historian. We need not repeat Conzelmann's detailed exposition of this thesis here.[1] As we shall see, considerable qualification of the thesis in detail is required, in particular the view that Luke was a pioneer in this approach, but in broad outline it can stand, and it affords some confirmation of the position which we have advocated.

History and the Kerygma

In summary, therefore, Luke is to be regarded as claiming to write history and attaching importance to the accurate reporting of the crucial events associated with Jesus. But now two further points must be considered. The first of them raises an important objection to the kind of view of Luke which we have been developing. The second is concerned with the legitimacy of what he was doing over against the background of early Christianity.

(1). Our opening remarks on the modern emphasis in the study of the Gospels showed how the Gospel writers were being increasingly recognized as theologians rather than simply as compilers of existing traditions. Associated with this recognition has been the assumption that because they were theologians they could not have been historians. We have become accustomed to the statement that the Gospels are not biographies of Jesus and were never intended to be such. They are rather the testimonies of faith in Jesus.[2] To attempt to obtain historical information about Jesus from them is a task of the greatest difficulty, since it means using the Gospels for a purpose for which they were not originally intended.

Behind this assumption regarding the Gospels there lies the further assumption that the early church was not interested in history. At the centre of its life was its preaching. "Preaching" is in itself a fairly innocuous term, but clothed in Greek dress as "kerygma" ($\kappa\acute{\eta}\rho\upsilon\gamma\mu\alpha$), a word which can be used in the New Testament either of the act of preaching or of the content of preaching, it has taken on a mysterious character and seems to be

[1] H. Conzelmann, *Die Mitte der Zeit*, pp. 4–8 (Eng. Tr., pp. 12–15).
[2] So, for example, G. Bouwmann, *Das Dritte Evangelium: Einübung in die formgeschichtliche Methode*, Düsseldorf, 1968, p. 16.

regarded by some writers as the answer to every problem in early church history.[1] In particular, the point has been frequently made that the early church did not narrate the history of Jesus; it simply proclaimed Him as the risen and exalted One. Salvation depended upon acceptance of the kerygma rather than upon acceptance of historical facts about Jesus. Indeed, one cannot get back to Jesus, except *via* the kerygma; for the early church what mattered was not the historical Jesus but the Christ proclaimed in the kerygma. For a time it was the claim of some modern writers that the historical Jesus cannot be known and that we ought not to want to know Him; we must be satisfied with the kerygma in which Christ is present and is presented to us. Such at any rate was the position adopted by R. Bultmann, or at the very least the impression which he gave. A less rigorous position has been adopted by some of his followers, associated with the "New Quest of the Historical Jesus." They would claim that there are two avenues of access to Jesus. One is this approach through the kerygma. The other is through a historical enquiry which is able to find in the Gospels something of the existential significance of Jesus; from the Gospels we can deduce what were Jesus' intentions and how He understood human existence. Thus it becomes possible to have some check on the message found in the kerygma; we can see whether the understanding of Jesus' existence found in the preaching of the early church corresponds "to the understanding of existence implicit in Jesus' history, as encountered through modern historiography."[2] Nevertheless, it is still asserted that it is not historiography which saves a man by giving him reliable knowledge about Jesus; rather, what historiography does is to open up another route by which he may be confronted with the message found in the kerygma. The kerygma of the early church did not try to legitimate itself by appeal to the historical facts of the life of Jesus; it simply presented the same call to decision as was inherent in the ministry of Jesus. Nor should modern man seek to get behind the kerygma in order to find some facts which would substantiate it and thus legitimate his faith.

The Gospels are, then, to be understood as falling into this pattern prescribed in the kerygma. And if they give the impression of containing history and presenting historical facts, this is because they have "historicized" the kerygma. They have taken the assertions of the kerygma and clothed them in a secondary, historical form. But this means that what appears in the Gospels in the form of history is not to be taken at its face value and uncritically as historical narration. One writer, S. Schulz, has

[1] The basic study of C. H. Dodd, *The Apostolic Preaching and its Developments*, 1936, should not be blamed for the subsequent loose use of the term.
[2] J. M. Robinson, *A New Quest of the Historical Jesus*, p. 94.

even coined a phrase in claiming that the "historicizing" which goes on in Luke is really "kerygmaticizing" (*Kerygmatisierung*); that is to say, it is carried on for the purpose of preaching the Gospel.[1]

It is surely time that this false and self-contradictory view of the Gospels and of Luke in particular should be shown up for what it really is and dismissed from further consideration.

We may note, first, that the basis of this general outlook, namely that the tasks of proclamation and of writing history are incompatible, is pure assumption, and baseless assumption at that. What is being suggested to us is twofold. First, it is being denied that faith can be dependent upon historical facts. We have already shown above that this denial rests upon an inadequate understanding of the nature of faith. Faith contains an intellectual element. To believe in a message – the terminology is biblical (Mark 1:15) – or in a person (Acts 16:31) involves acceptance *that* the message is true or *that* the person is of a particular character or has done particular things. Faith, therefore, cannot be indifferent to historical facts. If the proclamation concerns Jesus Christ crucified and risen from the dead, then faith in the proclamation cannot be indifferent to the questions whether Jesus Christ was crucified and did rise from the dead. And if it should be the case that all the historical evidence was against these two facts, then faith would be reduced to obstinate and irrational fantasy. It is of course true that faith may face great obstacles including historical obstacles. "In hope Abraham believed against hope" (Rom. 4:18); faith is concerned with "things hoped for" and "things not seen" (Heb. 11:1) But this does not mean that faith is irrational or historically groundless. The person who believes has good reason for being like Abraham and not trusting to appearances; he has some particular ground for extending his faith to things for which he might otherwise only hope and believing in things which he cannot see. Faith is dependent upon historical facts. Moreover, this is true of biblical faith and not merely of a modern view of faith. Paul writes, "If you confess with your lips that Jesus is Lord and believe in your heart that God raised Him from the dead, you will be saved" (Rom. 10:9). The belief that is spoken of here is a belief that includes accepting certain things about Jesus as being true. The point on which stress is laid is that God raised Him from the dead. In this proposition there is both a factual element and a theological interpretation of it. If the factual element is not true, then there would be no event to be interpreted. If Jesus did not rise from the dead at all, then the question whether it was *God* who raised Him cannot even be discussed. As Paul puts it elsewhere, "If Christ has not been raised, then our preaching is in vain, and your faith is in vain" (1 Cor. 15:14). We may, therefore, be assured that

[1] S. Schulz, *Die Stunde der Botschaft*, pp. 251, 280.

the view of the content of faith which we have adopted is that of a New Testament writer like Paul himself.

The second suggestion that is being made in this assumption is that a person who is committed to proclamation or to theology cannot write history. The point is one that has been developed by N. Perrin in his discussion of contemporary scholarly methods of investigating the Gospel tradition. "The gospel form was created," he writes, "to serve the purpose of the early Church, but historical reminiscence was not one of those purposes . . . So far as we can tell today, there is no single pericope anywhere in the gospels, the present purpose of which is to preserve a historical reminiscence of the earthly Jesus."[1] What Perrin means is that the contents of the Gospels were preserved because of their theological importance for the early church. This in itself is true enough. But to argue that because this was the motive in the preservation of the material therefore there can be no place at the same time for historical reminiscence is palpably illogical. There is no reason why the interests of the theologian and the historian should be mutually exclusive. It is true that a sceptic could argue that the theologian invented the so-called facts and their interpretation. This is a case which must be tested in the light of the historical evidence available – is it fact or fiction? But this is quite different from making the arbitrary assertion that the writing of theology automatically excludes the writing of history. If Perrin means merely that the Gospel writers were not historians, in the sense of collecting and checking every fact purely out of a disinterested passion for researching into the past, then we would have to agree with him. By this narrow definition of what it means to be a historian, they were not historians. But if some problem arose in the early church and it was asked, "What did Jesus say or do about this?" then to supply an answer to that question by telling what Jesus said or did was to engage in historical reminiscence and to set down a piece of genuine history.

Perrin's error is due to a false understanding of the nature of historiography. A historian records what he considers to be significant and memorable. Historical facts are precisely those facts which a historian thought worthy of being recorded. Historians are *not* disinterested. Perrin's implicit definition of the activity of the historian as disinterested scientific investigation is out of date. This is why he draws his false antithesis between historical reminiscence from disinterested motives and inquiry into what Jesus said and did in order to help the needs of the church, and then supposes that the latter activity cannot lead to sound knowledge of the past. It is not a man's motive in studying the past which determines whether the result is history; it is his diligence, accuracy and

[1] N. Perrin, *Rediscovering the Teaching of Jesus*, 1967, pp. 15f.

insight as an investigator. We can, therefore, dismiss Perrin's case, and with it the assumption that the tasks of theological proclamation and of writing history are incompatible.

(2). We must now consider the legitimacy of what Luke was doing over against the background of early Christianity. We saw that according to the modern view the kerygma of the early church is to be regarded as pure proclamation without any historical content. It was not a summons to accept certain historical facts on which faith might be grounded but simply a challenge to accept a person. The evidence which is adduced in favour of this view is that in the kerygma of the early church there is little, if any, reference to the historical facts of the life and ministry of Jesus. We are presented merely with Bultmann's "*Dass.*" The Gospel tradition appears to have exerted no effect upon the content of the preaching. In the writings of Paul there is hardly any reference to the historical Jesus; he has indeed been held to repudiate knowledge of the historical Jesus on the basis of a dubious exegesis of 2 Cor. 5:16. Consequently, the sort of history which is presented by Luke must be regarded as a new venture in the church, and some scholars have suggested that it was an illegitimate venture.[1]

It lies beyond our present purpose to discuss in detail the apparent disjunction in the New Testament between the kerygma on one side and the Gospel tradition on the other. It must suffice to hint at a solution. The fact that Paul has little to say about the earthly ministry of Jesus in his Epistles cannot be taken to mean that he was ignorant of, or opposed to, the presentation of the gospel in this way.[2] Some other explanation of his silence must be found. The clue to a solution lies in the fact that the Epistles of John are free from the type of historical material found in the Gospel of John. This is a compelling indication that the two types of material were deliberately kept separate. One single writer (or school of writers, if the common authorship of the Epistles and Gospel is disallowed) carefully differentiated between Gospel tradition (even in its Johannine "developed" form) and the type of material appropriate to Epistles. It would seem legitimate to conclude that the Gospel tradition was a distinct stream in the early church with its own special channel of transmission.[3] Both Paul on the one hand and the Synoptic Evangelists on the other are witnesses to the fact of this differentiation.

---

[1] See U. Luck, *op. cit.*, p. 53; W. C. van Unnik in SLA, pp. 27f. Van Unnik himself does not share this point of view.

[2] See W. G. Kümmel, "Jesus und Paulus," NTS 10, 1963–64, pp. 163–181, especially pp. 175–177. Contra: W. Schmithals, "Paulus und der historische Jesus," ZNW 53, 1962, pp. 145–160.

[3] Here I find the view of H. Riesenfeld, *The Gospel Tradition and its Beginnings*, 1957, and B. Gerhardsson, *Memory and Manuscript*, Uppsala, 1961, more convincing than that of W. Schmithals, although it probably requires considerable qualification.

Next, we must observe that Luke was not "out on a limb" in "historicizing the kerygma." He was not in fact the first Christian historian. He was preceded by Mark whose Gospel takes the form of a history of Jesus in which the various units of tradition about Him are put into a chronological and geographical framework.[1] The process is thus earlier than Luke. This is of course in agreement with Luke's own reference to his predecessors who drew up accounts of what had happened.

We may trace the line further. Did the preaching of the early church contain any reference to the facts of the earthly ministry of Jesus? One prominent scholar who thought so was M. Dibelius, and his point of view is of especial value because it arose from form-critical considerations. According to Dibelius the *Sitz im Leben* of much of the Gospel material was to be found in the early preaching of the church. "In the beginning was the sermon" is an apt summary of his approach.[2] If so, it is likely that no disparity was seen between the kerygma and the "history" of Jesus; the latter would be used to illustrate and give content to the former.

It may well be that Dibelius over-emphasized the place of missionary preaching as the life-setting of the Gospel material, and that other situations in the church must also be taken into account. But, even if this is granted, his basic point still remains sound, namely that the kerygma was associated with the Gospel tradition.

It is, however, notoriously difficult to proceed further than this and to find actual examples of the connexion between the kerygma and the Gospel tradition. Consequently, H. Riesenfeld was prepared to deny the thesis of Dibelius.[3] In our opinion this reversion to the other extreme is unnecessary. The problem is that we have so little material – outside the Gospels themselves – for reconstructing the early preaching. Various scholars, notably C. H. Dodd,[4] have attempted a reconstruction of the outline of the preaching by utilizing primitive material preserved in the Epistles and the evidence of the speeches in Acts. But all that can be produced by such research is a brief sermon outline, and we have no evidence as to how it was filled out. It has indeed been argued that to speak of "*the* kerygma" is misleading and that we should think rather of several versions of the message as being current.[5] What this means is that we largely lack the materials to prove or to disprove Dibelius' theory.

[1] S. Schulz, "Die Bedeutung des Markus für die Theologiegeschichte des Urchristentums," in SE II, 1964, pp. 135–145.

[2] E. Fascher, *Die formgeschichtliche Methode*, Berlin, 1924, p. 54, cited by V. Taylor, *The Gospel according to St. Mark*, 1953, p. 18. See N. Perrin, *What is Redaction Criticism?* 1970, p. 15 n. 19.

[3] H. Riesenfeld, *op. cit.*, pp. 8–13.

[4] C. H. Dodd, *op. cit.*

[5] C. F. Evans, "The Kerygma," JTS n.s. 7, 1956, pp. 25–41; J. P. M. Sweet, "The Kerygma," Exp. T. 76, 1964–65, pp. 143–147.

One point, however, is worth pursuing. The specimen early sermons in Acts 10:34–43 and 13:23–31 both contain allusions to the earthly ministry of Jesus which could easily have been filled out with fuller historical detail. Recent scholarship, however, has claimed either that the speeches in Acts are Lucan creations or that they have been so heavily worked over by Luke that it is impossible to know what is primitive material in them. In[1] particular U. Wilckens has attempted to show that Acts 10:34–43 represents a sermon meant for Christians and that it is based on the historical scheme already used by Luke in his Gospel. So far is it from being the case that the Gospels represent an expanded kerygma that in fact the kerygma according to Luke is a summary of the Gospel according to Luke.[2]

Wilckens' case is certainly to be rejected. For in fact the outline of the speech in Acts 10 is in agreement with the outline of the kerygma as it can be reconstructed from the evidence of Paul.[3] Further, although the vocabulary and style of the speech is to be ascribed to Luke, the basic treatment of the earthly life of Jesus agrees not merely with the pattern of the Gospel of Luke but also with the pattern of the Gospel of Mark. Consequently it remains the more plausible thesis that the structure of the Gospel is dependent upon the kerygma than vice-versa. There is no need to abandon the view of Dibelius.

As we indicated earlier, the stress in the apostolic message did fall more upon the death and resurrection of Jesus than upon His earthly ministry. These were, however, historical events, and therefore they had to be established as such to the hearers. This, we saw, was why Luke had so much to say about the witnesses who attested them in Acts. The same point, however, is found in the earlier tradition. Rom. 10:9, discussed above, is widely recognized as primitive in origin.[4] 1 Cor. 15:3–5 is used by Paul as part of his argument concerning what is of primary importance in the Christian faith. But this passage too is an extract from primitive tradition. It consists of plain statements concerning what Jesus did. They are theological statements, for they speak of death "for our sins" and assert that Christ "was raised," namely by the Father,[5] but at the same time they are historical statements for they speak about death, burial and

---

[1] M. Dibelius, *Studies in the Acts of the Apostles*, 1956 (English translation of *Aufsätze zur Apostelgeschichte*, Göttingen, 1951); U. Wilckens, *Die Missionsreden der Apostelgeschichte*, Neukirchen-Vluyn, 1963².

[2] U. Wilckens, "Kerygma und Evangelium bei Lukas," ZNW 49, 1958, pp. 223–237.

[3] Cf. L. Goppelt, *Apostolic and Post-apostolic Times*, 1970, pp. 36–41; G. N. Stanton, *Jesus of Nazareth in New Testament Preaching*, Cambridge, 1974, Ch. 3.

[4] R. Bultmann, *Theology of the New Testament*, I, p. 81; A. M. Hunter, *Paul and his Predecessors*, 1961², pp. 28–30.

[5] The passive form is a circumlocution for the active, with God as the implied subject: C. K. Barrett, *The First Epistle to the Corinthians*, 1968, p. 341; cf. Romans 10:9.

resurrection "on the third day."[1] There is also reference to the Easter appearances of Jesus. It has been argued that Paul is not here attempting to prove that the resurrection of Jesus was a historical fact, since the resurrection of Jesus appears to have been accepted by his audience; it was the theological deductions which were to be drawn from it which were in question.[2] Whether or not this is true of Paul's use of the passage, it is not the case with the primitive use of the passage, for it is expressly stated to be part of the message to non-Christians. It is, however, likely that even Paul was incidentally "piling up the evidence" for the resurrection, since, if the quotation concludes at the end of verse 5, Paul nevertheless continues to cite various other appearances of the risen Christ.[3]

Naturally, as C. K. Barrett has observed, "these appearances . . . cannot prove more than that, after the crucifixion, certain persons believed that they had seen Jesus again; they cannot prove the Christian doctrine of the resurrection, since this involves a statement about the action of God incapable alike of observation and demonstration."[4] But this amount of proof is important, for even if faith "cannot be created simply by the discovery of an empty tomb," "it would be destroyed by the discovery of the dead body of Jesus."[5]

We are thus justified in asserting that the primitive preaching did contain historical references and that it included statements which were meant to confirm the historical character of these references.

One final point must be made. We saw that Luke was accused of having "historicized" the kerygma. We have already in large measure answered this accusation by showing that the kerygma itself is of the same character as the Gospel of Luke. Both were historical in character. One further argument may now be brought forward in more explicit fashion. This is quite simply that the main content of the Gospel of Luke is not material which could be regarded as the author's "historicizing" of the kerygma. For the most part the Gospel consists of traditional material taken over from earlier Gospels and other sources. If, therefore, "historicizing" was going on, it had begun to happen long before Luke started work. Indeed it was going on long before Mark set to work, for according to the premiss of this argument any attempt to clothe the proclamation

---

[1] The most probable origin of the reference to the third day lies in the fact that historically this was the day on which the risen Jesus first appeared to His disciples; cf. G. Delling, TWNT VIII, p. 219.

[2] H.-W. Bartsch, "Die Argumentation des Paulus in 1 Cor. 15:3-11," ZNW 55, 1964, pp. 261-274.

[3] Cf. R. Bultmann, *Theology of the New Testament*, I, p. 295. This understanding of Paul's procedure is not in accordance with Bultmann's own view that such proof ought not to be given; his exegesis of Paul here is consequently all the more convincing, since Paul's statement has not been brought into harmony with Bultmann's own views.

[4] C. K. Barrett, *op. cit.*, p. 341.   [5] C. K. Barrett, *op. cit.*, p. 349.

of the message in narrative, historical form must be regarded as "historicizing." But this process reaches back to such an early period in the life of the church that it becomes obvious that to speak of "historicizing" would be not only anachronistic but also completely inappropriate; what was going on was historical remembrance of the ministry and teaching of Jesus. The Gospel tradition after all was not created by the church; it was handed down by the church. There may have been freedom in handling it, but that is not the point. The point is that there was a tradition to be handled.[1] Essentially the Gospel tradents and writers were passing on history, and historicizing was a secondary phenomenon whose magnitude has been grossly exaggerated.

We must draw this discussion to a close. Our theme has been the relation of history to faith. We have argued that there is no necessary conflict between these two concepts, and that Christian faith is related to historically verifiable events. This was the view taken by Luke, and we have attempted to show that he was not adopting an individual outlook but was in agreement with the early church generally.

This means that Luke conceived his task as the writing of history and that we shall fail to do justice to his work if we do not think of him as a historian. Modern research has emphasized that he was a theologian. The evidence which we have considered has shown that because he was a theologian he had to be a historian. His view of theology led him to write history.

Two final comments must be made. The first is that we have no wish to deny that Luke was a theologian with his own distinctive ideas which mark him off to some extent from other New Testament writers. It will be our main task to explore his theology. The other comment is that although we have stressed the factual nature of the early preaching and its crystallization in the Gospels, this does not mean that no place has been left for faith. Our point is that the events which faith interprets as divine acts must be real, historical events, or otherwise they cannot be interpreted at all. The facts may be tested historically, but the ultimate decisions are matters of faith. It is faith which sees the resurrection as an act of God; it is faith which goes on to confess "Jesus is Lord." But, "if Christ has not been raised . . . faith is in vain." Luke was a historian because he was first and foremost an Evangelist: he knew that the faith which he wished to proclaim stands or falls with the history of Jesus and the early church.

[1] It will be clear from the above that we do not accept the more extreme claims of some advocates of form criticism; for a defence of this position see I. H. Marshall, *I believe in the Historical Jesus*, 1977. On the theme of the chapter see also L. Morris, *Studies in the Fourth Gospel*, Exeter 1969, ch. 2; J. Roloff, *Das Kerygma und der irdischer Jesus*, Göttingen, 1970, C. Brown (ed.), *History, Criticism and Faith*, Leicester, 1976; B. Gerhardsson, *Die Anfänge der Evangelientradition*, Wuppertal, 1977.

CHAPTER III

LUKE AS A HISTORIAN

WRITING SOME FIFTY YEARS AGO W. M. RAMSAY DESCRIBED THE QUALI-ties of the good historian in these terms: "His statements of fact (are) trustworthy; he is possessed of the true historic sense; he fixes his mind on the idea and plan that rules in the evolution of history, and proportions the scale of his treatment to the importance of each incident. He seizes the important and critical events and shows their true nature at greater length, while he touches lightly or omits entirely much that was valueless for his purpose."[1] These words were in fact written in description of the work of Luke, but it would be manifestly wrong to make them the starting point in a discussion of how Luke actually carried on his work. We must begin again at the beginning. Although the work of Ramsay deserves to be rescued from the comparative neglect into which it has fallen,[2] we cannot simply take over his assessment of Luke today without begging many questions.

On the one hand, it may be asked whether the historical qualities desiderated by Ramsay are those of today. It could be argued, for example, that in the positive development of his view Ramsay commends the sort of historical selectivity which leaves the later scholar at the mercy of what an ancient writer (like Luke) considered vital instead of furnishing him with all the relevant evidence on a particular problem. Further, the quotation says nothing whatever about the author's choice of sources and the way in which he has used them, and this is a point of very considerable importance. Yet one important point is to be noticed. When Ramsay speaks about concentrating attention on the critical events and discovering the plan that lies in the evolution of history, is he not saying in somewhat different terms what the modern exponents of redaction criticism are saying? Is not this a way of saying that the ancient author had his own view of what was going on in history and that he has let this come to expression in his work? The real question that arises will be whether the events justify the overall picture which the historian presents.

On the other hand it may be protested that it is wrong to assess an

---

[1] W. M. Ramsay, *The Bearing of Recent Discovery on the Trustworthiness of the New Testament*, p. 222; cf. F. F. Bruce, *The New Testament Documents*, p. 91.

[2] See W. W. Gasque, *Sir William M. Ramsay: Archaeologist and New Testament Scholar*, Grand Rapids, 1966.

ancient historian by the standards of contemporary history. There were different standards of accuracy and there was a different outlook on the world. It would be wrong to expect an ancient historian to measure up to the standards of a later period. The better comparison would be with his own contemporaries, and W. C. van Unnik has issued an appeal for a fuller assessment of Luke against this background.[1] Perhaps it should be sought not so much in Greek historiography as in Jewish.

It would appear, therefore, that an assessment of Luke must be carried on against two different standards. He must be placed against his own environment, and he must also be looked at from a modern standpoint. We shall then be able to see what kind of historian he was when measured by the kind of standard by which he may be fairly judged, and we may also assess his objective value in terms of modern historiography.

Ancient Historians

A study of the writings of ancient historians in relation to the work of Luke was made by H. J. Cadbury and the authors of *The Beginnings of Christianity*.[2] They treated separately the Greek and Jewish traditions of writing history. The former tradition offers much more material for comparison and reveals that a number of different goals were followed in the Greek and Hellenistic periods. The first essential for a history was the collection of material; a writer like Polybius was reasonably conscientious in such research, but he comments unfavourably on other historians who adopted the easy way out and simply made use of the work of their predecessors.[3] How far sources were critically evaluated, it is difficult to say. The problem was certainly recognized, but there were not the modern methods of critical study. Instead the historian concentrated on the presentation of his material. Quintilian could go so far as to describe history as being akin to poetry, and to say that its aim was narration rather than proof.[4] This may be rather an extreme judgment, and it is certainly not to be applied to the best of the ancient historians. Nevertheless, as we observed earlier, historians in general were reckoned with practitioners of rhetoric whose main aim lay in producing a pleasing effect for the readers or the listeners (since public readings were often held).

[1] W. C. van Unnik in SLA, p. 27.
[2] BC II, pp. 7–29. Cf. B. Gärtner, *The Areopagus Speech and Natural Revelation*, Uppsala-Lund, 1955; C. K. Barrett, *Luke the Historian in Recent Study*, pp. 9–12.
[3] Polybius 12:25e, cited in BC II, p. 9 n. 4.
[4] "Historia quoque alere oratorem quodam uberi iucundoque suco potest; verum et ipsa sic est legenda ut sciamus plerasque eius virtutes oratori esse vitandas. Est enim proxima poetis et quodam modo carmen solutum, et scribitur ad narrandum, non ad probandum, totumque opus non ad actum rei pugnamque praesentem, sed ad memoriam posteritatis et ingenii famam componitur." Quintilian 10:1:31.

One particular characteristic of ancient history which brings it close to rhetoric is the use of speeches, placed in the mouths of the principal characters. The practice goes back to Thucydides, who used the speeches to give his readers an insight into the particular issues involved at crucial points in his narrative, but at the same time sought as far as possible for verisimilitude in the composition.[1] Later writers were not so conscientious, and their speeches tended to be examples of their rhetorical skill instead of attempts to report what was actually said. It is even possible to find examples where the same writer, reporting the same incident in two different parts of his writings, has provided two different versions of the same speech.[2]

Alongside the historians proper mention must also be made of the writers of historical romances. C. K. Barrett has drawn attention to the importance of this comparison, and holds that the Hellenistic romance is perhaps to be claimed as providing the literary context of the writings of Luke.[3] The writings of Lucian and Philostratus, which describe the lives of religious preachers and miracle-workers, offer a parallel to the way in which the Gospels describe Jesus and the Acts displays His followers as wandering prophets with superhuman powers.

We may take it that Luke, claiming as he does a literary place for his writings, must be set against the background of contemporary literature. This is certainly true of his contemporary Josephus who, for all his Jewish background, displays the characteristics of the Hellenistic historians. Indeed the faults of Hellenistic historians can be well illustrated from Josephus; his account of the Jewish war with Rome is undoubtedly distorted in order to glorify his own people, and especially in the Antiquities he has made a careless use of his sources.[4] He did, however, have access to some good sources, and where he has made proper use of these his work is of great value.[5]

Comparison of Luke merely with Hellenistic writers would be onesided. His style of writing, which is frequently reminiscent of the Septuagint, demands that he also be compared with Jewish historians. The basic material here is to be found in the Old Testament. From the point of view of a first-century writer the most notable feature of the historical books in

[1] T. F. Glasson, "The Speeches in Acts and Thucydides," Exp. T 76, 1964–65, p. 165; cf. F. F. Bruce, *The Speeches in Acts*, 1942.

[2] Cf. the speech of Herod in BJ I, 373–379 (I:19:4) with the version in Ant. XV, 127–146 (XV:5:3); the speech of Mattathias in Ant. XII, 279–284 (XII:6:3) is also different from that in Josephus' source (1 Macc. 2:49–68); cf. BC II, pp. 13 f., 27.

[3] C. K. Barrett, *op. cit.*, pp. 12–15

[4] E. Schürer, *The History of the Jewish People in the Age of Jesus Christ* (revised and edited by G. Vermes and F. Millar), Edinburgh, 1973, Vol. I, pp. 57f.

[5] See the verdict of H. St J. Thackeray in his translation of Josephus, Loeb Edition, Vol. II, 1927, pp. vii–xxxii.

the Old Testament would be the way in which the course of events is given an interpretation in terms of the activity of God. The various stages in the narrative are seen to be under divine control, to take place under divine initiative, and to be prophesied by men of God. Alike in the so-called Deuteronomic history and in the work of the Chronicler[1] the stress is on the way in which piety is associated with prosperity and idolatry and immorality lead to judgment.

From the modern point of view, the Old Testament histories are compilations based on earlier sources. The facts, however, that they deal with considerable periods of history and that they were finally composed for the most part long after the events recorded mean that their historical quality is not of immediate relevance for the writings of Luke. More important in this respect are the two Books of Maccabees which display notable discrepancies in their accounts of the same period and show how quickly legendary accounts could spring up.[2]

The writings of Luke are plainly indebted to the Old Testament tradition. This is to be seen in the way in which Luke also sees the working out of a divine plan in history, and may even be held to have regarded his work as depicting the continuation of the history recorded in the Old Testament. He thus writes from a particular standpoint which traces the activity of God in historical events. Consequently, he not only records miraculous events in his narrative, but he also sees the general course of history as the effect of divine activity. This means that he gives a particular interpretation to historical events which would not be shared by a secular historian.

The comparison with other historians does not solve for us the question of Luke's reliability as a historian. Although the general tendency of contemporary historians was towards inaccuracy and even invention (especially in the speech material), this was by no means universally the case, and it is necessary to remind ourselves that there was a real concern for accuracy on the part of some of them.[3] It is legitimate to ask to which historian Luke stands nearer: Josephus or Polybius?

Two considerations should be mentioned at this point. The first is that in some of his speeches in Acts Luke is plainly not concerned with elegance of style or rhetorical effect. The crudity of style found in Acts 4:25, for example, speaks against a striving for effect, and F. F. Bruce comments,

---

[1] These terms are used for convenience, without prejudice to the complicated questions regarding the sources and authorship of these two strands of Old Testament history.

[2] The various Jewish historical works discussed in E. Schürer, *op. cit.*, I, 1, pp. 19–43, and R. H. Pfeiffer, *A History of New Testament Times with an Introduction to the Apocrypha*, 1949, pp. 200–206, are for the most part fragmentary and the fragments deal with past antiquity rather than with the immediate past. A work like III Maccabees, which is pure fiction, is irrelevant to a study of history.

[3] A. W. Mosley, "Historical Reporting in the Ancient World," NTS 12, 1965–66, pp. 10–26; H. Weiss, "History and a Gospel," Nov. T 10, 1968, pp. 81–94.

"It is curious how often the Gk. becomes obscure when the apostles are speaking."[1] Luke can, it is true, produce some interesting stylistic effects – witness the confusion in which the stump-orator Tertullus lands himself (Acts 24:1–8) – but he cannot be said to have sought after a lofty rhetoric.

The second point is made by B. Gärtner. In his important study of the speech of Paul at Athens he finds that the speeches in Acts differ considerably in style from those of contemporary historians, both Greek and Jewish, and that there are no real parallels to the missionary speeches.[2] At this point Luke stands in a different tradition. He is here the Evangelist, and the parallels to his material are to be found in religious literature rather than in history.[3] While, therefore, the *practice* of including speeches is paralleled in the historians, the *content* must be illustrated from elsewhere; consequently, it becomes doubtful how far Luke's practice in this regard should be compared with that of the historians.

Our conclusion so far is that the attempt to set Luke in the context of ancient historians does not lead to any firm results. Insofar as the comparison can be made, the variety of ancient writers prevents us from finding a single context for Luke. At the very least, however, we can say that the view that Hellenistic history writing was in general tendentious and that therefore Luke must also be tendentious and inaccurate is ungrounded, both in its assumption and in its logic. Better progress may be made by an examination of Luke's own methods.

The Sources Used in the Gospel

The value of a historian is very often the value of his sources. We must, therefore, attempt to identify the sources used by Luke, to estimate their value and to investigate how Luke has used them.

We start with the Gospel, where the position is much clearer than it is in Acts. On one point at least there is a considerable measure of unanimity among scholars. This is that Luke made use of the Gospel of Mark as a basic source in the writing of the Gospel. Even this conclusion, sometimes regarded as the most certain in literary criticism of the Gospels, has not gone unchallenged. A number of recent scholars have drawn attention to the indecisiveness of the criteria which are commonly employed for the solution of the Synoptic problem.[4] Other scholars have proposed different

[1] F. F. Bruce, *The Acts of the Apostles*, 1951, p. 126.
[2] B. Gärtner, *The Areopagus Speech and Natural Revelation*, Chs. 1–4; cf. H. Conzelmann, *Die Apostelgeschichte*, pp. 6–8.
[3] H. Conzelmann, *op. cit.*, p. 102, lists the parallels to be found in religious literature, especially the Corpus Hermeticum.
[4] H. Palmer, *The Logic of Gospel Criticism*, 1968; E. P. Sanders, *The Tendencies of the Synoptic Tradition*, Cambridge, 1969.

solutions of the Synoptic problem, usually involving the claim that Matthew (or an "Ur-Matthew") is the oldest Gospel.[1] For the most part, however, the writers in this latter group are more concerned to argue that Mark is dependent on Matthew than to disprove the dependence of Luke on Mark. A notable exception to this category is W. R. Farmer who argues that the relationship is the other way round. Mark is dependent on both Matthew and Luke, and Luke is dependent on Matthew. Thus the relationship between the three Gospels is not:

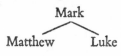

but rather:

This is a revolutionary hypothesis so far as current critical orthodoxy is concerned.[2] It will come as no surprise that it has not met with much acceptance. If it is correct, it means a very radical alteration in our approach to the Gospels.

In attempting to assess the matter we may observe, first, that the strength of Farmer's view lies in the area of the minor agreements between Matthew and Luke against Mark in passages where all three Gospels run in parallel. The explanations of these offered by earlier scholars do not seem adequate and sometimes give the impression of being desperate attempts to iron out the difficulties at any cost.[3] Until some satisfactory explanation of these from the point of view of Marcan priority can be found, that hypothesis must be judged insufficient to account for all the evidence.[4]

Second, a number of scholars have propounded the view that in the so-called "Q" material (i.e. where Matthew and Luke have parallels, mostly in discourse material, which are not in Mark) it is possible to account for

[1] B. C. Butler, *The Originality of St Matthew*, 1951; W. R. Farmer, *The Synoptic Problem: A Critical Analysis*, 1964; H. Meynell, "The Synoptic Problem: Some Unorthodox Solutions," *Theology* 70, 1967, pp. 386–397.

[2] See, for example, the comments of F. W. Beare in JBL 84, 1965, pp. 295–297. The statement by W. G. Kümmel, *Introduction to the New Testament*, p. 39, that Farmer advocates Augustine's theory of the composition of the Gospels rests upon an inference from Farmer's earlier articles.

[3] The classical treatment is B. H. Streeter, *The Four Gospels: A Study of Origins*, 1936³, Ch. 11; cf. R. M. Wilson, "Farrer and Streeter on the Minor Agreements of Matthew and Luke against Mark," SE I, 1959, pp. 254–257. For criticism of Streeter see N. Turner, "The Minor Verbal Agreements of Matthew and Luke against Mark," SE I, pp. 223–234; A. W. Argyle, "Agreements between Matthew and Luke," Exp. T 73, 1961–62, pp. 19–22.

[4] See further p. 76 n. 2.

the similarities by the hypothesis that Luke made use of Matthew.[1] This is a point to be discussed later, but if the hypothesis should be true it supports the view that Luke is dependent on Matthew in the wider area under consideration. On the other hand, if Luke is not dependent on Matthew in this limited area, it is extremely unlikely that he is dependent upon him in the wider area, especially as the distinction between Marcan and "Q" material can hardly have been as obvious to a first century reader of Matthew as it is to the modern user of a synopsis.

Third, the statistical investigations of the Synoptic problem undertaken by B. de Solages[2] and A. M. Honoré[3] both favour the theory of Marcan priority. It is significant that Honoré admits that the conclusion of his study was different from his earlier beliefs. However W. R. Farmer has argued against B. de Solages that his statistics merely prove that Mark occupies the middle position between Matthew and Luke, and not that it is prior to them[4]; criticisms have also been levelled against Honoré's treatment.[5] It is clear that further investigation is needed.

Fourth, if a personal opinion may be allowed, the result of a careful comparison of the Gospels is to suggest that the corresponding parts of the text of Luke can be accounted for in terms of the use of Mark as a source, whereas it is much less likely that the reverse is the case.[6] Further, it is the text of Mark which has been used, not the text of Matthew. If, as Farmer holds, Matthew is the source used by Luke, it is then necessary to ask where Mark fits into the development, since it is closely related to both the other Gospels. Farmer's view that Mark wove Matthew and Luke together remains quite incredible; consequently (in view of the statistics) it must have been a source for both Matthew and Luke. But if Luke used Mark as a source, there is then no reason to believe that he made use of Matthew, except perhaps to a very limited extent.

Our inclination, therefore, is provisionally to continue to maintain the hypothesis of Marcan priority, while admitting that the evidence is not completely in its favour. It still remains the view which has the least difficulties. In affirming this conclusion we would hold that it is possible to make use of literary-critical methods to study the Synoptic problem. It is true that some of the criteria are indecisive and that some of the arguments advanced in support of Marcan priority must be withdrawn, but this does

[1] See n. 4 on p. 60.
[2] B. de Solages, *A Greek Synopsis of the Gospels: A New Way of Solving the Synoptic Problem*, Leiden, 1959.
[3] A. M. Honoré, "A Statistical Study of the Synoptic Problem," Nov. T 10, 1968, pp. 95–147.
[4] W. R. Farmer, *op. cit.*, p. 197.
[5] See p. 76 n. 2.
[6] See GL, *passim*.

not mean that the problem is insoluble. Marcan priority is a reasonably based and fruitful hypothesis even if it can no longer be regarded as an absolute certainty.

A second main source is commonly recognized as having been used by Luke and Matthew, the so-called "Q" source. The general opinion is that behind the 200 or so verses common to Matthew and Luke, but not paralleled in Mark, there lies a lost document. Since the document has not survived, detailed reconstruction is not possible, but it is thought that the order of its contents roughly corresponds to the order of the material in Luke rather than in Matthew but that for its original wording Matthew is often the better guide.[1]

Once again, however, an "assured result" of early twentieth century study is in the melting pot, and there is a wide and well-supported range of other opinions. A middle position is adopted by those who have observed that the degree of agreement between Matthew and Luke varies widely in the Q material, and who would therefore postulate a variety of sources, some written, some oral, some in Greek, some in Aramaic, rather than one single written document.[2] At one extreme stand those who would deny the existence of any written source at all,[3] and at the other the advocates of the view that all the Q material in Luke was derived from Matthew.[4]

To come to a decision regarding these various possibilities would demand a minute examination of the textual evidence. It must suffice if we make some general observations. First, appeal has been made to the order of the Q material. Bearing in mind the fact that Matthew has grouped the sayings thematically, V. Taylor has shown that there is still a strong correspondence in order between the material in Matthew and in Luke.[5] The

---

[1] Cf. T. W. Manson, *The Sayings of Jesus*, 1949 (original edition, 1937), pp. 15–21. According to A. M. Hunter, *The Work and Words of Jesus*, 1950, pp. 131–146, the Lucan wording is more primitive, but in our view Matthew is often primitive; cf. W. Wilkens, *op. cit.* (n. 4 below), who uses this fact to argue that Luke was in fact dependent upon Matthew.

[2] M. Black, *An Aramaic Approach to the Gospels and Acts*, Oxford, 1967³, pp. 186–196; W. L. Knox, *The Sources of the Synoptic Gospels* II, Cambridge, 1957.

[3] J. Jeremias, "Zur Hypothese einer schriftlichen Logienquelle," in *Abba: Studien zur neutestamentlichen Theologie und Zeitgeschichte*, Göttingen, 1966, pp. 90–92 (originally published in ZNW 31, 1932, pp. 147–149); C. K. Barrett, "Q – A Re-examination," Exp. T 54, 1942–43, pp. 320–323; H.–T. Wrege, *Die Überlieferungsgeschichte der Bergpredigt*, Tübingen, 1968.

[4] K. H. Rengstorf, *Das Evangelium des Lukas*, Göttingen, 1937; A. Schlatter, *Das Evangelium des Lukas*, Stuttgart, 1960²; A. M. Farrer, "On Dispensing with Q," in SG, pp. 55–88; R. T. Simpson, "The Major Agreements of Matthew and Luke against Mark," NTS 12, 1965–66, pp. 273–284; W. Wilkens, "Zur Frage der literarischen Beziehungen zwischen Mt und Lk," Nov. T 8, 1966, pp. 48–57. See also p. 76 n. 2.

The converse view, that Matthew is dependent upon Luke is rarely held: see, however, H. P. West, "A Primitive Version of Luke in the Composition of Matthew," NTS 14, 1967–68, pp. 75–95.

[5] V. Taylor, "The Original Order of Q," in A. J. B. Higgins (ed.), *New Testament Essays in Memory of T. W. Manson*, Manchester, 1959, pp. 246–269 (reproduced in V. Taylor, *New Testament Essays*, 1970, pp. 95–118).

force of this argument is to preserve the unity of the Q material against attempts to divide it among several sources. It does not help us to discriminate between the theories of common use of Q by the two Evangelists and use of Matthew by Luke. It is, however, much more likely that Matthew has arranged the material thematically than that Luke has rewoven it into his particular pattern.[1]

The argument from order thus gives some support to the hypothesis of a Q document. But it is not necessary that all the material should fall into one source. There is the further factor of the variations in the amount of verbal agreement between Luke and Matthew. How is the distribution of the variation to be accounted for, and how is the variation itself to be explained? Some of the variation is undoubtedly due to the editorial habits of the two Evangelists. Other examples can be explained in terms of variant translations from Aramaic material,[2] but it is a nice question whether much that looks like variant translation may not be due simply to stylistic differences between the Evangelists. My impression is that the latter explanation may often be the more likely one. We have, however, a number of passages where the verbal dissimilarity between the two Gospels is so great that the hypothesis of a common source is less likely,[3] and we should probably think, therefore, in terms of two or more recensions of the same material being available to the Evangelists. At the same time it must be insisted that detailed analysis shows clear cases where sometimes Matthew and sometimes Luke have each preserved the more primitive text, thus demonstrating that neither Evangelist was dependent on the other but that both were dependent on common source material. The Q hypothesis thus remains the most probable explanation of the phenomena, with the proviso that Matthew and Luke may have access to different recensions of it.

It is customary to treat the birth stories in Luke 1–2 as standing on their own, a procedure which is justified by the probability that their back-

---

[1] The order of the Q material in Luke, as expounded by T. W. Manson, *The Sayings of Jesus*, gives an impression of coherence; the same cannot be said of the order in Matthew. It might be objected that there is no reason to expect any particular order in Q, any more than one might expect to find it in the Gospel of Thomas. But there are some traces of order in various series of sayings in the Gospel of Thomas, and the evidence adduced by V. Taylor shows that at the very least there were several ordered series of sayings in Q.

Other defences of Q will be found in E. Bradby, "In Defence of Q," Exp. T 68, 1956–57, pp. 315–318; F. G. Downing, "Toward the Rehabilitation of 'Q'," NTS 11, 1964–65, pp. 169–181. See also p. 63 n.3.

[2] M. Black, *An Aramaic Approach to the Synoptic Gospels and Acts*, pp. 186–196, gives several examples. On the other hand, N. Turner, "Q in Recent Thought," Exp. T 80, 1968–69, pp. 324–328, argues that the so-called Q material need not be a translation from Aramaic at all.

[3] Examples are: the Lord's Prayer (Matt. 6:9–13; Luke 11:2–4); the Great Supper (Matt. 22:1–14; Luke 14:15–24); various sayings (Matt. 18:6f, 15; 17:19f.; Luke 17:1–6). Cf. H.-T. Wrege, *op. cit.*

background appears to be Hebrew rather than Aramaic as in the rest of the Gospel.[1] The remainder of the material in Luke 3–24 is often designated by the symbol "L" in this country[2] and there is some reason to suppose that part of it at least may have been in a written source. The reason for this lies in the recurrence of certain basic themes throughout it, and these themes appear to be integral to the material rather than imposed upon it by Luke himself.

This brings us to a further question. It is a matter of simple observation that in Luke Marcan material and non-Marcan material alternate in "blocks." In particular "Q" material is scarcely ever found in a Marcan context but almost always in the context of "L" material, and in the resultant combination of "QL" the traces of material drawn from Mark are very few. The conclusion to be drawn from this evidence is that the combination of "Q" and "L" material took place independently of the linking of either with Marcan material. There is also some evidence that an alternative version of some parts of the passion narrative was available to Luke.[3]

From these facts it has been concluded that there was an earlier stage in the composition of Luke, a "proto-Luke" composed of "Q" and "L" material which may have been a miniature (or, in modern parlance, mini-) Gospel.[4] It has then been argued that proto-Luke was the first draft of the Gospel of Luke which was formed from it by the addition of material from Mark. Thus, whereas in Matthew the basic structure was provided by Mark, in Luke the basis was proto-Luke.

In its full form this theory must be pronounced "not proven." Against it the objection has been raised that the basic structure of Luke is provided by Mark and that the non-Marcan material gives the appearance of being inserted into a Marcan context rather than vice-versa.[5] Nevertheless, the less ambitious form of the theory stands proved, namely that "Q" and "L" were combined before they found their way into Luke, and that Luke on the whole prefers this source to Mark where they reported the same or similar incidents.

[1] See the summary of the debate in R. Laurentin, "Traces d'allusions étymologiques en Lc 1–2," Bib. 37, 1956, pp. 435–456, especially pp. 449–456; cf. R. M. Wilson, "Some Recent Studies in the Lucan Infancy Narratives," SE I, 1959, pp. 235–253.

[2] German writers prefer "S" for "Sondergut"; F. Rehkopf, Die lukanische Sonderquelle: Ihr Umfang und Sprachgebrauch, Tübingen, 1959, uses "L" to denote the combination of material common to Matthew and Luke and peculiar to Luke (English Q+L) which he believes to have been one of Luke's main sources.

[3] H. Schürmann, Der Paschahmahlbericht; Der Einsetzungsbericht; Jesu Abschiedsrede, Münster, 1953, 1955, 1957 (with full bibliography); F. Rehkopf, op. cit.

[4] B. H. Streeter, The Four Gospels, pp. 199–222; V. Taylor, Behind the Third Gospel, Oxford, 1926; G. B. Caird, Saint Luke, 1963, pp. 23–27.

[5] H. Conzelmann, Die Mitte der Zeit, passim; further difficulties are summarised by W. G. Kümmel, Introduction to the New Testament, pp. 91–95.

We do not need to go any more deeply into the question of what sources were used in Luke. We still need to discuss, however, the quality of the sources and the way in which Luke has employed them.

A discussion of the historical value of Mark in detail cannot be attempted here. It would, therefore, be unfair to offer dogmatic statements on the matter. The subject is one which is undergoing lively debate between those who would defend and those who would deny its historical value.[1] It must suffice to say that a critical evaluation of the radical position strongly suggests that its strength has been exaggerated, and that we can place a reasonable confidence in the value of Mark.[2]

Similar considerations apply to the "Q" material. Here the task is more difficult in view of our uncertainty about the character of this source. The source, however, reflects an Aramaic background at so many points that it is necessary to place its origin in Palestine; this affords some ground for claiming that it stands in fairly close proximity to the ministry of Jesus. The question whether it shows any particular *Tendenz* is hard to answer; attempts to show this are still decidedly exploratory.[3] Once again, therefore, caution in assessment is called for.

The situation is similar with the L material. It has a number of contacts with traditions found in John. If it is true that these contacts are not to be explained in terms of literary dependence between the written Gospels,[4] then we have some independent confirmation from the pre-Johannine tradition for the age of the traditions in the L material. Nevertheless, the whole question of the character and origin of the L material requires detailed investigation, and it would be rash to make any decisions about it.

Our estimate of the intrinsic quality of Luke's sources must accordingly be very tentative. We are not in a position to make a categorical pronouncement upon them, and the detailed investigation on which such a pronouncement must be based would go beyond the limits of the present volume. We must be content for the meantime to conclude that Luke's accuracy is dependent on the value of his sources, but that there are

---

[1] In England the debate is to be found in D. E. Nineham, *Saint Mark*, 1963; D. E. Nineham (ed.), *Historicity and Chronology in the New Testament*, 1965; A. T. Hanson (ed.), *Vindications*, 1966; D. E. Nineham, ". . . *et hoc genus omne* – an Examination of Dr A. T. Hanson's Strictures on Some Recent Gospel Study," in CHI, pp. 199–222; A. T. Hanson, "Non liquet: A Rejoinder to Professor Nineham," *The Modern Churchman* 11, 1968, pp. 212–222.

[2] Such a position is represented by V. Taylor in his comprehensive commentary, *The Gospel according to St Mark*, 1953; the positions upheld there are not so easily controverted as some subsequent scholars think.

[3] H. E. Tödt, *The Son of Man in the Synoptic Tradition*, 1965; P. Hoffman, *Studien zur Theologie der Logienquelle*, Münster, 1972; S. Schulz, Q, *Die Spruchquelle der Evangelisten*, Zurich, 1972; G. N. Stanton, "On the Christology of Q," in B. Lindars and S. S. Smalley, *Christ and Spirit in the New Testament*, Cambridge, 1973, pp. 27–42; A. P. Polag, *Die Christologie der Logienquelle*, Neukirchen, 1977.

[4] C. H. Dodd, *Historical Tradition in the Fourth Gospel*, Cambridge, 1963.

some good indications that they incorporated valuable, Palestinian tradition.

We must accordingly move on to the question of how Luke has used his sources. Here we are in the fortunate position of being able to compare Luke with Mark and also with the Matthaean version of the Q material. This gives a fair amount of scope for enquiry. The classical study of the subject is that of F. C. Burkitt who found that although Luke used Mark freely "what concerns us here is not that Luke has changed so much, but that he has invented so little."[1] This verdict appears to be unchanged by subsequent study, even though Burkitt wrote before the advent of the redaction criticism era.

In the first place, it is evident that Luke has subjected all his sources to a stylistic revision. Throughout his work there is a fairly uniform style. This has been analysed in detail by various scholars,[2] so that it is possible to give a very full list of the stylistic characteristics of Luke which has an objective basis in a comparative study of the texts of Luke and Mark. The extent of the revision varies. It would appear that Luke revised the beginnings and endings of pericopes more drastically than their central portions, and that he revised narrative material more heavily than sayings material; in particular he appears to have revised Mark more thoroughly than his other sources for the Gospel.[3]

Attempts have been made to trace stylistic constants in the QL material which have not been eliminated by Lucan revision.[4] But while it is possible to isolate individual features which can be regarded as pre-Lucan, the attempt to find a series of characteristics of a pre-Lucan source has met with very limited success.[5]

What does emerge, however, from a study of the Marcan parallels is that the presence of Lucan stylistic characteristics in a passage does not necessarily mean that the Evangelist has himself created the material. On the contrary, he has worked on existing material. Naturally this is not always the case; there are places in the Marcan material where Luke has added his own glosses, but this practice cannot justifiably be made into a general rule.

Second, it has already been noticed that Luke for the most part arranges his sources in blocks of material from each in turn. It is only rarely that he

---

[1] F. C. Burkitt, "The Use of Mark in the Gospel according to Luke," in BC II, pp. 106–120; quotation from p. 115.

[2] See my article "Tradition and Theology in Luke (Luke 8:5–15)," Tyn. B 20, 1969, pp. 56–75, with the references on p. 61 n. 10.

[3] This, however, may be due to the higher sayings content in the non-Marcan material.

[4] B. S. Easton, *The Gospel according to St Luke*, 1926; F. Rehkopf, *op. cit.*

[5] H. Schürmann, "Protolukanische Spracheigentümlichkeiten? Zu Fr. Rehkopf, Die Lukanische Sonderquelle," in *Traditionsgeschichtliche Untersuchungen*, pp. 209–227; cf. H. Conzelmann in *Gnomon* 32, 1960, pp. 470f.

intertwines material from two different sources. Here his practice stands in contrast with that of Matthew who groups material from different sources thematically. This consideration suggests that Luke was anxious to pass on the contents of his sources basically unchanged rather than to attempt an altogether new picture on the basis of a fresh combination of them.

There is of course intertwining of material at certain points. This happens especially in the passion narrative (in the broadest sense, i.e. Luke 19–24) where the Evangelist had on occasion two different accounts of the same incidents and had to fit them together; in the earlier parts of the Gospel his sources appear to have shown less overlap and he was able to use them alternately.

It might, however, be argued that in places (e.g. Luke 21) where two sources appear to be combined the Evangelist has simply been glossing one source (in this case, Mark) rather liberally. What looks like evidence for another source may simply be editorial activity. The same problem arises where there are passages in Luke which resemble passages in Mark (e.g. the call of Peter, Luke 5:1–11) but have been placed at different points in the narrative framework and have very different wording. Has Luke here transformed Marcan material or is he following independent sources? Although some scholars favour the former view,[1] it is the latter which is to be preferred.[2]

Third, for the most part Luke follows the pattern of the ministry already found in Mark. He omits two lengthy portions from Mark (Mark 6:45–8:26; 9:42–10:12), very probably because he thought them repetitive and parallel in content to other material. Otherwise, however, so far as the order of the sections is concerned, he follows Mark with the minimum of deviation; where he does vary in order from him, the reasons are usually fairly obvious.[3]

Nevertheless, Luke does not take over the chronological and geographical detail in Mark. His indications of time and place are much more vague and indefinite. To some extent the result is that the incidents in the ministry are generalized; it is more obvious that Luke is recording the kind of things that Jesus said and did. Luke, therefore, is not giving a detailed list of what Jesus did in chronological order. On the broader scale he is interested in chronology. He alone sets the ministry of Jesus in the broad context of Roman and Jewish history (Luke 3:1f.), but detailed references interest him much less. This incidentally is some reason for taking seriously the more detailed geographical and chronological

[1] H. Conzelmann, op. cit.
[2] See my article cited above (p. 64 n.), p. 62.
[3] J. Jeremias, "Perikopen-Umstellungen bei Lukas?" in *Abba*, pp. 93–97 (originally published in NTS 4, 1957–58, pp. 115–119).

references in Acts and claiming they demonstrate the use of sources.

Fourth, it does not appear that Luke has taken over much of what may be regarded as distinctly Marcan theology, whether features of the teaching of Jesus which Mark has particularly stressed or points which have been developed in his redaction. Thus the concept of the "Messianic Secret," which plays so important a role in Mark, is much less conspicuous in Luke, and other motifs have partly taken its place. The picture of Jesus and His teaching is thus different in Luke from what it is in Mark, and we shall attempt a characterization of it at a later stage.

Fifthly, Luke has inserted his own ideas into the Marcan material. On occasion he has altered the detail given by Mark. Thus "Herod the king" (Mark 6:14 et al.) receives his proper title of "tetrarch" (Luke 3:19; 9:7); the seed that fell on the rock had no *moisture* rather than no root (Luke 8:6, cf. Mark 4:6). The disciples do not appear as obtuse in Luke as they do in Mark. Luke too stresses the popular approval which was given to the mighty works of Jesus; they caused the crowds to fear and glorify God. The more "theological" changes will be considered below.[1]

It is less easy to be confident about the changes which Luke has made in his other sources. This is inevitable, since we have no means of checking what he has done against the originals. In the case of the Q material, which is mainly sayings of Jesus, there is less scope for change in historical detail. We have already suggested that Luke may have kept close to the original order of this material. This observation may be supported by a study of the section Luke 9:51–18:14, where it is notoriously difficult to establish a train of thought in the mind of the Evangelist himself, and the impression is given that he has taken over his sources largely as they stood.[2] On the other hand, comparison with Matthew shows that both Evangelists have adapted their common source or sources in wording.

Sixthly, one particular way in which Luke is thought to have altered his sources is by "Hellenization." There are one or two well-known examples of the alteration of Palestinian scenery to make narratives more easily intelligible in the outside world,[3] and in some cases the language and

---

[1] On Luke's use of Mark generally see R. Bultmann, *Die Geschichte der synoptischen Tradition*, pp. 384–392; W. G. Kümmel, *Introduction to the New Testament*, pp. 97–102.

[2] On this section see C. C. McCown, "The Geography of Luke's Central Section," JBL 57, 1938, pp. 51–66; J. Blinzler, "Die literarische Eigenart des sogennanten Reiseberichts im Lukas," in J. Schmid and A. Vögtle (ed.), *Synoptische Studien A. Wikenhauser dargebracht*, München, 1953, pp. 20–52 (full bibliography on p. 20 n. 3); J. Schneider, "Zur Analyse des lukanischen Reiseberichts," *ibid.*, pp. 207–229; C. F. Evans, "The Central Section of St Luke's Gospel," in SG, pp. 37–53; B. Reicke, "Instruction and Discussion in the Travel Narrative," SE I, 1959, pp. 206–216; W. Grundmann, "Fragen der Komposition des lukanischen 'Reiseberichts'," ZNW 50, 1959, pp. 252–270; W. C. Robinson Jr., "The Theological Context for interpreting Luke's Travel Narrative (9.51ff.)," JBL 79, 1960, pp. 20–31; I. H. Marshall, GL pp. 400–402.

[3] J. Jeremias, *The Parables of Jesus*, pp. 26 f.

thought are more Hellenistic than Palestinian,[1] but the total evidence for Hellenization is not particularly impressive, and in our judgment it would be wrong to suggest that a serious rewriting of the material had taken place.

We may sum up this section by claiming that the editorial work of Luke on his sources should not be unduly exaggerated. He is not the slave of his sources and he does not scruple to alter them when he thinks fit, but in general he appears to base himself fairly closely upon them. The resultant picture of Jesus is different from that in the sources, but (as we shall see) it is unmistakably the same Jesus.

The Sources of Acts

When we turn to the Acts it is very much more difficult to reach any certain conclusions regarding the sources used by Luke. The whole field has been admirably and comprehensibly surveyed by J. Dupont, and at the end of his investigation he concludes: "Despite the most careful and detailed research, it has not been possible to define any of the sources used by the author of Acts in a way which will meet with widespread agreement among the critics. . . . No theory has managed to impose itself by its probability and in virtue of the indications given by the texts."[2] So authoritative a conclusion demands caution on the part of any who venture into the same field.

The difficulty of course lies in the fairly uniform style which Luke has imposed upon his work. So thoroughly has this been done that it is almost impossible to discover pre-Lucan features of style which might suggest hypotheses to be confirmed by other types of investigation. Even the attempt to find residual Semitisms has produced the most meagre results.[3]

To conclude from this fact that Luke was largely independent of sources would be unjustified. The view of E. Haenchen that Luke exercised his inventive ability with few historical hints to guide him[4] has not commended itself generally. The fact is that the narrative bears the signs of origin in various sources. This is especially the case in Acts 13–28 where we have a detailed description of parts of Paul's journeys, sometimes couched in the first person plural (the "we" sections). It seems beyond question that

[1] W. C. van Unnik, "Die Motivierung der Feindesliebe in Lukas vi. 32–35," Nov. T 8, 1966 pp. 284–300.
[2] J. Dupont, The Sources of Acts, 1964, p. 167 (English translation of Les Sources du Livre des Actes, Bruges, 1960).
[3] M. Wilcox, The Semitisms of Acts, Oxford, 1965; R. A. Martin, "Syntactical Evidence of Aramaic Sources in Acts I–XV," NTS 11, 1964–65, pp. 38–59.
[4] E. Haenchen, Die Apostelgeschichte, pp. 73–80; cf. "Quellenanalyse und Kompositionsanalyse in Act 15," in W. Eltester (ed.), Judentum, Urchristentum, Kirche: Festschrift für Joachim Jeremias, Berlin, 1960, pp. 153–164.

some kind of itinerary or itineraries lies behind these sections, even if the limits and contents of such sources cannot be closely defined. Various explanations of the use of "we" in this area of Acts have been offered, but only one makes sense, namely that a source coming from a person who actually participated in the events described is being used.[1]

As regards the earlier part of Acts, matters are more obscure. There is no need here to repeat the details of the various hypotheses catalogued by J. Dupont since none is free from objection. We may suspect that material from the various church centres mentioned in the account lies at the basis of the story, but it is impossible with the means at our disposal to delimit these satisfactorily.[2]

In this connexion the question of the text of Acts should be mentioned. It is well known that Acts exists in two basic forms of text, that of the Egyptian witnesses and that of Codex Bezae and its "western" allies. It has sometimes been thought that these two forms of text, the latter fuller in detail than the former, may represent two successive editions of the work by the same author.[3] The result of recent investigation is to confirm that this hypothesis is most unlikely. The differences between the two forms of text are often of such a character that it is impossible to believe that the same person could be responsible for the divergent theological outlooks which are found in them. It is more likely that the western text represents a later redaction of Acts by a different hand.[4] At the same time, instead of operating with a simple choice between two types of text, critics are increasingly inclined to believe that both types may preserve true readings on occasion.[5] In any case, textual criticism affords no light on possible stages in the composition of Acts; the textual alterations are too late to witness to any activity which preceded the final editing of the book.

We are, therefore, left almost completely in the dark with regard to the sources of Acts. Consequently, it is impossible to characterize Luke's use of them in any detail, beyond noting that he will have written them all up in his own style. Other methods of investigation must be brought into play.

[1] C. K. Barrett, *Luke the Historian in Recent Study*, p. 22: "It is wildly improbable that this is merely a device of fiction."

[2] For a brief outline of this view see F. F. Bruce, *The Acts of the Apostles*, pp. 21–26.

[3] This was the view of F. Blass and T. Zahn. See also below, p. 157 n. 1.

[4] R. P. C. Hanson, "The Provenance of the Interpolator in the 'Western' Text of Acts itself," NTS 12, 1965–66, pp. 211–230; E. J. Epp, *The Theological Tendency of Codex Bezae Cantabrigiensis in Acts*, Cambridge, 1966.

[5] G. D. Kilpatrick, "An Eclectic Study of the Text of Acts," in J. N. Birdsall and R. W Thomson (ed.), *Biblical and Patristic Studies in Memory of Robert Pierce Casey* 1963, pp. 64–77, represents this tendency to an extent that many scholars would regard as extreme, but the principle in itself is sound. See B. M. Metzger *A Textual Commentary on the Greek New Testament*, 1971.

The History in Luke–Acts

One important line of research has been to examine the narrative in Acts in relation to the background which it describes. Historical romances such as the Book of Judith quickly betray themselves for what they are by the fact that the historical background of the tale is presented inaccurately. A writer who is careful to get the background right may be expected to tell a reliable story as well.

The Book of Acts has been intensively studied in this manner. The investigations of W. M. Ramsay, who began his research with the assumption that Acts was a tendentious production dating from the middle of the second century, convinced him that Luke was a first century historian with an accurate knowledge of Asia Minor and the Aegean area.[1] From this Ramsay concluded that in general the accuracy of Luke could be upheld, since a writer who was accurate in details which could be corroborated would also seek accuracy in more general matters and in areas where his statements could not be so easily confirmed or criticized.

More recent study has queried this assumption. The writings of E. Haenchen in particular have tried to show that Luke cannot be regarded as an accurate historian.[2] Nevertheless, the basic point made by Ramsay can still be defended and indeed stands beyond doubt. On matters of Hellenistic geography and politics, Roman law and provincial administration, Luke can be demonstrated to be for the most part a reliable guide. This is the verdict of a Roman historian, A. N. Sherwin-White,[3] and for this reason it demands all the greater respect. It is accepted, for example, by R. P. C. Hanson who cannot be accused of a blind conservatism in the matter.[4] There are, to be sure, a number of problems and difficulties in the narrative, such as the question of Quirinius and the census (Luke 2:1 f.)[5] but compared with other ancient historians Luke acquits himself very creditably. In matters of detail his historical stature is high.

[1] W. M. Ramsay, *The Bearing of Recent Discovery on the Trustworthiness of the New Testament*, pp. 37ff., 79.

[2] E. Haenchen, *Die Apostelgeschichte; Gott und Mensch*, Tübingen, 1965; *Die Bibel und Wir*, Tübingen, 1968; "The Book of Acts as Source Material for the History of Early Christianity," SLA, pp. 258–278.

[3] A. N. Sherwin-White, *Roman Society and Roman Law in the New Testament*, Oxford, 1963.

[4] R. P. C. Hanson, *The Acts*, Oxford, 1967. Other scholars adopting a similar point of view include: E. Trocmé, *Le "Livre des Actes" et l'Histoire*; T. D. Barnes, "An Apostle on Trial," JTS n.s. 20, 1969, pp. 407–419; C. J. Hemer, "Luke the Historian," BJRL 60, 1977–78, pp. 28–51. *Glaube und Leben der Urgemeinde; Bemerkungen zu Apg.* 1–7, Zürich, 1957; R. N. Longenecker "The Acts of the Apostles as a Witness to Early Palestinian Christianity ' *Themelios* 5:1, 1968, pp. 15–23. Cf. W. W. Gasque, "The Historical Value of the Book of Acts: An Essay in the History of New Testament Criticism," EQ 41, 1969, pp. 68–88.

[5] H. Schürmann, *Das Lukasevangelium* I, Freiburg, 1969, pp. 98–101, surveys the debate and warns against too easy acceptance of the conclusion that Luke has gone astray here; only the discovery of new historical evidence can lead to a solution of the problem.

One important objection to this verdict should be considered here. It is one of the theses of H. Conzelmann's book, *Die Mitte der Zeit*, that Luke betrays a defective knowledge of the geography of Palestine. On the basis of statements in the Gospel Conzelmann argues that Luke envisaged Galilee and Judaea as two adjacent areas, each bordering on Samaria which lay between them; he was unaware that there was no common border between Judaea and Galilee and that in order to get from one to the other it was necessary either to go through Samaria (John 4:3f.) or else to pass through Decapolis and travel down the east side of the Jordan through Peraea before crossing the Jordan westwards again near Jericho (cf. Mark 10:1, 46). This view of Luke's geographical conceptions is said to be confirmed by a similar muddle in other ancient writers (Pliny, Strabo and Tacitus; cf. the Epistle of Aristeas). Further, it explains the peculiar Lucan use of "Judaea": Jesus was able to work in Judaea and Galilee simultaneously since they were adjacent, and hence there is no need to assume with many commentators that for Luke Galilee was a part of Judaea.[1]

When this evidence is critically examined, it quickly becomes apparent that Conzelmann's conclusion cannot stand. The statements of Strabo and the Epistle of Aristeas are to the effect that the Jordan flowed out into the Mediterranean in the north, and, however misguided this notion may be, it is irrelevant to the particular geographical confusion which Conzelmann wishes to attribute to Luke.[2] More relevant is Pliny who writes: "Beyond Idumaea and Samaria Judaea stretches long and broad. The part of it near Syria is called Galilee, that near Arabia and Egypt is Peraea, scattered among rugged mountains and separated from the rest of the Judaeans by the river Jordan."[3] To deduce from this statement, however, that Luke thought of a territory stretching east of Samaria with Judaea and Galilee as direct neighbours is wrong. Pliny knows that Judaea is the name of an area which includes Peraea and Galilee, which is perfectly correct. So long as Galilee and Judaea (in the narrow sense) were under the same ruler they would be regarded as one land. This was the case from AD 41 onwards

---

[1] H. Conzelmann, *Die Mitte der Zeit*, pp. 12–86, especially p. 61 (pp. 18–94, especially p. 69). Conzelmann's primary aim is to discover geographical symbolism in Luke.

[2] Strabo 16:754 ff. states that the people of Arad (on the sea coast) carried on merchant shipping on the Jordan. The Epistle of Aristeas 116f. makes the Jordan join up with another river which flows into the sea. Strabo's other geographical statements are also irrelevant. He says that Jerusalem was near the sea and could be seen from Joppa (from which it is in reality 34 miles distant). Strabo also mentions the following place names in this order: Galilee, Jericho, Philadelphia and Samaria. Conzelmann (*op. cit.*, p. 13 n. 3 (not in Eng. tr.)) thinks that this illuminates Luke's description of Jesus' journey to Jerusalem from Galilee via Jericho. Luke has, however, taken this journey over from Mark. Although the main route from Galilee to Jerusalem was via Samaria (Josephus, Ant. xx:118 (xx:6:1), Bel. II:232 (II:12:3)), Josephus states that it was chosen for speed (Josephus, Vita 269 (53)), and Luke clearly states that Jesus avoided Samaria on this occasion (Luke 9:52–56). The fact that Jesus approached Jerusalem from Peraea and Jericho on his last visit is firmly established in the tradition.

[3] Pliny, NH 5:70.

when Galilee and Judaea were both under Herod Agrippa I, and then (from AD 44) under the Roman prefect or procurator[1] whose seat of government was Caesarea in Samaria. It was also the case during the reign of Herod the Great. It was only during the period immediately after the death of Herod the Great that Galilee was separate from Judaea, first under Herod Antipas (to AD 39) and then under Herod Agrippa I (AD 39–41). The areas north-east of the Sea of Galilee were under Herod Philip to AD 34, then for three years under Syrian administration, and then under Herod Agrippa I; on the latter's death they came under the Roman procurator until AD 53 when they passed to Herod Agrippa II, who also acquired some territory in Galilee in AD 61. This shows that the various parts of Herod the Great's kingdom continued to belong together. The name of Judaea was used for the whole area, a fact confirmed by Tacitus who speaks of Judaea being divided into Galilean and Samarian areas, each with their own governors.[2] Thus Judaea was a term used for the area which included Galilee, and this "wide" use is quite firmly attested.[3]

There is, therefore, nothing strange in Luke's use of the geographical terminology, once it is recognized that Judaea has both a broad and a narrow meaning. Conzelmann's picture of Jesus moving to and fro across an imaginary Judaean-Galilean frontier proves to be an illusion. Rather Luke uses "Judaea" as a term which includes Galilee, and the reason for this usage (which has involved him in altering his Marcan source at Luke 4:44) may lie in the fact that he does not ascribe theological importance to Galilee; it is the place where the gospel "begins" (Acts 10:37) but not its main theatre.[4]

[1] Before the reign of Claudius Judaea was governed by a Praefectus. From AD 44 to 66 it was under a Procurator, and after AD 70 it was placed under a Legatus Augusti Pro Praetore. In Luke 3:1 the verb ἡγεμονεύω is used of Pilate (cf. ἡγεμών in 20:20); it is the Greek equivalent for the activity of a Roman governor, including a Praefectus. The variant reading of the western text at 3:1, ἐπιτροπεύοντος, uses the correct technical term for the rule of a procurator, and was at one time regarded as a learned correction by the western reviser. But the discovery of an inscription at Caesarea which describes Pilate as "Praefectus" shows that this alteration was an error; Luke did not make the mistake of applying to Pilate the title by which governors of Judaea were known only after AD 44. Cf. J. Vardaman, "A New Inscription which mentions Pilate as 'Prefect'", JBL 81, 1962, pp. 70–71; A. N. Sherwin-White, op. cit., p. 12.

[2] Tacitus, Annales 12:54: "Atque interim Felix intempestivis remediis delicta accendebat, aemulo ad deterrima Ventidio Cumano, cui pars provinciae habebatur, ita divisis, ut huic Galilaeorum natio, Felici Samaritae parerent, discordes olim et tum contemptu regentium minus coercitis odiis." The preceding sentence describes Felix as "iam pridem Iudaeae inpositus."

[3] The "wide" use is found in Pliny (cited above), Strabo 16:21, and Dio Cassius 37:16:5 (cf. F.-M. Abel, Géographie de la Palestine, Paris, 1967³, I, pp. 312–315). Cf. Rom. 15:31; 2 Cor. 1:16; 1 Thess. 2:14. The "narrow" use is attested frequently in the Gospels and elsewhere (e.g. Matt. 2:22; Luke 2:4; John 4:3, 47, 54); see W. Gutbrod, TDNT III, p. 382; AG p. 379.

[4] In Luke 4:44 Judaea is named instead of Galilee, as in the parallels; it is likely that the broad sense is meant, especially in view of the description of the extent of Jesus' influence in 5:17. In 6:17 the use of "all Judaea" and the omission of the various place names given in Mark 3:7f. demonstrate that the wide use is again present; cf. 7:17; 23:5; Acts 1:8; 10:37.

Once this objection has been rebutted, we may reiterate that Luke's treatment of background details is basically reliable.[1] But can we go on from this fact to claim a broader accuracy for him? The answer must be that while the evidence so far may give us some ground to expect Luke to be generally accurate as a historian, such a conclusion can only be based on examination of all the relevant evidence. Even if the presumption is in favour of Luke's accuracy, it must still be proved in detail.

We turn, therefore, secondly to consider the speeches in Acts. This question is closely bound up with that of theology. Our earlier examination established two points: we cannot expect to find evidence for the use of sources by Luke any more easily in the speeches than in the rest of his writings as a result of the uniformity of style. Again, the background of ancient historiography cannot prove decisively whether or not Luke has aimed at Thucydidean verisimilitude in his speeches. The question is, therefore, largely one of determining the theological outlook present in the speeches; is it Lucan theology or is it a distinguishable theology (or theologies) which can be attributed to his sources? This is the approach which has been most favoured in recent study, and the general result of it has been to show that the speeches do contain much that is characteristic of Luke.[2] They can, therefore, be used as material for establishing the nature of Lucan theology. At the same time, however, it may be suggested that the type of approach practised has to some extent determined the results obtained. If a critic is primarily looking for evidence of Lucan activity, he will perhaps pay the less attention to evidence which inclines in a different direction; he will not ignore it, but he will not be so concerned to develop its implications. Disputed matter may be too easily linked with the Lucan material. In the event, this seems to be what has happened. U. Wilckens, for example, admits the use of traditional material in the speeches in Acts 14 and 17, but does not see that, if Luke has used tradition here, it is probable that he has also used it elsewhere. The more recent research of M. H. Scharlemann suggests that this probability should be regarded as a certainty in the case of Acts 7 where the speech of Stephen has by no means been fully assimilated to Lucan ideas but retains several individual characteristics.[3]

---

[1] Difficulties remain, however, at a number of points, for example, the site of Emmaus.

[2] U. Wilckens, *Die Missionsreden in der Apostelgeschichte.*

[3] M. H. Scharlemann, *Stephen: A Singular Saint*, Rome, 1968.

Conzelmann (*op. cit.*, p. 62 (not in Eng. tr.)) claims that the order "Judaea, Galilee and Samaria" in Acts 9:31 supports his reconstruction of Luke's geography in which Judaea and Galilee are adjacent. This is unlikely. Either the Jewish areas are named first before Samaria, corresponding to the order of evangelism in Acts 1:8, or the inclusive term is given first.

The meaning of Luke 17:11 (διὰ μέσον Σαμαρείας καὶ Γαλιλαίας) is difficult on any hypothesis; a journey along the border of Galilee and Samaria is perhaps indicated.

A further point may be made in this connexion. It is possible to look at the speeches in two ways. On the one hand, they may be regarded as component parts of a single theological scheme. Luke has a definite concept of the development of the early church, and he uses the speeches to bring out the theological significance of what is happening from time to time. They are complementary to each other, with the result that they must be considered together and in the total context of Acts. They are then seen to form a single, unified expression of Lucan theology.[1] On the other hand, they may be considered within their individual contexts. It is to be admitted that they are separable from their contexts, and may be regarded as insertions, although even this point is disputable. But the fact remains that they fit remarkably well into their contexts, and they do the task which they are required to do for the *hearers* at each stage in the narrative.[2] It would be hasty to argue from this fact to the historicity of each individual speech, but at least it is arguable that the type of speech is appropriate to its historical context.

Now it would be wrong to place these two approaches in contrast with each other, as if they were mutually exclusive. This is not the case. But it must be urged that the second approach deserves fuller consideration and emphasis. The speeches do have a primary function in their historical contexts, and the question of that function deserves discussion.

We have already seen that the parallels to the speeches in contemporary literature lie in religious teaching rather than in historiography. When, therefore, we ask why Luke included speeches in his history, the answer must lie in the fact that preaching was a part of the activity of the early church and not in the fact of historical convention. It is thus likely that Luke incorporated speeches not primarily to express his own theological viewpoint but rather because preaching was an integral part of the activity of the early church, as he saw it. But it is not merely a case of "as he saw it"; the fact of preaching, and the use of kerygmatic patterns akin to those found in Acts are amply attested from our other sources. In short, it is one-sided to look at the speeches in Acts merely as evidence for Luke's theology, they have a claim to be based on the practice of the early church.[3]

The third area which must be considered is that of Luke's general picture of the early church. There is general agreement among students that to some extent he has idealized and simplified the story of the development

---

[1] M. Dibelius, "The Speeches in Acts and Ancient Historiography," in *Studies in the Acts of the Apostles*, pp. 138–191, stresses these points. The speeches are Luke's method of preaching to the reader.

[2] F. F. Bruce, *The Acts of the Apostles*, p. 21 (quoting F. J. F. Jackson). U. Wilckens, *op. cit.*, p. 71, uses this fact to argue that both settings and speeches are attributable to Luke.

[3] Some of these points are discussed more fully in my article "The Resurrection in the Acts of the Apostles" (see p. 43 n. 1 above).

of the early church.[1] He has selected one strand in the history of the church, that which leads from Jerusalem to Rome and from the Jewish mission to the Gentile mission, and he has left us in ignorance of many matters about which we would gladly be better informed. To this extent he has simplified the movement of church history, and we do well to remember that he has not told us the whole story. Again, the story is on the whole one of progress in a forward direction. The church acts under divine guidance and achieves its appointed goal. It is sometimes said that there are no disagreements in it, and that everything proceeds smoothly without real opposition. Strife is glossed over and the impression is given that everybody lived in harmony. For example, Luke is said to have under-emphasized the degree of tension between the Jerusalem church and the Hellenists, and to have made out that nothing more than a mild dispute over charitable distribution to widows was involved.[2] Such a view should not be simply dismissed as a vestige of the Tübingen school's concept of Acts as a catholicizing document designed to heal the breach between Petrine and Pauline parties in the church. The fact that this theory of the early church is now rightly discredited,[3] should not absolve us from the need to look carefully at the kind of evidence which might be held to support it. In the event, however, the charge against Luke is often exaggerated. There are sufficient sinners within the church and persecuting opponents outside it in Acts to show us that the progress of the gospel was anything but smooth. The point is rather that Luke tends to relate typical incidents which express the particular problems and crises facing the church instead of giving a detailed account of the much greater number and variety of incidents which must have taken place; his history is selective and consequently open to misapprehension. The question is consequently whether the selection of incidents by Luke and the character of his narration may be regarded as showing historical acumen and judgment. It is, therefore, in our opinion a mark of right judgment that he has devoted a considerable amount of space to the incidents associated with the place of the Gentiles in the church. Evidence from elsewhere in the New Testament indicates that Luke has correctly assessed this as a crisis of great importance.

But it is precisely at this point that a further question arises. Much of Acts is concerned with the missionary work of Paul, and we have an independent check upon the career of Paul in his own letters. Today it is widely held that the picture of Paul presented by Luke is thoroughly

---

[1] E. Haenchen, *Die Apostelgeschichte*, pp. 88 f. ; cf. B. Reicke, *Neutestamentliche Zeitgeschichte*, Berlin, 1965, pp. 158 f. (English translation: *The New Testament Era*, 1969, p. 213).

[2] E. Haenchen, *op. cit.*, p. 92.

[3] J. Munck, *Paul and the Salvation of Mankind*, 1959 (English translation of *Paulus und die Heilsgeschichte*, Copenhagen, 1954).

inaccurate – so much so indeed that it is hardly credible that Acts embodies
the memoirs of a companion of Paul. Acts, it is held, cannot be used as a
primary source in the reconstruction of Paul's career.[1] In other words, the
historical capability of Luke is seriously called into question.

This is a verdict which we find it difficult to accept. That there are
differences between the picture of Paul in Acts and that in his own letters
nobody will deny; the two pictures are independent of each other and
cannot be harmonized in detail, since a man's self-portrait (even when
unconsciously undertaken) will not necessarily agree with the impression
of him received by other people. But this does not mean that the two
pictures are irreconcilable, and we believe that the two can in fact be
harmonized in general terms. The general outline of Paul's career in Acts
fits in well with what is disclosed in his letters. The principal problem is
that of the apostolic council recorded in Acts 15, but it is by no means
insoluble; the best reading of the evidence is still that which would place
the council after the composition of Galatians, so that there is no need to
try to reconcile the account in Acts 15 with that in Gal. 2:1–10.[2] The view
that Paul's theology is inaccurately presented in Acts is a palpable exaggeration, provided we do not ask too much of Luke and do not demand of
him a verbatim report of Paul's words. At the same time, it should be
remembered that there is no need to assume that the theology of a companion of Paul would be in all respects a replica of what Paul taught.
Luke was entitled to his own views, and the fact that they differ in some
respects from those of Paul should not be held against him at this point.
On the contrary, he is a theologian in his own right and must be treated as
such.

For the moment enough has been said to show that a blanket condemnation of Luke as a historian of the early church is uncalled for. We do not
wish to make exaggerated claims for his reliability, nor to suggest that his
views of the historian's task were identical with those of the modern
historian. But it is unfair to suggest that he is a thoroughly tendentious
and unreliable writer, freely rewriting the history of the early church in
the interests of his own theology. We may, therefore, proceed to examine
the contents of his writings with – at the very minimum – an open mind
regarding their historical value. While we do not wish to underestimate
the strength of the case that has been brought against him, there is in our
judgment sufficient evidence in his favour to demand a more positive
evaluation of his historical ability.

Throughout this discussion no attention has been paid to the problem
of the identity of "Luke." We have been content to state a case regarding

[1] J. C. Hurd, Jr., "Pauline Chronology and Pauline Theology," in CHI, pp. 225–248.
[2] See below, p. 184.

his historical abilities which does not rest on an appeal to his identity and chronological position. A judgment on these matters may be thought to belong more fittingly to the conclusion of the enquiry than to its presuppositions. Only when the contents of the Lucan writings have been examined in detail can the historical situation out of which they arose be identified. It is perhaps fair to state our conclusion in advance, namely that the discussion in the following pages in no way speaks against but rather supports the early tradition which identifies the author of the Gospel and the Acts with Luke the beloved physician and companion of Paul,[1] but this remains the conclusion of the discussion and not an assumption upon which the discussion depends.[2]

---

[1] This view of the authorship is cogently defended by E. E. Ellis, *The Gospel of Luke*, pp. 40–55; cf. B. Reicke, *The Gospel of Luke*, 1965, pp. 10–24 (English translation of *Lukasevangeliet*, Stockholm, 1962).

[2] Since 1970 the discussion of solutions to the Synoptic problem other than the two-source theory has gained momentum. (1). The view that Mark is dependent on Matthew and Luke has been defended by W. R. Farmer and his followers. For confrontations of this view and the traditional view see the essays by D. L. Dungan and J. A. Fitzmyer in D. G. Miller (ed.), *Jesus and Man's Hope*, Pittsburgh, 1970, Vol. 1, pp. 51–97 and 131–170; and also C. H. Talbert and E. V. McKnight, "Can the Griesbach Hypothesis be falsified?" JBL 91, 1972, pp. 338–368, with the reply by G. W. Buchanan, "Has the Griesbach Hypothesis been falsified?" JBL 93, 1974, pp. 550–572. W. R. Farmer has surveyed the discussion in "Modern Developments of Griesbach's Hypothesis," NTS 23, 1976–77, pp. 275–295. The 'minor agreements' between Matthew and Luke are discussed by a supporter of the two-source theory in F. Neirynck (et al.), *The Minor Agreements of Matthew and Luke against Mark with a Cumulatative List*, Gembloux, 1974. A. M. Honóre's statistical arguments have been weighed and found wanting by D. Wenham, "The Synoptic Problem Revisited: Some New Suggestions about the Composition of Mark 4:1–34," Tyn. B 23, 1972, pp. 3–38; on the topic generally see R. Morgenthaler, *Statistische Synopse*, Zürich, 1971, and W. R. Farmer's comments in Bib. 45, 1973, 417–433. (2). The Griesbach hypothesis dispenses with the 'Q' document. The existence of Q is also denied by other scholars who regard Mark as the earliest Gospel and hold that Matthew is dependent upon Mark and Luke is dependent upon both of them; on this view Luke derived his 'Q' material from Matthew. See M. D. Goulder, *Midrash and Lection in Matthew*, 1974; J. Drury, *Tradition and Design in Luke's Gospel*, 1976. These studies fail to account for the fact that there are passages in the 'Q' material where Luke's wording is obviously more primitive than Matthew's and hence cannot have been derived from the latter. (3). The case that Luke's special source material overlapped with his material from Mark, and that accordingly some of Luke's divergences from Mark may be explained by the use of a parallel source has been presented by T. Schramm, *Der Markus-Stoff bei Lukas*, Cambridge, 1971. (4). A fresh dimension has been added to discussion of Luke's sources in the Gospel and Acs by the claim that Luke has often moulded sections of his narrative to give parallelism with other sections; see C. H. Talbert, *Literary Patterns, Theological Themes and the Genre of Luke–Acts*, Missoula, 1974.

CHAPTER IV

THE THEOLOGY OF SALVATION

Recent Approaches to Luke's Theology

THE STUDY OF THE WORK OF LUKE FROM THE POINT OF VIEW OF ITS theological content has produced a variety of hypotheses regarding its central theme and basic thrust. A brief survey of some recent approaches will provide an introduction to our own discussion of the problem.

The most influential recent discussion of this kind is that of H. Conzelmann; his ideas have been taken up by several scholars, and even critics of his approach and conclusions must admit that his posing of the questions raised by Luke–Acts has been extremely fruitful for their own investigations.

The key word in Conzelmann's approach is *Heilsgeschichte*, variously rendered into English as "the history of salvation," "redemptive history" or "salvation-history." Whereas Mark offers what Conzelmann describes as "a commentary on the kerygma" and Matthew develops the theme of promise and fulfilment, the characteristic of Luke is that he traces the continuous development of the history of salvation.[1]

Conzelmann's thesis starts in effect from the assumption that the first Christians lived in hope of the imminent parousia of Jesus. A strong eschatological fervour animated the earliest Christians, but this was in danger of being replaced by disillusionment as the years went by and the parousia was delayed beyond all expectation. The thought of the church had to come to terms with the new situation; apocalyptic excitement had to be succeeded by a faith adapted to life in a world that went on in much the same way as it had always done.

Several early church theologians wrestled with this task, and Luke occupies a prominent place among them. He reinterpreted the eschatological content of the traditions which he incorporated in his Gospel in such a way that the parousia was regarded as sudden rather than soon and

---

[1] H. Conzelmann, *Grundriss der Theologie des Neuen Testaments*, pp. 160–172, especially pp. 163, 165 (Eng. Tr. pp. 140–152, especially pp. 143, 145). Some of Conzelmann's basic ideas are already to be found in R. Bultmann, *Theology of the New Testament*, II, pp. 116–118.

transferred to the indefinite future rather than expected at any moment. The concept of the kingdom of God was altered; instead of being an imminent event it was transformed into a transcendent, heavenly reality which would become manifest at some unknown future time. This meant that the parousia lost its earlier significance as a key factor in Christian hope and as a decisive motive in Christian living. The resultant vacuum was filled up in two ways. First, the time of delay which the church was now experiencing was not to be regarded as a period of negative significance before the parousia; it was not a time of useless waiting to be hurried through as quickly as possible, rather like a period of enforced waiting for the arrival of a late train, during which the traveller has nothing particular to do except "to kill time." On the contrary, it was a period of positive content, a vital stage in a developing plan foreordained by God and in process of fulfilment as He continued to act in history. Second, Luke drew attention to the role of the church, guided and empowered by the Spirit, as the institution through which God works in this present age until the parousia.

The important thing that Luke did, on this showing, was to take up the concept of history and to fit the period of the church into it. Luke regarded world history as running from the creation to the parousia and being divided into three periods. The period of Israel lasted up to and included the work of John the Baptist. Then came the ministry of Jesus, conceived of as a period free from the influence of Satan.[1] Finally, there was the period of the church. The development of this scheme had certain consequences.

First, there is the stress on history. The ministry of Jesus, once regarded simply as the content of the church's proclamation, now became a piece of history, indeed the central era in history – *Die Mitte der Zeit*. Thus the content of the kerygma was "historicized" and made into a part of world history.

This means that history had come to have a positive importance for theology. A community which expects the parousia to happen within the next week or month does not stop to write history, nor does it assign to itself a place within the general development of history, nor is its returning Lord regarded essentially as a figure of the past. But for Luke history, and history writing, had become important, and so he proceeded to "historicize" the message about Jesus.

Second, the placing of Jesus in the arena of history meant that his relationship to the past needed to be clarified. In the Gospel of Mark, there is little emphasis on the idea of promise and fulfilment as the link

---

[1] The period thus described by Conzelmann is that lying between the temptation and the passion, exclusive of these events themselves; cf. Luke 4:13; 22:3.

between the Old Testament and Jesus,[1] but in Matthew and Luke this theme is taken up and developed at length. There was also the problem of the existence of the Jews, who claimed to be the true descendants of the people of the Old Testament, and the relationship of the Christian faith to Judaism and of the Jewish people to the Christian church had to be examined.

Third, the relationship of Jesus to the church required elucidation. How was the continuity to be expressed? Luke's solution lay in the message of the church concerning Jesus. This message was based upon the preaching of the apostles and was handed down in the tradition of which they were the originators. Hence the church, with its message and its sacraments, became the custodian of the tradition and the channel of salvation.

Fourth, the church, now regarded as a historical institution, had to define its position within general history and over against the Roman Empire in which it existed.

Thus the general effect of Luke's writing was to replace the hope of the imminent parousia by a theory of the progress of Christian history through its various stages; he has shifted the emphasis in Christian faith from the future to the past, and given the present a positive significance.

Before considering various difficulties which are created by Conzelmann's understanding of Luke we may examine the views of other scholars which are closely related to his viewpoint. In an article published in 1954 E. Lohse adopted a similar point of view.[2] He describes Luke as "the theologian of salvation-history," and claims that he was the first to create a Christian literary work. Luke portrays the fulfilment of the promised saving events, which began with the ministry of Jesus and continues in the activity of the church. By this description of past events Luke intended to instruct the church of his own day how it ought to act in its preaching, in its inner life and in its relationship to the world.

A very similar standpoint is adopted by S. Schulz who deals with the individual characters of all four Gospels in his book *Die Stunde der Botschaft*.[3] In his handling of Luke he appears to be largely following in the steps of Conzelmann. His distinctive emphasis emerges at two points. First, he stresses most strongly the predetermined character of the history recorded by Luke. Whatever God ordains comes to pass, despite human sin and opposition. All is predetermined and will reach its appointed conclusion. Schulz claims that here pagan ideas of inevitable fate have coloured Luke's

---

[1] This is the thesis of A. Suhl, *Die Funktion der alttestamentlichen Zitate und Anspielungen im Markusevangelium*, Gütersloh, 1965. It is, however, an exaggerated point of view; see J. Rohde, *Rediscovering the Teaching of the Evangelists*, pp. 140f.

[2] E. Lohse, "Lukas als Theologe der Heilsgeschichte," Ev.Th. 14, 1954, pp. 256–275.

[3] S. Schulz, *Die Stunde der Botschaft*, pp. 235–296; "Gottes Vorsehung bei Lukas," ZNW 54, 1963, pp. 104–216.

thought; not election, as in the Old Testament, but the Hellenistic ideas of predestination and necessity are at work. Everything depends on God's will, and it is not for man to question it. The second point stressed by Schulz is that for Luke everything is bound up with the *una sancta*, the Christian church founded by the apostles and possessing the saving message handed down by an "apostolic succession" to the church's office-bearers as the representatives of the apostles. Outside this church there can be no salvation. These points are all present in Conzelmann, but they are brought out with greater clarity and force by Schulz. Whereas, however, Conzelmann makes as much, if not more, use of the Gospel of Luke than the Acts, it is interesting that Schulz, although he is ostensibly writing about the Gospel, draws most of his evidence from Acts.

A number of scholars have concentrated their attention on the Acts. This is an approach which has its dangers, since the Gospel and the Acts must be considered together, but which is clearly a legitimate one provided that the Gospel is not left out of sight. Here the massive work of E. Haenchen demands priority of attention.[1] In many respects. Haenchen stands close to Conzelmann. He emphasizes that Luke is first and foremost a theologian, a writer who sought to "edify" the church of his own day, and that historical considerations were subordinate to this purpose. The result is that Acts is less a guide to early church history than an expression of Lucan theology couched in historical form. Throughout his work Luke has made little use of historical sources and has engaged in creative literary work to a very considerable degree. What, then, was Luke's aim? Haenchen replies that once Luke had taken the step of regarding the life of Jesus as a period of past history he had to establish the relationship between it and the period of the church. The means by which he did this was the concept of the Word of God, the preaching of the message concerning Christ. Thus Acts is the story of the progress of the gospel as far as Rome. In taking up this theme, Luke attempted to deal with the actual problems of the church in his day, especially those caused by its relationship to Judaism. On the one hand, there was the theological question of the turning of the church to the Gentiles who were no longer required to keep the Jewish law: how then was the continuity of the church with salvation-history to be preserved? Luke's answer was that the leaders of the church had not broken with Judaism but rather grasped the true meaning of it, and that God Himself had called them to the Gentile mission. On the other hand, once the church broke free from Judaism it no longer stood in the favoured position assigned by the Romans to the Jewish religion and

[1] E. Haenchen, *Die Apostelgeschichte*, especially pp. 81–103, 670–689; cf. J. Rohde, *op. cit.*, pp. 194–202.

was liable to persecution. This political problem was faced by Luke and answered by showing both that Christianity was the continuation of Judaism and also that Christianity was politically harmless and recognized as such in the apostolic age by the authorities.

For Haenchen the picture which is thus painted by Luke is an idealized and even a misleading representation of what actually happened in the early church. This is seen particularly in Luke's portrayal of Paul, which Haenchen finds to be an uninformed idealization by a writer from a late generation. Here Haenchen joins hands with P. Vielhauer whose work may be conveniently mentioned at this point.[1] Vielhauer's principal contribution to the subject was an article on Paul and Luke in which he claimed to demonstrate in some detail the differences between the real Paul and Luke's portrait of him. A number of theological points are noted, in each of which Luke shows himself to be non-Pauline in outlook, and Vielhauer claims that he is typical of the later "early catholic" period, an adjective which in his usage appears to be pejorative.

The term "early catholic" requires some clarification. A number of writers have argued that in the later books of the New Testament there is a growth towards the type of Christianity found in the second century and later in which a great significance is attached to the church as an organized institution with fixed orders of ministry and carefully regulated sacramental practice. This institution dispenses salvation and stands over against any other groups which offer salvation on different terms. It is the church assuming a settled existence and establishing its place over against such heresies as gnosticism.[2]

The question then arises whether such "early catholicism" is to be found in Luke, and here opinions greatly differ, largely because the basic characteristics of the trend remain undefined, and consequently it is uncertain whether Luke's characteristics should be regarded as explicitly early catholic. Vielhauer's view that Luke falls within this description[3] is shared by E. Käsemann who claims that: "Luke is not, as Dibelius still believed, a late pupil of Paul, but the first representative of a nascent early catholicism."[4] He describes it as "a theology which is essentially different from that of primitive Christianity," formulated under the pressure of gnosticism and replacing eschatology (now in eclipse, thanks to the delay

[1] P. Vielhauer, "Zum 'Paulinismus' der Apostelgeschichte," Ev. Th. 10, 1950–51, pp. 1–15 (reprinted in P. Vielhauer, *Aufsätze zum Neuen Testament*, München, 1965, pp. 9–27; English translation in SLA, pp. 33–50).
[2] E. Käsemann, *New Testament Questions of Today*, 1969, pp. 21 f., 236–251 (English translation of *Exegetische Versuche und Besinnungen* II, Göttingen, 1965²); cf. J. H. Elliott, "A Catholic Gospel: Reflections on 'Early Catholicism' in the New Testament," CBQ 31, 1969, pp. 213–223.
[3] P. Vielhauer, *op. cit.* (English translation), p. 49.
[4] E. Käsemann, *op. cit.*, p. 21.

of the parousia) with salvation-history.[1] Other scholars, however, have felt that certain essentials of the early catholic position are missing from Luke's work.[2]

The question of Luke's eschatology is taken up by U. Wilckens in his study of the theology of the speeches in Acts.[3] He claims that the important question at the end of the first century was where salvation was to be found, in the past, future or present. Luke's answer to the question was that the decisive eschatological event had taken place in the ministry of Jesus; the eschatological content of the original apocalyptic tradition was seen to be fulfilled in Jesus, and the remaining apocalyptic imagery was reserved for fulfilment in the distant future. After the ascension of Jesus salvation is no longer directly present, but only indirectly by means of the Spirit and the "name" of Jesus. The salvation constituted by God in the past event of Jesus is mediated by the proclamation of the message. Nevertheless, Wilckens argues that at this point Luke is inadequate. He is unable to explain how the past event of Jesus can have saving significance now. Wilckens explains this weakness in Luke in two ways. On the one hand, Luke has no concept of the soteriological significance of the death of Jesus. On the other hand, his roots lie in Hellenistic historiography rather than apocalyptic theology, and consequently he views *Heilsgeschichte* as a closed system of events.[4]

The scholar who has perhaps made most use of the concept of salvation-history is O. Cullmann.[5] Cullmann finds in this concept an alternative way of understanding the essential message of the New Testament over against the "existential" view of Bultmann and his followers. The weakness of Bultmann's interpretation is that the existential interpretation will work only for certain New Testament writers, namely Paul and John, and that consequently much of the New Testament must be regarded as a

[1] E. Käsemann, *op. cit.*, p. 22. For Käsemann's view of Luke see also *Essays on New Testament Themes*, pp. 28f., 136–148; *Jesus Means Freedom: A Polemical Survey of the New Testament*, 1969, pp. 116–129 (English translation of *Der Ruf der Freiheit*, Tübingen, 1968³).
   That Luke is a representative of early catholicism is also the thesis of G. Klein, *Die Zwölf Apostel – Ursprung und Gestalt einer Idee*, Göttingen, 1961 (cf. J. Rohde, *op. cit.*, pp. 219–229). J. C. O'Neill, *The Theology of Acts in its Historical Setting*, 1961, 1970² dates Acts well into the catholic period (mid second century), but his arguments have not found acceptance.
[2] C. K. Barrett, *Luke the Historian in Recent Study*, pp. 70–76; H. Conzelmann, "Luke's Place in the Development of Early Christianity," in SLA pp. 298–316; E. Haenchen, *op. cit.*, pp. 46f., 202, 678f.; W. G. Kümmel, *Introduction to the New Testament*, pp. 102, 122.
[3] U. Wilckens, *Die Missionsreden der Apostelgeschichte*; "Kerygma und Evangelium. Beobachtungen zu Acta 10, 34–43," ZNW 49, 1958, pp. 223–237; "The Understanding of Revelation within the History of Primitive Christianity," in W. Pannenberg (ed.), *Revelation as History*, 1968, pp. 57–121, especially pp. 93–98 (English translation of *Offenbarung als Geschichte*, Göttingen, 1961).
[4] U. Wilckens, in W. Pannenberg, *op. cit.*, pp. 97f.
[5] O. Cullmann, *Salvation in History*, 1967 (English translation of *Heil als Geschichte: Heilsgeschichtliche Existenz im Neuen Testament*, Tübingen, 1965).

falling away from their insights. Early catholicism, as depicted by Käsemann and the other writers whom we have discussed, represents a shift
from the outlook of Paul, and the tendency among some scholars has been
to condemn it as a falling away from a higher insight into the nature of the
Gospel, while others have claimed that it was a necessary accommodation
to a changing era.[1] In any case the point is that the existential view cannot
be maintained successfully in interpreting the New Testament as a whole.
It is therefore legitimate to enquire regarding its validity and whether there
may not be some preferable method of understanding. This is what
Cullmann sets out to supply with his claim that salvation-history is the key
to the understanding of the New Testament. There is a divine sequence of
events which form the basis for faith, and this understanding of the nature
of faith is traced by Cullmann throughout the New Testament as a whole.
As he himself claims, salvation-history and the existential approach are
not irreconcilable alternatives. On the contrary, they are complementary;
it is the series of saving events which calls us to existential commitment,
and (pace Bultmann) faith cannot be independent of a historical basis.

The significance of this for the study of Luke will be apparent. On the
one hand, Cullmann is in general agreement with the approach which finds
Luke to be an advocate of salvation-history. He is able to accept much of
Conzelmann's approach to Luke, although he has certain qualifications to
make regarding it.[2] On the other hand, he insists that Luke was not an
innovator. The concept of salvation-history was already a part of Christian thinking; indeed in a rudimentary form it goes back to Jesus Himself.
Therefore Luke is not the individual thinker he is sometimes made out to
be. Cullmann would probably want to dissent from Käsemann's judgment that "considering the effect that he has had, (Luke) is the greatest
New Testament theologian'.[3] For, on Cullmann's view, the effect
ascribed by Käsemann to Luke should be ascribed to the New Testament
as a whole. Nor is Luke to be regarded as lapsing from the theology of the
early church; on the contrary, his work is to be evaluated positively as the
consistent development of the message of Jesus.[4]

[1] W. C. van Unnik, in SLA, pp. 27f.
[2] O. Cullmann, *op. cit.*, pp. 244f. It would be interesting to know how far Conzelmann's idea
of *"Die Mitte der Zeit"* has been drawn from O. Cullmann's earlier book *Christ and Time*
(1951; English translation of *Christus und die Zeit*, Zollikon-Zürich, 1946), where the thesis is
advanced that the Christ-deed is the midpoint of time. The differences between the two
scholars are: (1) Conzelmann attributes this theological understanding of the Christ-deed to
Luke, whereas Cullmann finds it to be characteristic of early Christianity generally. (2) Conzelmann holds that Luke has de-eschatologized the Christ-deed, but Cullmann preserves the
tension between its character as the mid-point of time *and* as the beginning of the new age
(*op. cit.*, pp. 82f.). Cf. O. Cullmann, *Salvation in History*, pp. 46f.
[3] E. Käsemann, *Jesus means Freedom*, p. 121.
[4] W. G. Kümmel, "Luc en accusation dans la théologie contemporaine," in EL, pp. 93-109
(German version in ZNW 63, 1972, pp. 149-165).

Problems raised by recent study

From this descriptive survey of some representative recent discussions of the work of Luke we must now turn to an examination of the problems which are raised by them. It is clear that something like a consensus of opinion exists regarding the theology of Luke, and that this agreement is expressed in the use of the term "salvation-history." The writings of Luke present the Christian message in the form of history, a history which embraces both the ministry of Jesus and the activity of the early church. There is no need to quarrel with this verdict. Undoubtedly a feature of Luke has here come to expression. What is open to question is whether this concept is the most fruitful one in an understanding of what Luke himself intended to do. Granted that he consciously set himself to write history, the question arises whether he thought of himself primarily as a historian or whether he unconsciously historicized the kerygma. In our opinion neither of these views is satisfactory. Much more suggestive is the plea of M. Dibelius and C. K. Barrett that Luke should be regarded as a preacher, even if he himself was not fully conscious of this motive.[1] Luke's purpose in writing was to present the gospel of salvation to his readers in order to lead them to faith or (as in the case of Theophilus) to confirm their faith.

This means that Luke's purpose was not so much to re-frame the Christian message in terms of "salvation-history" as to make the way of salvation plain to his readers. It could be objected at the outset that our distinction rests upon a confusion between Luke's conscious purpose in writing (to proclaim the gospel of salvation) and the underlying motif of his theology (the expression of the message in terms of "salvation-history"). But the ensuing discussion will make it clear that, while Luke does operate with a principle that may be termed salvation-historical, this motif was one that was already characteristic of the theology of the early church, so that it cannot be said that Luke's underlying motif was to re-frame the message in terms of salvation-history. Consequently, while we freely admit the presence of salvation-history in Luke–Acts, the idea is not distinctive of Luke, nor was it his theological purpose to bring it to expression. Rather, the emphasis falls upon the presentation of the story of Jesus, as in the other Gospels, in order to lead men to salvation.

Another objection may also be faced at this point. It could be argued that the emphasis which we are now placing on Luke as an evangelist and theologian runs contrary to the stress made in the earlier chapters of this book that Luke was a historian. But our concern there was to deal with

---

[1] M. Dibelius, *Studies in the Acts of the Apostles*, p. 137; C. K. Barrett, *Luke the Historian in Recent Study*, pp. 52f.

the false assumption that if Luke was a theologian he could not be a reliable historian, and to claim that Luke could be both a reliable historian and a good theologian. We then looked in a general kind of way at the evidence for his reliability as a historian and concluded that he could be credited with much more historical trustworthiness than he is often allowed by contemporary critics. In dealing with these points we were clearing the ground for an assessment of Luke as a theologian, since we believe that the validity of his theology stands or falls with the reliability of the history on which it is based. Granted that Luke has interpreted the historical facts, we have to ask both whether the facts have been reliably reported and whether the interpretation of them is justified by the facts themselves. Hence our stress from now onwards on the character of Luke as a theologian does not stand in tension with our earlier emphasis on his character as a historian. And, in terms of the distinction which we are making between the themes of "salvation-history" and salvation *simpliciter*, the point we are stressing is that Luke's concern is with the saving significance of the history rather than with the history itself as bare facts.

The difficulties which are inherent in the dominant modern conception of Luke, as represented especially by the work of H. Conzelmann, and which lead to our attempt to find a more appropriate characterization of his work may now be summarized. In the first place, the essential starting point for Conzelmann's view of Luke is his view that Luke wrote under the influence of the delay of the parousia. The theory that the delay of the parousia exerted a profound effect upon the theology of the early church and its writings was placed upon a solid foundation by the publication of E. Grässer's closely argued study in 1957. Grässer claimed that the teaching of Jesus made no allowance for any kind of interval before the coming of the end, and that in the Gospels and Acts we can trace the various successive attempts of the early church to reinterpret His teaching as a result of the fact that the eagerly expected denouement had failed to materialize.[1]

Grässer's presentation of the case has admittedly won much support.[2] Nevertheless, it is at the very least exaggerated, if not downright unconvincing.[3] In an early publication we have briefly offered our reasons for not accepting his reconstruction of the situation.[4] Since then the whole

[1] E. Grässer, *Das Problem der Parusieverzögerung in den synoptischen Evangelien und in der Apostelgeschichte*, Berlin, 1957.

[2] For example, W. Ott, *Gebet und Heil: Die Bedeutung der Gebetsparänese in der lukanischen Theologie*, München, 1965; G. Bouwmann, *Das dritte Evangelium*, Ch. II. The position is defended against the arguments of G. R. Beasley-Murray, *Jesus and the Future*, 1954, and W. G. Kümmel, *Promise and Fulfilment*, 1957 (English translation of *Verheissung und Erfüllung*, Zurich, 1956³) by C. K. Barrett, *Jesus and the Gospel Tradition*, 1967, pp. 74–76.

[3] O. Cullmann, "Parusieverzögerung und Urchristentum: Der gegenwärtige Stand der Diskussion," *Theologische Literaturzeitung* 83, 1958, cols. 1–12; *id.*, *Salvation in History*, pp. 209–230.

[4] I. H. Marshall, *Eschatology and the Parables*, 1963.

problem of the parousia has been discussed at length by A. L. Moore,[1] and, while certain aspects of his case may be open to criticism, in our judgment he shows up sufficiently the weakness in the case put forward by Grässer. The basic objection is that Grässer's argument depends upon denying to Jesus any saying which presupposes an interval before the parousia; every trace of such an expectation must be removed, but the critical methods used to carry out this removal are sometimes doubtful, and one is left with the impression that the evidence has been evaluated in the light of a pre-conceived theory.[2] Further, if the view of Grässer is sound, it becomes impossible to see how the early church ever developed the idea of the return of Jesus, since He Himself had never foretold this.

There are, then, grave difficulties surrounding the theory of parousia delay, and we are justified in enquiring whether the New Testament evidence may not be understood in a different manner.

This leads on to the second point. If the theory of the delay of the parousia is wrong, then it follows that we should not think of Lucan theology as being a reply to it. The notion that Luke has in effect replaced primitive eschatology by a historical scheme at once becomes suspect. We have to ask whether the Lucan scheme does not give the same kind of place to the parousia as the rest of the New Testament. This is the claim made by Cullmann.[3] He admits that in Luke there has been "interpretative reflection," but he denies that there is any alteration in principle from the theology of those who preceded Luke. In other words, the inclusion of the parousia as the end-term in a salvation-historical scheme corresponds to early Christian thought and is not an innovation by Luke.

This point is closely bound up with a third one. Cullmann's argument is that salvation-history is not a late development in the New Testament writings with Luke as a prime innovator. On the contrary, the concept of salvation-history is basic in the New Testament, and therefore Luke was not doing something radically new when he adopted it. Hence, the stress on history in Luke is not something new but is in line with earlier thought. It is significant to observe at this point that very similar claims have been made from within the circle of those who follow the general approach of

---

[1] A. L. Moore, *The Parousia in the New Testament*, Leiden, 1966; see also D. E. Aune, "The Significance of the Delay of the Parousia for Early Christianity," in G. F. Hawthorne (ed.) *Current Issues in Biblical and Patristic Interpretation*, Grand Rapids, 1975, pp. 87–109.

[2] That Jesus expected a period of time before the parousia is shown, for example by the command to repeat the rite given at the Last Supper. In favour of its authenticity see J. Jeremias, *The Eucharistic Words of Jesus*, 1966[2], pp. 237–255 (English translation of *Die Abendmahlsworte Jesu*, Göttingen, 1960[3]) ; H. Schürmann, *Der Einsetzungsbericht*, pp. 123–129. The objection raised by C. K. Barrett, *op. cit.*, p. 71 – that the words occur only in one Gospel in a textually uncertain verse – is without force. The longer form of Luke's narrative is almost certainly original, and the words in question are attested in 1 Cor. 11:25.

[3] O. Cullmann, *op. cit.*, pp. 237f.

Bultmann and Conzelmann: S. Schulz has argued that in Mark the gospel is already presented in historical form, and a similar claim has been made on behalf of Matthew by G. Strecker.[1] It follows that Luke would not necessarily have had his eye fixed on "history" as the key category in what he was attempting to do. His interest may have been elsewhere.

Fourthly, Conzelmann and Wilckens get themselves into difficulties over the realization of salvation in the present era of the church. Wilckens in particular finds it hard to see how salvation is possible in Luke's church since it depends upon a past event or series of events; while he is aware that Luke asserts the presence of salvation, he finds himself using words like "indirectly" to describe the way in which men receive it, and he argues that Luke has not raised the question of the rationale of present salvation based upon a past event. But may not the difficulty exist in the mind of the critic rather than in the mind of Luke? Wilckens' difficulty lies in his attributing too much importance to Luke's stress on the past history of Jesus as a period completely separate from that of the early church. He has not sufficiently appreciated the force of Acts 1:1f. with its implication that Jesus continues to be active in the period of the church.[2]

Linked with this criticism is, fifthly, the suggestion that too much emphasis has been laid upon Luke's schematization of the course of salvation history. Conzelmann's neat isolation of the "Satan-free" period in the ministry of Jesus between the temptation and the passion is undoubtedly to be rejected.[3] It overlooks the significance of Luke 11:16 and is forced to give an artificial sense to Luke 22:28.[4] More generally,

---

[1] S. Schulz, "Die Bedeutung des Markus für die Theologiegeschichte des Urchristentums," SE II, 1964, pp. 135–145; G. Strecker, *Der Weg der Gerechtigkeit*, Göttingen, 1966[2]; cf. R. Walker, *Die Heilsgeschichte im ersten Evangelium*, Göttingen, 1967.

[2] In Acts 1:1f. Luke relates that he wrote his first book concerning all that Jesus *began* to do and teach until the day when He ascended. The use of ἤρξατο is regarded by many critics as simply an example of Semitic or Greek redundancy (K. Lake and H. J. Cadbury, BC IV, p. 3; E. Haenchen, *Die Apostelgeschichte*, p. 106 n. 3; H. Conzelmann, *Die Apostelgeschichte*, p. 20). Others take it to mean "all that Jesus did as a beginning" (J. H. E. Hull, *The Holy Spirit in the Acts of the Apostles*, 1968, pp. 179f.). Luke, however, does not use ἄρχομαι redundantly when he is looking back on a completed episode, and it seems probable that the verb is here emphatic, so that (it is implied) the Acts describes what Jesus *continued* to do through His Spirit (F. F. Bruce, *The Acts of the Apostles*, p. 66). W. C. van Unnik, "'The Book of Acts,' the Confirmation of the Gospel," Nov. T IV, 1960, pp. 26–59, especially p. 49, finds that the continuity between Luke and Acts lies not in the activity of Jesus but rather in the salvation which took its rise in His ministry and was confirmed in the activity of the early church.

[3] J. Rohde, *Rediscovering the Teaching of the Evangelists*, pp. 177f., 243; S. Brown, *Apostasy and Perseverance in the Theology of Luke*, Rome, 1969, pp. 5–12; E. E. Ellis, *The Gospel of Luke*, p. 248.

[4] Conzelmann ignores Luke 11:16 with its reference to temptation by the human opponents of Jesus; although there is no explicit reference to Satan here, it is unlikely that he is regarded as inactive in the temptation (*pace* E. Best, *The Temptation and the Passion: The Markan Soteriology*). In any case Conzelmann does not enquire closely into the origin of the temptation, whether in Satan or in men.

(Footnote continued at foot of p. 88)

however, S. Schulz, who accepts the essential correctness of Conzelmann's threefold division of salvation history, has to admit that the scheme is not explicitly presented by Luke at any point.[1] G. Braumann has attempted to show that certain lines of continuity run through the various periods and prevent any simple, rigid separation of them from one another.[2]

The whole concept of salvation-history is denied to Luke by H. Flender in his extremely obscure book, *Heil und Geschichte in der Theologie des Lukas*.[3] He claims that Luke does not see a unilinear development in salvation-history, but rather has a dialectical approach. In spite of many useful observations, it is far from clear what Flender understands by salvation-history and what he wishes to substitute for it. Even the summary by J. Rohde in his account of redaction criticism fails to enlighten, and, since Rohde offers no critical appraisal of Flender's work (as he does with many of the authors whom he discusses), we may be pardoned for wondering whether he too could not understand him. We cannot, therefore, make much use of Flender as a critic of the Conzelmann approach.

These various considerations suggest that justice is not done to Luke by the current critical orthodoxy, and that the fault may lie in attributing to him the wrong kind of interest in salvation-history. There is room for a fresh approach to his thought.

Towards a Fresh Approach

A new look at the theology of Luke may concentrate its attention on the Gospel or on Acts or attempt to deal with both. We have already suggested that some studies of Luke have concentrated overmuch on Acts. The attraction of this approach is of course that, since here Luke was less bound by his sources, his distinctive approach may come to light more readily. The danger is that since we have very little knowledge of what Luke's sources were, and no way of comparing how other writers may have dealt with the same sources, such an approach can be very subjective. In the case of the Gospel we have not only one of Luke's sources available

[1] S. Schulz, *Die Stunde der Botschaft*, pp. 275 f.

[2] G. Braumann, "Das Mittel der Zeit," ZNW 54, 1963, pp. 117–145.
While operating with a scheme similar to that of Conzelmann, E. Käsemann, *New Testament Questions of Today*, p. 21, finds the mid-point of time not in the ministry of Jesus but in the hour of the church; cf. U. Luck, "Kerygma, Tradition und Geschichte bei Lukas," ZTK 57, 1960, pp. 51–66, especially p. 66.
For further criticism of this view see E. E. Ellis, *op. cit.*, pp. 15 f.

[3] H. Flender, *Heil und Geschichte in der Theologie des Lukas*, München, 1965 (English translation: *St Luke: Theologian of Redemptive History*, 1967). Cf. J. Rohde, *op. cit.*, pp. 229–236.

At Luke 22:28 Conzelmann attempts to make a perfect tense refer purely to the present. Despite the defence of this view offered by W. Ott, *Gebet und Heil*, pp. 85–89, this view remains grammatically impossible; the "remaining" and the temptations must both belong to the past and extend into the present. Cf. S. Brown, *op. cit.*, pp. 8 f.

for inspection but also another Gospel which has made use of some of the same sources as Luke. This gives us a double check on a large proportion of Luke's material and enables us to work with a greater degree of objectivity than in the case of Acts. We must, therefore, dissent from the approach of S. Schulz who holds that Luke's theology is more easily traceable in Acts since Luke was less bound by his sources or predecessors there.[1] Gospel and Acts must be treated together, but we shall be on surer ground if we concentrate attention on the Gospel.

When we approach the Gospel in this way, it is of interest to see whether there is any theme which is particularly emphasized by Luke over against the other Gospels and which may afford us a clue regarding his main interest.

In his commentary on the Gospel A. R. C. Leaney singled out the theme of Christ as King as the major emphasis of Luke. "His theme was the reign of Christ, how it is established, how it must be maintained."[2] So the principal theme of the Gospel is seen to be the Kingdom of God with Jesus as the king who acts in a royal manner during His ministry and then bequeathes His kingdom to the apostles (Luke 22:18). He goes up to Jerusalem as a king, but it is through crucifixion and resurrection that He reaches His throne. As king He is surrounded by glory; and His entrance into glory at His exaltation (Luke 24:26) is more significant in this regard for Luke than the future parousia in glory which is emphasized by Mark and Matthew.

Here we undoubtedly have an important theme in the Gospel of Luke, but we may well doubt whether it is the most important one. The statistics alone make it doubtful whether Luke ascribes much more significance to this theme than do the other Synoptists. It is true that the concept of glory is especially prominent in Luke, but this is not so of kingship. The usage of the word group is as follows:[3]

	Matthew	Mark	Luke	Acts
βασιλεία	55	20	46	8
βασιλεία τοῦ θεοῦ/τῶν οὐρανῶν	36	14	32	6
total references to God's kingdom[4]	43	14	35	8
kingdom of Christ/Son of man[5]	3	—	4	—

[1] S. Schulz, *Die Stunde der Botschaft*, p. 242.

[2] A. R. C. Leaney, *A Commentary on the Gospel according to St Luke*, 1958, pp. 34–37, quotation from p. 34. Cf. G. Voss, *Die Christologie der lukanischen Schriften in Grundzügen*, Paris, 1965, p. 61.

[3] Statistics are taken from R. Morgenthaler, *Statistik des neutestamentlichen Wortschatzes* Zürich, 1958, with corrections.

[4] Including references to "His kingdom" and the like.

[5] Matt. 13:41; 16:28; 20:21; Luke 1:33; 22:29, 30; 23:42. To this list Matt. 25:34 should perhaps be added. No distinction has been made between references to the Son of Man and to Jesus, since it is agreed that the Evangelists made none.

	Matthew	Mark	Luke	Acts
βασιλεύειν	I	—	3	—
βασιλεύς	22	12	II	20
βασιλεύς directly used of Jesus[1]	8	6	5	I

A glance at these figures will show that the concept of the kingdom of God is not any more prominent in Luke than it is in Matthew, although in both Gospels it occupies a more important place than it does in Mark. References to Jesus as king and to His kingdom are no more frequent in Luke than in Matthew, and the concept appears only once in Acts. It can scarcely be said on the basis of this evidence that Luke is significantly interested in the kingship of Jesus as compared with his Synoptic counterparts.

The actual usage must also be examined. Luke introduces the idea of the preaching of the kingdom by Jesus in places where it is not mentioned by Mark (Luke 4:43; 8:1; 9:2, 11; 16:16; 18:29), but there is nothing here which goes beyond the teaching of Mark and "Q."[2] It may be that Luke thinks of Jesus as the ruler in the kingdom of God, but, if this is so, it is still within the realm of ideas common to the other Synoptists.[3] Nevertheless, at the outset of the Gospel attention is drawn to the kingdom of Jesus, the Son of the Most High, which shall have no end (Luke 1:31–33), and in an important passage peculiar to Luke Jesus speaks of the kingdom which has been entrusted to Him by His Father (Luke 22:29f.). Even during His earthly ministry Jesus is king (Luke 19:38 par. Matt. 21:5), although His claim is disregarded. This, however, is a theme which receives greater emphasis in Mark's account of the Roman trial and crucifixion of Jesus. In any case, as Luke 23:42, "when you come into your kingdom,"[4] makes plain, this kingdom is essentially a future one; it is in Luke's view the kingly rule and glory which Jesus received at His ascension.

We may say, then, that Jesus is the destined king during His earthly ministry and assumes His kingly throne at His ascension, but it is only this latter idea which Luke uniquely brings to the fore, particularly in the parable of the pounds where the nobleman departs to a far country to obtain a kingdom for himself (Luke 19:11–27, especially vs. 12, 14, 15, 27).

[1] We take Matt. 25:34 and 40 as references to Jesus, but 18:23 and 22:2–13 apparently refer to God (K. L. Schmidt, TDNT I, p. 579). The references in Luke are: 19:38; 23:2, 3, 37, 38.

[2] The texts listed simply stress that the kingdom of God was the theme of Jesus' preaching, a theme which is sufficiently familiar from (for example) Mark 1:15; 4:26, 30; Matt. 5:3; 6:10, 33.

[3] In the Gospels the phrase "the kingdom of God" is rarely connected with the thought of God Himself ruling; the stress is much more on the blessings associated with His reign.

[4] Some MSS have "when you come in (i.e. with) your kingdom"; in this case the thought is of the parousia of Jesus, already enthroned as king, or of His entry into visible kingship at the parousia.

Here we do have a special development which shows that for Luke the entry of Jesus into kingly power at His ascension was significant. It is, incidentally, a factor which suggests that the view that for Luke Jesus is inactive between His ascension and parousia[1] is a false one. Nevertheless, our main contention remains unaffected, namely that for Luke the kingship of Jesus is neither a unique theme nor the most central one.

Another view of Luke's main interest is offered by E. E. Ellis. "The main theme of the Gospel," he writes, "is the nature of Jesus' Messiahship and mission."[2] The various episodes in the Gospel bear witness to the meaning of the person of Jesus and of the coming kingdom of God. In Ellis's view the part played by the Holy Spirit is central to this witness.

Here again we encounter one of Luke's interests. He does devote considerable attention to the Holy Spirit.[3] There are 17 references to the Spirit in the Gospel compared with 12 in Matthew and 6 in Mark. But it must be carefully noted that Luke does not stress the relation of the Spirit to Jesus Himself as much as is popularly thought. Seven of the references occur in the birth stories, and six of them speak of prophetic inspiration (Luke 1:15, 41, 67; 2:25, 26, 27). Within the main body of the Gospel Luke has references to the activity of the Spirit in connexion with Jesus in Luke 4:1, 14, 18; 10:21, and that is all. The references are important, Luke 4:18 being of programmatic significance: Jesus quotes Isa. 61:1 to show that the Spirit of God rests upon Him as anointing for His work. This verse to some extent counterbalances Matt. 12:28 which attributes Jesus' exorcisms to the Spirit of God; the parallel in Luke 11:20 has instead "the finger of God."[4]

The allusions to the Spirit are thus concerned primarily with the witness which is borne to Jesus at His birth and there is also restrained reference to the power which activated His ministry. But this latter concept is already fully present in the baptismal narrative in Mark, and Luke has done nothing more than make it explicit. It is the former concept which is perhaps more important. Here the manifestations of the Spirit which dominate the life of the early church in Acts are seen to begin right from the commencement of the new age which dawned with the birth of Jesus. From the outset the activity of the Spirit is the characteristic of the new age.

[1] H. Conzelmann, *Die Mitte der Zeit*, pp. 164f. (pp. 176f.), comes near to this thought. Cf. S. Schulz, *op. cit.*, pp. 290f., for a more positive statement. See below, pp. 179–82.

[2] E. E. Ellis, *op. cit.*, p. 10.

[3] G. W. H. Lampe states that "the activity of the divine Spirit is the essential theme of his writings" ("The Holy Spirit in the Writings of Luke," in SG, pp. 159–200).

[4] Most scholars hold that "finger" is original in Q, but C. S. Rodd, "Spirit or Finger," Exp. T 72, 1960–61, pp. 157f., argues for the originality of "Spirit." G. Strecker, *Der Weg der Gerechtigkeit*, p. 168, holds that here, as elsewhere, the difference is due not to the editorial activity of Matthew or Luke but to their use of different recensions of Q.

In Acts the place of the Spirit is of great importance,[1] but it is vital to notice that He is the Spirit of Jesus (Acts 16:7) and that He is subordinate to Jesus. He witnesses to Jesus and fills up His place, as in John, but He is not the central figure. Ellis is right, therefore, in his cautious statement that it is in *witness* that the Holy Spirit is central. The Holy Spirit as such is not Luke's main theme.

Ellis's main point, however, is that the nature of Jesus' messiahship and mission is the central theme of the Gospel. This is not sufficiently precise, even as a statement regarding the Gospel, to lead us very far. Moreover, it applies only to the Gospel. If we are right in our belief that the Gospel and Acts belong closely together, it becomes necessary to find some theme that will be seen to run through both parts of Luke's work.

It is our thesis that the idea of salvation supplies the key to the theology of Luke. Not salvation-history but salvation itself is the theme which occupied the mind of Luke in both parts of his work.

Linguistically there is a good case for finding a distinctive trait of Luke here as compared with the other Gospels. It is true that the use of the verb "to save" (σώζω) itself is not particularly impressive. It is proportionately no more common in Luke than in the other Gospels,[2] but this is not surprising when it is remembered that it is frequently used with the meaning "to heal" and "to save from danger." Luke, however, does use the verb in a spiritual sense in a way that stands out by comparison with the other Gospels.[3] The other words in the group are much more his own property. "Saviour," (σωτήρ) and "salvation" (σωτηρία and σωτήρ-ιον) are not found in Matthew or Mark, but together occur 8 times in Luke and 9 times in Acts.[4] It is true that these words are to be found elsewhere in the New Testament, so that they are by no means the exclusive property of Luke. It is also the case that Luke's usage is largely taken over from his sources, and that he himself has not developed the usage greatly. But the point which we are making must not be misunderstood. It is not the case that Luke is unique in his use of this word group, but that his distinctiveness over against the other Synoptic Gospels stands out at this point. We would claim that this distinctiveness affords some clue to Luke's own main interest, and is therefore worth following up. Again, the use may often be that of Luke's sources, but this indicates a fact to which we shall continually return, namely that Luke's theology is firmly

---

[1] A. A. T. Ehrhardt claims that the purpose of Acts "is to serve as the Gospel of the Holy Spirit" ("The Construction and Purpose of Acts," in *The Framework of the New Testament Stories*, Manchester, 1964, pp. 64–102; quotation from p. 89).

[2] The verb is used 17 times in Luke; 13 times in Acts; 15 times in Matthew; 14 times in Mark; and 6 times in John.

[3] Cf. Luke 7:50; 8:12; 13:23; 19:10.

[4] σωτήρ: Luke 1:47 (of God); 2:11; Acts 5:31; 13:23; σωτηρία: Luke 1:69, 71, 77; 19:9; Acts 4:12; 7:25; 13:26, 47; 16:17; 27:34; σωτήριον: Luke 2:30; 3:6; Acts 28:28.

based in the traditions which he has inherited and through which his thought has been moulded. Our claim is not that salvation is a feature unique to Lucan theology in comparison with the rest of the New Testament, but that it is the central motif in Lucan theology. Here Luke is more articulate than the other Synoptic Gospels, but the theme which he develops is one which was implicit in the earlier tradition and which comes to expression frequently in the New Testament.

Linguistic usage is not of course sufficient to establish a case. We must also consider whether the contents of Luke and Acts can be arranged around this central, guiding motif of salvation. In other words, if we can account for the substance of Luke's theology in terms of this idea, then this will be some proof that we have laid hold of his key concept.

The point being made here is one that was developed in outline by W. C. van Unnik in his essay, "'The Book of Acts,' the Confirmation of the Gospel,"[1] which is one of the most discerning and stimulating recent studies of Lucan theology. According to van Unnik the purpose of the Gospel was to show forth the saving activity of Jesus, and the Acts describes how the church continued to proclaim and confirm this salvation. Thus the purpose of Acts (with which van Unnik is chiefly concerned) is to build a solid bridge between the facts recorded in the Gospel and the people who never saw Jesus incarnate so that they might realize that salvation was for them and come to embrace it.

Similarly, in his valuable study of *The Meaning of Salvation* E. M. B. Green claims that "It is hard to overestimate the importance of salvation in the writings of Luke," but goes on to state: "It is astonishing, however, that in view of the frequency with which Luke uses salvation terminology, more attention has not been paid to it." He then inquires briefly whether salvation may not be the key to the purpose of Luke–Acts.[2]

It will be obvious that our concern is not limited to one particular word group, that associated with salvation. Rather, Luke's central concern is expressed in a variety of terminology, but "salvation" is in our opinion the most convenient label for the main thrust of Luke's theology. Our interest, therefore, is in an idea rather than in a word group as such. The danger inherent in this approach is clear. "Salvation" is such a broad term that it could be used to cover almost the whole of Christian theology, and hence discussion of Luke's theology in terms of salvation could lead to a

[1] See p. 87 n. 2 above.
[2] E. M. B. Green, *The Meaning of Salvation*, 1965, pp. 125–131; quotation from p. 125. Cf. A. Hastings, *Prophet and Witness in Jerusalem*, 1958, p. 175. The treatment of the word group by W. Foerster, TDNT VII, pp. 965–1024, does not handle the Lucan usage as a category on its own. A fuller discussion of Luke from a slightly different angle is provided by L. Morris, *The Cross in the New Testament*, Exeter, no date (1965), pp. 63–143. See further R. Glöckner, *Die Verkündigung des Heils beim Evangelistren Lukas*, Mainz 1976.

very general treatment with no clear focus. We would claim, however, that the use of the word group will indicate where Luke's main interest lies, and that it will then be possible to take up the various other aspects of his theology and see how they are related to this central concept.

Finally, it might be argued that Luke's interest is not so much in a theological idea as in a person, namely Jesus Himself. The point is a fair one, for the main theme of the Gospel is undoubtedly Jesus Himself. But our concern is with Luke's particular view of Jesus, and for Luke He is the Saviour. Emphasis on the abstract noun "salvation" should not be allowed to obscure the fact that it is Jesus, as the giver of salvation, who is the central figure in the theology of Luke.

In the remaining part of this chapter the theme of salvation will be introduced with a survey of Luke's use of the word group, particularly in the birth narrative at the beginning of the Gospel which acts as a kind of prologue to the main narrative in Luke–Acts. The following chapter will consider the doctrine of God and His plan of salvation which forms the underlying basis of Luke's theology. Thereafter successive chapters will deal with the revelation of salvation in Jesus as recorded in the Gospel, the proclamation of salvation by the early church as recorded in Acts, and the way in which salvation becomes a reality in the experience of believers.

Luke's Concept of Salvation

The background to the New Testament usage of the various words expressing salvation has been so well and so fully described by other writers that it is unnecessary to traverse the same ground here. We may conveniently make use of the summary statement offered by G. Walters: "(Salvation) means the action or result of deliverance or preservation from danger or disease, implying safety, health and prosperity. The movement in Scripture is from the more physical aspects towards moral and spiritual deliverance. Thus, the earlier parts of the Old Testament lay stress on ways of escape for God's individual servants from the hands of their enemies, the emancipation of His people from bondage and their establishment in a land of plenty; the later parts lay greater emphasis upon the moral and religious conditions and qualities of blessedness and extend its amenities beyond the nation's confines. The New Testament indicates clearly man's thraldom to sin, its danger and potency, and the deliverance from it to be found exclusively in Christ."[1]

[1] G. Walters, "Salvation," in NBD, pp. 1126–1130; quotation from p. 1126. See the works of W. Foerster and E. M. B. Green referred to above; R. M. Wilson, "Soteria," SJT 6 1953, pp. 406–416; A. George, "L'emploie chez Luc du vocabulaire de salut," NTS 23 1976–77, pp. 308–320.

From such a summary as this it emerges that the word salvation had a wide range of meaning, and it is not surprising that it came to be used in a rather general sense to denote the sum of the blessings which God bestows upon men in rescuing them from every human distress and from divine judgment itself. The word thus took on a more positive significance than might have been expected. In particular it was used to refer to the bliss which God would confer on His people at the end of the age.

In the Gospels a considerable number of occurrences of the verb σῴζω refer to healing from disease or to deliverance from other threats to life and safety. Thus in Luke it is used in 6:9 (Mark 3:4) of the preservation of life, in 8:36 (Luke only; cf. Mark 5:23, 28) of the cure of a demoniac, in 8:48 (Mark 5:34); 17:19 (L); 18:42 (Mark 10:52) of the healing of various afflictions, and in 8:50 (cf. Mark 5:23, 28) of the raising of Jairus' daughter; it is also used when the bystanders and the dying thief call on Jesus to display His power by saving Himself from death on the cross (Luke 23:35, 37, 39; cf. Mark 15:30f.). In this last set of examples it is noteworthy that Jesus is bidden to save Himself on the grounds that He had the power to save others, a fact which shows how the simple sense of "healing" merges into the broader one of deliverance. Similarly, the formula "your faith has saved you," which is used in a number of healing stories (Luke 8:48; 17:19; 18:42; cf. 8:50) is also found in Luke 7:50 at the conclusion of the anointing story where there is no suggestion of physical healing.[1] This shows that there is some link between the healings wrought by Jesus and the spiritual salvation which He brought to men, a link which is not merely linguistically easy but has its deeper roots in the fact that common to both sets of activity is the power of God revealed in Jesus in response to faith. The power to heal and the authority to save both reside in God.

The same usage is found less frequently in Acts. The verb is used of healing in Acts 4:9 and 14:9, and of rescue from mortal danger in Acts 27:20, 31; the compound διασῴζω and the noun σωτηρία also occur in this latter connexion in Acts 27:43, 44; 28:1, 4 and Acts 27:34 respectively.[2] Here again it is noteworthy how the use of σῴζω to express bodily healing in Acts 4:9 is followed by the description of Jesus as the only person in whom there is σωτηρία since only through His name may men

---

[1] W. Foerster, TDNT VII, p. 990. In its present form the content of salvation in the story is the forgiveness of sins; cf. Luke 1:77. But the church tradition which identifies the woman in the story with Mary Magdalene, who had been cured of demon possession (Luke 8:2), might perhaps claim support from the normal physical meaning of σῴζω in this phrase; did an earlier form of the story refer to the healing of the woman (without of course identifying her with Mary Magdalene)?

[2] The verb διασῴζω is also used in Luke 7:3 of healing the centurion's servant, and in Acts 23:24 of conveying Paul safely on a journey.

be saved (Acts 4:12). In the latter verse a broader sense is surely intended, but the healing miracle is clearly subsumed under this activity of the risen Lord. We may conclude that the healing ministry of Jesus is definitely seen as a part of His broader power to save.

This broader sense must now occupy us. We may put it in its context by noting first that Luke is aware of the use of salvation in the Old Testament to describe the action of God or the results of that action. In Acts 7:25 Stephen refers to the way in which Joseph's Israelite comrades did not realize that it was through him that God was going to grant them deliverance from their bondage. Again, in Acts 13:47 Luke quotes a passage from the so-called Servant Songs in which the function of the Servant is to bring salvation to the end of the earth (Isa. 49:6). The Old Testament reference is to the task of the Servant in restoring Israel and then in extending the blessing of God to the Gentiles (cf. Isa. 45:22)[1] Here particularly we may see how "salvation" has become a description of the bliss in the new order inaugurated by God and has been given a universal application. Similarly, in Acts 2:21 Peter quotes from Joel 3:5 to give the significance of the events at Pentecost: The prophecy has been fulfilled in which God promised to pour out His Spirit upon all mankind; there would be portents before the coming of the day of God's judgment, but whoever called upon the name of the Lord would be delivered. The passage refers to deliverance from the judgment associated with the day of the Lord, but it seems likely that to readers in New Testament times it would represent the negative aspect of the salvation associated with the end time. In this context it is a future blessing, but (as other texts confirm) it has a present aspect in that the person who calls on the name of the Lord may be sure *now* that he will be rescued from the judgment of God.

These passages give us some insight into the context of ideas against which the teaching of Luke is to be seen. It is essentially an Old Testament context, although it should not be overlooked that similar ideas and longings were to be found in the Hellenistic world and found expression in many of the religious cults of the time.[2] Since, however, Luke explicitly moves in an environment formed by the Septuagint, it is right that we should regard it as exercising the more important influence upon his ideas.

It is no surprise, therefore, that we plunge into an Old Testament and Jewish world at the outset of the Gospel. The birth narrative in Luke 1–2 reflects a piety nourished upon the Old Testament and the action of God

---

[1] One or two scholars have attempted to deny the universalism which is usually seen in these passages, but there is no doubt that the New Testament writers interpreted them in a universalistic sense – rightly, in our opinion. See H. H. Rowley, *The Faith of Israel*, 1956, pp. 182–187.

[2] E. M. B. Green, *op. cit.*, Ch. 4.

recounted in it is depicted in Septuagintal terminology.[1] To begin our discussion here may seem illegitimate. H. Conzelmann has stated quite emphatically that the birth stories play no role in Luke's economy of salvation, and in his discussion of Luke's theology he virtually ignores them.[2] But this denigration of the birth stories to the level of a prelude is unjustified. As early as 1952 P. Vielhauer had claimed that Luke's presentation of John the Baptist in them was an expression of his basic theology of salvation-history.[3] Then in 1964 H. H. Oliver devoted an article to showing more generally that the birth stories contain the main themes of Luke's theology and that he used them to introduce his purpose at the outset of his work.[4] Oliver's arguments are convincing, and they justify us in treating the birth stories not so much as a prelude to what follows but rather as the theme which is to be elaborated in the ensuing "symphony of salvation."

The opening reference to salvation in the Gospel is found in Mary's description of God as her Saviour (Luke 1:47).[5] The phrase comes from the Old Testament, but no one passage can be regarded as the direct source of the language here.[6] The hymn of praise is modelled in general terms on 1 Sam. 2:1-10, but the phrases used are paralleled in many passages, and the hymn gives the impression of being composed by someone whose mind was steeped in Old Testament piety.[7] Consequently we should not

---

[1] These features make it less likely that the essential motifs in the narrative are drawn from Hellenism. The discussion by M. Dibelius, "Jungfrauensohn und Krippenkind: Untersuchungen zur Geburtsgeschichte Jesu im Lukasevangelium," in *Botschaft und Geschichte*, I, Tübingen, 1953, pp. 1-78, does not refute the case against pagan derivation of the birth stories advanced earlier by J. G. Machen, *The Virgin Birth of Christ*, 1932². Cf. H. Schürmann, *Das Lukasevangelium*, I, pp. 61-63, 118f.

[2] H. Conzelmann, *Die Mitte der Zeit*, p. 9 n. 2 (p. 16 n. 3); p. 160 (p. 172); cf. *Die Apostelgeschichte*, p. 20.

[3] P. Vielhauer, "Das Benedictus des Zacharias (Lk 1, 68-79)," in *Aufsätze zum Neuen Testament*, pp. 28-46 (originally in ZTK 49, 1952, pp. 255-272).

[4] H. H. Oliver, "The Lucan Birth Stories and the Purpose of Luke-Acts," NTS 10, 1963-64, pp. 202-226. Oliver discusses the following themes which reflect the theology of Luke: John and the Period of Israel; John and the Middle of Time; Jesus and World History; Jesus and Jerusalem; Jesus and the Salvation of the Gentiles; Jesus and His identity; the power of the Most High. Similarly, P. S. Minear has argued for the integration of the birth stories within Luke's work as a whole and shown how the effect of this is to correct certain of Conzelmann's views ("Luke's Use of the Birth Stories", in SLA, pp. 111-130). W. B. Tatum, "The Epoch of Israel: Luke i-ii and the Theological Plan of Luke-Acts," NTS 13, 1966-67, pp. 184-195, claims support for Conzelmann's view of Luke in the birth stories.

[5] We accept the ascription of the hymn to Mary; cf. E. E. Ellis, *The Gospel of Luke*, p. 72; H. Schürmann, *op. cit.*, pp. 72f. The arguments of W. Grundmann, *Das Evangelium nach Lukas*, Berlin, 1966, pp. 63f., to the contrary are without force.

[6] See Psa. 24:5; 25:5; 27:9; Mic. 7:7; Hab. 3:18; Isa. 12:2. If the hymn is here basically following 1 Sam. 2:1, the author has changed "salvation" to "Saviour."

[7] In this respect the hymns in Luke 1-2 resemble the Qumran hymns, but the resemblance goes no further than this, the contents being quite different. Cf. A. J. G. Dreyer, *An Examination of the Possible Relation between Luke's Infancy Narratives and the Qumran Hodayot*, Amsterdam, 1962, who concludes that the only link lies in a common Old Testament heritage.

expect too precise a content to be attached to the idea of God as Saviour here. Nor is it certain that the description is anything more than a conventional or stylized form of address to God. Nevertheless, the hymn makes it plain that Mary is thinking of the mercy shown by God to His people in conformity with His promises, and she describes His action in terms of the blessings associated with the future era. We may, therefore, state with some confidence that the thought of God as Saviour is related to His eschatological action in exalting the humble and filling the hungry with good things. And Mary speaks of God as her Saviour because the angelic promise of the birth of the Son of God to her is proof that God has already begun to act and that His saving purpose includes her and is to be wrought through her.

Theologically the thought of God as Saviour is the correct place to begin. But it is possible that the first reference to salvation should be found at an earlier point in Luke 1. In verse 31 the prophecy of Gabriel to Mary regarding her son includes the instruction that she is to call His name Jesus. The Greek form corresponds to Hebrew $j^e h \hat{o} \check{s} u a^{\prime}$ or $j \bar{e} \check{s} \hat{u} a^{\prime}$ and has the meaning "Yahweh saves."[1] In Matt. 1:21, which furnishes a close parallel to the present verse, the etymological significance of the name is made explicit: the child is to be called Jesus because He will save His people from their sins. R. Laurentin has claimed that the various names in the Lucan birth narrative carry theological significance.[2] This would certainly be true in a Hebrew version of the narrative,[3] and is a point in favour of the existence of such a version, but would it also be true for Greek readers in the absence of an explanation such as Matthew gives? It is difficult to be certain. With the exception of Matt. 1:21, the meaning of the name is not taken up in the New Testament, and in the immediate context of the present verse the thought is not directly soteriological. It is thus on the whole unlikely that we should lay too much stress on the concept of Saviourhood at this point.

The next clear use of the word group is in the hymn of Zechariah, expressing his praise to God at the birth of his son, John. At the outset of the narrative the unusual circumstances accompanying the announcement of his birth and the content of the angelic message had indicated that John was to occupy a particular place in the purpose of God. Again we should not press the meaning of the name with its reference to the graciousness of God,[4] but attention should be given to the description of John's role. He

---

[1] See W. Foerster, TDNT III, pp. 284–293; SB I, pp. 63f.

[2] R. Laurentin, "Traces d'allusions etymologiques en Lc 1–2," Bib. 37, 1956, pp. 435–456; 38, 1957, pp. 1–23.

[3] H. Sahlin, *Der Messias und das Gottesvolk: Studien zur protolukanischen Theologie*, Uppsala, 1945, p. 113.

[4] The name corresponds to Hebrew *jôḥānān* and Aramaic *jûḥannān*. The meaning is variously

would be specially dedicated to God and filled with the Spirit in order to prepare the people for the coming of their God by converting them from their disobedience. He would fulfil the prophecy regarding the coming of Elijah found in Mal. 4:5 and treasured in Judaism (Sirach 48:10f.). Thus he would be the sign that God's final intervention in history was at hand, and consequently many would rejoice at the news of his birth.

In the Benedictus (Luke 1:68–79) these ideas are taken up and carried further by Zechariah. The hymn begins by celebrating the fact that God has visited His people and obtained redemption for them. The aorist tense used here may represent a prophetic perfect or indicate that the action of God has already begun with the birth of John; in either case the thought is of what God is about to do, and His action is conceived as one of redemption. Then in verse 69 Zechariah indicates how God is acting, namely by raising up "a horn of salvation for us in the house of His servant David." "Horn" is a metaphor referring to the strength of a fighting animal, and the whole phrase is tantamount to "a mighty Saviour," since a personal meaning is obviously intended. The reference to the house of David takes us into the realm of Messianism, with the hope of a Davidic Messiah. Here, therefore, the Messiah is identified as a Saviour through whom God delivers His people. In the following verses the content of this deliverance is described in Old Testament terms with a political flavour like that in Mary's hymn (Luke 1:46–55): salvation means deliverance from enemies (Luke 1:71) and the consequent opportunity to worship and serve God by righteous living.

In the final part of the hymn (Luke 1:76–79) John is addressed directly and his task is described. It is to bring salvation to God's people by means of the forgiveness of their sins. This corresponds with the historical actuality of John's mission, which was to preach a baptism of repentance leading to the forgiveness of sins. It may be doubtful how far the political language earlier in the hymn is to be pressed; here at any rate the language is spiritual and, as W. Foerster has observed, it assigns to a central place in the messianic salvation something which was much less significant in Judaism.[1]

It is not certain whether John's activity is further described in verses 78 and 79. It is probable that verse 79a ("to give light . . .") is dependent upon verse 78b ("the dayspring will visit us . . ."), in which case it refers to the activity of the dayspring. Verse 79b ("to guide our feet into the way of

[1] W. Foerster, TWNT VII, p. 991.

given as "whom Yahweh favours" (SB II, p. 79), "Jehovah's gift" (A. Plummer, *St Luke*, Edinburgh, 1901⁴), or "God is gracious" (K. H. Rengstorf, *Das Evangelium nach Lukas*, p. 20, and others).

peace") is generally taken to be epexegetical of verse 79a, in which case it also refers to the work of the dayspring. P. Vielhauer, however, has a two-fold argument that the reference is to John. First, he argues that verse 79b follows on from verse 77 after the virtual parenthesis in verses 78–79a describing the dayspring. This is possible, but perhaps not very likely, since it demands a more complicated connexion of thought than is likely in a simple hymn; it is more probable that the ideas are simply added to each other. Second, Vielhauer argues that in the original intention of the hymn the dayspring was none other than John himself;[1] the Baptist sect whom Vielhauer believes to have been responsible for the hymn saw in John the Messiah.[2] John was to be the forerunner of God ("the Lord," verse 76), and there is no place for another messianic figure.

This view is in itself unlikely. For the hymn refers clearly enough to the advent of the Davidic Messiah in verse 69, and there is no suggestion anywhere that John was of Davidic descent.[3] In any case, however, Viel-hauer admits that in its Lucan context the hymn takes on a different meaning, facilitated by the ambiguity of κύριος in verse 76, and that Luke uses the hymn to present John as a forerunner of Jesus.[4] On our view, this was not only Luke's intention but also the original intention of the hymn.

From the forerunner we come at last to Jesus Himself. In Luke 2:11 the angelic message to the shepherds at the birth of Jesus proclaims that a Saviour has been born in the city of David who is Christ the Lord. Here the thoughts already present in the Benedictus are taken up. The birth of Jesus is seen as that of a Saviour associated with the city of David, and the use of Christ makes this messianic idea explicit. O. Cullmann has objected that the usage here must have arisen on Greek soil since the Hebrew for "Jesus Saviour" would be "Jeshua Jeshua,"[5] but this objection is irrelevant since the name "Jesus" is not in fact present in the text. A bigger problem is raised by the phrase "Christ the Lord" (Χριστὸς κύριος). A small amount of textual evidence supports the reading Χριστὸς κυρίου, "the Lord's Christ," and, while the evidence is too weak to allow this to be the original text, it has suggested a plausible conjectural emendation to

---

[1] If this argument stands, then the first argument is obviously redundant.

[2] P. Vielhauer, *Aufsätze zum Neuen Testament*, pp. 34–41.

[3] Our objection assumes that the hymn is regarded as a unity. Vielhauer himself, in common with most recent scholars (so, for example, H. Schürmann, *op. cit.*, pp. 88f.), appears to regard the hymn as a combination of two parts; he argues that they display two different types of messianology (*op. cit.*, p. 39, n. 60). J. Jeremias, however, in a seminar held in 1959–60, de-fended the unity of the hymn, pointing to the frequent use of the 1st person plural throughout the hymn, which gives it the form of a community hymn. Cf. A. Vanhoye, "Structure du 'Benedictus'," NTS 12, 1965–66, pp. 382–389.

[4] P. Vielhauer, *op. cit.*, pp. 44–46.

[5] O. Cullmann, *The Christology of the New Testament*, 1959, pp. 244f. (English translation of *Die Christologie des Neuen Testaments*, Tübingen, 1957).

many scholars.[1] Such a reading would also fit in with Luke's usage in 2:26. But the apposition is not unparalleled, and a similar phrase is found at Luke 23:2.[2] It is wiser to retain the existing text[3] and to interpret it to mean that the Saviour is "the Messiah (and) the Lord."[4] The meaning of "lord" in Luke must concern us at a later stage, but we may anticipate the discussion by saying that it seems likely that for Luke κύριος was a title expressive of divinity, indicating that God was active in Jesus. Throughout the birth narrative Jesus is depicted as the Son of God through whom God acts. Already in Luke 1:43 the designation κύριος is applied to Jesus. There is consequently no objection to applying it to Him here. H. Sahlin has argued that here "Messiah-Yahweh" constitutes one idea, and finds the same concept expressed in Acts 2:36 and Psalms of Solomon 17:36.[5] What we have here, therefore, is the thought of an epiphany, and an important parallel is presented by T. Levi 2:11: "And by thee and Judah shall the Lord appear among men, saving every race of men."[6] Hence the force of the angelic announcement is that the Saviour is the Messiah, the personal presence of the God who has promised to visit His people. His coming means joy for "all the people" (Luke 2:10), a phrase which refers to Israel. The thought here, therefore, is restricted rather than universalistic, but universalistic ideas are found elsewhere in the birth narrative (Luke 2:32).[7] In gratitude for the news the choir of angels give praise to God and ascribe glory to Him (Luke 2:13f.), and their message is echoed by the shepherds (Luke 2:20). The appropriate response to the message of salvation is praise to God, a feature which constantly recurs in Luke. Finally, the effect of the tidings is to bring God's peace to men (Luke 2:14); the aged Simeon is prepared to be dismissed from his earthly service for God in peace because he has seen the salvation of God with his own eyes (Luke 2:29f.);

[1] Despite the wretchedly poor attestation it is mentioned as a variant reading in NEB. Some scholars regard the phrase in the text as a mistranslation from Hebrew (a possibility raised by J. M. Creed, St Luke, 1930, p. 35; E. Klostermann, Das Lukas-Evangelium, Tübingen, 1929², p. 37; P. Vielhauer, op. cit., p. 40). P. Winter, 'Lukanische Miszellen," ZNW 49, 1958, pp. 65–77, especially p. 75, holds that the error is due to a later scribe of the Gospel.

[2] At Luke 23:2 the translation "an anointed king" has been suggested; according to J. M. Creed, op. cit., p. 35, B. Weiss suggested the translation "an anointed Lord" for Luke 2:11. But B. Weiss, Markus und Lukas, Göttingen, 1885, p. 310, takes both words as nouns: "Ein Gesalbter, ein Herr."

[3] Lamentations 4:20 LXX, where the phrase is a mistranslation for "the Lord's anointed;" in Psalms of Solomon 17:36, a mistranslation is also likely.

[4] So H. Schürmann, op. cit., pp. 111f.

[5] H. Sahlin, op. cit., pp. 214–218.

[6] The thought of God appearing on earth is found in T. Simeon 6:5; T. Levi 5:2. It is uncertain whether the thought here is Jewish or the result of Christian redaction.

[7] H. Sahlin, op. cit., pp. 258–265, discusses the phrase "a light for revelation to the Gentiles" at length in an attempt to avoid finding universalistic ideas here (and throughout the Proto-Lucan document which he finds behind the birth narrative); his arguments are fully answered by H. H. Oliver, NTS 10, 1963–64, pp. 221f.

the idea of departure in peace is an Old Testament one (Gen. 15:15),[1] but the usage here seems to contain the more profound thought of the messianic salvation which brings to men peace with God so that they can cheerfully face death.[2]

We have now glanced over the line of thought created by the occurrences of the salvation word-group in the birth narrative. We have seen that the ultimate source of salvation is God the Saviour, that His Son Jesus has been born into the world as Saviour to bring men peace and lead them to glorify God, that this salvation is for God's people but also reaches to the Gentiles, that salvation is in accord with the divine promises in the Old Testament, and that it is heralded by the activity of John the Baptist as the fore-runner of the Lord. It is our claim that these are the ideas which run through the work of Luke as a whole and constitute its main theme. Our task now will be to justify and expound this thesis by a consideration of the contents of Luke-Acts as a whole.[3]

[1] See the references in W. Foerster, TDNT II, p. 402, n. 17.

[2] *Pace* W. Foerster, *op. cit.*, p. 411, who holds that a formal phrase is being employed here.

[3] On salvation in Luke see further J. Navone, *Themes of St. Luke,* Rome, 1970, especially pp. 141–150; F. Bovon, "Le salut dans les écrits de Luc," *Revue de Théologie et de Philosophie* 23 1973, pp. 296–307; R. P. Martin, "Salvation and Discipleship in Luke's Gospel," *Interpretation* 30, 1976, pp. 366–380.

CHAPTER V

GOD MY SAVIOUR

BEFORE WE DISCUSS LUKE'S ACCOUNT OF THE REVELATION OF SALVATION in the ministry of Jesus, as recorded in the Gospel, it will be helpful to examine what he has to say about God. Some justification for this procedure might be found in the recent suggestion that there is a strong element of subordinationism in Luke's view of Jesus Christ,[1] but in fact it is doubtful whether Luke accentuates the subordination of Christ to the Father as compared with the other New Testament writers.[2] The purpose of our discussion at this point is rather to place the work of Jesus within the context of God's plan of salvation, and thus at the outset to establish a correct understanding of Luke's concept of salvation-history. This will enable us to see how history and eschatology are related in Luke before we move on in the following chapters to a positive exposition of the teaching about salvation in Luke–Acts.[3]

The Sovereign Will of God

Luke views God the Father as the ultimate source of salvation, a fact which we have already noted in the description of Him as Saviour (Luke 1:47). Whether or not this description is taken over from tradition,[4] it admirably expresses his concept of God. The use of the title with respect to God is found elsewhere in the New Testament only in the Pastoral Epistles and Jude, where Hellenistic influence has been suspected,[5] but

---

[1] H. Conzelmann, *Die Mitte der Zeit*, pp. 161–172 (pp. 173–184); cf. U. Wilckens, *Die Missionsreden der Apostelgeschichte*, p. 139; S. Schulz, *Die Stunde der Botschaft*, p. 285.

[2] I. H. Marshall, "The Resurrection in the Acts of the Apostles," in AHG, pp. 92–107, especially pp. 101–103.

[3] On history and eschatology in Luke–Acts see P. Borgen, *Eschatology and Redemptive History in Luke–Acts* (Duke dissertation, 1957). See also E. E. Ellis, "Die Funktion der Eschatologie im Lukasevangelium," ZTK 66, 1969, pp. 387–402; J.-D. Kaestli, *L'eschatologie dans l'oeuvre de Luc*, Geneva, 1969; E. Franklin, Christ the Lord, 1975; cf. id., "The Ascension and the Eschatology of Luke–Acts," SJT 23, 1970, pp. 191–200.

[4] Luke has undoubtedly made use of tradition in the composition of the birth narrative, but it is extremely hard to form a verdict on the extent of his editing of his sources. In the present case the usage is firmly rooted in the Old Testament like that of the rest of the hymn, and therefore it is probably traditional. The use of the title fits in admirably with the description of God's activity in verse 48a, and probably belongs closely with it. Cf. H. Schürmann, *Das Lukasevangelium*, p. 78.

[5] M. Dibelius (and H. Conzelmann), *Die Pastoralbriefe*, Tübingen, 1955³, pp. 74–77; here, however, it is admitted that there is no Hellenistic influence in Luke 1:47 *ibid.*, p. 75).

we need not suspect this in Luke, whose usage stems from the O.T. He sees a link between the saving activity of God in the N.T. and His same activity in the O.T.

What Luke stresses is the supremacy of God over the world, especially in bringing salvation to mankind. The comparatively rare designation of God as "sovereign lord" (δεσπότης) is found twice in Luke–Acts. This term is one which expressed absolute lordship, such as a master has over his slaves, and in the Septuagint it indicated the omnipotence of God. K. H. Rengstorf claims that it was too abstract a title to be readily applied to a God whose omnipotence is seen in concrete acts in history.[1] It is therefore interesting that it does occur in Luke. It is the term used by the church in prayer when it wishes to praise the God who enables the gospel to continue its way unhindered by persecution; they speak of Him as the sovereign Lord who made all things (Acts 4:24). In the same way, the aged Simeon addresses God in prayer as Lord (Luke 2:29).[2]

The use of "Lord" (κύριος) of God is apparently more common in Luke than in the other Gospels. But this greater frequency is almost entirely due to the presence of the word in the birth stories. The N.T. use of κύριος is primarily in O.T. quotations or allusions.[3] It is the deeply biblical style of Luke 1–2, which is responsible for the intensity of the usage here. Otherwise Luke's usage is no different from that of the other Evangelists, and the same is essentially the case in Acts, although the position is complicated here by a number of texts in which Christ may be designated rather than God. It follows that Luke does not use κύριος as a means of expressing the sovereignty and supremacy of God.

What is more typical of Luke is his emphasis on the way in which events unfold at the behest of God and in accordance with His plan. This interpretation of history is of course familiar from the Old Testament where past

---

[1] K. H. Rengstorf, TDNT II, pp. 44–49.

[2] The title is used of Jesus in 2 Pet. 2:1 and Jude 4, a fact which might suggest that it arose comparatively late in the church. However, the two uses in Luke–Acts and the only other use with reference to God in the New Testament (Rev. 6:10) all occur in the context of prayer; this may be taken as an indication that the title belonged to liturgical usage. The use in prayer has a long history (LXX, Josephus). It is thus likely that Luke is here making use of Christian liturgical language. Nevertheless, although the use of the title is probably pre-Lucan, it fits in so well with Luke's doctrine of God that we are justified in including it in the evidence for this doctrine. Put otherwise, Luke's doctrine reflects early church usage.

[3] W. Foerster, TDNT III, pp. 1039–1095, especially pp. 1086–1088.

Recently it has been argued that the Septuagint, long regarded as the source of the title, did not originally use κύριος as the equivalent of JHWH (P. Vielhauer, Aufsätze zum Neuen Testament, pp. 147–150; H. Conzelmann, Grundriss der Theologie des Neuen Testaments, pp. 101–103 (Eng. tr. pp. 82–84)). The origin of the Greek title remains obscure at present, but it was being used by Christians from an early date (Paul uses it as something familiar that does not need explanation from 1 Cor. (1:31; 2:16; 3:20; et al.) onwards). See J. A. Fitzmyer, "Der semitische Hintergrund des neutestamentlichen Kyriostitels," in G. Strecker (ed.), Jesus Christus in Historie und Theologie, Tübingen, 1975, pp. 267–298.

history is regarded as expressing the purpose of God, and future history is the object of prophecy by men with an insight into the intentions of God. The sermon of Paul in Pisidian Antioch reflects this understanding of Old Testament history. It describes how God chose the patriarchs and made Israel His people; He brought them out of Egypt and established them in their land, and He gave them their rulers in due order (Acts 13:16–22). It is the same in the speech given by Stephen before his martyrdom; although Stephen is more concerned with the attitude of the people to God and dwells on what they did, the action of God in raising up Moses and later giving up the idolatrous Israelites to worship the host of heaven is described (Acts 7:35, 42). The analysis of historical events given here is essentially the same as that in the Old Testament, and shows where the roots of Luke's thinking are to be found. Where Luke perhaps goes beyond the Old Testament conception is in his references to one single plan of God which encompasses all His dealings with His people. Acts 13:36 suggests that David did his share in fulfilling the will of God during his own generation; it is implied that the purpose of God extended beyond David and continued to function long after him. Paul speaks of declaring the whole will of God to the church (Acts 20:27), a phrase which suggests that the whole content of Christian preaching and teaching is regarded as an exposition of the purpose of God.

As a result of the activity of the will of God, what happens in the world can be said to be pre-ordained and determined by the purpose of God. Thus it is God who has ordained the allotted periods of human life on the earth (Acts 17:26),[1] and whatever happens in the church has been ordained by His will (Acts 4:28). The progress of the gospel, moving from Jews to Gentiles, is in accord with divine necessity (Acts 13:46).

The story of the life of Jesus fits into this pattern. The births of Jesus and of His forerunner took place in accordance with the will of God revealed by the angel to their parents, and the various stages in the story are set in motion by the intervention of angelic messengers or the guidance of the Holy Spirit. The birth of the children was also accompanied by prophecy through Zechariah and Simeon which expressed in general terms the character of their work. All this fits in with the way in which in the Old Testament the birth of children with a particular destiny is accompanied by signs of the fulfilment of God's will in their birth.

It follows that the life of Jesus was seen as being a fulfilment of the will of God expressed in the Scriptures. The opening scene of His ministry at Nazareth has as its central content the reading of a portion from the Old Testament by Jesus with the comment, "Today this scripture has been

---

[1] The interpretation of the "periods" (καιροί) and "boundaries" (ὁροθεσίαι) is much disputed, but this does not affect the point at issue.

fulfilled in your hearing" (Luke 4:17–21). The closing scene finds Him telling His disciples "that everything written about me in the law of Moses and the prophets and the psalms must be fulfilled" and opening their minds "to understand the scriptures" (Luke 24:44–46 cf. 24:27). The Old Testament is thus regarded as prophetic of the ministry of Jesus. It was written that He should suffer and rise from the dead on the third day, and that subsequently repentance and forgiveness of sins should be preached to all nations, beginning from Jerusalem (Luke 24:46f.).

The fact of this divine plan for the life of Jesus is seen further in the various references to events which take place "as it is written" (Luke 18:31; 22:37, cf. also Luke 3:4; 7:27 applying the same principle to the ministry of John the Baptist). A final piece of evidence is to be found in the frequent use of the verb "must" ($\delta\epsilon\hat{\iota}$) in relation to the activity of Jesus. It was necessary for Jesus as a boy to be in His Father's house (Luke 2:49), to preach the gospel during His ministry (Luke 4:43), to cure the sick (Luke 13:16), and to visit Zacchaeus with salvation (Luke 19:5). His whole ministry lay under this constraint (Luke 13:33), but especially His suffering and death as the prelude to His glorification (Luke 9:22; 17:25; 22:37; 24:7, 26, 44; Acts 17:3).

The situation is the same with regard to the early church. The first preachers were conscious that what had happened to Jesus could be regarded from one point of view as the act of lawless and wicked men, but that at the same time it had taken place by the counsel of God (Acts 2:23; 4:28) and in accordance with the Scriptures (Acts 3:18; 13:27–33); it was God who allowed Him to be delivered up to death and then raised Him from the dead. Jesus Himself had spoken of future history being under the control of God (Luke 21:9, 22). The early church saw that its own life was similarly under divine control, and ranged it alongside the ministry of Jesus as the sphere of God's activity. Throughout Acts the notes of divine fore-ordination and necessity are if anything stronger than in the Gospel. God foretells what is to happen through Old Testament prophecy (Acts 1:16), and therefore it must take place. He pours out the Spirit (Acts 5:32), and it is He who takes the initiative in saving men, granting them repentance (Acts 11:18). He chooses the men who are to be His witnesses in the church (Acts 10:41; 22:14; 26:16), and hence what takes place in their lives is a matter of divine necessity (Acts 9:6, 16; 14:22; 27:24).[1]

The main feature of Luke's teaching about God thus lies in the thought of His plan, announced in the Old Testament and presently being fulfilled

[1] The evidence at this point should not be exaggerated. The statistics indicate that Luke has a preference for the use of προ- compounds and for δεῖ, but the concordance shows that many of these cases are entirely without theological significance. Luke uses προ- as a means of saying that one event preceded another (e.g. Luke 21:14; Acts 8:9; 20:38; 21:5) or to indicate spatial priority (e.g. Luke 19:4; Acts 7:40).

in history by His obedient servants. We must now inquire into the kind of thought which is thus brought to expression. In his discussion of this theme H. Conzelmann has made two points. First, he claims that the kind of necessity found in Luke is not eschatological, but rather characteristic of salvation-history. "It is in the very passages where the word occurs that the change from eschatology to redemptive history is obvious."[1] Second he notes the comparative absence from Luke of the terminology of "election" and "calling," and concludes that in Luke predetermination has replaced the idea of election. This latter point has been reinforced by S. Schulz who, as we noted earlier, argues that Luke's thought reflects pagan ideas of fate and necessity rather than the biblical tradition of election.[2]

Eschatology and Salvation-History

With regard to the first of these points, we would suggest that Conzelmann has been led to make a false dichotomy between eschatology[3] and

---

[1] H. Conzelmann, *Die Mitte der Zeit*, p. 143 n. 3 (p. 153 n. 3).

[2] *Ibid.*, p. 145 (p. 155). S. Schulz, *op. cit.*, pp. 275–283; "Gottes Vorsehung bei Lukas," ZNW 54, 1963, pp. 104–116.

[3] It may be useful to comment briefly here on the meaning of the term "eschatology."
(1). In its traditional use in Christian theology it refers to the doctrine of the last things, namely those events which come at the end of human history – the parousia, resurrection of the dead, the final judgment, heaven and hell.
(2). Since these last things represent the final intervention of God into human history in order to wind it up, there is a tendency on the part of some writers to stress the fact of divine action rather than the fact of finality. "'This is an eschatological event' thus comes to mean that the event is in a very special sense the work of God" (D. E. H. Whiteley, *The Theology of St Paul*, Oxford, 1964, p. 233).
(3). A different extension of meaning appears when C. K. Barrett claims that in modern biblical discussion eschatological thinking takes place when "the significance of a series of events in time is defined in terms of the last of their number" ("New Testament Eschatology," SJT 6, 1953, pp. 136–155, 225–243; quotation from p. 136). Thus the "great tribulation" (Rev. 3:10) takes its significance from the fact that it is an event which ushers in the final intervention of God in world history and is thus a forward-looking event.
In the expectation of Jesus the final event was seen primarily as the coming of the Kingdom of God or the coming of the Son of man. But the evidence is open to various interpretations:
(a). The advocates of "thorough-going eschatology" (A. Schweitzer, J. Weiss) hold that Jesus looked forward to the coming of the kingdom in the near future. Consequently, both He and His followers regarded themselves as living in the last days – days whose significance was eschatological in terms of Barrett's definition. When, however, the kingdom failed to come in the expected manner (the "delay" of the parousia), the early church had to adapt its theology to the situation and allow for a lengthy interval, with the result that the coming of Jesus tended to lose its eschatological significance. The ultimate result of this tendency in theology was the relegation of eschatology to refer to the events of the distant future, as in traditional dogmatics (cf. (1) above).
(b). Advocates of "realized eschatology" hold that Jesus saw His own ministry as the final intervention of God in history and thus as *the* eschatological event. "There is no coming of the Son of man in history 'after' His coming in Galilee and Jerusalem, whether soon or late, for there is no before and after in the eternal order" (C. H. Dodd, *The Parables of the Kingdom*, 1961², p. 81). While certain early church theologians (John and the later writings of Paul) retained this insight, others proceeded to look for a further coming of Jesus after His death

salvation-history by an article on "must" (δεῖ) by W. Grundmann. Here Grundmann claims: "The word δεῖ expresses the necessity of the eschatological event, and is thus an eschatological term."[1] The first half of this sentence is sound enough; δεῖ is used to express the fact that certain future events must take place because God has ordained them (Mark 13:7, 10; Rev. 1:1; 4:1; et al.). But the second half of the sentence is not the logical consequence of the first, as Grundmann apparently assumes, and is in fact false. For the fact that a word gains a certain nuance of meaning in one particular context does not automatically make it a technical term, even in that context, still less in different kinds of context. The eschatological flavour which Grundmann claims to find in certain contexts is not something that has become inherent in the word itself but is due to the associations of the context; while a word may gain fresh nuances of meaning from such a use in one context which will persist when it is used in other contexts, it has not been shown that this is the case with δεῖ. Indeed, the wide variety of its use in the New Testament speaks against its ever having become a technical term of eschatology. Grundmann has apparently assumed that an element of meaning found in one or several

---

[1] W. Grundmann, TDNT II, pp. 21–25; quotation from p. 23.

and resurrection, and when this failed to materialize, the theology of the church developed as in (a) above.

It should be noted that in later publications Dodd clarified his position in order to allow of further eschatological events in the future. The main thrust of his position was to claim that the ministry of Jesus actually was the *decisive* eschatological event, in which God finally intervened in history, and not a prelude to it. Later Dodd recognized the fact of a second coming of Jesus "beyond history," "outside our system of time-reckoning altogether" (*The Coming of Christ,* Cambridge, 1951, pp. 17, 7): but this form of statement is unsatisfactory, since it refuses to discuss the relation of time to eternity.

(c). Neither of the views discussed above does full justice to the teaching of the Gospels. Hence a third view of the teaching of Jesus is that He spoke of the kingdom both as having arrived in His ministry and also as yet to be consummated at the parousia (W. G. Kümmel, *Promise and Fulfilment*).

The question then arises: how long an interval did Jesus envisage between the ministry and its consummation? Some (W. G. Kümmel; G. R. Beasley-Murray, *Jesus and the Future*; O. Cullmann, *Salvation in History*) allow for a lengthy interval (though admittedly not much more than a generation); others (C. K. Barrett, *Jesus and the Gospel Tradition*) believe that Jesus expected the consummation immediately after His passion, and thus come close to the position of "thorough-going eschatology." Whereas the latter group emphasize the feeling of "delay" in the early church and its consequent effect upon theology, the former group (especially O. Cullmann) minimize it.

H. Conzelmann belongs in group (a). Jesus expected the End almost immediately, and saw the events associated with His ministry as eschatological in terms of Barrett's definition. (Thus for Conzelmann the kingdom had not yet come during the ministry of Jesus.) His argument is that as the End was delayed the various events which the first Christians (in agreement with Jesus) had regarded as eschatological were reinterpreted to form episodes in the slow and gradual development of salvation-history and lost their eschatological significance, since the End was now regarded as being in the indefinite and distant future.

On the theme of eschatology in general see T. F. Torrance, "The Modern Eschatological Debate," EQ 25, 1953, pp. 45–54, 94–106, 167–178, 224–232; C. Brown, NIDNTT II, pp. 901–935.

occurrences of a word may be presumed to be present in most occurrences. It is precisely this sort of approach which has led to some of the recent criticism of the *Theologisches Wörterbuch* in which his article appears.[1]

Conzelmann, therefore, is right in implicitly condemning Grundmann's sweeping claim regarding the meaning of δεῖ. But he has been led astray from this correct observation into a dubious distinction between eschatology and salvation-history (or redemptive history). The antithesis between them is largely of his making. For the "necessity" which is expressed in the "eschatological" statements really finds its basis in the nature and purpose of God and nowhere else. In other words, the necessity is concerned with what takes place in history at God's command. Insofar as the events which must take place in the New Testament are regarded as fulfilling the prophecies of God's final intervention in the world in the Old Testament, they may rightly be called eschatological, but since at the same time they are directed towards the redemption of God's people they must also be regarded as part of redemptive history. There is no reason to differentiate between eschatology and redemptive history.

However, Conzelmann would no doubt defend his position by claiming that certain events which were regarded as eschatological (i.e. associated with the End) in the earlier traditions are no longer eschatological in Luke; they have lost the significance derived from their assumed close proximity to the End, and have instead become events occupying particular places in God's continuous plan of redemptive history; the End, now transferred to the indeterminate future, has become largely irrelevant. For example, Conzelmann claims that "tribulation" (θλτψις), understood as a definitely eschatological term in Mark 13:24, where it is associated with the parousia, has been given a present, non-eschatological meaning ing in Acts. Again, he examines the preaching of John the Baptist and claims that "the eschatological call to repentance is transposed into timeless ethical exhortation." The threat of judgment in Luke's version of John's message is independent of the time when judgment will take place.[2]

This claim that Luke has reinterpreted the tradition obviously rests on the assumption that the tradition was eschatological and not redemptive-historical. But this is precisely the assumption which we have already had cause to question. There is no either/or in primitive Christianity between eschatology and salvation-history. The eschatological events form part of salvation-history. In the tradition the ministry of Jesus is eschatological because in it God has begun His final action in the world. Such events as persecution and the ministry of John are eschatological because of their relation to the first coming of Jesus and not simply because of their relation

[1] J. Barr, *The Semantics of Biblical Language*, Oxford, 1961.
[2] H. Conzelmann, *Die Mitte der Zeit*, pp. 90, 92–94 (pp. 98 f., 101 f.).

to His second coming or parousia. Further, if Luke was dependent upon the tradition for his knowledge of Jesus, the question of how Jesus Himself may have understood the eschatological events and the imminence of the End becomes irrelevant; we are concerned with how Luke has interpreted the tradition. But, whatever Jesus may have taught, the tradition certainly reckoned with an interval between His resurrection and the parousia.[1] There is in our opinion no evidence that Luke's interpretation of the situation was significantly different. For Luke, as for the tradition, the events beginning with the ministry of Jesus are the eschatological events. Hence the alleged difference between eschatology and salvation-history does not exist for Luke, any more than it does for the other New Testament writers.

This is a point which needs to be borne in mind throughout our study, since Conzelmann has endeavoured to sustain his view for Luke-Acts as a whole. Meanwhile, it may suffice to mention that neither of the two examples which we cited supports his theory. So far as θλῖψις is concerned, it is already a recurring event in the life of believers in Mark 4:17, and throughout the New Testament it means tribulation in general rather than one specific final "great tribulation," a sense found only in Rev. 7:14. All such tribulation is to be regarded as eschatological, since it takes place in the last days which have already begun.[2]

The second example was the preaching of John the Baptist. The facts that Conzelmann adduces in favour of his explanation are two. First, Luke includes the moral preaching of John (Luke 3:10-14) which Conzelmann regards as timeless ethical exhortation. Second, Luke omits the words "after me" (ὀπίσω μου) from the statement about the coming of the mightier One. Otherwise Luke's account agrees exactly with that in Matthew in all essentials, and is in line with that of Mark. We would submit that there is no case to answer here. The threat of judgment is clearly present, and the explication of John's call to repentance in terms of what it would mean for various types of hearer in no way transforms the message; the omission of ὀπίσω μου, found in Matthew and Mark, may be due to its absence from Luke's source here, but is in any case not of the slightest consequence for the point at issue.

From these considerations we may conclude that Luke has not abandoned eschatology in favour of salvation-history; in reality these are two sides of the same coin. Nor is the alleged distinction relevant to the

---

[1] It is the merit of E. Grässer, *Das Problem der Parusieverzögerung*, to have shown that the consciousness of an interval between the resurrection and the parousia is to be found at all stages in the tradition; his error, in our judgment, is in failing to allow that Jesus foresaw this interval, and in holding that it was regarded as a delay rather than as an interval.

[2] H. Schlier, TDNT III, pp. 144-146; cf. H. Seesemann, TDNT VI, p. 31; S. Brown, *Apostasy and Perseverance in the Theology of Luke*, pp. 13-15.

understanding of δεῖ in Luke–Acts. It is neither peculiarly eschatological, as Grundmann claimed, nor associated with the elimination of eschatology, as Conzelmann argued. Rather, it brings to expression the fact that the course of history, including those events which may be termed eschatological, is dependent upon the will of God, so that what He decides becomes as a result of His decision something that "must" happen.

Election and Fate

We now turn to the second point, namely that the kind of necessity found in Luke–Acts is based on pagan ideas of fate rather than the Old Testament idea of election.

If the material for evaluation at our disposal were confined to the Gospel, it would not be difficult to show that the view of Conzelmann and Schulz is a misinterpretation of the facts. For the evidence on which their view is based is confined almost exclusively to Acts. In the Gospel the emphasis is on the way in which the ministry of Jesus and the succeeding events take place as it is written in the Scriptures. The obligation of divine necessity hangs over the life of Jesus and the course of the eschatological programme, but this element is one which is already found in Mark (8:31; 9:11; 13:7, 10), and there is no doubt that it is to be interpreted in terms of conformity to a scriptural pattern.[1] The key words, in which Schulz finds the idea of ineluctable fate and irresistible divine movement, are almost completely lacking in the Gospel, and in any case stand in the context of the Old Testament pattern.[2] It is to be noted that Luke's thought goes beyond the thought of conformity to a pattern laid down in the Old Testament. The necessity which imposes certain conditions upon Jesus may sometimes lie in the will of God which has not been revealed to men rather than in the will of God as revealed in the Old Testament. But this is not surprising. There was never any suggestion that everything in the life of Jesus must have its complement in Old Testament prophecy or typology, and indeed the early church was often unable to find Old Testament texts to accompany specific events in the life of Jesus. Jesus Himself

[1] Luke has certainly interpreted the δεῖ in the passion predictions in terms of conformity to Scripture (cf. Luke 18:31 with Mark 10:32; Luke 17:25 and 24:7); Luke 24:44–46 brings the two ideas together. In Mark the two ideas are synonymous: cf. Mark 8:31 with 14:21. Cf. H. E. Tödt, *The Son of Man in the Synoptic Tradition*, pp. 188–194. It should be noted that this tradition is older than Mark, and that our view is further guaranteed by the presence of elements drawn from the Old Testament in the passion sayings.

[2] The προ- vocabulary is almost entirely absent from the Gospel; in Luke 2:21 nothing more than temporal priority is meant. βουλή occurs at Luke 7:30; it refers to God's saving plan by which John the Baptist was sent to bring the Jews to repentance. In Luke 22:22 κατὰ τό ὡρισμένον is Luke's alteration for Mark's καθὼς γέγραπται περὶ αὐτοῦ (14:21), but it simply brings out the element of necessity inherent in events prophesied in the Old Testament.

is represented as being intimately acquainted with the will and purpose of His Father (Luke 10:21 f. = Matt. 11:25-27), and therefore it is natural that He should have been conscious of specific divine purposes which He must fulfil.

When we turn to Acts, the picture is slightly different. Here we do encounter more of the language of predestination.[1] We also come upon the motif that it is futile for men to attempt to resist God; the opponent of the Gospel will find that it is hard to kick against the goads, and despite all opposition the Gospel will progress unhindered (Acts 5:38 f.; 26:14). At every critical stage the church and its missionaries are guided by God, through His angel, the Spirit or a prophet, and hence they move in the divinely ordained direction. Schulz finds a tell-tale use of "necessary" (ἀναγκαῖος) at Acts 13:46.

Now Schulz admits that this Hellenistic-Roman ideology of destiny which he finds in Luke is modified to the extent that it has a christological orientation,[2] but this is not the only difference. In Hellenistic thought there is often a certain arbitrariness about fate, or else its content becomes highly abstract.[3] But in Acts, as in the Gospel, the content of God's will is essentially related to His revelation in the Scriptures. The fates of Jesus and of Judas are explained in terms of Old Testament prophecies, and the most important crisis in Acts, the acceptance of the Gentiles into the church, is justified by reference to the Old Testament and to the working out of the prophecies contained in it (Acts 1:16-20; 2:30 f. et al.; 13:46 f.; 15:14-21; 28:25-28). Yet again, the thought of divine necessity is complemented by the way in which God Himself leads the church. It is not so much that the church follows a prescribed line of action as that God Himself shows the way which it ought to go; He pours out the Spirit upon the Gentiles as a sign that He accepts them, and Peter can only say, "If then God gave the same gift to them as he gave to us when we believed, who was I that I could withstand God?" (Acts 11:17).

It is within this context that the undoubted contacts between Acts and the Hellenistic motif of theomachy are to be seen, and when this is done, they fit into place. Luke is not controlled by pagan ideas but by the biblical concept of God. Within the biblical tradition itself the motif is not absent (2 Kings 19:20-28),[4] so that the thought found in Acts in a Hellenistic form is not alien to the biblical tradition.

---

[1] Note the use of βουλή in Acts 2:23; 4:28; 5:38f.; 13:36; 20:27.
[2] S. Schulz, op. cit., p. 280.
[3] Cf. R. A. Pack, "Fate," in OCD, pp. 357f.
[4] The thought that God will accomplish His will regardless of men and that their resistance is futile is frequent. Assyria and Babylon were His instruments for judgment and redemption, although they themselves were unconscious of it and thought that they were behaving freely (Isa. 10:5-19; 44:28; 45:4). Man may not strive with his Maker (Isa. 45:9; Job 15:25-30; et al.).

What, however, of the concept of election? Conzelmann begins his brief discussion by remarking that Luke is not familiar with the concept of a limited number of the elect.[1] This statement is largely evacuated of its force when it is remembered that such a concept is hardly common elsewhere in the New Testament. The word is found only in one passage in Mark (13:20–27) where it refers to God's people in an eschatological context. The idea of limitation is not present here.[2] In any case, however, precisely the same use of the word is found at Luke 18:7, and Conzelmann's claim that the meaning here is different from that elsewhere is quite unconvincing.[3]

Conzelmann further claims that in Luke the group of words associated with election is relatively rare. A glance at a concordance will show that statistically this is a dubious statement. Luke uses the verb to describe God's choice of the patriarchs (Acts 13:17) and the choice by God (or by the church under His guidance) of men to carry out special service within the church (Acts 1:24; 6:5; 15:7, 22, 25); the choice of the apostles by Jesus is also indicated by the same verb (Luke 6:13; Acts 1:2; cf. Acts 9:15). It is wrong to contrast this usage with that of the other Synoptic Gospels, as Conzelmann does, since the verb occurs elsewhere only once (Mark 13:20).[4] Luke certainly uses the word of election to particular functions in God's service rather than of election to membership of the church (as in the rest of the New Testament). This, however, is the way in which the Old Testament uses the concept when it speaks of the call of particular men to specific tasks for God (Neh. 9:7; Psa. 78:70; 89:3; 105:26; 106:23; Isa. 49:7; Jer. 1:4–8; Hag. 2:23). Similarly, Luke's designation of Jesus as the Elect One (Luke 9:35; 23:35) stems ultimately from the description of the Servant of Yahweh (Isa. 42:1). Luke's concept of election, while largely different from that of the rest of the New Testament, is in fundamental continuity with the Old Testament. To this extent Conzelmann is correct in stating that Luke is less interested in the idea of individual election to salvation and is more interested in the saving events as a whole. But this does not mean that Luke is disinterested in election to specific service or in the salvation of the individual. Above all, there is no reason to see in Luke's view of election any confirmation for attributing to him a Hellenistic idea of necessity in history.[5]

---

[1] H. Conzelmann, *op. cit.*, p. 144 (p. 154).

[2] The idea of limitation may be found in Matt. 22:14, but the thought is perhaps primarily of the need for obedience to God by those whom He calls; K. L. Schmidt, TDNT IV, pp. 181–192, especially pp. 186f. The saying was probably not known to Luke.

[3] K. L. Schmidt, *op. cit.*, pp. 187f. Luke's omission of the other uses of the word from his Marcan source (Mark 13:20, 22, 27) does not appear to be due to dislike of the word as such.

[4] Here it refers to God's choice of the elect for whose sake He shortens the final tribulation. The choice itself, however, is not necessarily an act of the End time, even if it looks forward to it.

[5] H. Conzelmann refers in a footnote (*op. cit.*, p. 145 n. 1 (p. 155 n. 1)) to Luke's use of the

The conclusion to be drawn from these considerations is that Luke's idea of God is drawn from the Old Testament tradition, and that Hellenistic influences are peripheral. He is the God who exercises sovereign control over history, and He has a purpose which finds expression in salvation-history. The various events in salvation-history are all related to this plan of God, so that it is correct to see a certain unity running through the history.

It remains to add that this conception of the work of God in history is shared by Luke with other New Testament writers. The closest parallel is to be found in Ephesians where Paul speaks of the God who accomplishes all things according to the counsel of His will, and describes His purpose which He has brought into effect in Jesus Christ (Eph. 1:9–11; 3:9–11). But the earlier letters of Paul also bear witness to the same idea. Paul is aware that his journeys as a missionary take place in accordance with the will of God which is revealed to him from time to time (Rom. 1:10; 15:32; cf. 1 Cor. 16:12), and His call to apostleship rests upon the will of God (1 Cor. 1:1, et al.) who separated him to this work even before he was born (Gal. 1:15). He is aware of the purpose of God which found expression in the sending of Christ to deliver men from the present evil age (Gal. 1:4), but his own particular use of the word ($\theta\acute{\epsilon}\lambda\eta\mu\alpha$) is to describe the spiritual and moral purposes of God for His people (Rom. 2:18; 12:2; 1 Thes. 4:3; et al.). Similar ideas are found elsewhere in the New Testament, and we may refer particularly to Rev. 4:11 where the creation of the world is ascribed to the divine will.[1]

Indeed we may go a stage further back and assert that the basis of this view of God is to be found in the teaching of Jesus Himself. He was conscious of His place in the purpose of God, and His prayer in Gethsemane, "Yet not what I will, but what thou wilt" (Mark 14:36; cf. Luke 22:42),[2] reflects this consciousness. The Synoptic statements about the sense of mission which informed His ministry and the constraint of divine necessity

[1] In Heb. 10:5–10 we have an interesting combination which shows the close link between the will of God for the conduct of an individual and the will of God for Jesus which leads to salvation. 1 Pet. relates the sufferings of the church to the will of God (3:17; 4:19). Luke does not use the verbs $\beta o\acute{u}\lambda o\mu\alpha\iota$ and $\theta\acute{\epsilon}\lambda\omega$ which occur elsewhere of God's saving plan (Jam. 1:18; 2 Pet. 3:9; Rom. 9:18, 22; 1 Tim. 2:4; et al.).

[2] We find no good reason for questioning the authenticity of this part of the prayer; contra: D. E. Nineham, Saint Mark, p. 392.

$\kappa\alpha\lambda\acute{\epsilon}\omega$ word group, and claims that it is not eschatological. This, however, does not set Luke apart from the rest of the New Testament, since the usage elsewhere is neither more nor less eschatological than in Luke. Conzelmann claims that there is a shift of meaning in Luke 5:32 (from Mark) and in Acts 2:39 (where an eschatological call (Joel 2:32b) has become ecclesiastical): but this argument fails to recognize that for Luke repentance and the call of God through the church are both eschatological and salvation-historical events.

which hung over Him are summed up in the Gospel of John where the task of Jesus is defined as the doing of the Father's will (John 4:30; 5:30; *et al.*). Perhaps too we may refer in this connexion to the petition in the Lord's Prayer, "Thy will be done." The fact that this phrase is found only in Matthew's version of the prayer (Matt. 6:10) has been made a reason for doubting its authenticity as a part of Jesus' original prayer.[1] This, however, is by no means a foregone conclusion, and the exposition of E. Lohmeyer in particular has shown how readily the ideas expressed may be fitted into the teaching of Jesus. The petition speaks of the achievement of the eschatological consummation which it is God's will to bring about.[2] It refers to the outworking of a divine plan which is concerned to bring history to its climax.

It thus appears likely that there was for Jesus Himself a sense of necessity in the course of His own personal life and in the progress of history to its divinely intended consummation. We may fairly claim that in the main theme of his doctrine of God as the sovereign ruler in history Luke was faithfully reflecting the teaching of the early church and very probably of Jesus Himself.

[1] J. Jeremias, "Das Vater-Unser im Lichte der neueren Forschung," in *Abba*, pp. 152–171 (English translation: *The Prayers of Jesus*, 1967, pp. 82–107). Contra: E. Lohmeyer, *The Lord's Prayer*, 1965, pp. 131–133 (English translation of *Das Vater-Unser*, Göttingen, 1952); W. Ott, *Gebet und Heil*, pp. 120–122.

[2] E. Lohmeyer, *op. cit.*, pp. 111–133.

CHAPTER VI

TO SAVE THE LOST

THE CENTRAL THEME IN THE WRITINGS OF LUKE IS THAT JESUS OFFERS salvation to men. If we were looking for a text to sum up the message of the Gospel, it would undoubtedly be Luke 19:10: "For the Son of man came to seek and to save the lost." With this verse Luke concludes the story of the ministry of Jesus in Galilee and Judaea. The immediately following section, which contains the parable of the pounds (Luke 19:11–27), looks forward to the entry to Jerusalem and belongs to the new section which begins here rather than to what has preceded. The saying of Jesus, therefore, stands as the climax of his evangelistic ministry and sums up its significance: Jesus came to save.

In singling out this feature as the decisive characteristic of the ministry, Luke was doing something novel as compared with the other Evangelists, and yet at the same time he was not imposing a new motif upon the Gospel tradition.

The emphasis of Mark is somewhat different. At the present time there are many different theories regarding the purpose and characteristics of Mark,[1] but we may surely regard it as significant that Mark uses the word "gospel" in connexion with the contents of his book. He regards himself as presenting a message, just as Jesus presented a message, and the content of the message is good news for those who receive it. But Mark does not go into much detail regarding the content of the message once he has summed up its essential ingredients (Mark 1:14f.). His concern appears to be much more with the person of Jesus; his purpose is to depict Him as the Christ and supremely as the Son of God. The all-important question is, "Who do you say that I am?" (Mark 8:29). The evidence consists partly of what have been called "secret epiphanies" in which the divine authority of Jesus is revealed to those who have been given eyes to see it. It also consists of teaching in which Jesus reveals that His task consists in suffering before He may attain to heavenly glory and victory, and that discipleship involves readiness on the part of men to follow the same path of suffering. If a generalization may be allowed, we can perhaps say that Mark is very much

---

[1] See the surveys: J. Rohde, *Rediscovering the Teaching of the Evangelists*, pp. 113–152; R. S. Barbour, "Recent Study of the Gospel according to St. Mark," Exp.T 79, 1967–68, pp. 324–329; R. P. Martin, *Mark: Evangelist and Theologian*, Exeter, 1972.

concerned with the person of Jesus; to know who Jesus is constitutes his Gospel.

The various motifs that come to expression in the Gospel of Matthew are not easy to sum up.[1] Two main themes predominate. The one is that Jesus is the promised Messiah of the Old Testament and Judaism. It seems certain that one major purpose of Matthew was to demonstrate to the Jews that Jesus was the Messiah and that consequently the church was the true people of God. Matthew therefore repeats much of the content of Mark and accentuates the features which indicate that Jesus is the Jewish Messiah. His other main theme is the teaching of Jesus. Matthew, it appears, has consciously brought together the sayings of Jesus and arranged them by subject-matter, so that the dominating impression which is given of the activity of Jesus is that He was a teacher who gave fairly systematic instruction to His followers. This does not mean that Matthew is presenting a new legalism; rather he believes that salvation lies in the words of Jesus.[2]

It is appropriate to consider briefly the Gospel of John also, since there are certain contacts between it and Luke which indicate that the two Evangelists, or at least the traditions underlying their Gospels were related in some manner. Here Jesus is seen as the One who reveals God and conveys the eternal life of God to men. The category of eternal life is the fundamental soteriological concept in John, and Jesus is presented basically in terms of His close filial relationship to His Father. The purpose of the Gospel is strongly evangelistic, although it also has wider interests.

From this brief characterization of the other Gospels it will be apparent at the outset, even before we have unfolded the teaching of Luke in greater detail, that the theme of salvation and Jesus as the dispenser of salvation is a distinguishing feature of Luke. The stress is more on the positive quality of what Jesus came to do in the world and to offer to men, and the vocabulary which Luke uses to express this is not so conspicuous in the other Gospels.

At the same time it is clear that the aim of Luke is not essentially different from that of the other Gospels. Each of the Gospels is evangelistic; each of them is concerned to present Jesus as the Saviour. But, whereas the stress in Mark is on the person of Jesus, in Matthew on the teaching of Jesus, and in John on the manifestation of eternal life in Him, Luke's stress is on the blessings of salvation which He brings. In general terms, therefore, the approach of Luke is not fundamentally different from that of the other Evangelists. All are concerned with salvation in the broad sense.[3]

[1] R. P. Martin, "St Matthew's Gospel in Recent Study," Exp. T 80, 1968–69, pp. 132–136.
[2] E. P. Blair, *Jesus in the Gospel of Matthew*, New York, 1960.
[3] C. F. D. Moule, *The Phenomenon of the New Testament*, 1967, p. 113.

Nor is Luke entirely an innovator in his terminology. The concept of salvation is fundamental to the teaching of the New Testament. 1 Thessalonians is among the oldest writings in the New Testament, and many scholars would consider it to be the earliest extant Epistle of Paul. Even, however, if it is not Paul's earliest writing – in our opinion Galatians probably preceded it – its date makes it significant for our present purpose of establishing the age of the terminology of salvation in the early church. For here we find Paul speaking of the Gentiles "being saved" in a manner which indicates that it was a current term for Christian conversion (1 Thes. 2:16). The same terminology reappears throughout his Epistles, being absent only from Galatians and Colossians. Of the other New Testament writings only 2 and 3 John fail to use the word group. This shows not only that the terminology arose early, but also that it was widespread throughout the church.

We can go further back. There is good reason to believe that in Rom. 10:9 Paul is making use of an existing formulary: "If you confess with your lips that Jesus is Lord and believe in your heart that God raised him from the dead, you will be saved." Here what is undoubtedly a primitive confession of faith is being quoted.[1] We note too that Paul prefaces his summary of the earliest preaching in 1 Cor. 15:3 ff. with the comment that it is by this gospel that men are saved (verse 2). This suggests that for him the primitive summaries of the gospel were bound up with the idea of being saved.

The Promised Saviour

If the story of Zacchaeus forms the climax of the ministry of Jesus before His entry to Jerusalem and the events leading to the passion, the opening scene, which sets the pattern for what follows, is the preaching of Jesus in the synagogue at Nazareth (Luke 4:16–30). It is usually supposed that the incident recorded here is the same as that in Mark 6:1–6, and that Luke has brought it forward in his narrative because of its programmatic character for his description of the ministry. Some would go further and regard the narrative at this point as being largely due to Luke's own redaction of the story in Mark. If these two points are sound, then the incident in its present form clearly has great importance in indicating how Luke wished his readers to approach the story of the ministry.[2]

However, neither assumption can been left unquestioned. The analysis

---

[1] See p. 50, n. 4. It is not clear how much of the verse, apart from the content of the Christian confession, should be regarded as pre-Pauline, but the use of the concept of salvation in similar contexts (1 Cor. 15:2) strongly suggests that there was a primitive connexion between the confession and the idea of being saved.

[2] R. Bultmann, *Die Geschichte der synoptischen Tradition*, pp. 387 f.

of tradition and redaction in the story is much disputed, but many scholars would agree that another source than Mark has been utilized for some or all of the story.[1] Further, H. Schürmann has presented a case for the existence of an alternative source narrating how the ministry of Jesus began, used by both Matthew and Luke; it included at least Luke 4: 14–16 and established a visit to Nazareth at the outset of the ministry.[2] If these suggestions are correct, then it follows that a strong part of the case for arguing that Luke himself constructed this scene to set the pattern of the ministry is deprived of support. Nevertheless, it is still true that Luke chose to use this particular report of the opening of the ministry rather than any other, and that therefore it must have had some significance in his eyes. We may legitimately examine it from this point of view.

The opening part of the narrative relates how Jesus stood up to read the lesson from the prophets in the synagogue service; he read from Isa. 61:1f.[3] and then astounded the company by declaring, "Today this scripture has been fulfilled in your hearing." It is with this section of the story that we are immediately concerned.

(1). The first thing to be observed here is that Jesus quotes from the Old Testament and speaks in terms of its *fulfilment*. The passage quoted was spoken by the prophet in the first person and therefore apparently refers to his own sense of mission.[4] It would, however, also be possible to identify the speaker with the Servant of Yahweh who figures so prominently in the immediately preceding chapters of the prophecy.[5] In any case the passage is here regarded as prophetic in the sense of being predictive, and the claim is made that the passage is fulfilled in Jesus Himself. His person and activity are described in the prophecy.

This means that the activity of Jesus may properly be described as eschatological. That is to say, His activity is regarded as something which was

[1] B. Violet, "Zum rechten Verständnis der Nazareth-Perikope Lc. 4, 16–30," ZNW 37, 1938, pp. 251–271; W. Grundmann, *Das Evangelium nach Lukas*, p. 119; I. H. Marshall, GL, pp. 177–181.

[2] H. Schürmann, "Der 'Bericht vom Anfang': Ein Rekonstruktionsversuch auf Grund von Lk 4, 14–16," in *Traditionsgeschichtliche Untersuchungen*, pp. 69–80 (originally in SE II, pp. 242–258); *Das Lukasevangelium*, pp. 241–244, 258f.

[3] The form of the quotation diverges slightly from the LXX and includes a phrase from Isa. 58:6. The conflation of two prophetic passages can hardly have taken place in a synagogue reading, and it is probably due to Christian exegetical activity. R. Bultmann (TDNT I, p. 511) suggests that while the thought is primarily of liberation the idea of forgiveness is also included.

[4] This is the interpretation in the Targum: SB II, p. 156; cf. Pesikta 125b (SB I, p. 470).

[5] The passage certainly uses language reminiscent of the Servant passages (Isa. 42:1–7), and was used by S. Mowinckel as evidence for his (earlier) view of the identity of the Servant with the prophet himself (see C. R. North, *The Suffering Servant in Deutero-Isaiah*, Oxford, 1956², p. 74). Cf. E. E. Ellis, *The Gospel of Luke*, p. 97; F. F. Bruce, *This is That: The New Testament Development of Some Old Testament Themes*, Exeter, 1969, p. 90. That Luke at least saw in the passage a reference to the Servant is the view of F. J. F. Jackson and K. Lake, BC I, p. 390.

prophesied as taking place in the future in the Old Testament, and, since a period of several hundred years separated the prophecy from the fulfilment, it is certain that the prophecy was regarded as referring to the time of the End, so that the appearance of Jesus would have been seen as an event of the End time. This is an important conclusion; it means that the ministry of Jesus is regarded as an eschatological event in the strict sense of the term. It is confirmed by the evidence of other passages in Luke. We may recall the birth narrative in which John the Baptist is regarded as preparing the way for the Lord in terms taken from the Old Testament prophecy of the coming of Elijah, and Jesus Himself is stated to be the promised Messiah of the house of David. These points are both taken up in Luke 7:18ff. where Mal. 3:1 is quoted to explain the work of John the Baptist and the ministry of Jesus is described in a series of phrases from Isa. 29:18f.; 35:3f. and 61:1. Here again the passages cited are those for which a fulfilment was expected in the time of the End. Similarly, in Luke 10:23f. Jesus says to His disciples, "Blessed are the eyes which see what you see! For I tell you that many prophets and kings desired to see what you see, and did not see it, and to hear what you hear, and did not hear it."

The interpretation of these passages is disputed by H. Conzelmann. He argues that Luke regards the time of salvation as something which is now over and finished in contrast with Paul who sees his own time as the eschatological time, and further that the coming of Jesus is not the End but only a picture of the future time of salvation.[1] The reason given for this statement is that in Luke 22:35f. Luke distinguishes between the period of Jesus and the present time. However, this reference will not bear the weight which Conzelmann tries to impose upon it. It does, to be sure, make a distinction between the period of the ministry and the period which began with the passion of Jesus. But its primary reference is to the immediately following events, including the scene in Gethsemane,[2] and it is a warning that persecution and suffering are at hand. There is certainly nothing in the text to suggest a distinction between a past time of fulfilment and the presence of salvation on the one hand, and a present time of a different kind on the other. There is no indication that the era of fulfilment has come to an end; in fact the reverse is the case, for over the new period there hang the words of prophecy: "For I tell you that this scripture must be fulfilled in me, 'And he was reckoned with transgressors;' for what is written about me has its fulfilment." This passage, therefore, so far from

---

[1] H. Conzelmann, *Die Mitte der Zeit*, pp. 25–32, 94 (pp. 31–38, 103). Contra: H. Schürmann, *Das Lukasevangelium*, p. 233 and n. 79.

[2] P. Minear, "A Note on Luke 22:36," Nov. T 7, 1964, pp. 128–134. According to F. Schütz, *Der leidende Christus*, the themes of the passion narrative, including the rejection of Christ and the suffering of the disciples, are to be found throughout the Gospel; consequently no rigid distinction between the various stages in the life of Jesus should be sought.

proving Conzelmann's case actually works against it, for it places the period after the ministry in the category of fulfilment; the point is confirmed by Luke 24:46f., where the post-resurrection mission is said to be in fulfilment of Scripture. Conzelmann's mistake is that he has made a distinction between the ministry of Jesus, which (in his view) Luke has de-eschatologized, and the future time of the End. It is more correct to say that Luke has broadened out the time of the End so that it begins with the ministry of Jesus, includes the time of the church, and is consummated at the parousia. Luke has not pushed the End into the distant future; he has lengthened it to include the whole era of salvation from the time of Jesus onwards. Salvation is not a thing of the past, belonging to the ministry of Jesus. It takes its start from then; the "today" of fulfilment continues right through into the time of the church.[1]

(2). Second, the time of fulfilment is to be characterized as *the era of salvation*. It is a positive view which is adopted by Jesus. J. Jeremias has drawn attention to the way in which the closing part of Isa. 61:2, which proclaims "the day of vengeance of our God", is omitted from the quotation in Luke 4:18f.[2] It is not enough to say that this phrase is omitted because it refers to the parousia rather than to the ministry of Jesus; the point is rather that the ministry of Jesus is primarily concerned with salvation.

This is brought out in the wording of the quotation. There is a certain amount of overlap with the quotation in Luke 7:22 mentioned above, so that both passages must be considered together. The latter passage is concerned exclusively with the works done by Jesus and refers to various classes of unfortunate people whose needs were met by the mighty works and the preaching of Jesus. It gives a list of actions which according to the Gospel tradition were actually carried out by Jesus. He gave sight to the blind (Luke 7:21; 18:35–43), restored the lame (cf. Luke 5:17–26; Acts 3:1–10; 8:7; 14:8–10), cleansed lepers (Luke 5:12–16; 17:11–19), made the deaf hear (not in Luke; cf. Mark 7:31–37; 9:25), raised the dead (Luke 7:11–17; 8:40–56) and preached the good news to the poor (cf. Luke 6:20).[3] Some commentators have held that the prophecy was originally

---

[1] "Today" (σήμερον) in Luke 23:43 has been held to refer to the "now" of salvation rather than to a particular "today" (E. E. Ellis, "Present and Future Eschatology in Luke," NTS 12, 1965–66, pp. 27–41, especially pp. 36f.). F. Schütz, *op. cit.*, traces the links between the ministry of Jesus and the time of the church, and shows that they are in effect continuous with each other.

[2] J. Jeremias, *Jesu Verheissung für die Völker*, Stuttgart, 1956, pp. 37–39, following a suggestion by K. Bornhäuser (English translation: *Jesus' Promise to the Nations*, 1958).

[3] The healing of lepers and the raising of the dead are not signs of the "messianic" age in Isa. 29, 35, 61, but for the latter see Isa. 26:19. Both activities are, however, associated with the prophets Elijah and Elisha. It would not be surprising if the eschatological prophet were to follow this pattern; cf. F. Hahn, *Christologische Hoheitstitel*, p. 393.

taken metaphorically of the effects of preaching, but there is no evidence that such a stage of understanding ever existed; it is an unlikely hypothesis.[1] Rather both the mighty works and the preaching of Jesus are regarded as the fulfilment of the prophecy, and the way in which the various parts of the quotation have been brought together from a number of Old Testament passages is proof that the ministry itself has dictated the choice of Old Testament texts, rather than that the description of the ministry was influenced by the wording of the prophecy. There are, as we have seen, incidents illustrative of nearly every aspect of the prophecy in Luke itself, and in every case further evidence may be given from the different streams of Gospel tradition. This means that, if the tradition is correct in narrating that Jesus did such acts, then it is wholly possible that the use of the quotation may go back to His own estimate of what He was doing. The attempt by P. Stuhlmacher to upturn the general consensus of scholarly opinion that the saying goes back to Jesus Himself is scarcely convincing.[2] In his characterization of the ministry Luke is thus making use of traditional material which in all probability stems from Jesus.

The climax of the saying comes in the reference to the preaching of the gospel to the poor. Here two important terms demand our attention. The objects of the preaching are the poor (πτωχοί). The occurrence of this term in the opening verse of the Sermon on the Mount (or Plain) (Luke 6:20 par. Matt. 5:3) has caused great discussion, especially by E. Percy, J. Dupont and H.-J. Degenhardt.[3] The word in the Old Testament refers to those who were literally poor. It took on the nuance of "oppressed," since the poor were helpless against the exploitations practised by the rich. This meant that the poor were forced to depend upon Yahweh as their helper, since they had no human help. The word thus combines the ideas

[1] J. Wellhausen, *Das Evangelium Lucae*, Berlin, 1904, p. 53; E. Klostermann, *Das Lukas-Evangelium*, p. 95. Against this view see E. Percy, *Die Botschaft Jesu*, Lund, 1953, pp. 187–189. E. Schweizer's view that in Luke 4:18 only preaching is regarded as the fulfilment of the prophecy (TDNT VI, p. 407) rests on a faulty interpretation of Luke 4:23–27.
[2] P. Stuhlmacher, *Das paulinische Evangelium: I. Vorgeschichte*, Göttingen, 1968, pp. 218–222. Stuhlmacher starts from E. Käsemann's claim that the "blessing" form (Luke 7:23) is a sign of early Christian prophecy (*New Testament Questions of Today*, pp. 100f.). He then claims that the purpose of the saying is to establish over against the claims of John the Baptist's followers that Jesus was the true eschatological prophet, as attested by His works. Finally, the form of the saying presents Jesus in a "hidden" manner, so that the hearer must make up his own mind about the saying if he is to penetrate its meaning. None of these points gives any reason for denying the authenticity of the saying. If Jesus Himself acted as a prophet, Käsemann's case promptly falls to the ground. Even if there was polemic between Baptists and Christians, this in no way implies that the present scene must be unhistorical. And the self-revealing, self-hiding manner of speech is characteristic of Jesus Himself. See further I. H. Marshall, GL, pp. 287–289.
[3] E. Percy, *op. cit.*, pp. 82–89; J. Dupont, *Les Béatitudes*, Louvain, 1954, pp. 142–148; H.-J. Degenhardt, *Lukas-Evangelist der Armen: Besitz und Besitzverzicht in den lukanischen Schriften*, Stuttgart, 1965, pp. 43–53; see also F. Hauck and E. Bammel, TDNT VI, pp. 885–915.

of weakness and dependence upon Yahweh; those who are poor depend upon God's favour. E. Percy has strongly contested the view that the word had come to mean "pious," but he has made his point in a somewhat exaggerated fashion; the point is that the word does not stress the positive performance of pious actions calculated to win God's favour but rather draws attention to the needy condition of the sufferer which God alone can cure. The poor are thus the needy and downtrodden whose wants are not supplied by earthly helpers. As Matthew makes clear, the meaning of the word is not restricted to literal poverty.

It was to such people that Jesus preached good news ($\varepsilon \dot{v} \alpha \gamma \gamma \varepsilon \lambda i \zeta o \mu \alpha \iota$). Here again we come upon a concept which has been the subject of considerable debate. Both the meaning and the origin of the concept are disputed.[1] Etymologically, the root is connected with the proclamation of good news. But this fairly generally accepted meaning has been thought to run into difficulty when the usage in Rev. 14:6 (cf. 10:7) is considered; here the content of the message is judgment rather than salvation. A fresh survey of the evidence by P. Stuhlmacher has suggested that the connotation of *good* news is not as securely tied to the root and to its Hebrew equivalent as was generally thought, and that the verb can therefore be used in a somewhat neutral sense. As to the origin of the word, despite the use in Hellenism which in some respects comes close to that of the New Testament, Stuhlmacher concludes that the Jewish influence was primary. He then argues that the use in Rev. 14:6 is, from a traditio-historical point of view, the most primitive in the New Testament: here there is a proclamation by an angel in which the coming judgment is announced and the peoples of the world are summoned to worship God. Whether this is good or bad news for them is not clear. In Rev. 10:7, however, we have a message of hope for the humiliated and persecuted church that God is about to act in kingly power for their benefit.

It is this "eschatological" use of the verb which Stuhlmacher finds in Luke 7:22. The message for the poor is the announcement that the Kingdom of God is at hand bringing salvation.

The exposition given by Stuhlmacher is not completely convincing. It should perhaps be emphasized more strongly that two factors are at play in the New Testament. There is, first, the etymology of the word in Greek which would undoubtedly lend weight to the thought of *good* news. Then, second, the primary source for the New Testament use of the word lies in Isaiah where the word is used especially of good tidings (Isa. 40:9; 41:27; 52:7; 60:6; 61:1). Although the indications of joy associated with the tidings may lie in the context rather than in the verb itself, it seems likely that the result of this would be to associate the verb with good

[1] G. Friedrich, TDNT II, pp. 707-737; P. Stuhlmacher, *op. cit.*

tidings. We would, therefore, be more positive than Stuhlmacher in affirming the positive note of joy which is to be found in Luke 7:22.[1]

This has implications for our estimate of other passages in Luke. Stuhlmacher holds that in a number of passages in Luke (1:19; 2:10; 3:18; 4:43; 8:1; 9:6; 16:16; 20:1) we have the same "neutral" sense of the word, which is sometimes used in parallel with the verb "to preach" (κηρύσσω) and conveys the same meaning.[2] One may agree with this statement in so far as it is clear that Stuhlmacher's aim is to deny that the technical sense "to preach the Christian gospel" is present in these passages. It is questionable, however, whether the verb has no connotation of *good* news in these passages. This is certainly not true for Luke 1:19 (cf. Jer. 20:15) and Luke 2:10 where the thought of joy is clearly present. Moreover, once the basic meaning of the term has been established at Luke 4:18, the same sense is likely in the following passages, especially in those where the content of the preaching is named as the kingdom of God (Luke 4:43, 8:1; 16:16; for 9:6 compare 9:2). The problem passage is Luke 3:18 where the activity of John the Baptist is described as preaching good news to the people (εὐηγγελίζετο τὸν λαόν). Conzelmann in particular had already denied on more general grounds that John could be regarded as preaching the gospel, since this would contradict the Lucan scheme of salvation-history and since no object is given to the verb.[3] Neither objection is valid. The immediately preceding verses (Luke 3:16f.) contain John's answer to the question whether he was the Messiah; they are a statement promising that the Messiah is coming. The general content of John's preaching was an exhortation to prepare for the coming of the Lord, the time at which all men would see the salvation of God (Luke 3:4–6). This was undoubtedly good news, the announcement of the coming of the deliverer.[4] Thus the description of John given by Luke is at variance with Conzelmann's view of Luke's historical scheme and at the same time Luke has in fact supplied the content of John's preaching of good news.

(3). We have now established that the prophecy from Isa. 61:1f. used in Luke 4:18f. and 7:22 shows that the time of Jesus is the era of salvation.

---

[1] P. Stuhlmacher's interpretation of Rev. 14:6 (*op. cit.*, pp. 210–218) is doubtful. As he admits (p. 212), the Jewish use of the word refers to the coming of God to judge and save. It is unlikely that the verb could be used in the New Testament without the idea of salvation being present. In Rev. 16:9, 11 a last chance to repent is offered to men; it is likely that Rev. 14:6 is to be taken in the same sense. The attempt to remove the positive sense from Rev. 10:7 is even less successful. Cf. G. B. Caird, *The Revelation*, 1966, pp. 181–184.

[2] P. Stuhlmacher, *op. cit.*, pp. 229f.

[3] H. Conzelmann, *Die Mitte der Zeit*, p. 17 n. 1 (p. 23 n. 1), pp. 206f. (pp. 221f.), following R. Bultmann, *Theology of the New Testament*, I, p. 87; cf. P. Stuhlmacher, *op. cit.*, pp. 229 n. 4; p. 234 n. 2.

[4] Cf. H. Schürmann, *Das Lukasevangelium*, pp. 178f.

Before this statement receives further clarification from the rest of the Gospel we must establish a third fact which arises particularly from Luke 4:18 f. This is that *Jesus Himself* is regarded as the fulfilment of the prophecy He is the person promised in the prophecy, for He does not merely prophesy that God is going to save His people, but He actually brings salvation to them by His preaching. The quotation describes the effects of His preaching in metaphorical terms as bringing release to the captives and sight to the blind. He announces that the year of God's favour has come. But the important thing is that this activity is inseparable from Jesus Himself. It is not a prophetic proclamation that something is going to happen. The Gospel as a whole makes it plain that salvation actually comes to men through the activity of Jesus. J. Wellhausen rightly saw that in Luke the message of Jesus is about Himself rather than about the kingdom of God.[1]

But what significance is attached to the person of Jesus here? Since the passage quoted is one in which the prophet himself speaks, it is tempting to think of Jesus as the eschatological prophet. It is surprising that G. Friedrich in his article on "prophet" ($\pi\rho o\phi\acute{\eta}\tau\eta\varsigma$) does not refer to Luke 4:18 f. in this connexion.[2] For the fairly considerable use of the category of a prophet to interpret the person of Jesus in Luke affords some presumption that the idea is present in this passage. Twice in Mark (6:15 par. Luke 9:8; Mark 8:28 par. Luke 9:19) the people refer to Jesus as a prophet. Once He likens His fate to that of a prophet (Mark 6:4; cf. Luke 4:24). Friedrich claims that Jesus does not explicitly call Himself a prophet here, but uses a proverbial saying to compare His fate with that of a prophet.[3] This is an inadequate verdict, for the saying is not really different in form from the independent saying in Luke 13:33; moreover, so long as no precise parallel to the saying is produced, it cannot be labelled proverbial, but must rather be regarded as a fresh creation in which Jesus deliberately likens Himself to a prophet. There is no reference to Jesus as a prophet in the Q material (unless Luke 13:31-33 be ascribed to Q), but Matthew has the concept twice (Matt. 21:11, 46). However, in Luke's special source, the crowds at Nain say of Jesus, "A great prophet has arisen among us" (Luke 7:16), and Simon the Pharisee has such an estimate in mind when he thinks that Jesus' lack of clairvoyance is inconsistent with His being a prophet (Luke 7:39); Luke 13:33 likens the fate of Jesus to that of a prophet slain in Jerusalem, and finally the opinion of the disciples on

[1] J. Wellhausen, *Das Evangelium Lucae*, pp. 9 f.
[2] G. Friedrich (and others), TDNT VI, pp. 781–861. Cf. F. Hahn, *Christologische Hoheitstitel*, pp. 351–404, especially pp. 394 f.; R. H. Fuller, *The Foundations of New Testament Christology*, pp. 125–131, 140, 193. Luke 4:24-27 shows clearly enough that prophetic ideas are present in the passage.
[3] G. Friedrich, *op. cit.*, p. 841.

the road to Emmaus is that Jesus was "a prophet mighty in deed and word before God and all the people" (Luke 24:19).

That such a view of Jesus continued in the early church and was taken over by Luke himself is apparent from Acts 3:22f. and 7:37; it is also a feature of Johannine christology (John 4:19; 6:14; 7:40; 9:17). It can satisfactorily account for much of Jesus' activity, as Luke 24:19 makes clear. There the mention of words and deeds reminds us that the activity of a prophet was not restricted to the proclamation of a message by word of mouth. Such features as the visionary experiences of Jesus, His supernatural knowledge of men's thoughts and His foreknowledge all fit into this pattern.[1]

It is fitting, therefore, to understand Luke 4:18f. in terms of Jesus being a prophet. But we must go further and ask whether Jesus is regarded in Luke as *the* prophet of Jewish expectation. The description of Jesus as a *great* prophet in Luke 7:16 may imply this, but it is doubtful whether this is implied in Luke 7:39.[2] So far as Luke 4:18f. is concerned, this explanation is probable. It receives some confirmation from the use of the same passage from Isaiah in a Qumran hymn, if it is correct to take the reference here as being to the Teacher of Righteousness.[3]

Stuhlmacher claims that the same description of Jesus as the eschatological prophet is found in Luke 7:22 where Jesus is described as the wonder-working prophet of the End. But a difficulty arises here because John the Baptist's question raises the question whether Jesus is "the coming one" (Luke 7:19f.); could this phrase be used to indicate the eschatological prophet, or did it refer to the Messiah?

In favour of the former view it is argued that the deeds described in Luke 7:22 are not those of the kingly Messiah but rather those of the prophet who restores the paradisial conditions of the wilderness period.[4] But, on the other hand, in John's preaching the coming one must be identified with the Messiah, unless we accept the unlikely view that John thought himself to be the prophet who announced the coming of the eschatological prophet rather than the eschatological prophet himself. Again, the evidence shows that the word "coming" was certainly used of the Messiah.[5] If, then, Jesus is the Messiah, how do we account for His "prophetic" deeds?

---

[1] *Ibid.*, pp. 843–845.

[2] In Luke 7:39 Codex Vaticanus has the article ὁ before προφήτης; the reading is accepted by W. Grundmann, *Das Evangelium nach Lukas*, p. 171, who holds that Luke is concerned with the question whether Jesus is the eschatological prophet. See, however, G. Friedrich, *op. cit.*, p. 842.

[3] 1QH 18:14; cf. 11QMelch 6; P. Stuhlmacher, *op. cit.*, pp. 142–147.

[4] G. Friedrich, *op. cit.*, p. 847; cf. F. Hahn, *op. cit.*, p. 393.

[5] Psa. 118:26; Hab. 2:3 LXX; cf. Dan. 7:13; Mal. 3:1; Heb. 10:37; Rev. 1:4; the Messiah is probably meant in Luke 3:16, and Matt. 11:2 makes it clear that in the Evangelist's opinion

The solution to this problem lies in uncovering a confusion that lurks in the idea of *the* eschatological prophet. Actually two streams of tradition can be unravelled here, showing that there were expectations of the return of Elijah and of the coming of a prophet like Moses.[1] This tension is reflected in the early church.[2] In the early church John the Baptist was regarded as the coming Elijah (even though he himself modestly disclaimed the role), but not as the new Moses. Although some of the actions of Jesus were understood in terms of Elijah (and Elisha) typology, He himself was not identified with Elijah but with the new Moses.

While Elijah was not generally identified with the Messiah,[3] the prophet like Moses was described in "messianic" terms as the eschatological deliverer. In Luke 24:19–21 the description of Jesus as a prophet is followed by the account of His death and then the words, "But we had hoped that he was the one to redeem Israel." G. Friedrich takes this to mean that the prophet like Moses was to redeem the people in the same way as Moses had done (Acts 7:35–37).[4] If so, the task of the Messiah could be understood in terms of the functions of the Mosaic prophet. Hence the distinction which has been drawn by various scholars in their discussions of Luke 7:19–22 between the deeds of the eschatological prophet and the Messiah proves to be a false one. As the eschatological prophet, Jesus is the Messiah.

If we now return to Luke 4:18 f., it will be remembered that we earlier raised the question whether the speaker in Isa. 61:1 f. was regarded as the Servant. If this is the case, then the task of the Servant is already understood in Isaiah as a repetition of that of Moses and as being prophetic. He restores the conditions of the wilderness period as idealistically conceived, and he takes on the role of a prophet who opens blind eyes and sets free the prisoners (Isa. 42:1–7). The early church made the identification between the Servant and the Messiah, an identification which in our opinion was

---

[1] R. H. Fuller, *The Foundations of New Testament Christology*, pp. 46–49, 50–53. The complexity of popular expectations is stressed by R. Schnackenburg, "Die Erwartung des 'Propheten' nach dem Neuen Testament und den Qumran-Texten." SE I (TU 73), pp. 622–639.

[2] Cf. J. A. T. Robinson, "Elijah, John and Jesus: an Essay in Detection," in *Twelve New Testament Studies*, 1962, pp. 28–52 (originally in NTS 4, 1957–58, pp. 263–281).

[3] J. Jeremias, TDNT II, pp. 928–941, especially pp. 931 f., claims that the expectation of Elijah as the Messiah was much less common than the view that he would be the forerunner of the Messiah.

[4] G. Friedrich, *op. cit.*, p. 846. But the passage may mean that the disciples, having been disappointed in their hope that Jesus would redeem Israel, had fallen back on the view that He was merely a prophet.

---

the coming One was the Messiah. Cf. J. Schneider, TDNT II, pp. 666–675, especially p. 670. H. Schürmann, *op. cit.*, pp. 408 f., claims that the phrase is quite indefinite and refers here to the coming One expected by John (Luke 3:16).

already made by Jesus.[1] This means that in Luke 4:18f. and 7:19–22 we have a description of the work of the Messiah in terms of the activity of the eschatological prophet like unto Moses and of the Servant of Yahweh. The claim has often been made that Jesus understood the activity of the Son of man in terms of the work of the Servant of Yahweh who suffers and dies; our investigation has shown that the influence of the Servant concept is wider than this, and extends to the ministry of Jesus as a whole; the "Messianic" activities of Jesus were those of the Servant, as Matthew (8:17; 12:17–21) correctly perceived.[2]

In our discussion we have gone back behind Luke to the traditions which he inherited. The result has been to show that Luke took up a view of Jesus which saw Him not merely as a prophet but as the final prophet, the Servant and the Messiah. This is the significance which is attached to the person of Jesus, and it is of such a character that we are bound to conclude that in the view of Luke the message of Jesus was very much concerned with His own person. It is true that these titles are not applied to Jesus, or applied only with restraint, in the Gospel,[3] but the activities associated with them are plainly present and have been shown to rest on tradition. In Acts these hints could be made more precise. The Gospel, however, says sufficient to make it clear that Jesus is the fulfilment of the Old Testament prophecies which in varied terms promise the coming of a Saviour.[4]

The Kingdom of God

In all three Synoptic Gospels the Evangelists state that the preaching of Jesus was principally concerned with the kingdom of God. Although Luke does not have the summary of the preaching of Jesus contained in Mark 1:14f. (par. Matt. 4:17), his general statements in 4:43; 8:1 and 9:11 show

---

[1] J. Jeremias (and W. Zimmerli), TDNT V, pp. 654–717. Against the arguments of M. D. Hooker, *Jesus and the Servant*, 1959, to the contrary, see R. T. France, "The Servant of the Lord in the Teaching of Jesus," Tyn.B 19, 1968, pp. 26–52.

[2] The understanding of Jesus in terms of the Servant is also to be found in the baptismal saying Luke 3:22. It is unlikely that the substitution of Psa. 2:7 found in Codex Bezae goes back to Luke; it is a typical assimilation of a quotation to the LXX form, frequently found in the western text (cf. J. Jeremias, TDNT V, p. 701 n. 349).

[3] C. F. D. Moule, "The Christology of Acts," in SLA, pp. 159–185.

[4] Luke's use of χριστός should be mentioned. He identifies Jesus with the Messiah (Luke 2:11, 26; 4:41), and he reproduces the questions and problems regarding the Messiah and Jesus' own status found in Mark (Luke 9:20; 20:41; 22:67; 23:35; cf. 3:15; 23:2, 39). He allows the risen Jesus to speak of Himself as the Messiah (24:26, 46). The usage thus fits in with the pattern established by C. F. D. Moule.

The title "Son of man" is taken over by Luke from tradition and reproduced accurately; he does not add the title to his sources (C. Colpe, TWNT VIII, pp. 461f., cf. p. 456).

The use of κύριος in narrative to describe Jesus will be mentioned later; it reflects Luke's own view of Jesus as already possessing in His earthly life the status which was confirmed at His resurrection and exaltation (see pp. 166–168).

that he shared this point of view. Luke's presentation has subordinated the theme of the kingdom to that of the proclamation of good news, but the kingdom remains the subject of the good news. It is, therefore, important to determine the meaning of the concept in Luke.

The main lines of the teaching of Jesus are not in doubt and can be briefly presented.[1] The term kingdom is used mainly of the action of God in intervening in human history to establish His rule. It refers to the action of God rather than to the realm which He establishes, although the latter idea is present in sayings which speak of entering the kingdom, and it finds its background in the apocalyptic expectation of the establishment of God's rule at the End rather than in the rabbinic concept of God's eternal rule in heaven with the Torah as the expression of His royal will for His people (although this idea too is not absent from the Gospels). But the concept of *God* ruling is remarkably infrequent in the Gospels, and it is fair to conclude that the emphasis is more upon the Agent of God through whom God's rule is made manifest. There is no doubt that the tradition before Luke regarded Jesus in this manner, and there is every reason to believe that this tradition was accurately representing Jesus' own understanding of His role.[2] Much more important for our present purpose is the question of when the kingdom was expected to appear.

A number of texts show that Jesus regarded the End and the manifest coming of the kingdom as imminent. On this point there is complete agreement among scholars.[3] Another set of texts indicates that Jesus saw His own ministry as a time of fulfilment with regard to the coming of the kingdom. Some scholars would interpret this time of fulfilment as being the period immediately before the coming of the kingdom, a period of fulfilment and of eager expectation, but not yet the time of the kingdom. This is the view of H. Conzelmann.[4] Other scholars argue – correctly, in our opinion – that these texts imply that the kingdom had already come during the ministry of Jesus, and they draw the conclusion that Jesus spoke both of the presence and of the future coming of the kingdom. Some way of explaining this polarity is required, and the most satisfactory is that

[1] W. G. Kümmel, *Promise and Fulfilment*; H. Ridderbos, *The Coming of the Kingdom*, Philadelphia, 1962; N. Perrin, *The Kingdom of God in the Teaching of Jesus*, 1963; *Rediscovering the Teaching of Jesus*, 1967; R. Schnackenburg, *God's Rule and Kingdom*, 1963 (English translation of *Gottes Herrschaft und Reich*, Freiburg, 1963); G. E. Ladd, *Jesus and the Kingdom*, 1966.

[2] On the questions whether Jesus related the figure of the Son of man to the concept of the kingdom of God and whether He regarded Himself as the Son of man see our surveys, "The Synoptic Son of Man Sayings in Recent Discussion," NTS 12, 1965–66, pp. 327–351; "The Son of Man in Contemporary Debate," EQ 42, 1970, pp. 67–87.

[3] The view of C. H. Dodd, noted earlier, namely that eschatology is fully realized in the ministry of Jesus, is no longer held, even by its proponent. See especially R. Morgenthaler, *Kommendes Reich*, Zürich, 1952.

[4] H. Conzelmann, *Grundriss der Theologie des Neuen Testaments*, pp. 125–134 (Eng. tr. pp. 106–115); cf. R. Bultmann, *Theology of the New Testament*, I, pp. 4–11.

which uses the terminology of fulfilment and consummation to refer to the coming of the kingdom in the ministry of Jesus and to its future coming respectively.[1]

Conzelmann's exposition of Luke's treatment of the theme of the kingdom proceeds from his assumption that the earlier tradition regarded the kingdom as exclusively future and also as imminent. He then contends that Luke has modified the tradition so that the concept has become even more transcendental than in the other Gospels; it has lost its contact with history and has been shifted into the distant future, away from history, in a manner which enables Luke to elaborate the eschatological, apocalyptic element. Luke's stress is not on the coming of the kingdom but rather on the nature of the kingdom. What belongs to the present time is not the coming of the kingdom but only the image of the kingdom. "It is the message of the Kingdom that is present, which in Luke is distinguished from the Kingdom itself."[2]

It is our contention that this is a misunderstanding of Luke's view. Conzelmann's mistake is that he has failed to do justice to the teaching about the presence of the kingdom which was already part of the tradition. This is evident in his treatment of Luke 11:20 (par. Matt. 12:28), "But if it is by the finger (Spirit) of God that I cast out demons, then the kingdom of God has come upon you." Faced by this unambiguous statement the best that Conzelmann can do is to claim that we do not know the Hebrew equivalent of "has come" ($\ddot{\epsilon}\phi\theta\alpha\sigma\epsilon\nu$); the saying may simply refer to the present signs of the coming kingdom. There is no justification for this manifest weakening of the saying. One may be less confident about the meaning of Luke 17:21, "The kingdom of God is in the midst of you," but there is a growing consensus of opinion that it refers to the presence of the kingdom.[3] A third text to be considered is Matt. 11:12 (par. Luke 16:16), "From the days of John the Baptist until now the kingdom of heaven has suffered violence, and men of violence take it by force." The interpretation of this saying is notoriously difficult, but Conzelmann's view, namely that, since people are trying to bring in the kingdom by force, therefore it must be a future entity, is among the least plausible views of the text.[4] Luke's interpretation of the saying is that the kingdom of God is being proclaimed and that men are pressing into it. This interpretation implies that the kingdom is present rather than future. Similarly, Matthew's version states that the kingdom is presently being attacked or

[1] So G. E. Ladd and R. Schnackenburg.
[2] H. Conzelmann, Die Mitte der Zeit, p. 113 (p. 122); cf. pp. 92–116 (pp. 101–125).
[3] H. Riesenfeld, TDNT VIII, pp. 149–151; R. Schnackenburg, op. cit., pp. 134–137; N. Perrin, Rediscovering the Teaching of Jesus, pp. 68–74.
[4] H. Conzelmann, op. cit., p. 103 (p. 112); Grundriss der Theologie des Neuen Testaments, pp. 130f. (Eng. tr. p. 112).

exercising its force and again implies the presence of the kingdom. Since both Matthew and Luke agree in the tense of the saying, we may be certain that the kingdom is here spoken of as a present entity.

The evidence of these texts is sufficiently clear. They are not awkward embarrassments to be explained away; rather they must be taken in conjunction with the sayings of Jesus which speak in a more general way of the present as a time of fulfilment and with the actions which He regarded as signs of the present activity of God through His Agent. They demonstrate that for Jesus the kingdom was already present in His ministry.

It will be observed that the texts so far quoted which speak unambiguously of the presence of the kingdom come in the Q material and Luke's special source rather than in Mark. The teaching of the parables recorded in Mark 4 is not absolutely certain. Probably they contain both present and future elements in that they teach that the kingdom which has come quietly and secretly in the ministry of Jesus (like seed beginning to grow in the ground) will come to a glorious consummation (like an abundant harvest). If this is the correct interpretation, then Mark also bears witness to both the present and the future aspects of the kingdom.[1] Since, however, Conzelmann claims that their teaching is "timeless," he finds no evidence for the presence of the kingdom in Mark. It may be this fact which has partly led to his conclusion that Luke has altered the tradition which came to him.

The presence of the kingdom is, then, firmly rooted in the tradition. But Conzelmann claims that for Luke what belongs to the present time is not the kingdom itself, but only the message of the kingdom. Luke, however, has taken over the texts already cited which refer to the presence of the kingdom without erasing this idea from them; even Luke 16:16 which speaks of the preaching of the kingdom, also refers to the presence of the kingdom. When Conzelmann speaks of "the foreshadowing of the Kingdom in the ministry of Jesus,"[2] he has in effect conceded our point.

On the other hand, Luke has not, as Conzelmann avers, shifted the future coming of the kingdom into the distance so that it is no longer relevant to present life. It must be remembered that the view that the earlier tradition expected an *immediate* rather than an *imminent* parousia is one that we have already found reason to reject. Luke too is aware that the parousia and the coming of the kingdom are not immediate. We should not attach any significance in this connexion to Luke 19:11, since the point of this editorial comment is that the disciples were wrong in expecting the kingdom of God to come when Jesus entered Jerusalem; it is not

[1] See O. Cullmann, *Salvation in History*, p. 203, for a discussion of other sayings which contain both present and future elements.
[2] H. Conzelmann, *Die Mitte der Zeit*, p. 108 n. 2 (p. 117 n. 2).

concerned with the expectations held by Luke's readers at a later date.[1] But we do find a period of waiting for the End presupposed in the parable of the pounds (Luke 19: 12–27); here, however, the important point is that the parable already had this sense when Luke received it, as is demonstrated by the presence of the same motif in the parable of the talents (Matt. 25:14–30).

In Luke 21:8 there is a warning against deceivers who will come and say "The time has drawn near," but, although this phrase is not found in the parallel in Mark 13:5, it does no more than bring out the thought, already explicit in Mark, that there will be a time before the End when deceivers will appear. Similarly, there is no real difference in emphasis between Mark 13:28 and Luke 21:28, 31, where the kingdom is said to be near from the standpoint of a still future situation.

This leaves Luke 9:27 (par. Mark 9:1) to be considered. Here Conzelmann makes much of the fact that Luke has omitted the words "coming in power," leaving the simple statement "until they see the kingdom of God." He claims that this refers to the timeless kingdom visible in Jesus.[2] Against this view A. L. Moore has argued that, if the saying were embarrassing for Luke, he could have omitted it altogether, and that its present context requires that it refers to the coming of the Son of Man and the transfiguration (regarded as a proleptic manifestation of the Son of man in His glory).[3] E. E. Ellis also notes that the use of "until" implies that the "some" in Mark 9:1 will die after they have seen the kingdom; hence a direct reference to the parousia is unlikely. He also observes that Luke has omitted "in power" because in his view the kingdom always comes in power.[4] These points make it doubtful whether Mark 9:1 was a direct reference to the parousia, so that Luke's "present" interpretation of the saying may well be in line with its original meaning.

One further passage must be considered at this point. In the mission instructions to the Seventy, they are commanded to preach, saying "The kingdom of God has come near to you" ($\ddot{\eta}\gamma\gamma\iota\kappa\epsilon\nu$ $\dot{\epsilon}\phi$' $\dot{\upsilon}\mu\hat{a}s$ $\dot{\eta}$ $\beta\alpha\sigma\iota\lambda\epsilon\acute{\iota}\alpha$ $\tau\upsilon\hat{\upsilon}$ $\theta\epsilon\upsilon\hat{\upsilon}$); if their message is rejected, they are to repeat the announcement in the form "nevertheless know this, that the kingdom of God has come near" ($\pi\lambda\dot{\eta}\nu$ $\tau\upsilon\hat{\upsilon}\tau\upsilon$ $\gamma\iota\nu\acute{\omega}\sigma\kappa\epsilon\tau\epsilon$ $\ddot{\upsilon}\tau\iota$ $\ddot{\eta}\gamma\gamma\iota\kappa\epsilon\nu$ $\dot{\eta}$ $\beta\alpha\sigma\iota\lambda\epsilon\acute{\iota}\alpha$ $\tau\upsilon\hat{\upsilon}$ $\theta\epsilon\upsilon\hat{\upsilon}$) (Luke 10:9, 11). Does this saying refer to the presence of the kingdom, or to its imminence, or to its presence in the message of the missionaries? Conzelmann's analysis is not very clear. He begins by observing

---

[1] It may be intended to correct the false view that the parousia had already taken place. See below pp. 153f.

[2] H. Conzelmann, *Die Mitte der Zeit*, pp. 95f. (pp. 104f.).

[3] A. L. Moore, *The Parousia in the New Testament*, pp. 125–131.

[4] E. E. Ellis, "Present and Future Eschatology in Luke," NTS 12, 1965–66, pp. 27–41, especially pp. 30–35.

that the form of the saying in Q, attested by Matt. 10:7, lacked the words "to you" (ἐφ'ὑμᾶς), which Luke has added to conform the saying to Luke 11:20. The saying may then refer either to the coming of the kingdom which took place at the first advent of Jesus or to its presence in the preaching. Conzelmann prefers the second interpretation, and this is also upheld by E. Grässer who argues that the ἐφ'ὑμᾶς means that the futurity of the kingdom is coupled with its present existence, as demonstrated in the activity of the missionaries.[1] In a further discussion of the same text Conzelmann begins by observing that Luke has omitted the similar statement in Mark 1:15, and then goes on to assert that Luke has omitted the section about the nearness of the kingdom from the Q saying Matt. 10:7, since here it is a matter of instructions about the preaching of the gospel, but he uses it in Luke 10:9 since the instructions here concern the future.[2] The point of this obscure remark appears to be that Luke has omitted this Q saying from his instructions for the Twelve in Luke 9:2, but has retained it in the instructions for the Seventy in Luke 10, since this passage deals with the future.

If we may take up this final point first of all, it is hard to see why the instructions to the Seventy should be regarded as dealing with the future and hence of a different character from the instructions to the Twelve, since Luke envisages the mission of the Seventy as being completed within the ministry of Jesus (Luke 10:17–20). Nor can it be said that Luke 10 contains "esoteric teaching for disciples,"[3] since the Seventy are explicitly told to preach that the kingdom has drawn near.

We are then brought up against the problem of "has come near" (ἤγγικεν). The question is bound up with the interpretation of Mark 1:15, a verse whose omission from Luke may be due to no more significant cause than the Evangelist's preference for his non-Marcan source at this point. The verb ἐγγίζω means "to draw near", but sometimes it can mean "to arrive, reach" (Jon 3:6). The problem is then whether the perfect tense means that the kingdom has drawn near (but has not yet arrived fully)[4] or has actually arrived. Is the reference to the nearness of the future, glorious manifestation of the kingdom or to the actual presence of the kingdom in the ministry of Jesus? Support for the latter view is supplied by Luke 11:20 par. Matt. 12:28, where the Greek phrase used unambiguously affirms that the kingdom has arrived.[5] On the other hand, it has

---

[1] H. Conzelmann, *op. cit.*, p. 98 (not in English translation); E. Grässer, *Das Problem der Parusieverzögerung*, pp. 140f.
[2] H. Conzelmann, *op. cit.*, p. 105 n. 3 (p. 114 n. 3).
[3] *Ibid.*, p. 105 (p. 114).
[4] W. G. Kümmel, *Promise and Fulfilment*, pp. 19–25.
[5] C. H. Dodd, *The Parables of the Kingdom*, pp. 36f.
[6] W. G. Kümmel, *op. cit.*, p. 24.

been argued that in view of the different Greek verb which is used ($\ddot{\epsilon}\phi\theta\alpha\sigma\epsilon\nu$ in Luke 11:20; $\ddot{\eta}\gamma\gamma\iota\kappa\epsilon\nu$ in Luke 10:9.11), we should not interpret the present passage in the light of Luke 11:20.[6] Despite this linguistic difference, however, it seems best to take the two passages in Luke together. Both make essentially the same point. In 11:20 the presence of the kingdom is attested by the exorcisms performed by Jesus and its power is available for the hearers, whereas in Luke 10:9, 11 the power of the kingdom is said to have drawn near to those who hear the message and it may be experienced by them if they respond to the message. In the preaching of the disciples the kingdom thus comes near to the hearers ($\dot{\epsilon}\phi'\ \dot{\upsilon}\mu\hat{\alpha}s$). One might almost say that whereas the nearness in Mark 1:15 is temporal here it is more spatial. In both cases, however, the point is that God's saving and sovereign power is at hand for those who will respond to the message. It is not, therefore, the message of the kingdom which is present, but the kingdom itself.

From this survey of the kingdom texts, therefore, it emerges that the presentation in Luke is not significantly different from that in the earlier tradition where the presence and the imminence of the kingdom were both affirmed. We must admit that the hope of the future coming of the kingdom (Luke 11:2; 22:29f.; 23:42) is not at the centre of Luke's thought but he has certainly not given up the idea. His emphasis is on the presence of the kingdom. Through the preaching of Jesus the power of the kingdom is manifested.

This fits in with the Old Testament concept of God's word which in itself is powerful and effects the will of God. The powerful word of Jesus is effective in bringing the kingdom to men. But this does not mean that the kingdom of God has become a timeless entity. Luke associates the coming of the kingdom not only with the preaching but also with the mighty works of Jesus which are the signs of the activity of God. The coming of the kingdom is firmly tied historically to the ministry of Jesus. From now on, the kingdom is at work, and in the future it will come openly.

One important point remains to be considered. We have argued that Luke retains the idea of the imminence of the kingdom found in the tradition. But there is a strong objection to this view, namely that the other eschatological teaching in Luke implies that the events associated with the coming of the kingdom have been pushed away into the indefinite future. Although Luke has retained the traditional terminology about the coming of the kingdom, he has in effect given up the idea. Whereas in the earlier apocalyptic teaching, represented by Mark 13, the fall of Jerusalem and the desecration of the temple are regarded as eschatological events closely associated with the coming of the Son of Man, in Luke the situation is different. The fall of Jerusalem has been "historicized" and carefully separated off from the predictions about the coming of the Son of man which belongs to the distant future after the completion of "the times of the Gentiles." (Luke 21:24).

In our view this objection represents an exaggeration of the situation. In the first place, despite the way in which Luke has ordered the material in ch. 21 the fall of Jerusalem is still regarded as an eschatological event. It retains its character as an event associated with the End. In Mark it is described as the "desolating sacrilege," and it is followed by cosmic signs, and then by the coming of the Son of man. In Luke this pattern is retained; the Old Testament colouring of the language is more pronounced, thus stressing the note of fulfilment,[1] and the cosmic signs and the parousia follow, as in Mark. In both Gospels the fall of Jerusalem is included among "all the things" that must take place. At the same time, the fall is part of the historical development which leads up to the parousia. But this is already the case in Mark, as has been demonstrated by E. E. Ellis, who rightly claims that Luke is not here "historicizing" Mark.[2]

Second, the Lucan stress on an interval before the parousia should not be exaggerated. We should not read too much into the phrase "but the end will not be at once" in Luke 21:9; it is Luke's equivalent for Mark's "but the end is not yet" (Mark 13:7), and the change is simply stylistic.[3] The reference to the enigmatic "times of the Gentiles" shows that an interval after the fall of Jerusalem is in mind.[4] Yet in essence Luke has not moved beyond Mark. E. E. Ellis has argued cogently that the "generation" in Mark 13:30 and Luke 21:32 is the last generation, a phrase which may cover several life-times; the point of the saying is to assure the hearers that they are part of the last generation, and that therefore the eschatological events are already taking place.[5] Consequently, the period of expectation of the parousia is not delimited in Mark (e.g. to a period of one generation)

[1] Contra: H. Conzelmann, op. cit., p. 126 (p. 135). Cf. H.-W. Bartsch, "Early Christian Eschatology in the Synoptic Gospels," NTS 11, 1964–65, pp. 384–397, who argues that "for the historian it is impossible that a past event should be also an apocalyptic event," (p. 396); for Bartsch "apocalyptic" in this context is tantamount to "eschatological." But the statement is quite arbitrary, and ignores the fact that a historian can regard himself as living in the last times which have already begun; cf. 1 Cor. 10:11.

[2] E. E. Ellis, The Gospel of Luke, pp. 244f.

[3] Luke does not like Mark's οὔπω; cf. 8:25 (par. Mark 4:40); 19:30 (par. Mark 11:2); the use in 23:53 may be from Luke's source (cf. John 19:41).

[4] The "trampling" of a holy place is a stereotyped theme in prophecy. It recurs in Rev. 11:2, a passage which is probably to be understood symbolically in its present context but which uses language drawn from a prophecy of the fall of Jerusalem; here the city is handed over to the Gentiles and they trample it for a fixed period of forty-two months. This passage gives us the key to Luke 21:24; the times of the Gentiles will then be a fixed apocalyptic period, as in Dan. 8:13. It is uncertain whether the thought that during this period the Gentiles will be evangelized is present here (cf. E. Grässer, op. cit., p. 162 for this view).

[5] E. E. Ellis, op. cit., pp. 246f.

any more than it is in Luke.[1] Mark says nothing about how near the End is; the accent is on its sudden, unexpected coming (Mark 13:36), a point that is still true for Mark's readers (Mark 13:37). In fact Mark makes it clear that a number of events must take place before the final denouement.

The fact that there is an interval before the End, that the End is imminent rather than immediate, does not mean that the End has been deferred so far into the distant future as to lose its relevance for the disciples. Luke has preserved a considerable number of sayings in which blessings and woes associated with the End are significant for the contemporaries of Jesus. We may briefly refer to the beatitudes and woes in the Sermon on the Plain (Luke 6:20–26), the sayings about the future coming of the Son of man (Luke 9:26; 12:8f., 40; 18:8), the warnings about future judgment (Luke 11:29–32) and the sayings about admission to and exclusion from the kingdom (Luke 13: 25–30; 14:14, 15–24; 16:9; 18:24; cf. 19:11–27; 22:28–30). The End is thus relevant for the life of men now. They must not grow slack in waiting for its coming (Luke 18:8), an exhortation which is not to be explained as a late community formation occasioned by the delay of the parousia, but which is authentic teaching of Jesus who Himself expected an interval before the End.[2] The disciples are to govern their behaviour in the light of the hope of the coming of the Son of man. Naturally this does not mean that they will be motivated simply by the hope of heavenly blessing or the fear of future woe, or that the imminence of the End is what basically animates their conduct. It is not the nearness of a crisis which animates New Testament ethics, but the character of God.[3]

We may briefly draw together the results of this section. It has emerged that in the Gospel of Luke the teaching of Jesus regarding the presence and the future coming of the kingdom is faithfully reproduced. While Luke retains the hope of the future coming of the kingdom, he also stresses the presence of the kingdom as a reality in the ministry of Jesus.

---

[1] A. L. Moore, *The Parousia in the New Testament*, pp. 131–136, holds that "generation" means the contemporaries of Jesus in both Mark and Luke, but argues that it is the signs of the parousia which are imminent rather than the parousia itself.

[2] W. Ott, *Gebet und Heil*, pp. 32–34, 41 f., 63–66, argues that verse 8b is an addition to the parable, verse 8a is Lucan, and that the parable, which originally referred simply to the need for importunity in prayer, has been turned by Luke into an exhortation to remain faithful until the parousia. Ott, however, has not shown that verse 8b is inauthentic, even if it is out of context. For a defence of the whole section see J. Jeremias, *The Parables of Jesus*, pp. 153–157; C. Colpe, TDNT VIII, p. 435.

[3] A. N. Wilder, *Eschatology and Ethics in the Teaching of Jesus*, New York, 1950[2], p. 133: "The nearness of the Kingdom of Heaven, viewed both as promise and as menace, is the dominant sanction for righteousness. This dominant eschatological sanction is, however, a formal sanction only, secondary to, if closely related to, the essential sanction. The essential sanction for righteousness is the nature of God."

The Blessings of Salvation

In the previous section we have established that for Luke the kingdom of God was manifested as a present reality in the ministry of Jesus. We must now enquire more closely into the character of the kingdom as it is presented by Luke.

We have already observed that two of the main signs were the performance of works of healing and preaching to the poor. The miracles wrought by Jesus are described in traditional language as signs (Luke 11:16, 29; 23:8) and mighty works (Luke 10:13; 19:37), but no particular stress is laid on this. They were carried out as a result of divine power (Luke 4:14, 36; 5:17; 6:19; 8:46; 9:1), a power which Luke ascribes to the Holy Spirit (Luke 4:14; cf. 24:49; Acts 10:38). They were thus the token that God was at work. Luke, for example, comments that on a certain occasion the power of God was present to heal (Luke 5:17). When such wonders were performed, as for example at Nain, the impulse of the people was to glorify God and to claim that He had visited His people (Luke 7:16). Thus the activity of Jesus was evidence of God's saving power.

The obverse of this fact is that the activity of Jesus represented an attack upon Satan and the powers of evil. The exorcism of demons was a sign that the kingly power of God had come among men (Luke 11:20). Jesus regarded Himself as setting free those who had been taken captive by Satan (Luke 13:16), and later the task of Paul was to be defined in similar terms (Acts 26:18). Satan is presented as the foe of Jesus. At the outset of the ministry he tempted Jesus (Luke 4:1–13), and at the conclusion it is he who, according to Luke and John, instigated Judas to betray Him (Luke 22:3; John 13:2; cf. 6:70). He is pictured as warring against the disciples (Luke 22:31). But Jesus is triumphant over Satan. On the return of the Seventy from their mission with the news that even the demons were subject to them, Jesus replied with the climactic statement that He had beheld Satan falling like lightning from heaven, and went on to promise them power over all his might (Luke 10:17–19). It is hard to say precisely what Jesus had in mind when He spoke of the fall of Satan, but it is probable that the story of the fall of Lucifer (Isa. 14:12) provides imagery which Jesus used to depict the defeat of Satan.[1] The evidence, it will be observed, provides no substantiation for the view that the central part of the ministry of Jesus was Satan-free.[2]

[1] The defeat of the demons is the sign that their master, Satan, has been overcome. Probably Jesus is using metaphorical language rather than describing an ecstatic vision.

[2] Against H. Conzelmann, *Die Mitte der Zeit*, p. 175 (p. 188). There is no evidence that the present saying refers to the temptation narrative. Conzelmann's claim that Luke 11:17–23 refers not to the time of the ministry but to the time of the church is quite arbitrary.

Outstanding among the blessings brought by Jesus to men is the for-giveness of sins. This is probably hinted at in Luke 4:18f., and it was of course associated with the ministry of John the Baptist (Luke 3:3; cf. 1:77). In Mark Jesus speaks of the need for divine forgiveness (Mark 3:28; 4:12; 11:25), but only once does He Himself actually offer forgive-ness to a man (Mark 2:1–10). Luke takes over these references, and to them he adds the story of the sinful woman whom Jesus forgave (Luke 7:36–50). The structure of the story places the emphasis upon the fact that Jesus forgives, and thus (Luke 5:21) assumes the prerogative of God. Forgive-ness through Jesus is a characteristic blessing of salvation in Acts; Luke shows in the Gospel that such forgiveness was already being offered by Jesus during His earthly ministry.

The older studies of the Gospels used to draw out their individual characteristics, sometimes in a rather haphazard and non-theological manner. One such feature of Luke, to which attention has frequently been drawn, is his stress on the concern of Jesus for the outcasts and the univer-sality of the offer of salvation. At a later stage we must give further consideration to the problem of Jew and Gentile as it appeared to Luke, but for the moment we must observe that this particular feature of univer-sal salvation is amply attested in the Gospel.[1]

Within Israel itself it is a matter of plain historical fact, admitted by all, that Jesus ate with the tax-collectors and sinners, and thus demonstrated the love of God to them. This aspect of Jesus' ministry has been admirably surveyed in a brief monograph by O. Hofius who claims that the table fellowship of Jesus with such people was a sign of the extension of God's forgiveness to them and at the same time an anticipation of the eschato-logical meal in the kingdom of God.[2] What interests us is that Hofius draws much of his evidence from the Gospel of Luke. The concern of Jesus for tax-collectors and sinners is of course attested in Mark 2:13–17 (par. Luke 5:27–32) where Jesus calls Levi to be His disciple and then dines in his house with his friends and associates. But it is also brought out in Luke 15:1f. where it is reported of Jesus that He received sinners and ate with them. Similarly, Jesus made Zacchaeus come down from his tree and asked that He might be his guest. He announced that His coming to Zacchaeus meant salvation for his household, and stated that His purpose was to seek and to save the lost (Luke 19:1–10). Two things are apparent here. First, Jesus claimed that Zacchaeus was a son of Abraham, a member of the Jewish race, and therefore every bit as much entitled to salvation as the respectable members of society. The saying should not be regarded as setting a barrier between the sons of Abraham and non-Jews with regard

[1] See, for example, W. Barclay, *The First Three Gospels*, 1966, pp. 284–291.
[2] O. Hofius, *Jesu Tischgemeinschaft mit den Sündern*, Stuttgart, 1967.

to eligibility for the grace of God. It is rather an *ad hominem* statement addressed to Jews who reckoned sinful Jews as being beyond the reach of divine mercy and forgiveness, and it claims that such people can be forgiven by God and must be treated by their fellow-Jews as members of God's people. The second point is that Jesus describes His concern for such people as Zacchaeus in terms of the activity of a shepherd – more precisely, of the shepherd of the flock of God (Ezek. 34:16); it is the same picture as He uses in Luke 15:3-7 when He justifies His eating with sinners to the Pharisees. His task is to seek out the lost and to bring them back to God.

The thought of forgiveness also arises in the parable of the prodigal son (Luke 15:11-32); although the actual word does not occur in the parable, the theme is the pardoning love of God for the sinner, and so tellingly is the point made that New Testament scholarship cannot be content merely to chronicle the fact but must echo the hymn of Samuel Davies:

> Who is a pardoning God like Thee,
> Or who has grace so rich and free?[1]

The parable describes the divine compassion revealed in Jesus – for it is He who tells the parable and makes known the character of His Father to men. It is God who rejoices when the lost sheep is found (Luke 15:24).

It is no wonder, therefore, that in the Q material Jesus earns the obloquy of being "a glutton and a drunkard, a friend of tax collectors and sinners" (Luke 7:34). It is this thought, deeply embedded in the tradition, to which Luke gives expression.

The same thought is found in the parable of the great banquet (Luke 14:15-24) where the householder commands that the poor, maimed, blind and lame be brought in to his supper when the rich and respectable have failed to respond to the invitation; the list of people here closely resembles that in Luke 7:22, and shows that the invitation of such people to the banquet is a sign of the fulfilment of God's promised salvation. We may perhaps also see in the meals held by Jesus with such people an anticipation of the messianic banquet on earth.[2] Certainly the thought of table-fellowship is important in Luke, although in our opinion clear signs that this is a foretaste of the heavenly banquet are lacking; the nearest indication that we have is the way in which the thoughts of the guests at the dinner in the house of the Pharisee turn to the eschatological banquet (Luke 14:15).

If Jesus is presented as the friend of sinners, He is also in Luke the One who cares especially for women. The significance of this may easily escape

---

1 "Great God of Wonders," *Methodist Hymnbook*, No. 356.
2 O. Hofius, *op. cit.*, pp. 19f.

the modern reader to whom the equality of women with men, at least in the majority of countries, is normal experience. In the ancient world, however, it was otherwise, and it was not uncommon for women to be despised.[1] Luke has two stories peculiar to his Gospel in which Jesus brings forgiveness and healing to women (Luke 7:36–50; 13:10–17). He produces the story of Mary and Martha serving Jesus (Luke 10:38–42), and of the concern of Jesus for the widow of Nain in the loss of her son (Luke 7:11–17). It is he who tells us of Jesus' cure of Mary Magdalene from demon possession (Luke 8:2) and especially emphasizes the place of the women who helped Jesus in His travels (Luke 8:1–3). Luke alone has the story of the women who wept for Jesus on His way to Calvary (Luke 23:27–31).

Other touches from time to time indicate that Luke himself shared the compassion which he saw in Jesus. It is he who mentions that Jairus's daughter and the epileptic son were both only children (Luke 8:42; 9:38), whose illnesses would be all the more distressing to their parents.[2]

For Luke the compassion of Jesus did not stop at the boundary of Israel. Although it is well-attested historically that for the most part Jesus confined His mission to the Jews, Luke indicates that there was also a place for the Samaritans, the particular enemies of the Jews, in His concern.[3] Jesus was prepared to visit a Samaritan village, but when the people refused to welcome Him He rejected the suggestion of His disciples that He should take vengeance upon them (Luke 9:51–56). His healing miracles included the cure of a leper who was a Samaritan (Luke 17:11–19), and the hero of the parable of the Good Samaritan is implicitly praised above the Jewish priestly aristocracy (Luke 10:30–37).

Finally, in the Gospel the ultimate scope of the ministry is made plain. We have seen earlier that Luke 2:32 witnesses to the fact that the advent of Jesus was to bring light to the Gentiles. All three Synoptic Gospels use a quotation from Isa. 40:3 to describe the ministry of John the Baptist as the herald of the coming of the Lord; only Luke carries the quotation through to its triumphant conclusion, "And all flesh shall see the salvation of God" (Isa. 40:5; Luke 3:6; contrast Matt. 3:3; Mark 1:3). Luke also relates the story of the healing of the centurion's servant, and stresses the character of the centurion as a godly non-Jew who showed greater faith than could be found in Israel (Luke 7:1–9).[4] The vision of Gentiles in the kingdom is also taken over by Luke from tradition when he includes the saying of Jesus

---

[1] A. Oepke, TDNT I, pp. 776–789.

[2] The detail is generally regarded as a legendary addition by Luke; it may, however, spring from oral tradition.

[3] Luke may have regarded the Samaritans as "The Lost Sheep of the House of Israel" rather than as Gentiles: see J. Jervell, *Luke and the People of God*, Minneapolis, 1972 pp. 113–132.

[4] Matt. 8:1–13 stresses perhaps more the exclusion of unbelieving Israel from salvation.

about men coming from all over the world to eat in the kingdom of God (Luke 13:28f.). Finally, the risen Jesus commands His disciples that repentance and forgiveness should be preached in His name to all the Gentiles. (Luke 24:47). This motif should not be regarded as peculiar to Luke; it is present in both Mark (13:10) and Matt. (24:14; 28:19). The characteristic of Luke is rather that in various ways He has illustrated this theme from incidents in the ministry of Jesus and developed its significance in concrete terms.[1]

The Rich and the Poor

At the beginning of the Sermon on the Plain Luke sets out a series of blessings and woes in which Jesus promises to those who are needy and down-trodden that they will experience a reversal of their present unhappy lot, and threatens the rich and prosperous with the loss of their present possessions (Luke 6:20–26). The statement is all the more striking when it is compared with its counterpart in the Sermon on the Mount (Matt. 5:3–12) where the teaching is much more concerned with spiritual virtues and their reward.[2] It appears that Luke teaches that there will be a reversal of places in the kingdom of God.

This impression is confirmed by quite a number of passages of a similar nature. In the Magnificat Mary praises God because "He has put down the mighty from their thrones, and exalted those of low degree; he has filled the hungry with good things, and the rich he has sent empty away" (Luke 1:52f.). The parable of the rich fool likewise speaks of a reversal of conditions for a rich man (Luke 12:13–21), whereas the disciples are promised that God will care for them (Luke 12:22–34). Again, when giving teaching at dinner in the house of a Pharisee, Jesus told a parable which referred to a reversal of places at table between the more and the less honoured guests and advised guests to take the lowest places in order that they might be summoned to move up higher (Luke 14:7–11); this should not be regarded simply as a piece of good advice for guests (in the manner of Prov. 25:6f.), but is rather a parable concerning the messianic banquet. But the chief passage in which this theme occurs is the parable of the rich man and Lazarus. Here nothing is said about the piety or impiety of the rich man or indeed of Lazarus, but in the next world there takes place a reversal of roles: "Son, remember that you in your lifetime received your good things, and Lazarus in like manner evil things; but now he is comforted here, and you are in anguish" (Luke 16:25).

[1] W. Barclay, op. cit., pp. 28f., also cites the fact that Luke omits the material in Matt. 7:6; 10:5; 22:14; Mark 7:24–30, but would all these passages have been known to Luke?
[2] J. Dupont, Les Béatitudes, passim; H.-J. Degenhardt, Lukas – Evangelist der Armen, pp. 43–53.

From all this it might be concluded that Luke teaches a simple reversal of conditions. Wealth is a bad thing; it leads to loss in the next world, and therefore it is better to renounce it now in the hope of spiritual reward: "Sell your possessions and give alms" (Luke 12:33). It might almost appear that wealth in itself is evil, and that Luke attacks it, regardless of the spiritual condition of its owners.

This would be a hasty conclusion. Luke is not guilty of "Ebionitism."[1] Nor does he think of a simple reversal of conditions in the next world. The teaching about wealth and poverty must be set in its context. We have already seen that the "poor" to whom the gospel is preached are those who are needy and dependent upon God. By the same token the rich are those who are self-satisfied and feel no need of God. The key to the parable of the rich fool lies in the concluding verse: "So is he who lays up treasure for himself, and is not rich toward God" (Luke 12:21).[2] The fool is the man who feels no need of God; moreover, the stress on almsgiving (Luke 11:41; 12:33; cf. Acts 9:36; 10:2, 4, 31) as the positive attitude which is required of the wealthy indicates that the rich fool and others like him most probably ignored their obligation to the poor who surrounded them. It has been denied that this motif is present in the story of the rich man and Lazarus (contrast Luke 16:21 Vulgate: "et nemo illi dabat")[3] but this is incorrect. For at the end of the parable the rich man asks that a messenger be sent to his brothers so that instead of coming to the same place of torment, they may *repent* (Luke 16:28, 30). The implication is that the rich man himself had failed to repent. The parable is surely to be seen as an indictment of a social situation in which the rich man was content to be in luxury while the beggar at his door was in deprivation and misery. J. Dupont, who in our opinion exaggerates the thought of reversal of values in the next world, is surely right to detect a social concern on the part of Luke here, and to connect it with the social situation in which he wrote the Gospel.[4]

A further point to be noted is that the teaching about rich and poor is set in a wider context. The idea of reversal of situation is not confined to wealth and poverty. In the beatitudes and woes Luke has retained the sayings about persecution (Luke 6:22f., 26). Although J. Dupont has tried

---

[1] So rightly H. Conzelmann, *op. cit.*, p. 218 (p. 233).

[2] Though omitted by the western text, the verse is undoubtedly original. Many scholars regard it as a Lucan addition (J. M. Creed, *op. cit.*, p. 173; E. Klostermann, *op. cit.*, p. 137; J. Jeremias, *The Parables of Jesus*, p. 106). Against Jeremias, the verse is not a moralizing addition; the parable is concerned with the danger of riches blinding a man to the approach of death or judgment, and the verse expresses this fact. H.-J. Degenhardt, *op. cit.*, pp. 78 f., holds that the verse is pre-Lucan.

[3] J. Dupont, *op. cit.*, pp. 193–210. Contra: J. Jeremias, *op. cit.*, p. 185; E. Bammel, TDNT VI, p. 906.

[4] J. Dupont, *op. cit.*, pp. 239–244. But see E. Bammel, *op. cit.*, p. 907.

to suggest that it is the situation of persecution and oppression in itself (as contrasted with the situation of enjoying popular favour) which is meant,[1] he is not able to explain away the words "for the sake of the Son of man" in the beatitude; these words prove plainly enough that it is the persecuted disciple who is meant.

We must also take into account the experience of the early church. The Jews knew well enough that it was the rich and powerful who were their oppressors. In the same way the Epistle of James shows that the rich were the persecutors of the Christians (Jam. 2:6f.), and the early church generally was aware of the great temptation caused by riches (1 Tim. 6:9f., 17–19).[2] It may, therefore, be suggested that often the use of the word "rich" carries with itself the notion of exposure to temptation and even of actual wickedness.

This is proved finally by the parable of the Pharisee and the tax-collector, which is peculiar to Luke (Luke 18:10–14). The parable is directed to the self-righteous who despise other men, but it is significant that one of the main actors, the Pharisee, belonged to a group whom Luke expressly designates as avaricious people, full of self-justification (Luke 16:14f.).[3] But the contrast in the parable is not between riches and poverty; it is not the poor man who is commended, for we may certainly assume that the tax-collector was not poor. Rather the contrast is between legal righteousness and sinfulness, and it is the sinner who is justified, not the righteous person. This is the real paradox presented in Luke, and the explanation of it lies in the difference between the self-righteousness of the Pharisee and the utter dependence upon God's mercy by the tax-collector. It is thus the attitude towards God which matters, and it is in this context that the teaching on wealth and poverty must be seen. Luke does not present poverty as an ideal in itself, nor wealth as intrinsically evil. When his teaching on wealth and poverty is seen in the context of the Gospel as a whole, the underlying attitude to God is what really matters. Outwardly, the Pharisee with his zeal for the law was on the same place as Cornelius who gave much in alms (Acts 10:2); the difference lay in the dependence of the latter upon God, expressed in his constant prayer.

We took up this problem of the rich and the poor in Luke in connexion with our discussion of the blessings of salvation. The conclusion to which we have come does not prejudice in any way the findings of the previous section where the universality of salvation was affirmed. A new feature

[1] J. Dupont, *op. cit.*, pp. 230–239.
[2] F. Hauck, TDNT VI, pp. 318–332; M. Dibelius, *Der Brief des Jakobus*, Göttingen, 1957⁹, pp. 37–44 (with the criticism by E. Percy, *Die Botschaft Jesu*, pp. 70–73).
[3] T. W. Manson, *The Sayings of Jesus*, pp. 295f., 350, holds that the description fits the Sadducees rather than the Pharisees. But the avarice of the Pharisees is attested by T. Menahoth 13:22 (533) (SB I, p. 937).

has appeared, however, with regard to the character of the blessings. Although our previous discussion has established that for Luke "now" is the era of salvation and the associated blessings, the reversal of conditions for the rich and the poor is associated with the future. In the Beatitudes it is those who suffer *now* who will be recompensed *then*. The afflicted on earth will have treasure in heaven. Those who are self-satisfied now will experience future deprivation. This is an important fact. It should not be explained simply as due to the presence of two points of view in the Gospels, deriving from the prophetic and wisdom traditions, the one promising present bliss and the other promising future blessings.[1] Rather, it serves to indicate how present and future are closely tied together in the Gospels. Already in the time of Jesus' ministry the blessings of the kingdom are there to be experienced by the disciples, and they include a measure of release from physical affliction; but along with blessing Jesus also envisaged persecution and oppression for the disciples, and the removal of these belongs to the final coming of the kingdom. There is thus a tension in the experience of the disciples between what is realized and what is still future in the way of blessing. It is a tension which Luke has inherited from the tradition: "There is no one who has left house or wife or brothers or parents or children, for the sake of the kingdom of God, who will not receive manifold more in this time, and in the age to come eternal life" (Luke 18:29f.).

EXCURSUS

THE COURSE OF JESUS' MINISTRY IN LUKE

In the preceding chapter we have considered the general character of the salvation brought by Jesus. We saw how great importance is attached to the preaching of the gospel by Jesus, and that the message of the kingdom is taken up into it. Both the present blessings of the kingdom and those associated with its future consummation find their place in the message. Through the preaching and the accompanying mighty works Jesus set men and women of all types free from the power of Satan.

We must now digress from our main theme to examine the form which was taken by the ministry of Jesus and see how Luke charts its course. The historical presentation in Luke differs from that in the other Gospels: what factors have governed the presentation? It will be our task to examine especially the way in which H. Conzelmann has claimed that Luke has rewritten the story of Jesus to bring out various salvation-historical points, and to suggest that his picture needs considerable

---

[1] J. Dupont, *op. cit.*, pp. 210–213.

qualification. In other words, the presentation of the ministry by Luke is not an argument against our view that Luke's purpose was to present the gospel of salvation rather than a particular view of salvation-history.

Jesus and John the Baptist

Two points of view regarding John the Baptist's place in Luke may be found in recent scholarship. H. Conzelmann argues that Luke has sharply separated the ministry of John from that of Jesus both geographically and historically, so that John no longer appears as the forerunner of Jesus and the inaugurator of the era of salvation; he is rather the last of the Old Testament prophets who brings the epoch of the Law and the Prophets to its conclusion. Geographically, he belongs to the Jordan, a region which Jesus does not enter. Historically, his ministry is given the appearance of terminating before that of Jesus, and as far as possible the historical link between John and Jesus at the baptism of the latter is played down (cf. Luke 3:19-20/21-22). Theologically, he is no longer presented in the role of Elijah, the eschatological forerunner of the Lord, but is simply a prophet excluded from the era of salvation: the point is summed up in Luke 16:16: "The law and the prophets were until John; since then the kingdom of God is preached, and every one enters it violently."[1]

On the other hand, W. Wink in his recent redactional study of the place of John the Baptist in the Gospels comes to different conclusions. While he agrees that Luke does not view John as the eschatological Elijah, he finds reason to question the rest of Conzelmann's case. He shows that the geographical argument propounded by Conzelmann will not stand; both John and Jesus are associated with the wilderness, and the locales of both of them are largely prescribed by tradition. Nor will the theological separation stand investigation. Wink propounds the view that Luke 16:16 dates the beginning of the new era from the time of John's manifestation, and claims that other evidence supports this view of the text itself. The note of fulfilment in Luke 3:1-7 shows that here something important is beginning, and in Acts 1:22; 10:36-43 and 13:23-25 this view of John is confirmed. His ministry is separated both from the period of promise in Old Testament times and from the ministry of Jesus, and is best regarded as a period of preparation within the second main era of history (the era of fulfilment). The importance of John is further seen in Luke 7:26 where he is declared to be more than a prophet.

In a second main section of his study Wink examines the birth narrative, which Conzelmann had precluded from discussion; he finds no evidence

[1] H. Conzelmann, *Die Mitte der Zeit*, pp. 12-21, 92-94, 103 (pp. 18-27, 101 f., 112).

there for a Baptist community which preserved legends and hymns about John, and claims that the stories of John and Jesus grew up together in Christian circles. He discusses whether John is presented in a messianic role, but is unwilling to find in him more than a prophet on the basis of the scanty evidence; the view that he was regarded as the priestly Messiah alongside Jesus as the Messiah of David falls short of proof.

In a brief, third section Wink finally argues that Luke did not regard the disciples of John as rivals to the Christian church; he does not conduct polemic against them.[1]

There can be little doubt which of these two presentations is to be preferred. It is safe to say that Conzelmann could not have come to his estimate of John if he had taken the birth narrative into account, and we have already seen that he has no justification for bracketing it off as irrelevant to the study of Lucan theology. From a linguistic point of view the crucial text Luke 16:16 could be taken in Conzelmann's sense; that is to say, "until John" (μέχρι Ἰωάννου) could be inclusive, and "from then" (ἀπὸ τότε) could be exclusive.[2] But it is equally possible to understand the latter phrase in an inclusive sense,[3] and this sense is the one required in view of other considerations. In particular, Luke 3:18 is relevant here: the use of εὐαγγελίζομαι ("to preach good news") here by Luke himself to describe John's preaching would be a piece of gross carelessness if in Luke 16:16 he had intended to exclude him from the era of the preaching of the gospel.[4]

We must therefore accept Wink's view of the place of John as occupying a place in the era of fulfilment, yet one which partakes of the nature of preparation. Perhaps, however, a better form of expression to clarify the position would be to say that John is a bridge between the old and the new eras.[5] He belongs to both, but essentially to the new one since he is the immediate forerunner of the Messiah. He is portrayed both as a prophet and as the first preacher of the gospel.[6]

---

[1] W. Wink, *John the Baptist in the Gospel Tradition*, Cambridge, 1968, pp. 42–86.

[2] G. Schrenk, TDNT I, pp. 609–613; E. E. Ellis, *The Gospel of Luke*, p. 204.

[3] K. Chamblin, "John the Baptist and The Kingdom of God," Tyn. B 15, October, 1964, pp. 10–16. Cf. G. Braumann, "Das Mittel der Zeit," ZNW 54, 1963, pp. 117–145; G. Strecker, *Der Weg der Gerechtigkeit*, p. 91 n. 1.

[4] Cf. W. Wink, *op. cit.*, pp. 52f. His argument is not refuted by the discussion in P. Stuhlmacher, *Das paulinische Evangelium*.

[5] Some support for thinking that Luke saw John in this way may be drawn from the manner in which Luke uses bridge-passages in the Gospel; see, for example, Luke 19:11–27, which has been grouped by different exegetes with the preceding and following sections; it may be best to think of it as belonging to both.

[6] The traditional passage in Luke 7:26f. teaches that John is more than a prophet and identifies him with the eschatological messenger of Malachi 3:1; Luke has taken over this tradition unaltered. The meaning of Luke 7:28 is uncertain; cf. R. Schnackenburg, *God's Rule and*

How, then, is his role to be explained? Both Conzelmann and Wink draw attention to the playing down of the Elijah typology, and the latter draws attention to a number of passages in which it is applied to Jesus instead. Yet it must be said that, while there is no explicit identification of Jesus as an Elijah-like figure, Luke does take this step with John in 1:17 and 76. He says as clearly as possible that John is to do the task of Elijah. Why then has he omitted the material found in Mark 1:6 and 9:9-13 which identifies John with Elijah? We suggest that the answer may be that Luke was unwilling to make a direct identification of John with Elijah in a literal manner. He took the prophecy of Malachi to mean the coming of a person like Elijah, not of Elijah himself. In the context of the transfiguration story in which Elijah appears he may have felt it incongruous to identify Elijah with John; at the same time he may have regarded the passages already cited from the birth narrative as an adequate equivalent for this difficult pericope in Mark. As for the description of John's Elijah-like clothing in Mark 1:6, the awkwardness of this verse is seen in the fact that Matthew has transposed its position (Matt. 3:4); Luke has in fact omitted the whole of Mark 1:5f. and transposed 1:7f., perhaps as a result of following a different source. We conclude, therefore, that Luke does retain the identification of John with Elijah, freed from any literalistic misunderstanding. At the same time, he is free to use Elijah-typology to describe the ministry of Jesus without any sense of logical impropriety.

If these conclusions are sound, it follows that for Luke the era of salvation begins with the announcement of the births of John and Jesus. The birth narrative indicates that the era of fulfilment has begun. Here Luke has a new emphasis which is not shared by the other Gospels; Matthew's birth narrative cannot be said to show the same motif. But this period is introductory. Luke knows and accepts the tradition that the ministry of Jesus, beginning from Galilee after the baptism preached by John (Acts 10:37), is *the* eschatological event. The preparation, however, belongs inextricably to the ministry proper, since it is already the era of fulfilment in which good news is announced and the Saviour is born.

Kingdom, pp. 132-134. The saying can hardly mean that John is excluded from the future kingdom, for this would conflict with the principle in Luke 13:28 par. Matt. 8:11. Its point is probably the same as in Luke 10:17-20, where the disciples are told that a place in heaven is worth more than authority over the demons; so possession of a place in the kingdom is more important than being the greatest of the prophets. The saying is of a kind frequent in the Gospels where men are exhorted not to speculate or to boast, but to make sure that they themselves enter the kingdom (cf. Luke 13:23f.); hence the question whether John is or is not in the kingdom is not raised.

The Way of Jesus

Luke's account of the ministry of Jesus differs from that found in Mark. In the earlier Gospel the ministry is divided geographically between Galilee, Judaea and Jerusalem. In the opinion of Conzelmann we are to think basically of a two-stage ministry divided between Galilee and Jerusalem, and this distinction is eschatological in character.[1] A similar view is taken by W. Marxsen in his study of Mark, but he has to admit that the boundary between the two parts is uncertain.[2] In reality the situation is probably much more complicated. The climax of the Galilean ministry comes in the scene at Caesarea Philippi, but this is situated well within the Galilean section. The teaching about the passion, which belongs to the Jerusalem motif, comes as early as chapter 8, and there may be earlier allusions. In other words, a simple thematic distinction between the two parts of the Gospel is not to be found. Again, the tendency of recent scholarship has been to give a more complicated analysis of the contents of Mark, and while all commentators find a break between chapters 10 and 11 at the entry to Jerusalem, not all of them give the impression that this is the major caesura in the Gospel.[3] Finally, the geography of the first half of the Gospel, while centred on Galilee, is not confined to it, so much so that W. G. Kümmel rather woodenly entitles the section 6:1–9:50 "Jesus' journeyings inside and outside of Galilee."[4] From all this it emerges that the precise structure of Mark is an open question, and that it is disputable whether geography is the main factor involved.

Nevertheless, one geographical factor is certain. After the transfiguration, which Mark evidently locates in the area of Caesarea Philippi, Jesus and His disciples journey secretly through Galilee and He has no more dealings with the crowds (Mark 9:30–50). They then depart from Galilee and go to Judaea and Peraea where Jesus taught the crowds and instructed His disciples. Their goal is Jerusalem (Mark 10:32, cf. 17) and they eventually reach Jericho in the course of their journey (Mark 10:52) from where they approach Jerusalem (Mark 11:1). Chapter 10 thus describes a journey from Galilee to Jerusalem; several incidental notices convey the

---

[1] H. Conzelmann, "Zur Lukas-Analyse," ZTK 49, 1952, pp. 16–33, especially pp. 19, 25.

[2] W. Marxsen, *Der Evangelist Markus*, Gottingen, 1959², p. 34.

[3] Most commentators divide up the Gospel into half a dozen or more major sections, rather than into two or three major sections each with further subdivisions. A number of scholars make 8:27–10:52 into such a major section (E. Lohmeyer, *Das Evangelium nach Markus*, Gottingen, 1959¹⁵; V. Taylor, *The Gospel according to St Mark*, 1953; C. E. B. Cranfield, *St Mark*, Cambridge, 1963²; D. E. Nineham, *Saint Mark*, 1963; E. Schweizer, *Das Evangelium nach Markus* (NTD) Göttingen, 1967); the more the independent character of this section is emphasized, the less significant does the break at 10:52/11:1 become. The theme of the path to suffering takes on major proportions in Mark.

[4] W. G. Kümmel, *Introduction to the New Testament*, 1966, p. 61.

impression of a journey. But the individual pericopes are not necessarily tied into this context by their internal characteristics (Mark 10:2–12, 13–16, 35–45), and it may be argued that their original historical placing could have been otherwise. In any case, it is certain that the motif of a journey to Jerusalem is consciously present for Mark, and that he has filled it out at least to the extent of a chapter.

In Luke this same structure appears, but there are differences. If we may ignore certain differences of detail in the Galilean ministry,[1] the most important arise from the place assigned to the journey of Jesus from Galilee and the destination. These must be considered separately.

In Luke the journey of Jesus has expanded to fill the whole of the section 9:51–19:10; the change of theme at 19:10 suggests that the end of the section should be seen here rather than at 19:27, but the precise point of division is unimportant. The section runs to 390 verses, approximately one third of the entire Gospel. The contents of the section are very varied, mostly from non-Marcan material, and it cannot be said that the motif of a journey is present in many of them.

The existence of this section in Luke is hard to explain, and it is doubtful

[1] These differences are mainly concerned with a certain stylizing of the geographical references. Conzelmann argues that natural features (mountain, sea and plain) are mythicized and the concept of "the Holy Land" is developed; Jesus' activity is confined to Galilee-Judaea.

While some interesting points are made here, there is much eisegesis. Thus it is wrong to claim that the plain has special significance as a place of meeting with the crowds (*Die Mitte der Zeit*, p. 38 (p. 44)), when the word occurs but once in Luke (6:17; quite fanciful is the suggestion of J. Manek, "On the Mount – on the Plain," Nov. T 9, 1967, pp. 124–131: since "neither mountain nor sea in Luke's expectation will share in the coming age, where only level ground will exist," the sermon could not be located on a mountain). Rather, Luke's point may be the negative one that the mountain is not a place where the crowds meet Jesus but a place where He seeks solitude and reveals Himself to His disciples. Even this statement, however, must not be exaggerated: Luke does not go beyond Mark in this respect, for he does not introduce the mountain into narrative by himself (for Luke 6:12 cf. Mark 6:46). On the other hand, W. Foerster, TDNT V, pp. 475–487, is possibly too drastic in excluding all symbolical reference from the word.

Conzelmann has correctly drawn attention to the way in which the sea (i.e. Galilee), so frequently mentioned in Mark, disappears in Luke except as a place of epiphany and as the abode of demons. Even here, however, a correct observation is spoiled by extravagant assertions: the calling of Levi is removed from the seaside, for "Evidently no normal human activity takes place by the lake, therefore there are no tax-gatherers there" (*op. cit.*, p. 37 (p. 44)).

Conzelmann's claim that Jesus confines Himself to Galilee–Judaea (except for the specific journey to the country of the Gerasenes) loses much of its force when people from outside this area come to hear Jesus (Luke 6:17). His case is also weakened by the contact of Jesus with Samaritans and the fact that Jesus was willing to enter Samaria (Luke 9:52; 17:11). Conzelmann's claim that it is not Galilee but the Galileans who are significant for Luke (*op. cit.*, p. 35 (p. 41)) needs to be extended in scope.

On Galilee and Judaea see our earlier discussion. Conzelmann's suggestion (*ibid.*) that Judaea has significance as a locality for Luke is quite false; nowhere in Luke is the word Judaea used theologically. It is Jerusalem (or, according to Conzelmann, the temple), if anywhere, which is significant.

whether the various recent studies of it have adequately accounted for its nature.[1] For Conzelmann the section is the creation of Luke himself who has transformed Mark's two eschatological phases into a three-stage historical account of the ministry of Jesus.[2] He finds the theological motivation for the account in christology: "Jesus' awareness that He must suffer is expressed in terms of the journey ... The purpose of the journey is not merely to bring about the inevitable change of place, in order to reach the place of suffering; it is also in itself something of divine appointment."[3] Again, the journey "is primarily symbolical, and is meant to express the changed emphasis in Jesus' ministry. In particular it expresses Jesus' awareness that he must suffer ... The original, apologetic demonstration that the Passion is according to plan is expanded on a grand scale into a picture of the whole activity of Jesus."[4]

It seems to us that, while there is some truth in this suggestion, it is not an adequate explanation of the phenomena. It must be insisted, first of all, that the traditional material should be analysed somewhat differently. Conzelmann has argued that the journey material available to Luke was meagre, and finds in this an argument for Lucan redaction.[5] He ignores the fact that specific journey material in Mark is also meagre, and yet Mark emphasizes the idea of the journey. This can only mean that the idea of the journey was firmly embedded in the tradition; with C. H. Dodd we are inclined to believe that there was a traditional outline of the ministry of Jesus,[6] and that this outline included the journey. Hence Luke did not invent the journey, nor, we may add, the fact that it was a significant journey. Already in Mark the journey is of twofold significance. It is the path to martyrdom for Jesus (Mark 10:32f.), and thus it is brought into connexion with the divinely appointed destiny of the Son of man. It is also significant for the disciples, since Mark implies that they must be prepared to travel the same way as Jesus (Mark 10:17, 52). It is this same significance which we find in Luke. Like Mark he sees the journey as the path to the passion, and he brings out the point that it is divinely ordained (Luke 13:33). Jesus "sets his face" to go to Jerusalem, a phrase which indicates firm resolve to do something unpleasant. From the outset the goal of the jour-

---

[1] See the literature cited above, p. 66 n.2.
[2] H. Conzelmann, "Zur Lukas Analyse," pp. 19, 25.
[3] H. Conzelmann, *Die Mitte der Zeit*, pp. 57, 60 (pp. 65, 68); see the whole section, pp. 53–66 (pp. 60–73).
[4] *Ibid.*, p. 184 (p. 197). Conzelmann does allow that the section has some significance as a journey for the disciples in which Jesus teaches them about discipleship (*op. cit.*, p. 59 (not in English translation)).
[5] *Ibid.*, p. 54 (p. 62).
[6] C. H. Dodd, "The Framework of the Gospel Narrative," Exp. T 43, 1931–32, pp. 396–400 (reprinted in *New Testament Studies*, Manchester, 1953, pp. 1–11); cf. *Historical Tradition in the Fourth Gospel*, p. 233 n. 2.

ney is His passion and resurrection (Luke 9:51).[1] It is strange that Luke has not taken over Mark's references to the "way" in connexion with discipleship,[2] but the motif is to be found in Luke 9:57 where a would-be disciple offers to accompany Him.[3]

E. E. Ellis has observed that it is not the journey as such which is of interest to Luke. Jesus does not suddenly become a traveller at Luke 9:51; He has been on the move from 4:42 onwards.[4] This point is in effect allowed by Conzelmann who admits that Jesus still travels in the same area as at first, only in a different manner.[5] In other words, it would be a more precise statement of the situation to say that from 9:51 onwards Jerusalem is continually in sight as the goal of Jesus' journeyings.

We have already seen that the journey motif was present in Mark, and have thus negated the suggestion that it is basically a creation by Luke himself.[6] It is worth noticing that the motif was also present in Luke's other sources. The content of Luke 9:53 which speaks of Jesus journeying through Samaria to Jerusalem may well be traditional.[7] The concept of the homelessness of Jesus, expressed in the Q saying Luke 9:58, fits in with the travel motif, and it may be legitimate to see in this saying an allusion to the impending passion also.[8] More importance must be attached to the saying in Luke 13:31-33 which refers to Jesus continuing His activity undeterred by fear of Herod, since the death of a prophet must take place in Jerusalem rather than elsewhere. The saying is unquestionably traditional; it speaks not so much of a journey to Jerusalem, as of a ministry which will be brought to its end in Jerusalem.

The motif of travel is accordingly present in various traditional items in the Q and L material. But we have already seen that this material was probably formed into a unity before it was incorporated in the present Gospel. We cannot be certain whether at this stage the material spoke of a single journey to Jerusalem being undertaken by Jesus, but we can be sure that some parts of the material at least were cast in the form of a journey. The last piece of QL material before the journey begins in the present form of Luke at 9:51ff. is to be found at Luke 8:1-3, a passage

---

[1] On ἀνάλημψις see G. Delling, TDNT IV, pp. 7-9. But his restriction of the meaning of the word to the death of Jesus with only a possible reference to His "taking up" or "taking back" to God seems unduly narrow. The Elijah typology in the context suggests that the ascension is included; the whole event of the passion and resurrection is probably involved.

[2] Mark 10:17, 52.

[3] The point is noted, but not stressed by H. Conzelmann, *op. cit.*, p. 59 (not in English translation).

[4] E. E. Ellis, *The Gospel of Luke*, pp. 148f.

[5] H. Conzelmann, *op. cit.*, p. 57 (p. 65).

[6] Contra: W. C. Robinson, Jr., "The Theological Context for Interpreting Luke's Travel Narrative," JBL 79, 1960, pp. 20-31.

[7] H. Conzelmann, *op. cit.*, pp. 58f. (pp. 65f.).

[8] R. H. Fuller, *The Mission and Achievement of Jesus*, 1954, pp. 104f.

which describes how Jesus went through the cities and villages preaching with the Twelve and the women. Then at Luke 9:52 it is related how He came to a particular Samaritan village and was not received there. It is a fair inference that the latter passage is the continuation of the former in Luke's source.[1] This means that the motif of a journey was originally present in the structure of the source. In the original form of the source the journey may not have been the last journey to Jerusalem. Luke has probably placed the theme of Jerusalem as a kind of motto over the whole section.

But the extent of this editorial work by Luke should not be exaggerated. The actual references to Jerusalem in the travel narrative are few, and they are all found in contexts in which the tradition implied that Jesus was journeying to Jerusalem. Thus the references in Luke 9:51, 53 and 17:11 are all linked to the journeyings of Jesus in or near Samaria, and the assumption in each case is surely that a Jew would not be in this area unless he was travelling from Galilee to Judaea (or vice versa); similarly, the reference in Luke 13:22 is added to prepare the way for the sayings in Luke 13:31-35 where Jesus anticipates martyrdom in Jerusalem. The final reference in Luke 18:31 comes from Mark and is placed shortly before the arrival in Jericho. Luke has used these markers to indicate that from the first prediction of the passion onwards (Luke 9:22) Jesus was conscious of the shadow of Jerusalem hanging over His ministry and had His ultimate destination in view. His consciousness of the path of suffering is expressed more clearly in the editing than in the tradition utilized.

What is new in this section is, then, the stress on Jerusalem as the ultimate goal of Jesus, the place where He must suffer. Earlier in the Gospel the same consciousness of rejection is to be found, a fact especially stressed by F. Schütz who has assembled the evidence and shown that the thought of suffering and rejection runs throughout the Gospel.[2] What we find in the "journey" section is a heightened consciousness of suffering on the part of Jesus.

Finally, we must observe that the actual content of the section bears little relationship to the suffering of Jesus. The traditional material which is incorporated here covers a wide range of other themes, and it may be argued that Luke was too much of an artist to have filled up this section with such diverse material if his main theme was the situation of Jesus Himself. It is in fact extraordinarily difficult to trace clearly the themes which run through this section, but the most convincing suggestion is that of B. Reicke, who is followed by E. E. Ellis; the main theme of the section is the teaching of Jesus, and it alternates between the instruction of the

[1] W. Grundmann, *Das Evangelium nach Lukas*, p. 173.
[2] F. Schütz, *Der leidende Christus.*

disciples and discussion with the opponents.[1] This point is important, because it shows that Luke is not concerned here simply with the character of discipleship, as was the case in the corresponding section in Mark. The polemic against the Pharisees and the justification of the preaching of the gospel to the outcasts do not fit into Mark's pattern. The themes rather fit into Luke's broader concept of salvation, and the material stresses both the grace of God and the need for a radical response on the part of the hearers. It is significant that the term "way" (ὁδός), which is a characteristic feature of the vocabulary of Acts does not figure in this section to describe the path of Jesus or the life of the disciples, and this must raise doubts as to how far Luke regarded the journey of Jesus which forms the framework of the section as a pattern for the disciples to follow in daily life.[2]

We need not go more deeply into the structure and content of the so-called journey section for our present purpose. The conclusion which has emerged is that a variety of themes run through this section, and that the rejection and suffering of Jesus at Jerusalem is not the controlling factor. Rather the theme is the broader one of salvation, and within this theme Luke gathers together material on a number of topics to give a picture of the Jesus, who will be rejected by the Jews, preaching and defending the gospel and instructing His disciples.

Jerusalem and the Passion

The final stage in the career of Jesus is His entry to Jerusalem, His death and resurrection. We must enquire what theological significance is ascribed to this stage within the context of Luke's theme of salvation. H. Conzelmann has again suggested that Luke has used geography in a symbolical manner to express theological statements. We must accordingly test the validity of his conclusions.

Conzelmann opens his discussion by arguing that Luke is concerned to deny that Jerusalem will be the place of the parousia (Luke 19:11).[3] But this is a misconception. Luke does not say anything here about *where* the parousia will take place, only about *when* it will do so. His point is that the expectation of the disciples that it would be the denouement of the journey to Jerusalem was mistaken. It is possible that there is an implicit correction of the view which may have been held by some members of the early church, namely that the resurrection itself was the final coming of

[1] B. Reicke, "Instruction and Discussion in the Travel Narrative," SE I, 1959, pp. 206–216; E. E. Ellis, *op. cit.*, pp. 146f. Cf. V. Taylor, *Behind the Third Gospel*, pp. 151–159.

[2] *Pace* W. C. Robinson, *op. cit.*

[3] H. Conzelmann, *op. cit.*, p. 67 (p. 74); on Jerusalem in general see pp. 66–86, 124–127 (pp. 73–94, 132–135): cf. E. Lohse, TDNT VII, pp. 331f., 335f.

the kingdom.[1] However, the main point to be noted at the outset is that Luke is not here affirming or denying any particular theological significance of Jerusalem in connexion with the parousia.

Second, Conzelmann notes positively the significance of the temple for Luke in the concluding ministry of Jesus. In Luke's view Jesus does not enter Jerusalem itself until the Last Supper; previous to the Supper He merely goes into the temple by means of an outside gate and thus avoids entering the city as such.[2] The temple is the scene of His teaching, and the city of Jerusalem is merely the place of His death. The Mount of Olives takes on symbolical significance as "the mountain" in the passion story, while Bethany and the anointing scene disappear from view.[3] At the same time the eschatological significance of the Entry and the cleansing of the temple is lost, and these events become the prelude to the passion and the preparation of the temple for Jesus' ministry there. The temple is the place where Jesus teaches, and the eschatological discourse is transferred there from the Mount of Olives.[4]

This fits in with the importance given to the temple earlier in the Gospel. At the beginning of the Gospel the birth narratives were closely associated with the temple. Jesus was presented in the temple, and His significance as the Saviour was there revealed to Simeon and Anna. As a boy He claimed that it was His Father's house where He must stay. Now the temple becomes the place where He teaches the people on the eve of His passion, and afterwards His disciples continued to pray and to preach there (Luke 24:52f.).

Some of the details here are doubtful,[5] but of the importance assigned to the temple there can be no doubt. Two points must be made by way of correction and supplement. The first is that Conzelmann's dissociation of the temple from Jerusalem is misleading. It would be a more accurate representation of the situation to say that for Luke the important place *in*

[1] H.-W. Bartsch, "Early Christian Eschatology in the Synoptic Gospels," NTS 11, 1964–65, pp. 387–397. It is unlikely, however, that the misunderstanding was quite so widespread as Bartsch thinks, or that its influence may be traced so widely in the New Testament. See further H.-W. Bartsch, *Wachet aber zu jeder Zeit*, Hamburg-Bergstedt, 1963; C. H. Talbert, "The Redaction Critical Quest for Luke the Theologian," in D. G. Miller (ed.), *Jesus and Man's Hope*, Vol. 1, pp. 171–222.

[2] H. Conzelmann, *op. cit.*, p. 68 (p. 75).

[3] *Ibid.*, p. 69 (p. 76).   [4] *Ibid.*, p. 116 (p. 125).

[5] A major difficulty is the mention of Bethany in 24:50–53. Conzelmann's claim that this is a later addition to the Gospel is untenable; the evidence of language and style favours Lucan authorship. The suggestion that the Mount of Olives has become the symbolical mountain of the passion narrative rests on the evidence of Acts 1:12; the location of the prayer of Jesus on the Mount rather than at Gethsemane reflects Mark 14:26. The encampment of Jesus at the Mount of Olives may mean that He prayed there, but it more probably reflects historical fact – the encampment of passover pilgrims outside the overcrowded city of Jerusalem (J. Jeremias, *The Eucharistic Words of Jesus*, p. 42). This detail, and the absence of reference to Bethany probably reflect the use of a non-Marcan tradition. It is not clear whether Mark and Luke have the same place of lodging in mind.

Jerusalem is the temple. The temple symbolizes Jerusalem in its religious aspect. Luke does not separate the temple from Jerusalem itself because he is not primarily interested in the theology of topography. On the contrary Luke's interest is primarily in people. Thus the teaching of Jesus in the temple is given to the people of Jerusalem. The significance of Jerusalem as the place of the crucifixion is that there the rulers of the Jews are to be found. The guilt of Jerusalem is the guilt of its people who refused to respond to the message. Jerusalem did not recognize the time of its visitation, and this visitation was precisely the presence of Jesus in the temple (Luke 19:44).[1] Hence it was entirely fitting that the doom of Jerusalem should be spoken in the temple (Luke 21).

The reason for this stress on Jerusalem and the temple lies in its presence in the tradition which Luke inherited. The sayings which he inherited from Marcan (Luke 21) and non-Marcan material (Luke 13:34f.) were sufficient testimony to the fate that awaited Jerusalem. Moreover, it was a simple fact of history that Jerusalem was the place where Jesus died. The significant place assigned to the temple is also traditional; the teaching of Jesus in the temple and His prophecies of its destruction were well-established in the tradition. It is therefore correct to see the temple as the focal point of the rejection of Jesus by the Jews.

The third question is that of the resurrection appearances. Luke locates these in and around Jerusalem. He records no appearances in Galilee, and he omits the sayings found in Mark which point in this direction (Mark 14:28; 16:7). There is a historical problem here which has not yet been satisfactorily cleared up. It would seem certain that there were traditions of resurrection appearances in both Galilee and Jerusalem. Luke stresses the fact that it is the Galilean disciples who are the witnesses of the Jerusalem appearances (Acts 1:11; 13:31).[2] Luke's treatment of the appearances is to some extent stylized, since he gives the impression in the Gospel that the appearances were confined to Easter Sunday; Acts, however, makes it quite clear that he knew of a longer period of appearances (Acts 1:3; 13:31). The conclusion seems likely that since the earliest appearances were in Jerusalem and since the descent of the Spirit was

---

[1] Conzelmann's view that for Luke Jesus did not enter Jerusalem before the Last Supper, but confined Himself to the temple, is possible, but improbable. Conzelmann has not shown *why* Jesus should not enter Jerusalem; Luke 13:34f. and various pieces of evidence in John show that He had been in Jerusalem on earlier occasions, and it is unlikely that Luke would contradict this. Nor is any evidence produced to show that Luke or his readers would regard the temple as distinct from Jerusalem and able to be entered without passing through the city (Acts 3:1ff. is no proof). It is true that Luke omits Mark's repeated statements about Jesus entering Jerusalem (Mark 11:11, 15, 27), but his omission of these is connected with his avoidance of Mark's Jerusalem-Bethany scheme in preference for his own.

[2] The form of the saying in Luke 24:6 (contrast Mark 16:7) indicates that it is the disciples who heard the prophecies in Galilee who are now the witnesses of their fulfilment in Jerusalem.

firmly anchored at Jerusalem, Luke has endeavoured to gain a stylistic unity for his narrative by omitting any story of the disciples' journey to Galilee and their return to Jerusalem.

The conclusions of this treatment of the progress of the ministry of Jesus from the time of John the Baptist to the resurrection contribute somewhat indirectly to our main theme. At the beginning of the previous chapter we argued that Luke's main concern was with the salvation revealed in Jesus. In this second area of discussion we have taken up the evidence which might be interpreted to suggest that Luke's concern was basically with salvation-*history*, and that his primary purpose was to historicize the story of Jesus and to attach symbolical or theological significance to the various stages in His work. Our conclusion has been that this interpretation of the evidence is unjustified. We have not found anything to suggest that Luke was primarily concerned with the history of salvation rather than with salvation itself. Luke is of course concerned with history, but he has not refashioned the history in any decisive way for the sake of establishing theological points.

A number of other topics in the Gospel of Luke should be considered in any detailed study of the doctrine of salvation. These are deferred for the moment in order that they may be discussed in the context of the same teaching in Acts; questions about the reception of salvation by men, about discipleship and the mission of the church are accordingly held over for later discussion.

CHAPTER VII

THE WORD OF THIS SALVATION

THE ACTS OF THE APOSTLES IS THE INTENDED SEQUEL TO THE GOSPEL OF Luke.[1] Its purpose must be understood in this context. Although a variety of motifs are present, some of them obviously of considerable importance as secondary themes of the book, the main theme is the good news of salvation which was the theme of the Gospel. By implication Acts is about what Jesus continued to do and teach (Acts 1:2).[2] The explicit statement of its plan comes in Acts 1:8 "You shall receive power when the Holy Spirit has come upon you; and you shall be my witnesses in Jerusalem and in all Judaea and Samaria and to the end of the earth."

Against any adherents of the view that the parousia was to follow immediately after the passion, Luke gives the statement of Jesus that the "restoration of the kingdom to Israel" was not to take place at a time

---

[1] This consideration in itself makes the theory of composition advocated by G. Bouwmann unlikely (*Das dritte Evangelium*, pp. 62–95). According to Bouwmann Acts was written before the Gospel. The attraction of this theory is that it allows the dating of Acts before the end of Paul's imprisonment although the Gospel was written after the fall of Jerusalem. But the arguments produced in its favour are far from compelling. (1). Bouwmann claims that certain aspects of the pattern of the Gospel (its three-fold division; the character of the travel narrative) are modelled on the pattern of Acts. But the fact that the pattern in Acts is not reproduced exactly in the Gospel is no proof that Luke was trying to reproduce in the Gospel what he had already done more expertly in Acts. (2). Certain incidents in the Gospel are based on the structure of incidents in Acts (e.g. the Nazareth scene (Luke 4:16–30) is modelled on the Antioch scene (Acts 13:15–51)), and gospel material already included in Acts is omitted from the Gospel. Bouwmann, however, has not reckoned sufficiently with the influence of Luke's other sources, and thinks too much in terms of Lucan redaction of Mark. (3). Bouwmann finds the solution of the problem of the western text in Acts in the suggestion that it represents Luke's own revision of Acts in connexion with the publication of the Gospel. But there are well-known difficulties in the way of attributing both the Egyptian and the western texts of Acts to the same hand. (4). Bouwmann claims that the theology of the Gospel is more developed than that of Acts, and that certain characteristics of the Gospel (e.g. its stress on the Spirit, on prayer and on the place of women) are to be explained in the light of the early church life reflected in Acts. The latter part of this argument, however, merely shows that early church life is reflected in the Gospel, not that the account in Acts is reflected in and precedes the Gospel. As for the former part, other scholars have come to the opposite conclusion (cf. S. Schulz, *Die Stunde der Botschaft*, p. 242, who states that Luke's theology is more easily discoverable from Acts, where he was less bound by his sources, than from the Gospel; C. F. D. Moule, in SLA, pp. 159–185, has shown that the christology of the Gospel is (consciously) less developed than that of Acts, and that Luke has not imposed a uniform view on his sources). Bouwmann's theory is accordingly not proved; the phenomena can be better explained on the view that the Gospel and Acts were composed simultaneously.

[2] See above, p. 87 n. 2.

known to men.[1] For the time being the apostles were promised the power of the Spirit and commanded to be the witnesses of Jesus to the end of the earth. The ensuing account describes the progress of the gospel in accordance with this pattern. The purpose of Acts is thus to describe the witness given by the apostles to Jesus and to relate its progress. It is an account of how the good news led to the conversion of men and women to the Christian way. It sets out to confirm the faith of a man like Theophilus by describing how the preaching of Christ corroborated the facts recorded in the Gospel;[2] when the good news of Jesus was preached, the Holy Spirit empowered the word and people were converted. The Book of Acts is indeed "the confirmation of the Gospel."

Since this is the writer's theme, we need not be surprised that he has chosen to narrate his story and select his material from this particular point of view. Two or three main characters dominate his pages – Peter, Stephen, James and Paul and his companions. The rest of the apostles are largely absent from Luke's account, and we are left to the apocryphal acts and other sources for a mixture of scanty historical fact and much fiction.[3] One main line of progress interests Luke, that which leads from Jerusalem to Rome. Even along the path which Luke has chosen to take us, much has been left in obscurity, so that many questions remain unanswered for the historian. We must, therefore, be sympathetic to what Luke was trying to do, rather than grumble that he has not done what we might have wished him to do.

We shall concentrate our attention on Luke's main theme, and largely ignore other aspects of Acts. Thus, while it is impossible to resist the conclusion that Luke had a definite apologetic purpose in mind, that of showing that the Christians were not guilty of any crimes that came within the purview of Roman law, we shall not take up this theme.[4] Again, while it may be the case that Acts is meant to some extent to defend the position of Paul within the church, it is hard to believe that this is the main purpose of a book which contains so much other material and which

---

[1] It is not made clear whether a "restoration" is to be expected in the future. A direct "No" is not voiced. On the whole Luke's view appears to be that the concern of the disciples should be with evangelism rather than with sovereignty. Luke 21:24 may leave open the possibility of some kind of future for the Jews after the fulfilment of the times of the Gentiles. Paul knows nothing of a sovereign position being assigned to Israel at the conclusion of the Gentile mission, but only of the conversion and salvation of "all Israel." See further below, pp. 186 f.

[2] Cf. D. P. Fuller, *Easter Faith and History*, pp. 188–261. Fuller's thesis that the evidence of changed lives, like that of Barnabas, is meant to constitute a historical proof of the resurrection is, however, carried too far.

[3] E. Hennecke, *New Testament Apocrypha*, II, 1965 (English translation of E. Hennecke, *Neutestamentliche Apokryphen* (ed. W. Schneemelcher), Tübingen, 1964).

[4] H. Conzelmann, *Die Mitte der Zeit*, pp. 128–139 (pp. 138–149). See, for example, B. S. Easton, *Early Christianity*, 1935; H. Sahlin, *Der Messias und das Gottesvolk*; F. F. Bruce, *The Acts of the Apostles*, pp. 30f.

as we have stressed, must be regarded as having the same ultimate purpose as the Gospel.[1] Similarly, while part of Luke's purpose may have been to refute heresy, he does not make explicit mention of particular errors which he opposed; we shall not, therefore, regard this as his main theme or as one of the central motifs in the composition of the book.[2] Much has been made of the "edifying" character of Acts by its most substantial recent commentator, E. Haenchen,[3] but this description is somewhat vague and does not bring us in sight of the main theme of Acts. We should also notice the view of J. C. O'Neill that the central purpose of Acts is evangelistic, with educated Romans as the intended audience.[4] This approach is very much in harmony with our own view, even if our understanding of several crucial problems with regard to the character of Acts differs rather considerably from that of O'Neill. One cannot doubt that Luke hoped that the effect of his book would be evangelistic, but on the whole it is more likely that Acts, with its considerable proportion of material intended for believers rather than for non-believers, is intended to prepare the church for evangelism. Its purpose is first of all to help the church to know the character of its message.

Word and Witness

Just as a central feature in the Gospel of Luke was the preaching of the good news by Jesus, so in the book of Acts a central place is occupied by the preaching of His disciples. This is true at a formal level from a consideration of the amount of space devoted to their words. It has been estimated that the speeches in Acts take up about one fifth of the book.[5] We have also seen that it is true from a theological point of view when at an earlier stage we considered Luke's concept of witness. The Acts contains the witness of the apostles to Jesus, and therefore their words occupy an important place in the total conception of the book. From the point of view of composition the same conclusion emerges. E. Haenchen observes that it is the word which binds the Gospel and Acts together: "This 'Word of God' binds the period after Jesus with the period of Jesus; for it is the message about Jesus, faith in whom leads to forgiveness of sins and deliverance from judgment. Thus we have found the link which holds the two epochs together and thus permits the continuation of the first book

---

[1] E. Trocmé, *Le "Livre des Actes" et l'histoire*; A. J. Mattill, Jr., "The Purpose of Acts: Schneckenburger Reconsidered," in AHG, pp. 108–122.

[2] C. K. Barrett, *Luke the Historian in Recent Study*, pp. 62f.; C. H. Talbert, *Luke and the Gnostics*, Nashville, 1966; "An Anti-Gnostic Tendency in Lucan Christology," NTS 14, 1967–68, pp. 259–271. Contra: W. C. van Unnik, "Die Apostelgeschichte und die Häresien," ZNW, 58, 1967, pp. 240–246.

[3] E. Haenchen, *Die Apostelgeschichte*, pp. 93–99.

[4] J. C. O'Neill, *The Theology of Acts in its Historical Setting*, pp. 166–177.

[5] H. J. Cadbury, BC V, p. 402.

(which described the life of Jesus as the period of salvation) in a second book, and indeed demands it: the salvation which has appeared must be preached to all peoples, and the presentation of this mission itself serves to awaken faith and the consequent reception of salvation."[1]

The content of the apostolic preaching is designated as "the word of God" (Acts 4:29, 31 *et al.*). This is a term which was already used in the Gospel to describe the message of Jesus, and the evidence shows that the phrase was one which the Evangelist himself applied to it.[2] Thus a common designation in primitive Christianity for the gospel message[3] is used to indicate the continuity between the message of Jesus and that of His disciples; this fact is further evidenced by the way in which Jesus sent His disciples out during His lifetime to preach the same message as He Himself proclaimed (Luke 9:2). These same disciples became the apostles who preached in the early church. In Acts the message may also be called "the word of the Lord", and it remains ambiguous whether God or Jesus is meant in this phrase; the ambiguity is perhaps deliberate.[4] In any case the source and authority of the word is indicated; it is not a human word, but it comes from God (cf. 1 Thess. 2:13).[5]

Continuity with the Gospel is further seen in the use of the verb εὐαγγελίζομαι, "to proclaim good news," to describe the activity of the apostles. The verb is construed either with the accusative of the content of the message (e.g. Acts 5:42) or with the accusative of the audience to whom the message comes; the English translation "evangelize" is used for this second sense (e.g. Acts 8:25, 40). The character of the message as good news is thus the same as in the Gospel.

The break comes when we consider the content of the message. To be sure, a formal link is maintained in a number of passages which describe the message as being about "the kingdom of God" (Acts 8:12; 14:22; 19:8; 20:25; 28:23, 31). The link is not of course purely formal for the same terminology is used by Paul and the other apostolic writers.[6] Luke is bearing witness to terminology actually used in the apostolic preaching, but there is a shift in meaning. In Acts 17:7 the preaching is summed up as being about "another king, Jesus." Here the apostolic preaching is brought into conflict with the imperial ideology of the Roman Emperor

---

[1] E. Haenchen, *op. cit.*, pp. 87f.

[2] Luke 5:1 is probably an editorial link; Luke 8:11 and 21 show editorial modification of Mark 4:14 and 3:35 respectively; there remains Luke 11:28. Cf. Luke 22:61.

[3] E.g. 1 Cor. 14:36; 2 Cor. 2:17; Phil. 1:14; Heb. 13:7; 1 Pet. 1:23; Rev. 20:4.

[4] J. C. O'Neill, "The Use of *KURIOS* in the Book of Acts", SJT 8, 1955, pp. 155–174, especially pp. 168–170, has argued that Jesus is meant in all the texturally certain examples (Acts 8:25; 13:49; 14:3; 15:35, 36; 19:10), but admits that God the Father may be meant.

[5] See further C.-P. März, *Das Wort Gottes bei Lukas*, Leipzig, 1974.

[6] Rom. 14:17; 1 Cor. 4:20; 6:9f.; 15:24, 50; Gal. 5:21; Eph. 5:5; Col. 1:13; 4:11; 1 Thess. 2:12; 2 Thess. 1:5; Rev. 12:10.

who brooked no rivals within his domain, but it is plain that the adversaries of the faith had formed an accurate idea of the terminology used in the preaching. The message of the kingdom brought to the fore the fact that Jesus was the king. There is little evidence that the early Christians did use the title "king" of Jesus, although it figured historically in His trial.[1] This fact in itself shows that the message was breaking the bounds of the original "kingdom" framework. For the point to which Acts 17:7 bears witness is that the message was less and less about the kingdom and more and more about Jesus. The title of king was perhaps politically dangerous, certainly open to misunderstanding (John 19:36–38), and possibly theologically inadequate. It was swallowed up in a variety of other titles which made clear the new significance of Jesus.

The Exalted Lord

The speeches of Peter in the opening chapters of Acts acquaint us with the view of Jesus which Luke regarded as definitive for the early church. If we follow the order of events adopted by Luke himself our attention is drawn in the first place to the speech given on the Day of Pentecost. The speech begins with an Old Testament passage cited in explanation of the descent of the Spirit upon the disciples. The passage begins with a prophecy that God will pour our His Spirit in the last days,[2] the implication obviously being that this prophecy, or rather this part of the prophecy, has been fulfilled in the event of Pentecost. The prophecy then goes on to speak of apocalyptic signs, which we may correlate with the similar events promised for the future in the apocalyptic discourse of Jesus in Luke 21:11, 25 f. It is reasonable to suppose that this portion of the prophecy is quoted not for its immediate relevance to the situation but because it forms a link with the final part of the passage which speaks of the coming of the Day of the Lord and then makes the promise that whoever calls on the name of the Lord will be saved (Joel 2:28–32 LXX; Acts 2:17–21; cf. 2:39). In the discourse which follows the main theme is

[1] For the "kingdom of Christ" see Col. 1:13; 2 Tim. 4:1, 18; Heb. 1:8; 2 Pet. 1:11; cf. Eph. 5:5. On Christ as king see K. L. Schmidt, TDNT I, pp. 576–579.
[2] The reading ἐν ταῖς ἐσχάταις ἡμέραις is to be preferred in Acts 2:17. E. Haenchen, *Die Apostelgeschichte*, p. 142, accepts the reading of B, μετὰ ταῦτα, which avoids the suggestion that Pentecost introduces the End-time. But it is extremely unlikely that a text which assimilates to the LXX form of Joel 2:28 is to be preferred, and Haenchen's theological objection to the "eschatological" text is unjustified.
Consequently, H. Conzelmann's view that the gift of the Spirit is merely a substitute for the possession of final salvation is deprived of support (*Die Mitte der Zeit*, p. 87 (p. 95); cf. p. 108 n. 3 (p. 117 n. 3), p. 127 (p. 136), p. 216 (p. 230)). Admittedly, Conzelmann's case is not based on this text only. See further G. Strecker, *Der Weg der Gerechtigkeit*, pp. 46f.; H.-J. Degenhardt, *Lukas – Evangelist der Armen*, p. 16 n. 11.

not so much the Spirit as the Lord; the Lord is identified as Jesus, and consequently it is He who has poured out the Spirit (Acts 2:33).

This, then, is the key point in the discourse. It is the fact that Jesus is the Lord. So the sermon begins by describing how Jesus was a man attested during His earthly ministry by the mighty works which God did through Him. But by the plan of God the Jews put Him to death. Nevertheless, He was raised from the dead by God, for, says Peter, it was not possible for Him to remain held by death. The explanation of this statement is then given. A quotation from Psa. 16:8–11 in which the speaker refers to himself as somebody who will not be abandoned to Hades is used to establish the point. Although the writer of the Psalm was David, he could not be speaking about himself, since it was common knowledge that he had died and remained dead. He must, therefore, have been speaking prophetically: but about whom? The answer is provided by reference to another passage, 2 Sam. 7:12f. (cf. Psa. 89:3f.; 132:11f.), which promised a descendant to David whose kingdom would last for ever. This descendant was understood to be "the Messiah," the promised king in the line of David. Consequently, the prophecy of David must be taken to apply to the Messiah. It is Jesus who fulfils this prophecy. It is not crystal clear, however, in which direction the argument goes at this point. Either Peter is arguing that since God raised Jesus from the dead, Jesus must be the Messiah. Or he is claiming that, since Jesus was the Messiah whose resurrection was prophesied, therefore death could not hold Him and it was inevitable that He should rise from the dead. The former argument gains support from Acts 2:36, which says that God has made Jesus Christ, and also from the probability that the equation of Jesus with the Messiah would be what needed to be proved to the Jews. But while this equation is the point at issue in verse 36, this is not necessarily the case in the earlier verses. The latter argument must therefore be seriously considered. In its favour is the fact that it provides the appropriate conclusion to the line of argument suggested by verse 24b: Jesus had to rise from the dead because He was the Messiah. Also, throughout Acts it is assumed that Jesus was already the Messiah during His earthly ministry; we may refer to Acts 3:18; 10:38, and also 3:13 and 4:27, where the status of the earthly Jesus is made clear. At this point, therefore, the argument is not from the resurrection of Jesus to His subsequent status as Messiah, but rather from His Messiahship to the fact that as Messiah He must rise from the dead.

This means that two lines of argument are to be traced here. The former one can now be restated. It is that the resurrection proves that Jesus was already the Messiah. To people who saw in Jesus merely a man who suffered crucifixion, the Christians replied that the resurrection proved that this estimate was inadequate: He was really the Messiah. The second argument is the one on which the first depends.

But Peter goes further and makes a second point. The previous argument concerned the status of Jesus as the Messiah. It culminated in the statement that the resurrection of Jesus was His exaltation at the right hand of God. We may ignore for the moment the reference to the Spirit. The significant point is that if Jesus is now at the right hand of God another Old Testament prophecy comes into focus. In Psa. 110:1 David said, "The Lord said to my Lord, Sit at my right hand, till I make thy enemies a stool for thy feet." Once again, the Psalm could not be about David himself, since he did not ascend into heaven. It must, therefore, be about the Messiah, and it shows that He bears the title of Lord. Hence, when the argument is summed up in verse 36 it is stated that God has made Jesus both Lord and Christ.

The use of this title brings us back to the beginning of the speech where we saw that Peter spoke in Joel's words of the coming of the day of the Lord and of the need to call upon the name of the Lord in order to be saved. The effect of the argument is to show that Jesus is the Lord in the prophecy of Joel. Consequently He is the One through whom men are saved. This is clarified by the reaction to the speech. The people, appalled at the thought that they have put to death the Lord and Christ, cry out, "What shall we do?" The answer given is that they are to repent and to be baptized in the name of Jesus. Obedience to this command will grant them forgiveness of sins, and the gift of the Holy Spirit, already poured out upon the disciples. In both cases the gift comes from Jesus. Forgiveness comes through baptism in His name, and it is He who pours out the Spirit (verse 33).

We may wonder how far this speech is an exact reproduction of what Peter actually said on the day of Pentecost. The indications are that it probably preserves the pattern of apostolic preaching, expressed in Lucan style, rather than that it is a verbatim report of what Peter said.[1] At the moment, however, we are interested in it primarily as a record of Lucan theology. The indications are that it offers a view of Jesus whereby He was attested to be Lord and Messiah by His resurrection and exaltation and received authority to bestow the Holy Spirit upon those who responded to the preaching of the apostles.

We must now compare the other, similar material in Acts to see what further light is shed upon this basic conception. A second example of Peter's preaching is given in Acts 3:12-26. The speech begins by

---

[1] On this point and for much of what follows on the significance of the resurrection see my article "The Resurrection in the Acts of the Apostles," in AHG, pp. 92-107.

explaining the healing of the lame man at the temple gate in terms of the activity of the exalted Jesus. God's Servant, the Holy and Righteous One, the Author of life, was put to death by the Jews, but God glorified Him by raising Him from the dead, a fact attested by the witness of the apostles. Faith in the name of Jesus is responsible for the cure of the lame man.

Having explained the point at issue, Peter proceeds further and launches into an evangelistic appeal. The Jews were acting in ignorance of who Jesus really was. Nevertheless, the plan of God for His Messiah to suffer was being fulfilled. Therefore, the opportunity was given to the Jews to repent, in order that their sins might be forgiven and they might enjoy times of refreshing. God would then send the appointed Messiah, Jesus, who is at present in heaven until the accomplishment of all that has been prophesied to take place first. This means that there is a promise of blessings associated with the parousia, although these are not to follow immediately.

There is then a fresh element in the speech. Peter takes up again the fact that the coming of the eschatological prophet was foretold by Moses and that the succeeding prophets also bore witness to the era of salvation. Consequently, the promise is in the first place to the Jews, to whom Jesus has been sent by God to turn them from their sins. The point of the addition seems to be to stress that the promise of salvation is for the Jews, but at the same time it is neatly linked to the preceding part of the speech, for it recounts the things spoken by the prophets of old which must be fulfilled before the parousia: first the good news must go to the Jews and also to all the families of the earth. If this is a correct interpretation of the structure of the speech we have here an indication of the progress of salvation history.

The brief remarks of Peter in which he defended the healing of the lame man before the Jewish authorities make two fresh points. The one is the introduction of the "stone" *testimonium* from Psa. 118:22 to indicate the unique position of Jesus as the One rejected by the Jews but accepted by God. The other is that in consequence of this fact Jesus is constituted as the only Saviour. He *healed* (i.e. "saved") the lame man; He is the only One who can *save* men in the broadest sense of the term (Acts 4:8–12).

A further brief speech, again before the Jewish authorities, is to be found in Acts 5:29–32. The christological pattern is the same as previously but it is interesting that the effect of the exaltation is said here to be the establishment of Jesus as Leader and Saviour so that He might give repentance and forgiveness to Israel.[1]

[1] It is not clear whether the implied subject of "to give" is God or Jesus; in such a case probably both subjects are implied.

The speech of Stephen in Acts 7 is irrelevant to our present purpose, but the vision of Stephen before he was stoned is significant. He claimed to see Jesus standing at the right hand of God, and described Him in this role as the Son of man, a title which takes up the idea expressed in Luke 22:69, where Jesus stated that "from now on the Son of man shall be seated at the right hand of the power of God." The fact that Jesus was standing rather than sitting has proved perplexing, but the most likely explanation is that He was standing in order to welcome and vindicate His martyr.[1]

One further speech by Peter claims our attention. In his address to the household of Cornelius (Acts 10:34-43) the interesting feature is the slightly more extended treatment given to the earthly ministry of Jesus. Having been anointed by God with the Holy Spirit, He was able to accomplish His mighty works and to preach good news of peace. Another significant fact is the reference to His appointment as judge of all men, both living and dead.

Finally in this connection, there is the speech of Paul at Pisidian Antioch (Acts 13:16-41, 46f.). It places the coming of the Messiah in the context of Jewish history, especially with regard to the desire of the people for a king, and designates Jesus, the offspring of David, as a Saviour. Though innocent, He was put to death by the Jews, but was raised from the dead. This is the sign that He is the fulfilment of God's promises made in the Old Testament. Here there is a repetition of the scriptural arguments used by Peter in Acts 2, making use of Psa. 2:7; Isa. 55:3 and Psa. 16:10. The first two of these quotations, however, are new. Psa. 2:7 which speaks of God begetting His Son is taken to be a reference to the way in which God gave new life to Jesus at the resurrection. The use of Isa. 55:3 is somewhat obscure; its point is probably the permanent nature of the Messiah's rule, which presupposes His resurrection to endless life.[2] Consequently, the resurrection of Jesus is to be seen as the fulfilment of the Old Testament promises. He is therefore the One through whom forgiveness of sins and justification is possible; He gives light and eternal life to men.

We have rehearsed these speeches in some detail because together they give a presentation of the christology accepted by Luke. It is now time to draw together their implications. The basic point which has emerged is that the exaltation of Jesus is the central point in the preaching in Acts. It is God who exalted Jesus, a fact which fits in with Luke's view that the

---

[1] C. F. D. Moule, *The Phenomenon of the New Testament*, pp. 60f., 90f. C. K. Barrett, 'Stephen and the Son of Man," in W. Eltester, *Apophoreta* (Festschrift for E. Haenchen), Berlin, 1964, pp. 32-38, adopts the view that the passage indicates a real anticipation of the parousia for the individual believer at death. See also C. Colpe, TDNT VIII, pp. 461-463.

[2] E. Lövestam, *Son and Saviour: A Study of Acts 13, 32-37*, Lund, 1961.

whole of salvation-history bears witness to the action of the Father. By His exaltation Jesus has been shown to be Lord, Christ and Saviour, and a variety of other titles are also used to describe Him, especially in order to characterize His person as the Saviour.

Among these titles the one which stands out most perhaps is that of Lord. At the outset its use is related to passages in the Old Testament where the same word is used of God (Acts 2:20f., 34). Elsewhere in Acts "the Lord" is a common designation of Jesus (Acts 1:21; 4:33 et al.). Thus what was in the Old Testament the name of God has been applied to Jesus. Naturally the word κύριος was also used on many occasions in the ancient world without any reference to God; it was a common secular term. But it seems likely that in Christian usage a title that was used for God was also used of Jesus. This is all the more probable if it is the case that Christians had something to do with the introduction of this equivalent for Yahweh into the Septuagint.[1] The word is used of both God and Jesus quite indiscriminately, so that it is often hard to determine which Person is meant. The conclusion appears to be that in the usage of Acts at any rate the title implied that the lordship belonging to God had been transferred in part to Jesus.

Earlier we suggested that Luke did not regard the status of Lord as having been conferred on Jesus for the first time at the resurrection. This point may now be confirmed by a reference to the evidence of the Gospel. It is a well-known fact that although the title of Lord is almost entirely absent from Matthew and Mark as a designation of Jesus (except in the vocative case, which is non-technical),[2] it is one of the most common designations of Jesus in Luke. It occurs in narrative for the first time in Luke 7:13, and thereafter some sixteen times, always in non-Marcan sections.[3] There does not appear to be any clear pattern in its usage as compared with other ways of referring to Jesus. It can be used of any

---

[1] See above, p. 104 n. 3.

[2] The word κύριος occurs in Mark 11:3, where a reference to Jesus Himself is not absolutely certain, and also in 12:36f. where Jesus is talking about the Messiah; in 2:28 there is an allusion to the function of the Son of man as Lord. The usage in Matthew is similar.
The vocative form is rare in Mark (7:28), but frequent in Matthew, who has been thought to use it with greater fulness of meaning.

[3] Narrative use is found at Luke 7:13, 19; 10:1, 39, 41; 11:39; 12:42; 13:15; 16:8(?); 17:5, 6; 18:6; 19:8, 31, 34; 22:61 bis; 24:3, 34. The Matthaean parallel to 17:5f. does not have the word. Luke 19:31 is parallel to Mark 11:3, and 19:34 is simply a repetition of this phrase. It is disputed whether Luke has mostly taken over the use of the title from his sources (so F. Rehkopf, Die lukanische Sonderquelle, p. 95; F. Hahn, Christologische Hoheitstitel, pp. 88-91) or has introduced it himself (P. Vielhauer, Aufsätze zum Neuen Testament, pp. 154-156). See further W. Ott, Gebet und Heil, pp. 35-38 (who analyses the link verses where the title occurs as Lucan compositions), and H. Schürmann, Das Lukasevangelium, p. 401. The fact that the title is not introduced by Luke into Marcan material strongly suggests that his usage rests to some extent upon his sources. See also I. de la Potterie, "Le titre ΚΥΡΙΟΣ appliqué à Jésus dans l'Évangile de Luc," in A. Descamps (ed.), Melanges Bibliques, Gembloux, 1970, pp. 117-146.

aspect of the ministry.[1] Jesus, therefore, is for Luke the Lord during His earthly ministry, although Luke is careful not to add the title in the Gospel so as to imply that the disciples spoke of Jesus in these terms during His earthly life; He allows that they had a different estimate of Jesus from that of the crowds by the forms of address which he places on the lips of the disciple and of the crowds,[2] but he does not make the disciples speak about Jesus as "the Lord," except in 19:31, 34, where the designation is taken over from Mark.

The exception to this rule is to be found in Luke 1:43 where Elizabeth speaks of Mary as "the mother of my Lord." This fits in with the angelic description of Jesus to the shepherds as Lord (Luke 2:11).[3] From His birth Jesus is the Lord, and there is no suggestion in Luke that He gained this status only at some later point. The disciples came to recognize Him as Lord in the full sense only at the resurrection, but what they recognized was not a new status but one already possessed by Jesus.

It is the same with the designation of Jesus as the Messiah. The resurrection is the proof that Jesus was already the Messiah during His earthly life. This is clear from Acts 4:26; 17:3 and 26:23. It is shown in the Gospel by the birth narrative (Luke 2:11, 26) and by the confession of men (Luke 9:20) and demons (Luke 4:41), as well as by a statement ascribed to Jesus Himself (Luke 23:2).

Luke does not make great use of the title "Son of God." It is remarkably rare in Acts. In Acts 13:33 there is a quotation from Psa. 2:7 which implicitly identifies Jesus as God's Son, but in the passage itself no stress is laid on this identification; it is something assumed by the author rather than a point to be emphasized. The only other reference is Acts 9:20 where we are told that Paul preached in Damascus that Jesus was the Son of God. The fact that the statement is not taken up or amplified anywhere else in Acts strongly suggests that this is a piece of tradition taken up by Luke and not integrated into any scheme of his own.

In the Gospel Luke has taken over the references to Jesus as the Son of God which he found in his sources (Luke 3:22; 4:3, 9, 41; 8:28; 9:35; 10:22; 22:70) except for Mark 13:32 and 15:39. The evidence shows that Luke shared the view of his sources that in His earthly life Jesus was the Son of God, but took care to avoid possible misrepresentations of what this meant. Of special importance is the statement at the annunciation to Mary that her child would be the Son of the Most High or the Son of

---

[1] Introducing authoritative statements by Jesus; used also of His power to heal and save.

[2] Luke uses διδάσκαλε as the form of address to Jesus by non-disciples. Disciples address Him as κύριε or ἐπιστάτα. Luke drops the Jewish form ραββί. E. Franklin, *Christ the Lord*, pp. 49–55, has argued that κύριε expresses a deep commitment to Jesus and comes close in meaning to ὁ κύριος.

[3] In Luke 1:76 κύριος is ambiguous. Luke probably saw it as a reference to Jesus.

God. It has been claimed that Luke 1:32 witnesses originally to an adoption-ist type of sonship, the description implying no more than it did in the case of the Old Testament references to the adoption of David's son by God (2 Sam. 7:14).[1] But it seems probably that the thought goes beyond this meaning, since verse 35 speaks of the divine begetting of Mary's Son by the Holy Spirit. The whole context, with its clear teaching that Mary was a virgin, implies that something more than the birth of a man destined to be Messiah and therefore adopted by God as His Son is meant.[2] It is through His conception by the Spirit that Jesus is born as the Son of God. Consequently, Sonship is not to be conceived here in terms of Messiahship, but rather the reverse. The office of Jesus as the Messiah is grounded in the fact that He is the Son of God. In this text something of the mystery of the person of Jesus as the Son of God comes to expression and we may perhaps be justified in seeing here the underlying "meta-physical" basis for Luke's view of the person of Jesus.

The christology which we find in Acts is one that is consonant with what we know of the development of theology in the early church. The attribution of the title of Lord to Jesus can be traced back to an early stage, as is shown by its use in the pre-Pauline texts Romans 10:9; 1 Corinthians 12:3 and Philippians 2:11. The first of these texts with its parallelism between confession that Jesus is Lord and belief that God raised Him from the dead suggests that the recognition of the Lordship of Jesus was connected with the fact of His resurrection; this is confirmed by Phil. 2:5–11 where the conferring of the name which is above every name is linked to the exaltation of Jesus. Moreover, here the title given to Jesus is taken from an Old Testament passage referring to Yahweh (Isa. 45:23). We have here, therefore, some proof that Luke's description of the risen Jesus as Lord rests upon early theology. Again, the way in which Luke speaks of the earthly Jesus as the Lord is paralleled by a similar usage in Paul when he speaks of "the brother(s) of the Lord" (1 Cor. 9:5; Gal. 1:19), or when he refers to "the Lord Jesus" in connec-tion with the historical institution of the Lord's Supper (1 Cor. 11:23).[3]

Luke's use of "Lord" is thus corroborated to some extent by that of Paul and pre-Pauline tradition. There is less need to discuss the use of "Messiah" in relation to the other New Testament evidence. Luke's usage

[1] F. Hahn, Christologische Hoheitstitel, p. 247; cf. G. Voss, Die Christologie der Lukanischen Schriften in Grundzügen, p. 79. E. Schweizer, TDNT VIII, pp. 376f, 380–382. On Luke's view in general see A. George, "Jésus, Fils de Dieu dans l'Evangile selon Saint Luc," Revue Biblique 72, 1965, pp. 185–209.

[2] B. S. Easton, The Gospel of Luke, p. 10; O. Procksch, TDNT I, p. 101, finds that "Son of God" is "a predicate which is not grounded in the Messianic office of Christ but in His origin." H. Schürmann, Das Lukasevangelium, pp. 47f., 54f., expresses himself more cauti-ously.

[3] Cf. F. Hahn, op. cit., pp. 91–94.

is basically that of his sources, and he does not show any independent development of it. As for the title of Son of God, the evidence of Paul shows that the application of the title to the earthly Jesus is early (e.g. Gal. 4:4f.). Where Luke differs from Paul is in the lack of any clear teaching on the pre-existence of the Son of God.

Jesus the Saviour

We now turn to the character of the saving work of Jesus as expressed in Acts. The most notable features of this are the ways in which salvation is linked with the exaltation of Jesus and with His Name. "God exalted him at his right hand as Leader and Saviour, to give repentance to Israel and forgiveness of sins;" "To him all the prophets bear witness that everyone who believes in him receives forgiveness of sins through his name" (Acts 5:31; 10:43) – these are typical statements of how salvation is bestowed according to Acts. Although salvation is the gift of God the Father (Acts 2:39; 5:32; 11:18), it is clearly linked with Jesus, the only Saviour; only through Him may men receive salvation (Acts 4:12).

But how does Jesus save? The clear view expressed in Acts is that Jesus saves men by virtue of His exaltation. Through His exaltation He has been shown to be the Lord. In the Old Testament, salvation is associated with the name of Yahweh, the Lord. In particular, forgiveness is His prerogative; it is the Lord who forgives iniquity and remembers sin no more (Jeremiah 31:34).[1] Now forgiveness is Luke's characteristic word for the content of salvation. The conclusion must be that God has given to Jesus the title of Lord and with it His own sovereign prerogative to forgive sins and to bestow salvation. Thus salvation is closely bound up with the person of Jesus. It is because He is the Lord that He has the right to forgive. Consequently, the exaltation of Jesus is the supreme saving event in Luke's eyes, since it is the act whereby God confirms the status of Jesus. What Jesus was privately shown to be at His birth (Luke 2:11) is now openly declared to all men.

This theory explains three aspects of Luke's teaching. First, Luke describes how Jesus referred to "Moses and all the prophets" as prophesying concerning Himself (Luke 24:27). While it is true that Old Testament passages may be found throughout the law and the prophets which were interpreted christologically – for Moses see Acts 3:22f. – it is not possible to find passages which speak of forgiveness as the prerogative of the Messiah in "all the prophets" (Acts 10:43). But there are passages in all

---

[1] See Exod. 34:7; Num. 14:18; I Kings 8:34; Isa. 33:24; 55:6f.; Jer. 36:3; Ezek. 36:25; Dan. 9:19; Amos 7:2; Mic. 7:18.

the prophets which tell how the Lord forgives, and it was these that the early church applied to Jesus.[1]

Second, the significance attached to the "name" of Jesus in Acts is justified. At the outset in Acts 2:21 Peter claims that everybody who calls on the name of the Lord will be saved. This idea governs the subsequent narrative. It is by the name of Jesus that mighty works are wrought (Acts 3:16; 4:30; 16:18), and by His name that salvation is offered (Acts 4:12; 10:43; 22:16). It is the Old Testament concept of the name as representing the person himself. It denotes the power and authority of the person. Hence the early church was claiming the authority of Jesus to do mighty works and to forgive when it spoke of His name.

Third, we have an explanation of the saving activity of Jesus in the Gospel. He performed His mighty works and saved men and women in virtue of His person as the Lord entrusted with the prerogative of God Himself. Thus there appears to be no essential difference between what Jesus did before and after His exaltation. In this way Luke accounts for what he found in the tradition, namely that the earthly Jesus wrought miracles and offered salvation to the needy.

But this view of the work of Jesus raises some problems. There is the question of the place of the cross in the thought of Luke. There is also the problem of whether his line of thought is his own arbitrary creation.

If Luke associates salvation with the person of Jesus as the exalted Lord, what becomes of the cross? At first sight it appears to be of minimal importance.[2] The evidence of the Gospel has often been taken to imply that the death of Jesus had little significance for Luke. It should be observed, however, that the situation is not so very different from that in Mark and Matthew. Direct references to the atoning aspects of the death of Jesus are found in Mark only at 10:45 and 14:22-25, although the concept is implicit elsewhere.[3] The former of these texts is missing from Luke, and its virtual equivalent in Luke 22:27 omits the crucial ransom clause.[4] But while it is true that Luke has not edited this saying in the light of Mark 10:45,[5] it must be stressed that here he is following a different tradition, and his procedure must be judged in the light of his preference for his special source over against Mark. The words of institution at the last supper are a true part of Luke's text in their full form (Luke

[1] See the previous note. But "all the prophets" is a stereotyped phrase in Luke (11:50; 13:28; 24:27; Acts 3:18, 24: 10:43; cf. Luke 18:31; 24:25, 44; Acts 24:14) and should not be pressed too literally.

[2] M. Kiddle, "The Passion Narrative in St. Luke's Gospel," JTS 36, 1935, pp. 267-280; H. Conzelmann, Die Mitte der Zeit, pp. 186-188 (pp. 199-201).

[3] V. Taylor, Jesus and His Sacrifice, 1937.

[4] Luke 22:24-27 in its context however emphasises that Jesus' death is his service for his disciples (R. Glöckner, op. cit., pp. 177-183).

[5] It is not Luke's habit to conflate his sources, although there are occasional examples of this.

22:19f.)[1] and indicate that the death of Jesus is associated with the new covenant.

In Matthew there is little more to be found than there is in Mark; the ransom saying is taken over unchanged (Matt. 20:28). The word of interpretation over the cup states that the blood is poured out for many "for the forgiveness of sins" (Matt. 26:28); this addition shows that Matthew understood the death of Jesus in terms of atonement for sin, but it is the only fresh indication of this fact in his Gospel.

As compared with Mark and Matthew, therefore, Luke's silence about the death of Jesus in the Gospel is not in any way remarkable. It is more significant that there is little about it in Acts. But the rather scanty evidence must be carefully scrutinized lest we take too superficial a view of Luke's teaching on this theme.

We observe first of all that Luke describes Jesus in terms of the suffering Servant. This is rendered certain by the explicit quotation of Isa. 53:7f. in the story of the Ethiopian eunuch (Acts 8:32f.) and the way in which Philip took up this scripture and beginning from it told the good news of Jesus. In the light of this passage there can be no doubt that the references to Jesus as God's παῖς (Acts 3:13, 26; 4:27, 30) speak of Him as God's Servant rather than as God's Son. But in Acts 4:25 the same word is used to describe David, and this might be taken to suggest that in the description of Jesus the word is being used in a general sense rather than in the particular sense of the Servant in Second Isaiah.[2] However, in Acts 3:13 there is a very probable reference to the glorification of the Servant taken from Isa. 52:13, and in Acts 4:27 the allusion to the anointing of Jesus probably takes us to Isa. 61:1, understood as a reference to the anointing of the Servant. Moreover, the Servant Jesus is described as righteous (δίκαιος) (Acts 3:14; cf. 7:52; 22:14), a phrase which reflects Isa. 53:11. The weight of these allusions strongly supports the view that Jesus is here thought of as the suffering Servant.[3]

According to J. C. O'Neill, the New Testament generally does not bear witness to a Servant Christology.[4] That is to say, the title of "Servant" did not become a major concept in elucidating the person of Jesus.

---

[1] H. Schürmann. "Lk. 22, 19b–20 als ursprüngliche Textüberlieferung," Bib. 32, 1951, pp. 366–392, 522–541; J. Jeremias, The Eucharistic Words of Jesus. Contra: A. Vööbus, "A New Approach to the Problem of the Shorter and Longer Text in Luke," NTS 15, 1968–69, pp. 457–463. See further I. H. Marshall, GL, pp. 799–801.

[2] H. J. Cadbury, BC V, pp. 354–375, especially pp. 364–370.

[3] The description of David as God's servant (Luke 1:69; Acts 4:25; Didache 9:2) may be drawn from Jewish liturgical usage (J. Jeremias, TDNT V, p. 700). If this is the case, the meaning of παῖς here is not necessarily determinative of passages in which the title is applied to Jesus (Acts 4:27, 30). Cf. V. Taylor, The Atonement in New Testament Teaching, 1945[2], p. 19 n.1. For a different point of view see C. F. D. Moule in SLA, pp. 169 f.

[4] J. C. O'Neill, The Theology of Acts in its Historical Setting, pp. 133–139 (not in second ed.).

But even if this point be granted, it does not foreclose the question of a Servant soteriology. That such a soteriology existed is beyond doubt. It is to be seen fully developed in 1 Peter, a fact whose significance is very much played down by M. D. Hooker in her book *Jesus and the Servant*.[1] The researches of J. Jeremias especially have shown that there are fairly widespread traces of its existence in the New Testament.[2] However, the saving work of the Servant is not very prominent in Acts. It has been observed that there are no references to the vicarious work of the Servant.[3] Rather, the Servant is a typical example of the humiliation and exaltation pattern; in the Servant in fact we see the supreme case of a person who goes to suffering by the will of God and is subsequently vindicated by God. This is the pattern which is followed by Luke who sees in the passion of Jesus the divinely appointed path which He must trace before being glorified by God in the resurrection. It is Luke who records in his passion narrative that Jesus applied the words of Isa. 53:12, "And he was reckoned with transgressors" to His impending death (Luke 22:37). He does not, however, go out of his way to emphasize the atoning aspects of the suffering of the Servant.

Yet it would be wrong to conclude that these aspects are completely absent from Luke. H. Schürmann has shown that elements of the Servant conception are to be found in the Lucan text of the Lord's Supper narrative.[4] The status of Luke 23:34a in Luke's text is uncertain; on the whole the textual attestation suggests that it is ancient tradition but leaves it doubtful whether it is from Luke himself.[5] If, however, it is genuine, it gives a prayer of Jesus for His executioners which exemplifies the statement of Isa. 53:12 that the Servant makes intercession for the transgressors.

The most that can be claimed for these references is that they show that Luke has incorporated traditions about the atoning work of the Servant; there is no evidence that he himself has positively evaluated the Servant concept in terms of redemptive suffering. In this respect Luke stands alongside Paul whose writings contain a number of traditional allusions to the Servant concept but who himself makes little use of this particular

[1] M. D. Hooker, *Jesus and the Servant*, 1959; cf. F. J. F. Jackson and K. Lake, BC I, pp. 384–392.

[2] J. Jeremias (and W. Zimmerli), TDNT V, pp. 654–717.

[3] M. D. Hooker, *op. cit.*, pp. 107–116.

[4] H. Schürmann, *Der Einsetzungsbericht*, pp. 75f., 101f. On the other hand, G. Voss, *Die Christologie der lukanischen Schriften in Grundzügen*, pp. 99–130, holds that in Luke the sufferings of Jesus are martyrological rather than sacrificial, and presented as an example to the disciples. The death of Jesus is a service for the disciples in so far as it opens up for them the possibility of a new life of commitment to God. Voss's treatment of Acts 20:28 in particular (*op. cit.*, p. 122) is quite unconvincing.

[5] So J. Jeremias, TDNT V, p. 713 n. 455. But the language and thought fit in so well with Lucan theology that one is tempted to accept the verse as an integral part of the Gospel despite the textual evidence; cf. G. Voss, *op. cit.*, p. 128 n. 1; I. H. Marshall, GL, pp. 867f.

mode of interpretation of the death of Jesus. Luke's attitude therefore is not very surprising. The evidence of the New Testament as a whole suggests that use of the Servant category to explain the death of Jesus was infrequent from the time of Paul onwards. Instead of the more subtle allusions of the earlier period we have the use of explicit quotations whose purpose is to see the whole ministry of Jesus and the mission of the church in terms of the Servant.

While Paul has used other ways of expressing the atoning significance of the death of Jesus, Luke has little to offer in this respect. The other material to be found in Acts is to be classified as traditional. This applies to the references to Jesus "hanging on a tree" (Acts 5:30; 10:39; 13:29). In each case the allusion is to the way in which the Jews crucified Jesus. But there can be little doubt that the choice of this unusual word to denote the cross rests upon the use in Deut. 21:22f.: "And if a man has committed a crime punishable by death and he is put to death, and you hang him on a tree, his body shall not remain all night upon the tree, but you shall bury him the same day, for a hanged man is accursed by God." This text is quoted by Paul in Gal. 3:13 where it is applied to the death of Jesus as the means whereby men are freed from the curse of the law. Similarly, 1 Pet. 2:24 combines ideas from Isa. 53 with the thought of Christ bearing our sins on the tree. It seems probable that the use in Paul and Peter, which associates the tree with the bearing of sin and its curse, is the oldest form of the tradition, and that Luke has taken over the term from tradition without expressing explicitly its soteriological significance.[1]

The unusual phrase in Acts 20:28 is likewise traditional. Here Paul refers to the church of God which He purchased with the blood of His own One. The translation of the phrase is doubtful. The difficulty lies in the phrase διὰ τοῦ αἵματος τοῦ ἰδίου, which would ordinarily be translated "with His own blood." Since such a reference to God's own blood would be quite unprecedented in the New Testament, one must either translate the phrase as we have done above, making τοῦ ἰδίου in effect into a noun,[2] or else assume that there has been a change of subject in the relative clause so that "Christ" must be supplied as the subject – "the church of God which (Christ) purchased with His own blood."[3] In either case it is probable that a traditional phrase is being used; this would account for the difficulty of the expression. It speaks of the purchase of the

---

[1] J. Schneider, TDNT V, p. 39, however, regards the use made of the quotation in Acts as more primitive than that in Paul.

[2] Cf. J. H. Moulton, *A Grammar of New Testament Greek*, I, Edinburgh, 1906², pp. 90f. The adoption of the widely attested reading κυρίου (so RSV) instead of θεοῦ (Aleph, B) is an inadmissible solution of the difficulty.

[3] E. Lohse, *Märtyrer und Gottesknecht*, Göttingen, 1955, p. 188 n.; H. Conzelmann, *Die Apostelgeschichte*, p. 119.

church at the cost of the blood of Jesus, phrases which lead into the realms of sacrifice and redemption.[1]

All this means that Luke has taken over certain traditions regarding the meaning of the death of Jesus but he has not in any way developed them or drawn attention to them. Now there is no doubt that teaching that "Christ died for our sins" formed part of the primitive gospel of the church (1 Cor. 15:3). Has Luke misrepresented this preaching in the sermons in Acts?

The answer appears to be that Luke has grasped hold of another aspect of the teaching of the early church which he has seen to be of central importance. The character of the passion narrative in Mark shows that the passion of Jesus was regarded from an early date as the divinely ordained path to His exaltation as the Messiah. Luke has emphasized the fact that as the exalted Lord and Messiah Jesus is the Saviour. But this emphasis too is primitive. The evidence of pre-Pauline kerygmatic material shows that the resurrection itself was not only closely linked with the death of Jesus as a saving event (Rom. 4:25; 1 Cor. 15:3-5) but was also given saving significance in its own right. This is apparent from Rom. 4:24 where faith is centred on the God who raised Jesus from the dead.[2] It is also to be found in Rom. 10:9-13 where Paul speaks of righteousness and salvation in connection with belief that Jesus, raised from the dead by God, is the Lord. Phil. 2:5-11 should also be understood in the same context. Although the hymn used here by Paul stands at present in the midst of an ethical exhortation, it is certain that its primary motivation was not to express the exemplary aspects of the career of Christ but to depict His humiliation and exaltation through which He is known to be Lord.[3] As the Lord He is sovereign over principalities and powers and has the right to dispense salvation: is it accidental that Philippians (3:20) contains the first Pauline reference to Jesus as the Saviour? Traditional material is also present in 1 Tim. 3:16, where again the significance of Jesus is expounded in terms of His exaltation without any reference to His vicarious death.

There are probably various strands of thought to be found in these passages. Some of the passages are liturgical and may well reflect the worship of the believing community rather than its evangelistic message. Even so it is significant that the praise offered to Jesus should dwell upon His humiliation and exaltation and not (as in the hymns in Revelation)

[1] Luke's use of the terminology of redemption (Luke 1:68; 2:38; 21:28; 24:21; Acts 7:35) is not linked to the death of Jesus. Perhaps there is heavy irony in Luke 24:21: the death which convinced the disciples that Jesus was not the Redeemer was in reality the means of redemption.
[2] The phrase is pre-Pauline: W. Kramer, *Christ, Lord, Son of God*, 1966, 3, pp. 20-26 (English translation of *Christos Kyrios Gottessohn*, Zürich, 1963).
[3] R. P. Martin, *Carmen Christi: Philippians ii. 5-11*, Cambridge, 1967.

upon the fact that He has redeemed men by His blood. Again, there may be indications of a presentation of the gospel message in terms of the victory of Jesus over the principalities and powers so that those who submit to Him as their Lord are set free from domination by the evil forces that formerly held them in thrall. Such a presentation of the gospel would have been especially relevant to Gentiles living in a world populated by idols and evil spirits. But the form of the message presented by Luke is one that is obviously appropriate to the Jews. It is in fact the Jews who are the principal recipients of the kind of message proclaimed in Acts; examples of preaching to a Gentile audience, which has not been reached by the message of the synagogue, are found in Acts 14:15–17 and 17:22–31, and these show that a different kind of approach was employed, at least initially.[1] For a Jewish audience, however, the fact that needed to be emphasized in the first place was the Messiahship of Jesus: although He had suffered and died, yet Jesus was the Messiah. He was the Messiah, first, because Scripture foretold the sufferings of the Messiah (Acts 3:18), and, second, because the resurrection positively demonstrated Him to be such.

It seems likely, therefore, that in Acts Luke has preserved one form of the early preaching in which particular stress was laid on the resurrection both as the certification of the Lordship of Jesus and as the token that through Him God offered forgiveness to men. The atoning significance of the death of Jesus is not altogether absent from Acts, but it is not the aspect which Luke has chosen to stress. His presentation of the saving work of Jesus is consequently one-sided. But it is going too far to say that he has no rationale of salvation. He demonstrates quite clearly that salvation is bestowed by Jesus in virtue of His position as the Lord and Messiah. What is lacking is rather a full understanding of the significance of the cross as the means of salvation.[2]

The Coming Christ

C. H. Dodd's attempt to reconstruct the pattern of early Christian preaching on the basis of fragments preserved in the Pauline Epistles together with the evidence of the speeches in Acts is well known. Among the fundamental points of the message was: "He will come again as Judge and Saviour of men."[3] A number of scholars have regarded

[1] Luke has reproduced general monotheistic considerations which would form the introduction (as in Acts 17:31) to more specifically Christian argumentation; the aposiopesis should not be taken to mean that Paul would have stopped short of the latter.

[2] R. Glöckner, op. cit., argues that Luke sees salvation as the exaltation of the lowly. It is brought about through Jesus who trod the path of lowliness in service for his disciples and was exalted to become Saviour and Lord. It remains unclear, however, how Jesus saves in virtue of his own humiliation and exaltation.

[3] C. H. Dodd, The Apostolic Preaching and its Developments, p. 17.

this hope as forming the centre of the earliest preaching, and F. Hahn has gone so far as to find in it the mainspring of the earliest christology: titles of dignity such as "Lord" were first applied to the One whose imminent arrival from heaven was expected by the church, and only later were they used in relation to His exaltation and resurrection. No significance was at first attached to the exaltation of Jesus or His sojourn in heaven; all the attention was centred on the hope of the parousia.[1]

If one were to judge the evidence of Acts on the basis of this hypothesis, one would probably conclude that it was out of touch with the atmosphere of the early church. As Dodd himself carefully stated: "It is to be observed that the apostolic Preaching as recorded in Acts does not (contrary to a commonly held opinion) lay the greatest stress upon the expectation of a second advent of the Lord."[2] Since Dodd is concerned to establish the content of the early preaching rather than to depict the theology of the author of Acts, he confines his references to those which may plausibly be regarded as representing primitive material, namely Acts 3:20f. and 10:42.

The second of these references is in effect dismissed from consideration by J. A. T. Robinson in his study of the origins of the concept of the parousia on the grounds that it refers merely to the ordaining of Christ as judge and says nothing about a second coming.[3] But this judgment fails to take into account the close interrelationship of ideas in the early church according to which the consummation of history, the parousia, the last judgment and the resurrection of the dead form parts of one indivisible event.[4] We may, therefore, retain this text as evidence for the future work of Christ. But we must also take into consideration verses which are relevant for the theology of Acts. Thus in Acts 17:31 we find repeated the fact that God has appointed a day on which He is going to judge the world by a Man whom He has appointed. The other important reference is in Acts 1:11 where it is promised that as Jesus ascended into heaven, so He will come in the same manner.

These texts establish clearly that in Acts the hope of the parousia and the associated judgment is an accepted part of the author's theology. They demonstrate that the fact of final judgment by Christ formed a sanction in view of which men were summoned to repent and believe the gospel. There is a real hope of the future coming of Jesus.

Nevertheless, it cannot be said that the future coming is the centre of the message. It is not an integral part of each and every presentation of the

---

[1] F. Hahn, *Christologische Hoheitstitel*, pp. 95–112 and *passim*.
[2] *Ibid.*, p. 33.
[3] J. A. T. Robinson, *Jesus and His Coming*, 1957, p. 28.
[4] See also the points advanced by A. L. Moore, *The Parousia in the New Testament*, pp. 59f.

gospel in Acts. On the contrary, the basic point in the preaching is concerned with the resurrection and exaltation of Jesus. It is the resurrection
indeed which is the basis of the status of Jesus as the judge; "Of this (God)
has given assurance to all men by raising him from the dead" (Acts
17:31).[1]

In one place the parousia is associated more positively with salvation.
This is in the difficult text Acts 3:20f.: Peter commands the Jews to repent
so that their sins may be blotted out, "that times of refreshing may come
from the presence of the Lord, and that he may send the Christ appointed
for you, Jesus, whom heaven must receive until the time for establishing
all that God spoke by the mouth of his holy prophets from of old." In this
text inducement to repent is given by the promise that conversion will
lead to the arrival of the messianic era associated with the coming of the
one who has been ordained as Messiah for the Jews, namely Jesus. Although
the text has been understood to mean that Jesus was foreordained to
become the Messiah at the parousia,[2] this would be an unparalleled conception and is an improbable interpretation of the text.[3] The main point
however, is the expectation of the messianic era with the refreshment and
rest which it brings to the people of God.[4] The coming of this era is
dependent upon the repentance of Israel, a thought which is found not
only in Jewish thought but is also attested in the New Testament where
the idea that the gospel must be made known and the full number of the
elect converted before the End can come is well attested.[5] Thus the coming
of the End with its blessings is here brought into close connection with the
offer of salvation. Conzelmann claims that the passage envisages the delay
of the parousia.[6] The evidence for this is the reference to the period during
which Jesus is in heaven until the appointed time of fulfilment. But, as we
have seen earlier, the existence of such an interval between the resurrection and the parousia is well attested in the tradition, and therefore there is
no reason to trace a specifically Lucan emphasis on the interval here. On

[1] Cf. Acts 10:42, where it is the risen Christ who claims to be the judge; the use of
ὡρισμένος points to a time of appointment, and this is to be linked with the resurrection as in
17:31; cf. Acts 1:4.

[2] J. A. T. Robinson, "The Most Primitive Christology of All?", JTS n.s. 7, 1956, pp. 177–
189 (reprinted in *Twelve New Testament Studies*, pp. 139–153); R. H. Fuller, *The Foundations of
New Testament Christology*, 1965, pp. 158f.; F. Hahn, *op. cit.*, pp. 184–186.

[3] C. F. D. Moule, in SLA, pp. 167–169. A. L. Moore, *op. cit.*, pp. 59f.; G. Voss, *Die Christologie der Lukanischen Schriften in Grundzügen*, pp. 151f.

[4] For the idea of rest associated with the messianic era F. Hahn (*ibid.*, following H. H.
Wendt) refers to 2 Thes. 1:7; Heb. 4:3–11.

[5] SB I, pp. 165–170, 599f.; W. Bousset and H. Gressmann, *Die Religion des Judentums in
späthellenistischen Zeitalter*, Tübingen, 1966³, p. 390. Cf. similar ideas in Mark 13:10; Rom.
11:25–27; Rev. 6:11; 2 Pet. 3:12.

[6] H. Conzelmann, *Die Apostelgeschichte*, pp. 34f.; similarly E. Haenchen, *Die Apostelgeschichte*, p. 158; E. Grässer, *Das Problem der Parusieverzögerung*, p. 214.

the contrary, it seems more likely that Luke is here making use of tradition.[1]

The association of a future hope with the gospel message is also demonstrated for Acts by the use of the verb "to save." W. Foerster notes that the quotation from Joel 2:32 in Acts 2:21 refers to salvation in the context of the coming Day of the Lord, and that salvation "from this crooked generation" (Acts 2:40) should be understood in the same context. Probably too Acts 15:1 and 11 point in the same direction.[2]

But the main interest of Luke is in the presence of salvation. If he looks forward to the future coming of Christ, he also knows that Christ is ready here and now to welcome the martyr Stephen into His presence. It is the same combination of eschatological hope and present realization which we find in Paul. For Paul too the content of Christian hope lies in the future coming of Jesus *and* in the prospect of entry to His presence at death: the juxtaposition of these two ideas in Phil. 1:23 and 3:20 shows that here a real tension in Christian hope is being expressed.[3] Similarly, Paul uses the concept of salvation to refer to both present and future.[4]

Thus, while the hope of the parousia and the future events associated with it is an integral part of Luke's theology, just as it is in the case of Paul, it is part of a wider view in which the central place is occupied by the presence of salvation. This, as we have seen, is corroborated by the way in which the hope of the parousia is made to be dependent upon the fact of the resurrection. This again is not a specifically Lucan trait. The connection between the resurrection and the parousia is established as being early by the evidence of Paul (Rom. 14:9; 1 Thes. 1:10);[5] a similar point may also be developed in the case of that most apocalyptic of New Testament writings, the Revelation, where the hope of the future victory of Christ can be shown to rest squarely upon the fact of His death and exaltation. Consequently, without entering upon the point in detail, we can see that there is considerable evidence against the view of Hahn that the future hope

---

[1] So J. A. T. Robinson, *ibid.* Lucan phraseology is nevertheless present (E. Schweizer, *Lordship and Discipleship*, 1960, p. 57 n. 3 (English translation of *Erniedrigung und Erhöhung bei Jesus und seinen Nachfolgern*, Zürich, 1955)). U. Wilckens develops the point made by O. Bauernfeind that a piece of Elijah speculation has been christianized here (*Die Missionsreden der Apostelgeschichte*, pp. 153-156).

[2] W. Foerster, TWNT VII, p. 997.

[3] The point is not greatly affected if it is claimed that Philippians is not a unity; even in this case the constituent parts of the Epistle would belong to the same general period of time. But the Epistle is probably not to be dismembered.

[4] Present: Rom. 8:24; 1 Cor. 15:2; 2 Cor. 6:2; Eph. 2:5, 8; 2 Thes. 2:10. Future: Rom. 5:9f.; 1 Cor. 3:15; 5:5; *et al.*

[5] G. Friedrich, "Ein Tauflied hellenistischer Judenchristen. 1 Thes. 1.9f.," *Theologische Zeitschrift* 21, 1965, pp. 502-516, argues that 1 Thes. 1:10 is pre-Pauline.

was decisive in primitive theology and formed the locus of the earliest christology.

The Presence of Christ and the Spirit

But what is happening in the meantime? We have established the importance of both the past and the future from the point of view of Luke and the early church which he describes. It can, however, be argued that he has little to say about any present work of Christ in the church.[1] In fact one of the most obvious differences between Luke and Paul emerges here. Whereas Paul attaches tremendous importance to the fact of a personal relationship between Christ and the Christian, such a relationship is not part of Luke's theology. The so-called "mysticism" found in Paul has not left a trace in Luke.

We should not exaggerate the importance of this omission. It is of course highly significant in any comparison of Luke and Paul,[2] but it should not be forgotten that only John of the other New Testament writers develops the same kind of concept to anything like as great a degree. Otherwise, it is more or less absent.

Yet in other ways Luke does know of the present work of Christ. This is seen by his emphasis on the "name" of Christ. The use of this phrase does not mean that Jesus Himself is inactive in heaven and that His name is some sort of independent hypostasis. Nor is it a mere "label," simply signifying the name of a superior person by whose mandate a person acts (as in Luke 19:38). The name is rather indicative of the living power of Jesus at work in the church. The signs that are done by the name of Jesus (Acts 4:30) are done by the Lord (Acts 14:3), that is to say by Jesus Himself.[3] The power of Jesus resides in His name, so that it is sufficient to pronounce it over demoniacs in order that they may be cured – provided, of course, that the exorciser has authority to use it, for there is nothing magical about its use (Acts 19:13). Thus too Peter healed Aeneas by saying to him, "Jesus Christ heals you" (Acts 9:34).[4]

But Luke also speaks of Jesus acting in the mission of the church. It is the Lord who appears to Paul in a vision at Corinth to encourage him (Acts 18:9) and who similarly appears to him at Jerusalem to assure him

---

[1] F. Hahn, *Christologische Hoheitstitel*, p. 112 and *passim*, claims that this was the view of the earliest church; it had no concept of the exaltation and present activity of Jesus. J. A. T. Robinson, *Jesus and His Coming*, p. 153, finds this view expressed in Acts 3, but admits that it was not Luke's own belief. H. Conzelmann, *Die Mitte der Zeit* (p. 176), states, however, that this view has often been attributed to Luke. Against Hahn see W. Thüsing, *Erhöhungsvorstellung und Parusieerwartung in der ältesten nachösterlichen Christologie*, Stuttgart, 1969.

[2] It is remarkable that there is no comment on it in P. Vielhauer's discussion of "Paulinism" in Acts (SLA, pp. 33–50).

[3] That "Lord" in Acts 14:3 means Jesus is shown by the parallel in 9:27f.; cf. J. C. O'Neill, SJT 8, 1955, p. 172.

[4] On Luke's use of ὄνομα see also below, pp. 196 f.

that he will reach Rome (Acts 23:11. We should probably also include in this category the vision of Jesus to Paul at his conversion, since it falls outside the forty days of the resurrection appearances, which might be thought to form a class by themselves).

A further fact pointing in the same direction is that prayer is offered to Jesus. Stephen addressed two brief petitions to Jesus at his martyrdom (Acts 7:59, 60), and Paul held a dialogue with Him on the Damascus road (Acts 9:4-6). In the same way He spoke to Ananias giving him directions with regard to Paul (Acts 9:10-17) and to Paul before he fled from Jerusalem (Acts 23:17-21).

These references may suffice to show that when Acts 3:21 speaks of Jesus being received into heaven until the time of the parousia there is no suggestion that He is inactive; the point is simply that He is in heaven and not on earth. The activity which is ascribed to Him is similar to that which Luke ascribes to the angel of the Lord or to the Spirit; Jesus is no less active than those who are elsewhere described as "ministering spirits sent forth to serve, for the sake of those who are to obtain salvation" (Heb. 1:14).

The suggestion may now be made that in some measure Luke's description of the activity of the risen Christ in Acts is his equivalent for what Paul describes in terms of life "in Christ." It must be remembered at the outset that the Pauline use of the key phrase "in Christ" (and its equivalents such as "in the Lord") is not always the expression of a mystical relationship. The outcome of the latest study is to suggest that a life "in Christ" is a life which is moulded by the Christ-event, a life in which the saving events of the cross and the resurrection have decisive force; it is a life which is governed ethically and spiritually by the standards established by the Lord.[1] Yet even when references which fall into these categories are discounted, it remains true that for Paul life means personal union with Christ and communion with Him. The aim of His life was to "know Christ." For him the living Christ was a reality. But what is spoken of here in one set of terms is surely the same thing as is meant by Luke when he describes how Paul and the risen Christ held communication with each other. Paul himself can use Luke's language when he describes how he besought the Lord regarding his thorn in the flesh and received his answer (2 Cor. 12:8 f.): this example should warn us against too readily dismissing Luke's account of visions and dreams received by Paul and others. In the same way, the conversion vision of Jesus given to Paul is referred to in his own way in Gal. 1:16, and if we want an analogy to Stephen's vision of the Son of man one may perhaps be found in Paul's experience of being caught up into Paradise (2 Cor. 12:2 f.).

[1] F. Neugebauer, "Das paulinische 'In Christo'," NTS 4, 1957–58, pp. 124–138; J. K. S. Reid, *Our Life in Christ*, 1963.

In Paul the activity of the Spirit is in some respects so similar to that of the risen Lord that it has even been possible for some commentators to argue that for Paul the two were really one entity (2 Cor. 3:17).[1] From what we have seen it would be possible to draw the same rash conclusion in the case of Luke, for certain of the activities reported of the risen Jesus are also ascribed to the Spirit. Thus to a certain extent the performance of mighty works is due to the Spirit. The Spirit is associated with power (Acts 1:8), and it was through possession of the Spirit and power that Jesus in His earthly ministry was able to heal all who were oppressed by the devil (Acts 10:38). By virtue of his filling with the Spirit Paul was able to pronounce the penalty of blindness upon Elymas (Acts 13:9).[2] Much more significance, however, is attached to the guidance of the church by the Spirit. The commandments of Jesus to the apostles were given "by the Holy Spirit" (Acts 1:2), and thereafter specific instructions to the missionaries are given by the Spirit (Acts 8:29; 10:19; 11:12, 28; 13:2, 4; 15:28; 16:6, 7; 19:21; 20:22,[3] 23; 21:4, 11). This is an impressive set of references and demonstrates how much in Acts the Spirit is the medium through which the will of God is declared to the church. There is nothing quite like this emphasis in the rest of the New Testament. The important point to observe for the moment is that the Spirit which so guides the church is the "Spirit of Jesus" (Acts 16:7); the phrase occurs in narrative, and in contrast to the form "the Holy Spirit" in the previous verse, so that it is likely that Luke is consciously expressing a viewpoint here, and not merely repeating a traditional phrase. E. Schweizer further notes how in Luke 12:21/21:15 and Acts 10:14/19 the Spirit is parallel to the risen Lord.[4] This is to be expected, since the gift of the Spirit is bestowed by God through Jesus (Luke 24:49; Acts 2:33).

We should also notice that the gift of the Spirit to the individual believer is closely associated with baptism in the name of Jesus (Acts 2:38; 9:17f.; 10:43f.; 11: 16f.; 19:5f.). This indicates that the power of Jesus is effective in the conversion of each individual. The gift of the Holy Spirit by Jesus was not a once-for-all act on the day of Pentecost, but is renewed by Him for each individual who is baptised in His name.

[1] "Christ and the Spirit are in some way identical" (J. Weiss, *The History of Primitive Christianity*, New York, 1937, II, p. 464 (English translation of *Das Urchristentum*, Göttingen, 1917). Recent commentators, however, are agreed "that v. 17a is not asserting the identity of two personal entities" (E. Schweizer, TDNT VI, pp. 418f.).

[2] Hence E. Schweizer's denial that Luke ascribes miracles to the working of the Spirit is too sweeping (TDNT VI, p. 407). The same idea is also present in Acts 5:9 where tempting the Spirit leads to judgment.

[3] In Acts 19:21 and 20:22 the Holy Spirit is probably meant (E. Schweizer, TDNT VI, p. 408 n. 491; p. 415). E. Haenchen, *Die Apostelgeschichte*, p. 503, and H. Conzelmann, *Die Apostelgeschichte*, p. 112 (cf. AG, p. 681) hold that in 19:21 a reference to Paul's own spirit is meant.

[4] E. Schweizer, TDNT VI, p. 406.

Through the Spirit, then, the power and presence of Christ are known in the church.[1] Luke does not speak as Paul does of a mystical relationship with Christ, nor of the spiritual effects of the gift of the Spirit in the life of the believer,[2] but he nevertheless has a positive concept of the continuing work of Christ directly and through the Spirit in the church.

Beginning from Jerusalem

Having considered the means by which salvation is offered in Acts, namely through the preaching of the Word accompanied by the work of the risen Christ and the Spirit, we must now look at the historical development of the church.

The New Testament generally bears witness to the priority of the Jews in the divine plan of salvation. It is not only a matter of historical fact but also of theological purpose that the gospel message came first to the Jews. Even Paul who knew that he was called to be the apostle to the Gentiles, having "received grace and apostleship to bring about the obedience of faith for the sake of his name among all the nations" (Rom. 1:5) asserted that the gospel was the power of God for salvation "to the Jew first and also to the Greek" (Rom. 1:16). While Paul insists that there is no partiality with God, he also allows that the Jews come first, even paradoxically to the point of being the first to suffer divine judgment (Rom. 2:9f.). Similarly, in the Gospel of John, the Greeks who wish to speak to Jesus are able to come to Him only indirectly through Philip and Andrew (John 12:20–22). Earlier we noted that it is historical fact that Jesus essentially confined His ministry to the Jews, although there were indications that He was not exclusivist in principle. Moreover, He looked forward to the inclusion of the Gentiles within the kingdom of God.

In the Acts of the Apostles this same priority is maintained. The historical course of the gospel given by Luke is from Jerusalem and Judaea to the end of the earth. The church begins with the Jews, but it spreads to include Samaritans, an Ethiopian eunuch, who may have been a proselyte, and a devout centurion with his friends. Whatever may be the situation with the former persons, this latter group is regarded as being composed of Gentiles, and the incident provoked the verdict, "Then to the Gentiles also God has granted repentance unto life" (Acts 11:18). Thereafter, the gospel was preached to Greeks at Antioch and to Romans

---

[1] Hence H. Conzelmann's claim to the contrary (*Die Mitte der Zeit*, p. 165 n. 2 (p. 178 n. 2)) cannot stand.

[2] C. F. D. Moule claims that "for Paul the Spirit is not the representative and substitute of an absent Christ but the mode of his very presence," and argues that Luke's christology is individualistic, whereas Paul's is inclusive (SLA pp. 179f.).

at Cyprus. A decisive point occurs when in Pisidian Antioch Paul preached to the Jews in the synagogue, and when they rejected the message he turned to the Gentiles: "It was necessary that the word of God should be spoken first to you. Since you thrust it from you, and judge yourselves unworthy of eternal life, behold, we turn to the Gentiles. For so the Lord has commanded us, saying, 'I have set you to be a light for the Gentiles, that you may bring salvation to the uttermost parts of the earth'" (Acts 13:47).

Two effects followed from this. In the first place, the news of the conversion of the Gentiles aroused criticism from some Jewish Christians who argued that such people must submit to circumcision and the law of Moses in order to be saved (Acts 15:1, 5). The criticism evidently arose from the fact that Jews were unable to eat with Gentiles; this appears from the story of Cornelius where the ground of complaint against Peter was that he went to uncircumcised men and ate with them (Acts 11:2). Since acceptance of this principle made entry to the church where common meals were a regular practice impossible, the practical effect of it was to declare that Gentiles must accept Judaism, and the theological consequence drawn was that apart from acceptance of Judaism they could not be saved. According to Luke, however, the criticism was rejected by the leaders of the church. In the story of Cornelius Peter had a vision which showed him that the Jewish ritual law concerning eating with Gentiles was now a thing of the past. The actual conversion of Cornelius demonstrated that God had accepted the Gentiles. Further proof of this latter point was given by the experience of Paul and Barnabas, and it was confirmed by recollection of Old Testament prophecies which spoke of the conversion of the Gentiles (Acts 15:16–18). It was therefore concluded by a gathering of the apostles and elders in Jerusalem that the Gentiles should not be required to accept the Jewish law, except for certain minimal conditions (Acts 15:19–21). The Gentiles were thus freed from any suggestion that they must keep the law of Moses in order to be saved. The issue is not heard of again in Acts.

In the second place, the ministry of Paul is described as following a pattern whereby in the first instance he preached the gospel in new mission centres in the synagogue or to the Jews. This was a regular practice according to Luke. Paul stayed in the synagogue until he was thrust out. Thus the Jews were given the first opportunity, although at the same time any Gentiles who attended the synagogues were also among the first hearers of the gospel. So much is this principle observed that even on arrival at Rome, although he had been met by Christian friends from Rome on the way to the city, Paul called together the Jewish leaders and spoke first of all with them. When they failed to accept the gospel, he uttered the words of Isa. 6:9f. as a condemnation upon them, and said "Let it be known to you then that this salvation of God has been sent to the Gentiles; they will listen" (Acts 28:25–28). Thus Luke's universalism is one in which the Jews come first.

Various problems arise from this presentation. There is first of all the historical one, whether it conforms to what actually happened. This is one of the burning questions of contemporary research into Acts, and it is argued that here in particular Luke has misrepresented the situation by idealization or downright misinterpretation of what happened. The historicity of the so-called council in Acts 15 has been sharply questioned, especially in relation to the evidence of Paul who does not seem to know of it.[1] And the account of Paul's missionary procedure has also been criticized; W. Schmithals can go so far as to say, "It is almost impossible to imagine Paul beginning his preaching in the synagogues."[2]

The problem of the council is too complicated for a full discussion in the present context.[3] It must suffice to express an opinion. It is in our view probable that the meeting described in Gal. 2:1–10, which is often thought to be a variant account of the council, is a previous meeting, and that the council in Acts 15 is not directly mentioned by Paul at all. What Paul describes in Galatians is an earlier meeting which was concerned with the same topic. There is no indication in Acts or anywhere else that the decree of the council was promulgated beyond the churches of Paul's first missionary campaign; it was not known, for example, at Corinth, although at a later date it appears to have been reflected in the messages of John to the churches at Pergamum and Thyatira (Revelation 2:14, 20).[4] The references in Revelation show clearly enough that the decree existed in some form. As for Acts 21:25 this is probably to be taken as a literary reference for the reader's benefit, since Paul himself would not need to be reminded of the provisions of the decree.

As for the second point, Schmithals' view has not commended itself to

[1] See the discussions in E. Haenchen, *Die Apostelgeschichte*, pp. 381–414; H. Conzelmann, *Die Apostelgeschichte*, pp. 81–87.

[2] W. Schmithals, *Paul and James*, 1965, p. 60 (English translation of *Paulus und Jakobus*, Göttingen, 1963). On Luke's representation of Paul generally see G. W. H. Lampe, *St Luke and the Church at Jerusalem*, 1969 (which I have been unable to consult).

[3] Among scholars who identify the council in Acts with the meeting in Gal. 2:1–10, but assess the reliability of Acts more positively are: L. Goppelt, *Apostolic and Post-Apostolic Times*, pp. 75–77; R. P. C. Hanson, *The Acts*, pp. 153–165.

[4] For this view see especially F. F. Bruce, *The Acts of the Apostles*, pp. 287–304; *New Testament History*, 1969, pp. 263–274; "Galatian Problems: 1. Autobiographical Data," BJRL 51, 1968–69, pp. 292–309. D. Guthrie, *Galatians*, 1969, pp. 29–37, finds the evidence very evenly balanced between this view and the one mentioned in the previous footnote.

On Paul and the decree see C. K. Barrett, "Things sacrificed to Idols," NTS 11, 1964–65, pp. 138–153; he argues that Paul was not present when the decree was composed and that 1 Corinthians demonstrates his rejection of it.

THE WORD OF THIS SALVATION

other scholars.[1] The plain meaning of 1 Cor. 9:20 is that Paul worked among Jews, and the churches founded by Paul certainly contained Jews. Schmithals' case is founded on his interpretation of Gal. 2:1–10 which (he holds) means that Paul gave up any attempt to evangelize the Jews and went exclusively to the Gentiles whereas Peter led a mission to the Jews. But such a rigid division of aim would be practically impossible, and it cannot be maintained that an exclusive mission to Jews or to Gentiles was practised. The situation at Antioch described in the immediately following verses of Galatians (2:11 ff.) shows that there at any rate Jews and Gentiles were together in the church. It seems likely that a roughly territorial division was in mind, with the Jerusalem church confining its attention to Palestine while Paul went further afield.

The second main problem concerns the place of the law in the church. Luke is clearly of the opinion that Gentiles do not need to keep the Jewish ritual law. This is the plain meaning of the discussion at Jerusalem. It is also the view of Paul. But this does not mean that Gentiles should not be prepared to make concessions for the sake of peace and harmony. This is evident from the regulations in the Jerusalem decree. The same point of view is expressed by Paul when he counsels the strong Christians to consider the best interests of the weak with regard to the eating of food sacrificed to idols (1 Cor. 8–10; Rom. 14). But Luke does not suggest that Jewish Christians are free from the law. Paul himself is represented as keeping the law: he circumcised Timothy to avoid offence to the Jews, but this should not be regarded as a surrender of principle, since Timothy's parentage made him a special case; the case is quite different from that of Titus who was a Gentile (Acts 16:3; Gal. 2:3). Again he undertook a Jewish vow at Cenchreae (Acts 18:18) and shared in a Jewish rite of purification at Jerusalem (Acts 21:26). Luke thereby seeks to avoid the Jewish accusation that Paul was teaching against the law and the temple (Acts 21:28), but there is no reason to doubt the truth of his account.[2] The situation, as Luke depicts it, is that Jewish Christians themselves keep the law, but they must admit that Gentile Christians do not need to be circumcised. It is consistent with this that the Jewish Christians are said to have worshipped in the temple, and that Paul preached in the synagogues until he was forced out. It was not the Christians who forced the break, but the Jews.

It is important to observe what Luke has related. He has shown that a *modus vivendi* was established. At the same time, there are hints that it was not permanent. Peter is the spokesman of the view that the Jewish law is

[1] G. Bornkamm, "The Missionary Stance of Paul in 1 Corinthians 9 and in Acts," in SLA, pp. 194–207, especially p. 200.
[2] *Pace*, G. Bornkamm, *ibid.*

a yoke "which neither our fathers nor we have been able to bear" (Acts 15:10). What Luke has shown is simply that the place of the Gentiles in the church – on the grounds of the grace of the Lord Jesus Christ alone (Acts 15:11) was assured. He does not, therefore, enter into the question of the continuing difficulties caused by Judaisers in the churches founded by Paul. Whether or not he knew of these, he has passed over them. It was not his purpose to go into these details; his main task was to show that in principle the Gentiles were accepted into the church. Nor again has Luke gone in any detail into the situation for the Jewish Christians. This situation must have become increasingly acute. The question of the necessity of circumcision and keeping of the Mosaic law inevitably arose, and raised acute problems. But at the point at which he was writing this problem was not Luke's concern. He had established that Christianity had not forced the issue of separation from Judaism. He showed that it was the fulfilment of Jewish hopes. He did not feel the need to do more.

The solution was thus not a lasting one. But we should not judge it by too modern a standard. The realization that in Christ circumcision was no longer necessary even for Jews must have taken a long time to establish itself. Paul reached this insight in Rom. 2:29, but it must have taken a long time to establish itself in practice. But would the establishment of it mean the denial of the theological position represented by Luke? This is not necessarily so. Luke's basic position is that Christianity is the fulfilment of what was prophesied in the Old Testament; the essential difference from Judaism lay in the question of the resurrection of Jesus and His attestation as the Messiah. But once this was admitted, and the full significance of Jesus as the Saviour was understood, then the way was open for a development to the position already reached by Paul without any breach of principle.

The third main problem concerns the place of the Jews in the plan of salvation. Do they have a place at all? Or is not Acts 28:28 a final verdict?[1] The Jews have rejected Christ, and therefore they are excluded from the church. This would be a false conclusion in the light of all the evidence. For Luke was perfectly well aware that the church began among the Jews and that its leaders were Jews. He has gone to pains to demonstrate that the gospel is the logical fulfilment of Judaism; the Jewish hopes of the Messiah and the resurrection have been fulfilled in Jesus. He lets the Jewish leaders of the church claim that the Gentiles have been admitted to the church on the same grounds as the Jews, namely by faith.

---

[1] So J. Gnilka, *Die Verstockung Israels. Isaias 6, 9–10 in der Theologie der Synoptiker*, München, 1961, p. 152; cf. pp. 119–154. Cf. P. Richardson, *Israel in the Apostolic Church*, Cambridge, 1969, pp. 160–165.

THE WORD OF THIS SALVATION

Consequently, there can be no question of Jews being excluded from the church.[1] Many did in fact become believers (Acts 21:20).

At the same time, Luke claims that if the Jews, who have the first right to the gospel, refuse it, then the mission must go to the Gentiles. As a nation the Jews have rejected Christ and His followers; consequently they are no longer God's people, but this does not mean that as individuals they may not become members of the new people of God, the Christian church.

Luke's point is, then, concerned essentially with mission. It is not a question of whether Jews can be saved. It is a question of the direction of the church's mission, and Luke's answer is that the gospel is for the Gentiles, since the Jews by and large have rejected it.

It should be obvious that this is in essence the same point as that made by Paul in Romans 9–11.[2] There Paul is conscious that his divine calling is to be the apostle to the Gentiles, and yet he longs that Israel too may be saved. He speaks as a man who would gladly evangelize the Jews but knows that he has a different calling. The basis for this different calling lies in the fact that a divine plan is being carried through. As a result of their unbelief a hardening has come upon the Jews, so that they are unable to believe for the time being. Meanwhile the Gentile mission prospers, and Paul's hope, based on the revelation of a "mystery" by God, is that the Jews will be envious of the Gentiles and that eventually, once the full number of the Gentiles has come in, the Jews too will be saved. Thus the Jews are not finally rejected, but at present the mission is primarily directed to the Gentiles.

Luke too possibly shares this hope of the final conversion of Israel. This is suggested by the reference to the fulfilment of the "times of the Gentiles" in Luke 21:24, and also by the question of the apostles in Acts 1:6: "Lord, will you at this time restore the kingdom to Israel?". It may well be that there is to be a "restoration of the kingdom," although not in the precise manner expected by the Jews at the time.[3]

Our survey has shown that the salvation which is proclaimed in Acts by the word of the Lord "with signs following" stands in continuity with the Old Testament hope of the coming of the Messiah. But the legal requirements of Judaism are no longer binding upon Christians (whether Jew or Gentile) for salvation. This statement poses our next question: how is salvation received by the individual and by the church?

[1] Cf. F. Schütz, *Der leidende Christus*, pp. 123–138.
[2] P. Borgen, "From Paul to Luke," *CBQ* 31, 1969, pp. 168–182.
[3] J. C. O'Neill, *The Theology of Acts in its Historical Setting*, p. 82 n. 2 (second ed., p. 87 n. 1). For the theme of this section, which some scholars regard as the central motif in Acts, see further J. Jervell, *Luke and the People of God*; S. G. Wilson, *The Gentiles and the Gentile Mission in Luke-Acts*, Cambridge, 1973; G. Lohfink, *Die Sammlung Israels*, München, 1975.

CHAPTER VIII

WHAT MUST I DO TO BE SAVED?

IN THE TWO PREVIOUS CHAPTERS WE HAVE SEEN HOW THE GOOD NEWS OF peace by Jesus Christ began with the proclamation of the word by Jesus Himself and was continued by the preaching of the witnesses whom He had commanded (Acts 10:36f., 41f.). The next task which must concern us is to inquire into the appropriation of salvation by the individual: what has he to do in order to be saved? The simple answer is that which Paul gave to this question when it was asked by the jailer at Philippi: "Believe in the Lord Jesus, and you will be saved, you and your household" (Acts 16:31). But this simple answer requires elaboration in order that its full significance may be appreciated.

The Divine Initiative

We must observe at the outset that there is a sense in which the individual can do nothing to save himself. The initiative lies entirely in the hands of God. Although, as we saw earlier, it has sometimes been argued that the ideas of calling and election are not prominent in Luke, the basic motif is both present and important. Throughout the writings of Luke it is God who takes the initiative in the work of His church; when the gospel is preached, it is at the behest of God (Acts 5:20), and the sending out of missionaries takes place by His command and guidance (Acts 8:26; 9:10–12; 10:19f.; 13:1–4; 16:6–10; 19:21; 20:22). In some of these cases the reference is to the conversion of specific individuals, the Ethiopian eunuch, Paul, and Cornelius; the personal circumstances which led to their meetings with Christians can be seen to reflect the providential arrangement of God. Cornelius received an explicit vision which set in motion the train of events leading to the arrival of Peter. Paul was the recipient of a personal vision of the risen Christ. And it was surely not fortuitous that the Ethiopian was reading Isa. 53 in his chariot. The divine ordering of circumstances is seen further in the word of the Lord encouraging Paul to continue his work in Corinth: "I am with you, and no man shall attack you to harm you; for I have many people in this city" (Acts 18:10). Here the thought is of God's election of men to salvation. The same idea may be present in Acts 13:48 where we are told that of the Gentiles in Antioch "as many as were ordained to eternal life believed"; here, however, the idea may be that these people were already marked out for salvation, like Cornelius, by their earlier acceptance of the grace of God.[1] In any case, however, the initiative is with God. Similarly, Lydia is described as a person whose heart the Lord opened to give heed to what was said by Paul (Acts 16:14). In the same strain are the passages which speak of God giving repentance to the Jews and to the Gentiles (Acts 5:31; 11:18); the opportunity to repent is God's gift.

The cumulative evidence of these passages is decisive. For Luke salvation is dependent upon the initiative of God who not only sends out the Word but also prepares the hearts of men and women to receive it. Any suggestion that here Hellenistic ideas of predestination are present is effectively refuted by the fact that in this context Luke stresses the divine grace which leads to salvation. The gospel is the gospel of the grace of God (Acts 20:24), and it is through grace that men come to faith (Acts 18:27).[2] Grace is also associated with the Lord Jesus as the means of salvation (Acts 14:3). It is the divine backing for missionaries (Acts 14:26 15:40) and it upholds the members of the church (Acts 20:32).

The same consideration is important in another respect. It has been alleged that Luke comes perilously near, or even actually embraces, a doctrine of salvation by works. In the Gospel he lays stress on alms as the way to secure inward cleansing (Luke 11:41), and he shows how those who are pious gain salvation (Luke 7:4f.; Acts 8:27; Acts 10:2–4, 22). In the same way he stresses the virtues of piety and devoutness on the part of disciples (Acts 9:36; 22:12). Consequently, the conclusion has been drawn that Luke is not free from a doctrine of salvation by works. Devout Jews who keep the law qualify for salvation, and Jewish Christians are singled out for their piety; we are reminded of the birth narrative where the blameless and God-fearing lives of the principal characters are stressed (Luke 1:6: 2:25, 37). It has, therefore, been claimed that "according to Luke . . . justification by faith is so to speak only complementary for Jewish Christians. It is necessary for them because and to the extent that

[1] This is suggested by the fact that in Acts 13:43 Paul's hearers were urged to "continue in the grace of God." But it is not certain that the same group of people are meant in both verses; the Gentiles in verse 48 may be a different group from the "devout converts to Judaism" in verse 43. In any case H. Conzelmann's claim (*Die Mitte der Zeit*, p. 144 n. 1 (p. 154 n. 2)) that the phrase "ordained to eternal life" is taken over from tradition and must not be pressed is dubious; the evidence rather suggests that the idea expressed is Lucan.

[2] It is debated whether "through grace" is to be construed with "who had believed" (RSV, NEB; BC IV ad loc.) or with "he greatly helped" (E. Haenchen, *Die Apostelgeschichte* p. 485; H. Conzelmann, *Die Apostelgeschichte*, p. 109).

they fall short of the fulfilment of the law or because the law provides no complete justification."[1]

This conclusion is completely unwarranted. The fact is indisputable that Luke places value on piety. To do otherwise would be to display moral frivolity. Doubtless he is not as daring in his expressions as Paul who categorically denies the value of works of the law as a means of justification (Rom. 3:20, 28), but this very stress made Paul liable to misinterpretation against which he had to defend himself. But Luke knows as clearly as Paul or John that salvation is through faith in Christ alone (Acts 15:11). What Luke is defending is not the value of works as a means of salvation. On the contrary he sees in piety and good works the indication of an attitude which prior to the coming of the gospel of faith in Jesus Christ is seeking salvation by trusting and serving God. When the devout people described by Luke heard the gospel or met Christ, their immediate reaction was to believe in Him; their earlier life was a preparation for faith (Luke 7:9; Acts 8:36; 11:17 cf. Luke 1:67–79; 2:28–32, 38). In each case piety came to its consummation in faith, and piety which was looking forward to God's salvation was rewarded by Him. Hence "in every nation any one who fears him and does what is right is acceptable to him" (Acts 10:34), but it was God Himself who took the initiative in bringing the gospel to them. The time of their devotion to Judaism was a period of experiencing the grace of God, and to accept Christ was to "continue in the grace of God" (Acts 13:43). Jews and Gentiles are accepted by God on precisely the same terms: Peter, a Jew, said, "We believe that we shall be saved through the grace of the Lord Jesus, just as they will" (Acts 15:11), and Paul would have agreed wholeheartedly: "God is one: and he will justify the circumcised on the ground of their faith and the uncircumcised through their faith" (Rom. 3:30).

Nor is there any suggestion that the works of the law and faith somehow complement each other.[2] This is an entirely false deduction from Acts 13:39, "by him everyone that believes is freed from everything from which you could not be freed by the law of Moses." To argue that this means that there are some things from which a person could be freed by the law of Moses, but that for others faith in Christ was necessary is to attribute to Luke a quibble which is unsupported by any other statement in his writings. The statement means that Christ offers full forgiveness. As F. F. Bruce comments: "Moses' law does not justify; faith in Christ does. Not only is this interpretation of Paul's words here supported by the not irrelevant consideration that this is how the doctrine of justification is

---

[1] P. Vielhauer, "On the 'Paulinism' of Acts," SLA, p. 42. Contra: E. Haenchen, *op. cit.*, p. 354 n. 4.

[2] P. Stuhlmacher, *Gerechtigkeit Gottes bei Paulus*, Göttingen, 1966[2], pp. 194f.

presented in his epistles; it is the interpretation required by the natural emphasis of the passage itself. Paul is not making partial but total claims for the power of the gospel over against the law."[1]

Luke's attitude to the law is expressed in the words of Peter who speaks of it as a yoke "which neither our fathers nor we have been able to bear" (Acts 15:10). It is true that he also knows of many thousands of Jewish believers who were zealous for the law (Acts 21:20) and that Paul himself kept the law (Acts 21:24). But the break in principle has been made when the Gentiles are no longer required to keep it, and we must judge that the words of Peter represent the ultimate principle accepted by Luke. It is true that some scholars have suggested that Luke has not made the same kind of break with the law in principle as was made by Paul. Luke, it is said, speaks only of the inadequacy of the law, whereas Paul speaks of the end of the law, which is Christ. For Luke the law has been done away with because men could not keep it (Acts 15:10), but for Paul it is done away with in Christ.[2] Or again it is argued that Paul saw in the law a means by which man sought to achieve his own grounds for boasting and thereby separated himself from God, but Luke regarded it as a list of commands and prohibitions which no man could fulfil.[3] But surely this contrast is overdrawn. Paul too can speak of the law as holy, just and good (Rom. 7:12); he knows that the way of righteousness by the law consists in fulfilment of its obligations (Gal. 3:12). He is prepared to admit that a man may keep the law (Rom. 2:7, 13; Phil. 3:6), but since Christ has come the law is no longer the way of righteousness (Rom 3:21). The law was inadequate – "God has done what the law, weakened by the flesh, could not do: sending his own Son in the likeness of sinful flesh and for sin, he condemned sin in the flesh, in order that the just requirement of the law might be fulfilled in us" (Rom. 8:3f.). At the same time the law still stands: "Do we then overthrow the law by this faith? By no means! On the contrary, we uphold the law" (Rom. 3:31), for it is taken up into the new relationship in Christ (Rom. 8:4; 1 Cor. 9:21; Rom. 13:8–10).

The Pauline position is surely not essentially different from that of Luke. Both affirm the value of the law, both deny that it is the way of salvation, both speak of faith in Christ as the only way of salvation, both agree that the law was inadequate to save men. One cannot deny that the deeper and more theological exposition is that of Paul, but this is only to be expected. It may well be, as Vielhauer argues, that Luke had never

---

[1] F. F. Bruce, *The Book of the Acts*, p. 279. What Luke is emphasizing is the completeness of the salvation offered in Christ. One may be justified from *all* the things for which there was no remedy in the law. Cf. U. Wilckens, *Die Missionsreden der Apostelgeschichte*, p. 184.

[2] P. Vielhauer, *ibid.*; H. Conzelmann, *Die Mitte der Zeit*, p. 149 (p. 160).

[3] E. Haenchen, *op. cit.*, p. 387 n. 1.

experienced the personal problem of the law as the way of salvation, and therefore he did not feel the need to go into it as deeply as Paul.[1] But his solution should not be dismissed as unpauline or even superficial because he has not wrestled with it at the same level as Paul. Both Luke and Paul agree on the central point: salvation is not by keeping the law but by the free grace of God.

Repentance, Faith and Conversion

We now turn to what may be called the human side of receiving salvation. A number of stories of the conversion of both groups of people and individuals are recorded in Acts, and from these we may construct a pattern of the essential steps in becoming a Christian.[2] It then emerges that there are a number of constant factors involved. The first of these is that the persons concerned hear the preaching of the Word. In every single case the first step in conversion is the preaching of the Word so that Christ is made known as Saviour; the case of Paul is only an apparent exception, since in his case there was a direct revelation of Jesus Himself (Acts 2:14–36; 4:2; 8:4f., 12, 35; 10:34–43; 13:12, 46; 16:14, 31f.; 17:2f., 11, 22–31; 18:5; 19:4, 8–10). Preaching in itself implies hearing (Rom. 10:14b), and it is therefore significant that Luke especially draws attention to the fact that men heard the Word that was preached to them (Acts 2:37; 4:4; 8:6; 10:33; 13:44, 48; 17:32; 18:8; 19:5, 10; cf. 13:12; 16:14; 17:4, 11). Luke here develops a motif that is important both in Paul (Rom. 10:14–17; Gal. 3:2, 5; Eph. 1:13; Col. 1:6, 23; 1 Thes. 2:13) and John (1 John 1:1, 3; 2:7, 24: 3:11) and also in the Gospels (Luke 5:1; 7:22; 8:4–21; 10:24)[3] Apart from hearing the word there can be no salvation.[4]

Those who hear the word may accept it or reject it, the latter fulfilling with regard to themselves the prophecy of Isa. 6:9f. (Acts 28:24–27).[5] Through their rejection of the word they cut themselves off from salvation. The response of those who accept the word is described as belief. From one point of view, it is belief in the message (Acts 8:12); from another it is belief in Jesus Christ. The latter expression is used to describe the act of commitment to Him. It means accepting that He is the Saviour, the Messiah and the Lord, but such acceptance of the message about Him

---

[1] P. Vielhauer, *ibid*. On the other hand, E. E. Ellis has claimed that Luke was not a Gentile but a Jewish Christian, *The Gospel of Luke*, pp. 52f. But Ellis's discussion of Col. 4:10–14, if valid, only *allows* that Luke was a Jewish Christian if this seems probable on other grounds.
[2] Cf. U. Wilckens, *Die Missionsreden der Apostelgeschichte*, pp. 178–186.
[3] G. Kittel, TDNT I, pp. 216–221.
[4] The implications of this statement for the practice of infant baptism should be noted.
[5] The prophecy is applied to the case of the Jews, but it may be applied more widely.

obviously implies personal commitment to the One who is the Lord. This point is stressed by R. Bultmann who argues that "faith in the kerygma is inseparable from faith in the person mediated thereby" and quotes in evidence Acts 14:23 ("They committed them to the Lord in whom they had believed") and the use of πιστεύειν ἐπί in Acts 9:42; 11:17; 16:31 and 22:19.[1] The personal character of this relationship is further indicated by the Lucan use of the word "disciple" to indicate the believer. This word is not found outside Acts to designate believers in the post-Easter situation; apart from Acts its use is confined to the Gospels where it describes the followers of the earthly Jesus who stood in a personal relationship to Him. Luke's use of it in Acts is a further example of the continuity which he traced between the periods of Jesus and of the early church, and indicates that he saw no essential difference between discipleship before and after Easter. The use of the term may well be due to a source used by Luke, but it accurately expresses his own viewpoint.[2] Disciples are those who believe in Christ (Acts 6:7; 14:22; 18:27) and stand in a personal relationship to Him as their Lord.

Alongside faith repentance is an important factor in conversion. Already in the Gospel of Luke there is a greater stress than in the other Gospels on the need for repentance. Luke alone gives details of the ethical teaching of John the Baptist in which he explained what was meant by "the fruits of repentance" in practical terms (Luke 3:8, 10-14). Luke alone adds the words "to repentance" to the saying of Jesus "I have not come to call the righteous but sinners" (Luke 5:32), and in a number of other places the word "repentance" figures prominently in his vocabulary.[3] This culminates in the command of the risen Lord that repentance should be preached in his name to all nations (Luke 24:47).

Thus on the day of Pentecost the Jews who listened to Peter were convicted of their corporate guilt in crucifying Jesus and were summoned to repent (Acts 2:37f.; cf. 3:19; 5:31). The message of repentance also was proclaimed to the Gentiles (Acts 11:18; 17:30), so that it was a basic part of the message to all men (Acts 20:21; 26:20).

The content of repentance is undoubtedly moral as well as religious. Repentance is concerned not only with the guilt of the Jews in crucifying Jesus but also with turning away from wickedness and evil (Acts 3:26; 8:22f.). It has to find expression in outward acts which indicate the reality of an inward change of heart (Acts 26:20). Sin must be confessed and given up (Acts 19:18f.) and a new way of life must begin (Luke 19:1-10).

[1] R. Bultmann, TDNT VI, pp. 211f.
[2] H. J. Cadbury, BC V, pp. 376-378; K. H. Rengstorf, TDNT IV, pp. 457-459. Peculiar to Acts is the absolute use of the phrase without a qualifying genitive. Cf. H.-J. Degenhardt, *Lukas – Evangelist der Armen*, pp. 33-41.
[3] Luke 13:3, 5; 15:7, 10; 16:30; 17:3f.

At two points Luke's view of repentance requires some justification. First, it is not correct to say, with H. Conzelmann, that Luke has changed the notion of repentance from being a concept describing the whole act of conversion, as in Mark, to a description of one pre-condition for salvation. Repentance for Luke has been narrowed down to mean penitence, an inward attitude that must be followed by a changed life.[1] This view of Luke rests on the acceptance of E. Lohmeyer's claim that in Mark repentance and forgiveness have much the same meaning.[2] But Lohmeyer's view of the meaning of repentance in Mark 1:4 is over-subtle and cannot bear the weight that Conzelmann places upon it.[3] Further, conversion in Mark involves both repentance and belief in the gospel (Mark 1:15).[4] So Luke and Mark do not differ essentially in usage. A further source of confusion lies in Conzelmann's apparent supposition that ἐπιστρέφειν refers to the change of life corresponding to the act of penitence (μετανοεῖν).[5] But Luke's usage demonstrates quite plainly that "conversion" is concerned with the act of turning to God rather than with the adoption of a different kind of behaviour. It is an expression which denotes the positive aspect of the act which is denoted negatively by repentance (Acts 26:18-20).[6] It is thus not precisely a synonym for repentance,[7] but denotes the positive side of conversion, and is consequently more suitable for use as a comprehensive term to describe the process of repenting and believing in God.

The second point is to observe that it is curious how a number of scholars speak of Luke moralizing the nature of repentance.[8] It is difficult to see how else repentance could be envisaged when it is a question of turning away from sin and disobedience to God's commands. What else is repentance concerned with if it is not concerned with a man's moral life in the sight of God? This is clear from the teaching of John the Baptist as recorded in the Q tradition where he demands that men show the fruit

[1] H. Conzelmann, *Die Mitte der Zeit*, pp. 90-92, 213-215 (pp. 99-101, 228-230).

[2] E. Lohmeyer, *Das Evangelium des Markus*, Göttingen, 1959¹⁵, pp. 14f.

[3] Lohmeyer's argument is that in the phrase "baptism of repentance" repentance cannot be a human attitude but is rather a gift of God to the baptized. Yet he claims that this divine gift does not exclude human penitence and repentance. This exegesis is too subtle. It does not fit in with the preaching of John which was a call to men to repent. It also requires the deletion of "for the forgiveness of sins" as an interpretative addition.

[4] Only in Mark 6:12 does Mark sum up the message of Jesus as one of repentance. But here, as E. Lohmeyer has noted (*op. cit.*, p. 115), we have merely a catchword which is meant to suggest to the reader the remainder of the message.

H. Conzelmann, *op. cit.*, p. 91 (p. 100), also holds that for Luke μετανοεῖν designates a once-for-all act. This is not the case in Acts 8:22.

[5] H. Conzelmann, *op. cit.*, pp. 91-93 (pp. 100-102). He does not discuss the usage of ἐπιστρέφω in detail.

[6] G. Bertram TDNT VII, pp. 722-729, especially pp. 726-728.

[7] Contra: U. Wilkens, *op. cit.*, p. 180.

[8] H. Conzelmann, *op. cit.*, p. 91 (p. 100); U. Wilckens, *op. cit.*, p. 181.

of repentance (Matt. 3:8 par. Luke 3:8), and it is also part of the teaching of Paul (2 Cor. 12:21) and Revelation (2:16, 21f.; 9:20f.; 16:11). Luke has not introduced anything new into the understanding of the word.[1]

Baptism and its Results

The preceding remarks have dealt largely with the inner disposition of the converted person. But this disposition is inseparable in Luke's thought from the act of baptism, an outward act which indicates a spiritual reality. The significant place of baptism is easily seen from the way in which it figures in the pattern of conversion in Acts. In almost every record of conversion it is explicitly mentioned; the exceptions are Acts 2:47; 4:4; 6:7; 9:42; 11:21-24; 13:48; 14:1, 21; 17:34, and in these cases we have to do for the most part with summary statements in which the interest is not in the fact of conversion as such but rather in the growth and spread of the church. The existing pattern of conversion shows that for Luke baptism was indispensable, and there is no reason to suppose that there was any other practice in the early church.

It is clear that baptism was an outward indication of the existence of faith. This is apparent from Acts 8:36 where faith is not mentioned but is implied in the act of baptism. U. Wilckens's statement that in Luke faith appears to follow baptism is quite unfounded.[2] Baptism is also closely linked with repentance (Acts 2:38). Here Luke preserves a link which is elsewhere attested of Christian baptism only in Hebrews 6:2f.[3] But the connection of repentance with John's baptism is fundamental for the understanding of the latter (Mark 1:4f.; Matt. 3:7f. par. Luke 3:7f.). Luke has closely related the substance of John's baptism with Christian baptism. This is a correct insight. In view of the contrast expressed in Mark 1:8 between water baptism and Spirit baptism it is hard to explain why the early church practised water baptism in connection with the reception of the Spirit unless it took over John's baptism, and with the act the meaning of the act. This is proved by the way in which forgiveness is associated with Christian baptism just as it was with John's-baptism (cf. Acts 22:16; 1 Cor. 6:11; Eph. 5:26; Titus 3:5; 1 Pet. 3:21). The connection between forgiveness and repentance is fundamental for Jewish thought, and it was taken over in Christian theology, where, however,

---

[1] On repentance in general see J. Behm, TDNT IV, pp. 975-1008.
[2] U. Wilckens, op. cit., p. 183 n. 2, quoting Acts 16:15, 33 f. It is clear, however, that in the first of these passages baptism is the evidence of faith; Lydia is speaking in a somewhat formal, courteous manner; in the second passage the use of the perfect form (πεπιστευκώς) implies that faith and baptism were simultaneous.
[3] U. Wilckens, op. cit., p. 182.

the human act of repentance took second place to the atoning act of God in Christ.[1]

Christian baptism is described as baptism in (ἐν) the name of Jesus Christ (Acts 2:38;[2] 10:48) or into (εἰς) the name of the Lord Jesus (Acts 8:16; 19:5); similarly forgiveness is bestowed through His name (Acts 10:43) on those who believe (Acts 10:43). This phraseology appears to have been known to Paul (1 Cor. 1:13, 15), but he prefers to use the form "into Christ" (Rom. 6:3; Gal. 3:27; cf. 1 Cor. 10:2). The meaning of the formulae used by Luke is obscure. It has been thought that ἐν τῷ ὀνόματι, refers to the invocation of the name of Jesus Christ by the baptized person or to the naming of Christ over the person who was baptized.[3] This would help to explain the connection of the name with baptism, but it does not elucidate the meaning of the phrase. The older view is that a well-known term from commercial papyri is here used, signifying that a person or thing is reckoned to the account (εἰς τὸ ὄνομα) of a particular person and thus becomes his possession.[4] More recently, a number of scholars have advocated the view that a rabbinic phrase meaning "with respect or regard to" is reflected; then Jesus Christ represents the goal of baptism, the person for whose sake it is carried out.[5] It seems likely that no one explanation should be adopted to the exclusion of the others. The name in baptism signifies Jesus as the One who becomes the Saviour and Lord of the baptized; He is the One confessed by the baptized, the One to whom he turns and in whom he puts his faith. At the same time Luke's usage is not necessarily delineated by that of his sources. We must take into account the rich use which he makes of the term ὄνομα in connection with the risen Jesus. Elsewhere in Acts the name of Jesus is used to indicate both the One by whose authority the early church acted and also the One through whose power mighty works were performed (Acts 3:6, 16; 4:7, 10, 30; 9:27; 16:18). It seems likely that these ideas are also present in the baptismal language. The name of Jesus indicates the power by which salvation (Acts 4:12) and forgiveness are made available to the baptized. The name of Christ is thus the

---

[1] For the Jewish view see E. Lohse, *Märtyrer und Gottesknecht*. In Christianity faith replaces repentance as the basic attitude, but faith implies that a prior act of God has taken place; cf. J. Denney, *The Christian Doctrine of Reconciliation*, 1917, pp. 284f.

[2] In Acts 2:38 it is not clear whether ἐν or ἐπί is to be read.

[3] F. F. Bruce, *The Book of Acts*, p. 76, interprets the use of ἐν τῷ ὀνόματι in this way. Compare the use of ἐπικαλέομαι to describe invocation of Christ as the means of salvation (Acts 2:21; 9:14, 21; 22:16; Rom. 10:12-14; 1 Cor. 1:2; 2 Tim. 2:22, cf. 1 Pet. 1:17). For naming the Name over the baptized see Acts 15:17; Jam. 2:7.

[4] J. Weiss, *Der erste Korintherbrief*, 1910, pp. 18f.; A. Oepke, TDNT I, pp. 539f.; F. F. Bruce, *The Book of Acts*, p. 181 n. 32.

[5] J. Jeremias, *Infant Baptism in the First Four Centuries*, 1960, p. 29 n. 9 (English translation of *Die Kindertaufe in den ersten vier Jahrhunderten*, Göttingen, 1958); H. Bietenhard, TDNT V, pp. 274-276.

effective power in baptism, just as it is in the performance of mighty works.

The immediate effects of baptism are forgiveness and the reception of the Holy Spirit. "Forgiveness of sins" is a typical Lucan phrase; we have previously noted its prominence in the Gospel. It also appears frequently in Acts to designate the content of salvation (Acts 2:38; 5:31; 10:43; 13:38 26:18). The use of this phrase brings the message of the early church into close connection with that of John the Baptist whose baptism mediated forgiveness (Mark 1:4; Luke 1:77) and with the teaching of Jesus, but the precise phraseology is remarkably rare elsewhere in the New Testament. It is not a part of Paul's vocabulary; Rom. 4:7 is a quotation from the LXX, and in Col. 1:14 and Eph. 1:7 traditional liturgical phraseology is probably to be found. Elsewhere forgiveness is mentioned in Hebrews (9:22; 10:18), James (5:15) and 1 John (1:9; 2:12). In the case of Paul the vocabulary of justification has almost completely ousted that of forgiveness, but the quotation from Psa. 32:1f. in Rom. 4:7f. in the context of justification indicates that for Paul the ideas were closely related.[1] It thus appears that Luke has preserved a term which was characteristic of the early preaching.

The other blessing closely associated with baptism is the reception of the Holy Spirit. Here again the connection with John the Baptist is made. At the beginning of Acts there is a promise by the risen Christ which is reminiscent of the words of John the Baptist: "John baptized with water, but before many days you shall be baptized with the Holy Spirit" (Acts 1:5; cf. Luke 3:16). The fulfilment "before many days" took place on the Day of Pentecost when the disciples were filled with the Holy Spirit accompanied by the signs of wind and fire. There is no mention of the baptism of the initial group of disciples with water. But the converts at the end of Peter's sermon were baptised with water and received the gift of the Spirit (Acts 2:38, 41). Thereafter, as we have seen, converts were regularly baptized. This baptism of converts was regarded as the fulfilment of John's prophecy; the prophecy was not exhaustively fulfilled in the original outpouring of the Spirit.[2] This is demonstrated by the repetition of the words of the Baptist and their application to the case of Cornelius and his household in Acts 11:17. Here the fact that Jesus has poured out the Spirit on the Gentiles is regarded as the fulfilment of John's prophecy, and therefore it is the justification for a baptism with water.

The association of the Spirit with baptism is made in Acts 9:17f.; 10:47f.; 11:16 and 19:5f. (cf. 8:15f.). It is, however, not made explicitly

---

[1] That forgiveness was a significant concept for Paul is apparent from the fact that he could have made his point about imputation by quoting Psa. 32:2 without including verse 1.

[2] Contra: F. F. Bruce, *The Book of Acts*, p. 76.

in the rest of the New Testament except perhaps in John 3:5. But too much should not be made of this apparent discrepancy. On the one hand, the assumption that reception of the Spirit is the decisive indication that a man is a Christian is basic to the theology of Paul, John and Peter; it is axiomatic that a believer possesses the Spirit: "Any one who does not have the Spirit of Christ does not belong to him" (Rom. 8:9) is a statement that would be confirmed by any of the New Testament writers.[1] The difference between Luke and the rest of the New Testament should not, therefore, be pressed too sharply.

On the other hand, it is a notorious problem that Luke's statements about the relation of the Spirit to baptism are incapable of being worked into one single pattern. While the pattern that Luke apparently wishes to regard as normal is that of water-baptism associated with the reception of the Spirit, he records several anomalies. The 120 disciples who shared in the Pentecostal outpouring were not baptized; at least Luke was not concerned to record whether or not they were. In Acts 8:14-17 the converts in Samaria who had been baptized with water in the name of the Lord Jesus did not receive the Spirit until a subsequent date when the apostles Peter and John laid hands on them. Cornelius and his household received the Spirit before they were baptized with water (Acts 10:44-48; 11:15-17).[2] Nothing is said about the Christian baptism of Apollos, a man who knew only the baptism of John; the commentators are deeply divided over the explanation of the incident (Acts 18:24-28).[3] But another group of "disciples" who had been baptized only with John's baptism were baptized by Paul and had hands laid upon them, with the result that the Spirit came upon them (Acts 19:1-7).[4] A further complication arises from the way in which the gifts of tongues and prophecy are associated with the reception of the Spirit in Acts 2:1-4; 10:46 and 19:6.

The attempt to discover what lies behind these varied reports has led to

---

[1] See the texts listed by U. Wilckens, *op. cit.*, p. 183 n. 4.

[2] E. Schweizer's view (TDNT VI, p. 413) that Acts 11:16 implies that no baptism followed (or was at least non-essential) is rightly rejected by H. Conzelmann, *Die Apostelgeschichte*, p. 67.

[3] E. Käsemann, "The Disciples of John the Baptist in Ephesus" in *Essays on New Testament Themes*, pp. 136-148, argues that Acts 18:25c is a Lucan fabrication, designed to denigrate Apollos from being an independent, authorized teacher of the church, by associating him with the defective disciples in Acts 19;1-7, and thereby making him require further instruction from Paul's colleagues; Luke, it is implied, would have liked to describe his rebaptism, but did not dare to do so. This theory goes too far. Luke is not concerned with denying the existence of free-lance teachers, but rather with showing that their teaching is in accordance with the apostolic tradition. The fact that Apollos is described as possessing the Spirit shows that he did not come into the same category as the defective disciples who did not possess the Spirit.

[4] K. Haacker, "Einige Fälle von 'Erlebter Rede' im Neuen Testament," Nov. T 12, 1970, pp. 70-77, has shown convincingly that "disciples" here signifies how the men appeared *at first sight* to *Paul*; his subsequent questioning demonstrated that his initial impression was incorrect, and therefore he gave them Christian baptism.

no very certain conclusions. Fortunately, we do not need to investigate the matter closely. What is important for us at the moment is Luke's point of view. It is clear that Luke had received several varying accounts of how the Spirit was received by men, but he has not tried to harmonize them and impose a pattern upon them. From a theological point of view this should not surprise us. Writing about spiritual gifts, Paul insisted that the Spirit apportions them "to each one individually as he wills" (1 Cor. 12:11), and the words of Jesus in the Gospel of John are to the same effect: "The wind blows where it wills, and you hear the sound of it, but you do not know whence it comes or whither it goes; so it is with every one who is born of the Spirit" (John 3:8). If Luke was wishing to fit the work of the Spirit into a pattern, he had no need to record these anomalous experiences. It is to his credit that he has left the commentators with a certain confusion to wrestle with. E. Schweizer correctly notes that in the end Luke was not too concerned with water baptism as the necessary means to the bestowal of the Spirit. He is more concerned to stress the importance of faith (always) and prayer (often) as the appropriate attitudes of men.[1] The significance of water baptism and the laying on of hands in connection with the reception of the Spirit is that these outward acts relate the experience of the individual to that of the church; this is a point to which we must revert later.

The Spirit and the Believer

At this point we must ask what is the practical effect of the reception of the Spirit by the believer. In an earlier discussion it became clear that an important aspect of the work of the Spirit was His guidance of the church. One other aspect of His work is especially prominent in Acts. The key text Acts 1:8 reminds us that the apostles were to receive power when the Holy Spirit came upon them and would in consequence be the witnesses of Jesus. The significance of the gift of the Spirit at Pentecost was that it enabled the apostles to bear witness in other tongues so that their message was heard by people from every nation under heaven (Acts 2:4–11) Thereafter, the apostles were filled with the Spirit in order to speak effectively as witnesses to Christ (Acts 4:8, 31; 5:32; 6:10; 7:55; 9:17–20) or to carry on the other work of the church (Acts 6:3, 5; 11:24).

Now the gift of the Spirit was not the prerogative of the apostles alone. We have just seen that it was so much the mark of every believer that, on the one hand, the reception of the Spirit by Cornelius and his household was the decisive indication that salvation was for the Gentiles as well as for the Jews, and therefore the Gentiles were to be welcomed into the

[1] E. Schweizer, TDNT VI, p. 414.

church; further, on the other hand, the lack of the Spirit on the part of certain disciples demanded that action be taken to remedy the deficiency. Every believer, therefore, possesses the Spirit. The suggestion which we now make is that this gift of the Spirit to every believer has the same effect as in the case of the apostles. Its purpose is to constitute a church composed of missionaries. This is substantiated by Acts 4:31, which shows that the task of speaking the Word of the Lord was not confined to the apostles, and by Luke 12:11 f., where the promise of Jesus regarding inspiration by the Spirit is meant for the disciples generally in situations of persecution.

It is true that other effects are ascribed to the gift of the Spirit. On three occasions Luke draws attention to speaking in tongues as the outward manifestation of the gift of the Spirit (Acts 2:1-4; 10:46; 19:6), and it may be that the gift of tongues was originally mentioned in the sources for certain other passages in Acts.[1] But it is unlikely that this gift was the universal or normal accompaniment of the reception of the Spirit, and it is certainly not so in Luke's thought. For Luke speaking in tongues appears to be connected with particular crises in the history of the church.[2] Again, consolation and joy are linked with the gift of the Spirit (Acts 9:31; 13:52), but no particular importance is attached to this, although it incidentally brings Luke's view of the Spirit close to that of the early church generally.[3]

It therefore seems likely that Luke especially understood the gift of the Holy Spirit as equipping the church for mission, and consequently that he regarded the essence of being a Christian as the activity of mission. "A church which does not engage in mission is not a church filled by the Spirit and hence not a church living in the new era."[4] It is true that Luke's use of the term "witness" is a special, restricted one,[5] but what we have uncovered here is something which is not bound to a particular terminology. Evangelism and speaking the word of the Lord were by no means confined to those who were witnesses in the technical sense; this is clear, if proof were needed, from Acts 8:4-6; 11:19-21 and 19:24-26, passages which show others than the apostles and the appointed missionaries of the

---

[1] At Acts 4:31 H. Conzelmann (*Die Apostelgeschichte*, p. 38) notes that the phrase καὶ ἐλάλουν suggests an original continuation γλώσσαις. A description of outward manifestations of the gift of the Spirit has also been suspected at Acts 8:17 (*Ibid.*, p. 55; E. Haenchen, *Die Apostelgeschichte*, p. 254). On this view Luke has suppressed these references in favour of a more edifying account. But if this is so, it is strange that Luke has not also suppressed the other references which he has allowed to remain.

[2] E. Schweizer, TDNT VI, p. 411.

[3] Cf. the description of the Spirit as the Paraclete in John 14:16, 26; 15:26; 16:7. For the linking of joy with the Spirit see Rom. 14:17; Gal. 5:22.

[4] E. Schweizer, "Gegenwart des Geistes und eschatologische Hoffnung," in BNTE, pp. 482-508; quotation from p. 505.

[5] See above, pp. 41-44.

church preaching the gospel. It is true that in each of these cases the leaders of the church took steps to ensure that what was being done was in accordance with the teaching of the apostles and in continuity with the work of the original community, but this does not affect the basic point at issue. It was not the messengers who had to be authenticated so much as the message itself. Presentation of the gospel might be done by anybody.

If there is substance in this point, it counters E. Schweizer's claim that Luke's view of the Spirit is limited. For Schweizer, fundamentally Luke "does not cease to regard the Spirit merely as the extraordinary power which makes possible unusual acts of power. . . . The Spirit . . . does not totally shape the existence of the believer as a completely new, eschatological existence. The Spirit gives the believer a special gift which makes him capable of certain additional expressions of his faith which are essential to and alone make possible, the ongoing and as yet incomplete history of mission."[1]

Despite the cautious way in which this is formulated, and the qualifications which surround it (the Spirit empowers for prophetic utterance; all members of the community possess the Spirit), it does not do full justice to the facts that the gift of the Spirit is *the* criterion of being a believer and that the task of the church is mission; all disciples have the Spirit so that all may partake in the task of the church. Luke does not go deeply into the "ethical" effects of the Spirit (as in Gal. 5:22f.) because for him the life of the church is to be understood in terms of mission, and it is for mission that the church has received the Spirit. Yet he does not completely ignore the ethical aspect of the Spirit's work, as is shown by the description of Barnabas in Acts 11:24 as a "good man". Nor is the gift of the Spirit an intermittent one; Schweizer is wrong in saying that it is merely this for Luke. His statement would be less open to objection if it claimed that the gift is both continuous and also specially bestowed in particular situations; this was certainly the case with Stephen (Acts 6:3, 5/7:55).[2] Nor again is it clear what on Schweizer's view the believer is able to do without the gift of the Spirit, since it is clear that for Luke a disciple who does not possess the Spirit is a contradiction in terms.[3] We must conclude that Schweizer's statement is at the very least a misleading overstatement;[4] the

---

[1] E. Schweizer, TDNT VI, p. 412; cf. BNTE, pp. 502–4.

[2] Cf. G. Delling, TDNT VI, pp. 130, 285f.

[3] The apparent exceptions in Acts 8:16 and 19:1–7 simply prove the rule, since in both cases steps were at once taken to right the situation.

[4] Schweizer's statement would be more capable of justification if it were the case that the initial reception of the Spirit by a believer was a momentary inspiration (expressed, for example, in a momentary outburst of joy or ecstatic speech) rather than the bestowing of a permanent possession. But there is no suggestion anywhere that the former of these alternatives is correct for Luke; on the contrary, the evidence shows that Luke like the other New Testament writers regarded the Spirit as the permanent possession of the believer.

truth is rather that for Luke the gift of the Spirit is both continuous and renewable in the life of the believer, and that it is the token that he has received the salvation offered by the risen Christ.

A further point which follows from this discussion is that for Luke the gift of the Holy Spirit is closely associated with the incorporation of the individual in the church. The possession of the Holy Spirit is the common gift which constitutes the church, and water-baptism is the outward symbol of integration in the church. While, therefore, Luke is not indifferent to the spiritual life of the individual and (for example) relates several accounts of the conversion of individuals, he is also greatly interested in the communal life and mission of the church. Conversion is not only for individuals, but also for their households (Luke 19:9; Acts 10:2; 11:14; 16:15, 31f.; 18:8). The individuals whose stories Luke relates are often those who took a prominent part in the mission of the church, whether as missionaries (Paul, Apollos) or as representatives of significant stages in the mission of the church (the Ethiopian eunuch, Cornelius). Moreover, as we shall see directly, Luke's description of the Christian life and the outworking of salvation in the lives of its recipients deals largely with the experience of the community.[1]

Praise and Prayer

The new life of the Christian has its foundation in the experience of the gifts of forgiveness and baptism, and the immediate effect of this experience is a joy which is closely related to the individual's attitude to God. Joy is mentioned by Luke not only in connection with the progress of the church's mission (Acts 5:41; 11:23; 15:3, 31; 12:14) but also as the result of conversion (Acts 2:46; 8:8, 39; 13:48, 52; 16:34). A note already sounded in the Gospel rings through Acts also. For in the Gospel rejoicing accompanies the hearing of the message of salvation (Luke 2:10; 8:13) and the knowledge that one's name is written in heaven (Luke 10:20); to receive Jesus as one's guest is an occasion for joy (Luke 19:6). Such joy on the part of the recipient and the spectators of God's grace (Luke 13:17)

---

[1] The teaching about the Spirit in Acts must be related to that in the Gospel. The Gospel has little to say about the Spirit in the life of the disciples, and Luke does not really go beyond the teaching in Mark and Matthew. This ties in with the general consciousness in the New Testament that the Spirit was not bestowed before the exaltation of Jesus (John 7:39). Luke's interest is rather in the work of the Spirit in relation to the coming of salvation in Jesus. The births of both John the Baptist and Jesus are surrounded by prophecies and praises inspired by the Spirit (Luke 1:41, 67; 2:25–27). John is filled with the Spirit for his task of turning men to God (Luke 1:15). The conception of Jesus is traced to the work of the Spirit (Luke 1:35) and in His ministry He is guided and empowered by the Spirit (Luke 4:1, 14, 18; cf. 10:21; Acts 1:2; 10:38). In this way the outpouring of the Spirit at Pentecost is prepared for by His activity in relation to Jesus. The ministry of Jesus and the mission of the church are firmly tied together by the activity of the Spirit in both. See further J. D. G. Dunn, *Baptism in the Holy Spirit*, 1970; *Jesus and the Spirit*, 1975.

is but an echo of the heavenly joy over the return of repentant sinners to the Father (Luke 15:5, 7, 10, 32). God and man share in joy.[1]

Such joy is closely connected with the praise of God. One of the most conspicuous Lucan features of the Gospel is the way in which the various scenes often culminate in an expression of praise or glory to God on the part of the people involved and the spectators. This is the case at the birth of Jesus, where both the angels and the shepherds glorified and praised God (Luke 2:13f., 20; cf. 2:28 of Simeon), and when he taught in the synagogues of Galilee (Luke 4:15). It is a frequent result of the mighty works performed by Jesus (Luke 5:26; 7:16; 13:13; 17:15, 18; 18:43). The triumphal entry is accompanied by praise to God (Luke 19:37f.), and His death caused the centurion at the cross to glorify God (Luke 23:47). Finally, after the parting of the risen Jesus from His disciples they returned to Jerusalem with great joy and were continually in the temple blessing God (Luke 24:52f.).

In the same way the effect of the healing of the lame man by Peter was that he praised God for what had been done for him in the name of Jesus, and his praise was echoed by the people who saw his cure (Acts 3:8f.; 4:21). But it is the salvation of the Gentiles which receives more stress in this connection. The Gentiles themselves glorified the word of God when they heard that salvation was for them (Acts 13:48), and the church glorified and praised God at the news of their conversion (Acts 11:18 21:20). Thus the praise of the individual is linked with that of the community.

The thought of praise leads naturally to that of prayer. Here again the fact which stands out is the close association between the individual and the community. S. Brown has argued that Luke is not greatly interested in the perseverance of the individual in the Christian life.[2] Luke sees the individual much more as a part of the church engaged in mission and the defence of the gospel. Consequently, while Luke records the prayers of individuals such as Stephen (Acts 7:59f.), Paul (Acts 9:11), Cornelius (Acts 10:4) and Peter (Acts 10:9), in most cases he is concerned with prayer in connection with the mission of the church. The first disciples prayed until the coming of the Spirit (Acts 1:14), and prayer accompanied the sending out of missionaries on their travels (Acts 13:3). But prayer is in fact the normal activity of the church when its members gather together, and it is entirely natural that Peter and John go to prayer in the temple (Acts 3:1) or that Paul and Silas sing and pray in prison (Acts 16:25). The prayer meeting which met while Peter was in prison (Acts

---

[1] R. Bultmann, TDNT I, pp. 19–21, links ἀγαλλίασις with eschatology: God's help is always the theme of the rejoicing. Cf. B. Reicke, *The Gospel of Luke*, pp. 75 ff.

[2] S. Brown, *Apostasy and Perseverance in the Theology of Luke*, p. 130.

12:5, 12) was not a panic measure of men driven to their knees by disaster; it was the intensification of the church's normal prayer to God (Acts 2:42). Through prayer the members of the church were committed to God (Acts 14:23, cf. 20:36; 21:5), and in response to it God acted, even by signs and mighty works (Acts 4:31; 9:40; 28:8).[1]

Thus in Acts the Christian life is characterized by expressions of joy and praise made in prayer to God. The private prayers of the individual believer are not forgotten, but the emphasis is on the way in which praise and prayer are activities of the community and are closely related to the mission in which it was engaged.[2]

One special aspect of this joyful relationship with God remains to be noted. Among the characteristics of the common life of the first believers is mentioned "the breaking of bread" (Acts 2:42). The phrase, which is apparently a Jewish one with no significant Hellenistic parallels,[3] refers to the necessary preparation for a Jewish meal; thus in Acts 27:35f. it forms part of the preliminaries to the meal which Paul took on board the ship to Malta, giving thanks and breaking off a piece of bread for himself in the normal Jewish manner before eating.[4] In Acts 2 the context of the phrase makes it clear that a religious act is intended; the breaking of bread is associated with the apostles' teaching, fellowship (see below) and the prayers. It has been suggested by J. Jeremias that these four elements together constituted the form of an early Christian service in which teaching and table fellowship were followed by the Lord's Supper and prayers.[5]

[1] On prayer in Acts see W. Ott, *Gebet und Heil*, pp. 124–136. He notes that the church fulfilled the command of Jesus to pray without ceasing, and that prayer is especially associated with the mission of the church. At the same time prayer is associated with conversion; in order to be saved it is necessary to call on the name of the Lord in prayer. Here there is a shift of emphasis compared with the Gospel where the stress is on prayer in relation to perseverance.

[2] In the Gospel the place of prayer in the life of the church finds a parallel in the place of prayer in the life of Jesus, just as there is a parallelism between the work of the Spirit in relation to Jesus and in relation to the church. Luke takes up the references to prayer in Mark and adds others. He shows how Jesus prayed at significant points in His ministry (Luke 3:21; 6:12; 9:18, 28f.; 22:32). He also includes teaching about prayer by Jesus, and it is clear that prayer is a main theme in this teaching rather than something which is mentioned only incidentally (W. Ott, *op. cit.*, pp. 137–139). See Luke 6:28; 10:2; 11:1–13; 18:1–14; 21:36, 40, 46. Ott argues that in the Gospel the stress is on the need for ceaseless prayer in order that the believer may not lose his faith or fall into temptation but may stand before the Son of Man; to this end he must pray especially for the gift of the Holy Spirit (cf. Luke 11:2 v. l., 13). Ott's book has brought out the importance of a theme which may easily be overlooked, but he has overstressed its importance within the thought of the Gospel as a whole (for example, he does scanty justice to Luke 18:9–14), and his stress on the delay of the parousia requires qualification.

[3] J. Behm, TDNT III, p. 728.

[4] J. Jeremias, *The Eucharistic Words of Jesus*, p. 133, argues that an ordinary meal is meant; the reference to the breaking of the bread indicates that Paul shared it with his Christian companions.

[5] J. Jeremias, *op. cit.*, pp. 118–122.

The arguments adduced by E. Haenchen against this interpretation of the verse are without force,[1] and the subsequent detailed exposition of his position by Jeremias has greatly strengthened his exegesis; the only proviso which we would make is that both Jeremias and Haenchen think rather too rigidly in terms of a fixed order of proceedings. We need not assume, for instance, that the prayers were always the final part of the proceedings. There is, however, a different objection to Jeremias' view: this is that in verses 43 to 47 we have elements described corresponding more or less exactly to the four items in verse 42 – wonders and signs done by the *apostles*, the holding of possessions in *common*, the *breaking of bread* in their homes, and *praising* God (sc. in prayer). This might suggest that we have here a brief description followed by an expansion of it in the following verses. Nevertheless, whether or not Jeremias's persuasive view be accepted, it is certain that "breaking of bread" represents a religious event here. This is confirmed by Acts 20:7, 11 where the breaking of bread follows a sermon from Paul.

There can be no doubt that the meal referred to is the Lord's Supper. This is proved by the name itself. The breaking of the bread is a fixed and constant part of the Lord's Supper (Matt. 26:26; Mark 14:22; Luke 22:19; 1 Cor. 10:16; 11:24). Moreover, the phrase is present in other texts where it is probable that overtones of the Lord's Supper have found their way into the wording (Mark 6:41; 8:6, 19; cf. Matt. 14:19; 15:36; Luke 9:16).[2] Thus every other mention of the breaking of bread in the New Testament contains an allusion to the Lord's Supper. But the same is also true for Luke.[3] In addition to the allusions in his account of the feeding of the five thousand, his story of the disciples walking to Emmaus describes a meal in which the Lord Himself "took the bread and blessed, and broke it and gave it to them" (Luke 24:30). This description of a Lord's Supper in which the risen Lord Himself is present must govern the meaning of the accounts in Acts. The phrase refers to the Lord's Supper. Moreover, the Emmaus story fixes the significance of the meal. It is one in which the Lord Himself is personally present, though unseen – a further indication of His living activity in the early church as described by Luke – and therefore the accompaniment of such a Supper is joy and praise to God.

The fact that the term "breaking of bread" implies the holding of a meal[4] means that no significance is to be attached to the omission of men-

---

[1] E. Haenchen, *Die Apostelgeschichte*, p. 153; W. Ott, *op. cit.*, p. 126.

[2] B. M. F. van Iersel, "Die wunderbare Speisung und das Abendmahl in der synoptischen Tradition," Nov. T 7, 1964, pp. 167–194.

[3] For Acts 27:35f., however, see p. 204 n. 4.

[4] J. Jeremias, *op. cit.*, pp. 119f., notes that "breaking of bread" does not refer in Jewish sources to a whole meal but to the opening rite. But in Christian usage at any rate it seems probable that the mention of the opening rite implied that a meal followed; this is the case in

tion of the cup of wine. F. F. Bruce quotes with approval R. Otto's comment that the emphasis on the breaking of the bread implies that this was "the significant element of the celebration. . . . But it could only be significant when it was a 'signum,' viz. of Christ's being broken in death."[1] This means that the meal described as the breaking of bread had the sacrificial character which is more explicitly associated with the cup of wine in the Lord's Supper, and consequently that, since there is no difference in meaning between them, the breaking of bread and the Lord's Supper are names for the identical meal. There is, therefore, no reason to suppose that Luke was referring to a non-sacrificial meal without the use of wine, separate from the Pauline Lord's Supper. On the contrary, the indications are that he has taken over an old Palestinian name for the Lord's Supper.[2] For Luke, as for Paul, it formed the principal part of the Christian gatherings, and figures as the "Sunday service" in Acts 20:7-11.

Wealth and Possessions

In an earlier part of our study we observed that in the Gospel Luke included a considerable amount of teaching regarding the rich and the poor. In the teaching of Jesus the good news of the kingdom of God was for the poor, and there were stern warnings to the rich about the danger of being kept outside the kingdom by their possessions. The corollary of such warnings is the command to use wealth in the right way. There is the injunction to give alms (Luke 11:41; 12:33), assumed by Jesus to be a normal religious activity that His followers would practise (Matt. 6:2-4; Mark 14:4-7). But this act of self-denial was intensified by Jesus into the command that His disciples should give up everything to follow Him; this is particularly evident in the story of the rich young man who was commanded to sell all that he had and give the proceeds to the poor (Mark 10:21), but it is also to be seen in the way in which Peter and the other disciples forsook everything when they followed Jesus (Mark 1:16-20; 10:28). In Luke this injunction becomes all the more stringent. This is to be seen in the stories of the call of the disciples (Luke 5:11, 28) who left their homes (Luke 18:28) to follow Jesus. It also finds expression in the sayings of Jesus which speak of the decisive break with the past involved in

---

[1] F. F. Bruce, *The Acts of the Apostles*, p. 100, quoting R. Otto, *The Kingdom of God and the Son of Man*, 1943, p. 315.

[2] See p. 204 n. 3 above. It is quite out of the question that Luke should have invented a Lord's Supper celebrated only with bread and without any sacrificial significance. Even the shorter text of Luke 22:17-19a still contains a cup.

---

1 Cor. 11:24f. and in Acts 20:7. Consequently, Acts does not give an "ideal" picture of the original unity of a daily meal with the Lord's Supper (so H. Conzelmann, *Die Apostelgeschichte*, p. 31); the so-called "ideal" was also practised at Corinth.

discipleship (Luke 9:57-62) and of the need to renounce all that one has in order to be a disciple (Luke 14:25-33).

This emphasis in the Gospel of Luke simply brings out the sharpness of the call to decision expressed by Jesus.[1] What it might mean in practice is shown by the case of Zacchaeus (Luke 19:8). We must now relate this teaching to the life of the disciples as recorded in Acts. Here at the beginning of the story of the church there is a description of how "all who believed were together and had all things in common; and they sold their possessions and goods and distributed them to all, as any had need" (Acts 2:44 f.). Similarly, we are told later that "the company of those who believed were of one heart and soul, and no one said that any of the things which he possessed was his own, but they had everything in common" (Acts 4:32). This summary statement is then amplified by the story of how those who were rich sold their real estate and distribution was made to the needy. The apostles were in charge of the distribution, but the task became so time-consuming that it had to be passed over to other officers (Acts 6:1-6).

It should be clear that the description in Acts is not quite the same as that in the Gospel. In the Gospel renunciation of wealth and the giving of alms to the poor in general is commanded. In Acts there is renunciation of wealth, but the proceeds are held in a common fund and used for the poor in the Christian community. The evidence strongly suggests that a feature peculiar to the life of the early church in Jerusalem is being described rather than a universally applicable practice.

The practice in Acts should not be misunderstood. In no sense was it a matter of a rigidly imposed condition upon members of the community. The selling of goods was voluntary, and it was undertaken by the rich. This is shown by the story of Ananias and Sapphira from which it emerges that the selling of the property was entirely voluntary and that the sin lay not in keeping back part of the proceeds but in pretending that the part was the whole (Acts 5:4). The way in which attention is drawn by contrast to Barnabas stresses the voluntary generosity of the giving. With this qualification, however, a voluntary sharing seems to have been practised initially, and this need cause no surprise when it is borne in mind that another religious group, that at Qumran, had a similar practice.[2]

[1] For detailed comment on the teaching in Luke see H.-J. Degenhardt, *Lukas – Evangelist der Armen*. The author, however, attempts to show that Luke's teaching is not meant for all Christians but rather for the *leaders* of the church (*op. cit.*, pp. 27-41); this view rests on an implausible narrowing of the meaning of the word μαθητής in the Gospel. Degenhardt draws a contrast between the disciples and the people (λαός) who heard Jesus gladly (Luke 19:48), but there is nothing to suggest that the people responded to His words with faith. Further, the stringent commands to self-denial in Luke 14:25ff. are clearly addressed to the crowds, and there is no ground for Degenhardt's claim that these commands are concerned with becoming missionaries rather than becoming followers of Jesus (*op. cit.*, p. 105).

[2] H.-J. Degenhardt, *op. cit.*, pp. 188-207. The Qumran practice, however, was compulsory and required total renunciation of possessions.

Later on it is implied several times that the church in Jerusalem was particularly poor, and the most probable explanation of this lies in the loss of capital by its members in the early days. This is shown as early as Acts 6 by the scale on which the distribution to the poor was being conducted and it is confirmed by the account of the famine in Judaea in Acts 11:27–30. The Jerusalem church was too impoverished to resist this new hazard, and help from outside was needed. The Epistles of Paul provide independent evidence of this same fact. In Gal. 2:10 we read of the Jerusalem leaders' concern that Paul should remember the poor and of Paul's willingness to do so. The later Epistles of Paul mention several times the collection which he took from the Gentile churches for the benefit of "the poor among the saints at Jerusalem" (Rom. 15:26; 1 Cor. 16:1–4; 2 Cor. 8-9). Whatever may have been the theological motives for this collection,[1] the practical reason which led Paul to organize such a demonstration of the unity of Jews and Gentiles in the church and the love of the latter for the former lay in the material need of the Jerusalem church. Luke's account of the early days in Jerusalem should not, therefore, be dismissed as a piece of idealism. The arguments adduced by H. Conzelmann in defence of this position are weak.[2] Luke's own description of the way in which the system worked qualifies the apparent absoluteness and idealism of the summary statement that the disciples had all things in common. And the point of this statement is not that they gave up all their wealth but rather that they lived a common life, meeting together and eating in each other's houses, even to the extent of sharing their property so that there were resources to help the poor. H.-J. Degenhardt suggests that there was a kind of family community in which each person held his goods at the disposal of the others without any legal change of possession or adoption of a communist system.[3] There is consequently no need to suppose that Luke is describing a state of affairs characteristic of an imaginary "ideal"

---

[1] K. F. Nickle, *The Collection: A Study in Paul's Strategy*, 1966, overemphasizes the function of the collection in promoting unity between Jews and Gentiles in the church and in providing a demonstration of the salvation of the Gentiles to the Jews so as to make the latter jealously seek for salvation; Paul never suggests that the second of these aims was in his mind.

[2] H. Conzelmann, *Die Apostelgeschichte*, p. 31. He argues that a communal organization of production is not mentioned, and therefore the picture is not historical. But this argument would hold good only if Luke intended to describe a permanent, communist way of life, such as was practised at Qumran; there is no indication that this was his intention. See further L. Goppelt, *Apostolic and Post-Apostolic Times*, pp. 49f.

[3] H.-J. Degenhardt, *op. cit.*, p. 167; Thus Luke is not suggesting that there was a general pooling of resources in a common fund, thus leaving individual Christians without any private property, but rather that each was willing to dispose of his possessions as need arose. Degenhardt, *op. cit.*, pp. 169–171, finds a tension between Acts 4:32 and 34f., but argues that in the former verse Luke has expressed the situation in Hellenistic terms, whereas the latter verses describe what actually happened in Jewish terms. The ideal of "having all things in common" is said to be Hellenistic rather than Jewish (p. 170), but it is found at Qumran; cf. 1QS 1:11–13. It is unlikely that Luke was aware of any tension.

beginning of the church; the principles which are expressed remained true
for the church of his own time, and these ideals of generosity and care for
the poor were taught throughout the early church.

Through Many Tribulations

The fact that Luke has not developed a doctrine of the atonement has
been taken to mean that he works with a *theologia gloriae* and has no real
theologia crucis.[1] The verdict is a false one in that Luke was certainly well
aware of the necessity of Christ's sufferings even if he has not developed
a doctrine of their saving efficacy. It is true that glory lay ahead for Christ,
but it was a glory that could not be attained other than by the way of
suffering and death.

The same pattern of suffering and glory is shared by Paul and other New
Testament writers.[2] The pattern is found for example in Phil. 2:5–11;
Heb. 12:2 and 1 Pet. 3:17–22. What was the divinely appointed way for
Jesus is also seen as the way which His followers must take. In 1 Cor.
4:8–13, for example, Paul speaks sarcastically about the Corinthian
Christians who thought that they had already entered into the bliss of the
kingdom and were reigning over the world. The reality of the situation
was somewhat different. As experienced by the apostles, it was a case of
being like men sentenced to death, weak and dishonoured in the eyes of
the world, suffering hunger, thirst and physical discomfort. The true
Christian always carries about in his body the death of Jesus, so that the
life of Jesus may also be manifested in his body. Death is at work in the
apostle so that his converts may enjoy life (2 Cor. 4:7–12). Paul sees the
tension in which the believer lives, for while he can speak of the present
enjoyment of resurrection life he also emphasizes that suffering and death
must precede the moment of resurrection into the presence of God
(Rom. 6: 1–11; 8:10f.; Gal. 2:20; Eph. 2:1–10; Phil. 3:10f.; Col. 2:12f.).
The faithful saying in 2 Tim. 2:11f. is an accurate summary: "If we have
died with him, we shall also live with him; if we endure, we shall also
reign with him." The same theme is to be found in Hebrews, where the
suffering of Jesus is presented as an example to the readers (Heb. 12:3);
they stand in the tradition of the Old Testament saints and martyrs who
did not receive what was promised, but glimpsed it from afar. Although
the people of the new covenant already know something of the reality,
the fulness of blessing comes only at the end of their pilgrimage. Similarly,
1 Pet. appeals to its readers to bear suffering patiently and to endure

[1] E. Käsemann, *New Testament Questions of Today*, p. 22; U. Wilckens, *Die Missionsreden der
Apostelgeschichte*, p. 127. See the discussion in F. Schütz, *Der leidende Christus*, pp. 90–96.
[2] E. Schweizer, *Lordship and Discipleship*, 1960 (English translation of *Erniedrigung und Erhöhung bei Jesus und seinen Nachfolgern*, Zürich, 1955).

the trials that are their present lot; they already know what it means to rejoice in the salvation and the living hope bestowed upon them through the resurrection of Christ, but their eyes are to be fixed on the salvation which is ready to be revealed in the last time (1 Pet. 1:3–9; 2:18–21; 4:12–16; 5:10). Finally, the theme is developed fully in the Revelation whose message is: "he who conquers, I will grant him to sit with me on my throne, as I myself conquered and sat down with my Father on his throne" (Rev. 3:21).

What does Luke know of this conception? The theme of suffering is one that is announced early in the Gospel. In the prophecy of Simeon regarding the destiny of Jesus His mother was told not only that He would be "for a sign that is spoken against" but also that "a sword will pierce through your own soul also" (Luke 2:35). The thought is undoubtedly of the anguish that Mary would suffer as she saw her Son rejected and crucified. A solemn note is thus sounded amidst the jubilation of the opening chapters of Luke with their strong accent on the good news of salvation. We have already had cause to mention the way in which Luke's Gospel testifies to both the present blessedness of the disciples and also the sufferings, persecution and deprivation which they would suffer. So too in Acts the disciples are told "through many tribulations we must enter the kingdom of God" (Acts 14:23). Paul knew that in every city imprisonment and afflictions awaited him (Acts 20:23; cf. 9:16). What is here stated in general terms as a possibility is shown to be stark reality by the narrative. Stephen perishes by stoning as a martyr. James is put to death with the sword. Peter is put in prison and is fortunate to escape with his life. From the outset the Jewish leaders persecute the church in Jerusalem, and after Stephen's death the pace quickens, so that many of the Christians have to flee elsewhere. When the story of Paul's missionary work is taken up, opposition and persecution continually face him and his converts, culminating in his arrest in Jerusalem, his subsequent imprisonment, and his journey as a captive to Rome. Paul himself lives under the threat of death, and is ready to meet his end when it comes (Acts 20:24; 21:13). Here is no account of a church which already lives in a state of heavenly glory or whose mission is uninterrupted by difficulty.

Nor is the church free from internal trouble. There are examples of gross sin to be found in Ananias and Sapphira and Simon Magus. There is dissension between the Hellenists and the Hebrews (Acts 6:1). Even missionaries quarrel with each other and go their separate ways (Acts 15:39f.). There are threats of false teaching and dissension in the church (Acts 20:29f.). It should be carefully observed that these dangers were already present in the apostolic church; Luke saw the stress on circumcision for the Gentiles as a real threat to the truth of the gospel, and his aim is to show how this danger was overcome.

There is, therefore, trouble in plenty. It is narrated from the point of view of its effects on the church and its mission.[1] Luke does not have much to say about the possible effects of persecution and false doctrine in tempting individual believers to apostatize from the faith.[2] The thought is not absent, but it is not especially stressed. This is in harmony with Luke's concept of the church as a missionary body. He is concerned with the mission of the church as affected by opposition, and with the need for the converts of the mission to be kept safe from temptations to sin and apostasy.

"But the word of God is not fettered" (2 Tim. 2:9). These words indicate the other side. Despite opposition and persecution the onward movement of the gospel triumphs. "But the word of God grew and multiplied" (Acts 12:24) is a typical comment on the result of persecution. Even when the disciples are scattered by persecution, the effect is simply to extend the preaching of the gospel more widely (Acts 11:19f.). So the story is one of triumph. But the fact that the gospel triumphs and that the church is confident of its ultimate success by the power of God does not obliterate the fact of suffering, nor does it mean that the *theologia crucis* is transformed into a *theologia gloriae*. The quotations from Paul and other writers a few lines earlier show that the authentic New Testament testimony is one which holds fast to the hope of the final triumph of Christ and His cause even in the midst of suffering and which knows an anticipatory joy despite every outward affliction. "The sufferings of this present time are not worth comparing with the glory that is to be revealed to us" (Rom. 8:18). The hope in the final triumph and the associated glory sustains the believer who groans in his present state. So too in Luke there is hope in the midst of persecution, but the reality of the persecution is not thereby minimized. The church is rather confident in the power of God to help it and to bring it through tribulation. Hence it prays to God not that it might be delivered from persecution but rather that despite the threats of opposition it may be able to speak the word with all boldness (Acts 4:29). And when a martyr looks death in the face, it is to see beyond death the welcome of his Lord into the presence of God (Acts 7:55f.). This is the theology of the cross.

---

[1] F. Schütz, *op. cit.*, argues that the parallel between the rejection of the message of Jesus by the Jews and the opposition to the mission of the church is meant to demonstrate to the church that it *is* the church of its suffering Lord and thus to encourage it in the midst of its own suffering. Suffering is the means by which God extends His kingdom. Consequently just as Jesus did find faith among some of His hearers, so the church must proclaim the call to repentance to its persecutors (the Jews).

[2] S. Brown, *Apostasy and Perseverance in the Theology of Luke*, carries this point too far.

Una Sancta Apostolica?

In our study of the nature of salvation as proclaimed and experienced in Acts we have been brought into frequent contact with Luke's doctrine of the church. Something must now be said more directly on this topic, although it will not be our purpose to deal with it exhaustively. Our concern is simply with the significance of the church for Luke's doctrine of salvation. The question put before us by contemporary scholarship is whether in Luke the church has become an institution dispensing salvation and through which alone salvation can be obtained.[1] Have we here the beginnings of the doctrine of "one holy, catholic and apostolic church"? Is it true that as a theologian Luke "can only be understood from his doctrine of a legitimate church"?[2]

The general pattern of the answer should be clear from the previous discussion. We have seen that all the way through Luke thinks of the disciples as being constituted into the church. He is as much concerned with the fate of the church as with that of the individual. He knows next to nothing of a solitary religion, although the case of the Ethiopian eunuch proves that such may exist.

Nevertheless, there is no special stress on the church as an institution. Men become believers through hearing the Word and responding to it. What matters here is not the activity of the church but the truth of the message. It is continuity with the apostolic teaching that is of supreme significance. For Luke this is preserved by a continuity within the church. The church sends out its missionaries and confirms the work of those already engaged in preaching the word. Thus the mission in Samaria is legitimated by the apostles, and the work in Antioch is confirmed by Barnabas (Acts 11:22f.), who was not one of the Twelve but was an apostle in the same sense as Paul (Acts 14:4). The church at Jerusalem is represented as having authority over the missionary churches to whom it sent its decree (Acts 15:22–29; 16:4), but it is not clear how Luke conceived of this authority in detail; it is noteworthy that the council at Jerusalem was held at the instigation of the church in Antioch, and that its purpose was to correct the false impression given by unauthorized men claiming to represent the church at Jerusalem.

The picture thus drawn is a natural one. The same problem arises in the modern church when a church raises up daughter churches for itself which are at first under its jurisdiction and later become independent. Luke reflects the early period when Jerusalem was thought of as the centre of

---

[1] E. Käsemann, *Essays on New Testament Themes*, pp. 136–148; S. Schulz, *Die Stunde der Botschaft*, pp. 255–275.
[2] E. Käsemann, *op. cit.*, p. 148.

the church. Later the mission churches became increasingly independent. What matters for Luke is not so much the church itself as the apostles who were the guardians of its doctrine.

The church of Luke cannot be said to dispense salvation by means of the sacraments. The Lord's Supper is not in Luke a means of salvation but a fellowship meal in which the Lord's death was remembered. Baptism is the outward sign of receiving the Spirit and becoming a Christian, but Luke demonstrates plainly that the reception of the Spirit was not rigidly tied to baptism. Moreover, the validity of baptism depends not on the person who performs it (cf. 1 Cor. 1:17) but on its character – whether it is administered in the name of Jesus. This is the point of the story of the disciples at Ephesus; the significance is not that they were baptized by Paul but that they were baptized in the name of Jesus (Acts 19:1-7). But what about the case of the Samaritan believers who did not receive the Spirit until they had had hands laid upon them by Peter and John (Acts 8:14-17)? Does this mean that apostolic confirmation (whether in the ordinary or in the technical religious sense) is required? It is most unlikely that this question should be answered affirmatively, since elsewhere in Acts Philip himself baptizes without the need for his action to be completed or confirmed (Acts 8:38), and the Spirit is given without the imposition of apostolic hands (Acts 19:1-7). On the contrary, the context of the story is a twofold one. On the one hand, there is the person of Simon Magus who wished to purchase apostolic power, and the story is concerned with his confrontation with Peter. There may be a polemical reference here to claims by Simon to possess powers that rivalled those of the apostles. On the other hand, the story is in the context of the development of the universal mission of the church; the coming of the gospel to the Samaritans was epoch-making, especially in view of Acts 1:8 where Samaria is especially mentioned, and this extension of the mission demanded clear legitimation by the apostles. The new fellowship between Jews and Samaritans had to be clearly demonstrated. The point of the story lies in this, and not in any prerogative of the apostles to dispense the Holy Spirit.[1]

It is of course true that evangelism is carried on by the church. But why should Luke be accused of "early catholicism" for making this clear, when the same assumption is made throughout the early church? Did anybody ever think otherwise? So the only ground that remains for the critic of Luke is to say that he has self-consciously stressed this point. But this is not true either. On the contrary, while Luke is certainly interested in the

---

[1] F. F. Bruce, *The Book of the Acts*, pp. 181-183; E. Schweizer, TDNT VI, pp. 414f.; G. W. H. Lampe, *The Seal of the Spirit*, 1951, p. 72, characterized the incident as "a Samaritan 'Pentecost'."

apostles and witnesses who preach the gospel, he does not reflect a developed view of the church and its officials.[1] E. Schweizer sums up his discussion of the structure of Luke's church by saying, "This almost casual mention of special office-bearers in the Church, and the absence of definite titles, show that the order of these forms of service is not fundamental to the Lucan church."[2] The conclusion is true at a more general level. The church does not figure in Acts as a saving institution which dispenses salvation through the sacraments.

It is also of course true that Luke assumes that converts will join the church. The function of water-baptism is precisely this. But again there is nothing that smacks of "early catholicism" in this, for there is no evidence that in the apostolic period any other understanding was ever entertained. To be a Christian was to be a member of the church. What matters for Luke is that Christians come together and share in the common life of the church – in fellowship, in prayer and in mission. Consequently, the term "the Way" which he has taken over as his characteristic description of the church appears to refer both to the teaching of the church and to the members.[3] These are the two things which are important for Luke. It is the apostolic teaching which constitutes the church. And if there is no salvation *extra ecclesiam* it is not because the church possesses the gospel but because salvation is through Christ and His word is committed to the apostles.

To say that the church is a missionary church is not to say that it has become an institution. Throughout Acts the church remains subject to the guidance of the Spirit and its work is done through the power of the name of Jesus. It does not "possess" these gifts. It is a church under the Word and subject to its Lord. It is called by God to proclaim salvation and to be the company of believers.

Thus in the end Acts is the story of the growth of the church because it is the story of the spread of salvation. In Acts salvation becomes a reality. The work of Jesus is continued by His disciples and embraces men and

---

[1] It is noteworthy how the apostles themselves tacitly disappear from view. There is no question of apostolic succession in Acts.

[2] E. Schweizer, *Church Order in the New Testament*, 1961, 5 l , p. 72 (English translation of *Gemeinde und Gemeindeordnung im Neuen Testament*, Zürich, 1959). See the whole of ch. 5.

[3] The meaning of ὁδός is "teaching" in Acts 16:17; 18:25f.; cf. 24:14. In 22:4 the stress appears to be on the company of believers. In Acts 9:2; 19:9, 23; 24:22 it appears to be almost a synonym for "Christianity." W. Michaelis, TDNT V, pp. 88–90, suggests the meaning "the mode of life which comes to expression in the Christian fellowship." The basis for this usage appears to be Jewish and has affinities with terminology used at Qumran: S. V. McCasland, "'The Way'," JBL 77, 1958, pp. 222–230.

For an exposition of Luke's theology of "the Way," see W. C. Robinson Jr., *Der Weg des Herrn – Studien zur Geschichte und Eschatologie im Lukas – Evangelium*, Hamburg–Bergstedt, 1964; cf. J. Rohde, *Rediscovering the Teaching of the Evangelists*, pp. 236–239; S. Brown, *Apostasy and Perseverance in the Theology of Luke*, pp. 131–145.

women of every nation. If Luke has restricted his story to the movement of the gospel to Rome, he nevertheless hints at its wider spread in the Pentecost narrative (Acts 2:5–11, 39). Luke's task was to show what men everywhere must do in order to be saved. Thus the Book of Acts is itself a means of salvation to those who hear the gospel in it and make the same response as the Philippian jailer and many another: "Believe in the Lord Jesus, and you will be saved."[1]

[1] W. C. van Unnik, Nov. T 4, 1960, pp. 41 f., 53, following M. Dibelius, *Studies in the Acts of the Apostles*, pp. 133, 179 f.

CHAPTER IX

LUKE THE EVANGELIST

WE HAVE NOW COMPLETED OUR SURVEY OF LUKE'S CONCEPT OF salvation, and it is time to summarize our conclusions and indicate their significance. The study which we have undertaken may be regarded as falling within the sphere of *Redaktionsgeschichte*, since our concern throughout has been with the ideas and concepts of Luke himself. Our aim was to isolate and discuss the central motif of Lucan theology. We have identified this as being the concept of salvation, and the justification for this choice must lie in deciding whether the foregoing exposition has in fact uncovered the basic theme of Lucan theology. We would claim that it has proved possible to organize the contents of Luke-Acts in terms of this central concept without forcing the material into an unnatural mould, and that the fact that we have been able to do this is proof of our thesis.

For Luke the concept of salvation is closely bound up with history. We found it necessary at the outset of our study to clarify the relationship of theology to history not simply for its own sake but because this was an important issue for Luke himself. We found that it was possible to justify Luke's claim that theology rests upon history in the sense that the salvation of God is revealed in historical events; theology reflects upon those events and establishes their significance. Consequently, theology cannot be separated from history, although this is not to say that the establishment of the historical facts is necessarily the same thing as the acceptance of their theological import.

For Luke the chief historical event in which salvation was revealed was the ministry and person of Jesus. We examined his presentation of Jesus in the Gospel and concluded that the message and work of Jesus were presented in terms of salvation. The salvation associated with the messianic age in the Old Testament had become a reality in the ministry of Jesus. In Him the new era had arrived. We then saw that after His passion and exaltation the message of salvation bestowed by Him was the theme of the preaching of the early church. Those who accepted the message and believed in Christ experienced the forgiveness of their sins and the gift of the Holy Spirit.

This theological interpretation of what was happening in Jesus and in the early church was presented as historical by Luke. Its validity as interpretation depends upon its validity as history. Throughout our study, therefore, we have been concerned with the historical basis of Luke's account. It was not enough to establish that Luke was trying to write reliable history, although this in itself is an important pointer that he was more likely to be a reliable historian than somebody who professed other aims and was indifferent to questions of historicity. It is necessary to examine what Luke actually achieved. At the beginning of our study in Chapter III we produced evidence that suggested Luke's general reliability as a historian. In the subsequent exposition of his thought we have continually drawn attention to the question of historicity.

With regard to this question our aim has been a somewhat limited one. It is notorious that today questions regarding the ministry and teaching of the historical Jesus have become immensely complex and difficult, so much so that some scholars (wrongly, in our opinion) have despaired of ever answering them. The result is that the attempt to justify fully the theology of Luke in terms of its being a faithful development from the message of Jesus would be an undertaking that would stretch the limits of a study of Luke's theology to breaking point. We have therefore had to be content with a more limited aim. Our procedure has been at each point to examine Luke's use of the traditions which were available to him. Since Luke had no direct contact with the historical Jesus and was entirely dependent on traditions of various kinds, both oral and written, the most that could be demanded of him is faithful use of the sources at his disposal; this is not to exclude, of course, the probability that he sifted and criticized them. The basic question, therefore, is simply what Luke has done with the traditions at his disposal. The result of this enquiry has been to show that Luke was generally conservative in his use of tradition. Time and again we have seen that the characteristics of Lucan theology reflect motifs already present in the sources. The tendency of *Redaktionsgeschichte* – an understandable one – is to emphasize the individuality of an author over against the sources which he used. Our study, however, has suggested that Luke was basically faithful to the traditions which he was using; he was drawing out motifs already present in them rather than radically reshaping the material and adding to it from his own ideas. We may quote with regard to Luke C. E. B. Cranfield's estimate of Mark: "He possessed, to an outstanding degree, that without which one cannot begin to be a true theologian, namely, a deep humility before God's self-revelation, and ... he tried to state the facts of what he believed to be God's self-revelation as accurately as he could, refraining from all attempts at improving on them by artistry, precisely because he was a serious theologian – too good a theologian not to recognize the folly of trying to paint the lily or (to borrow an expression of B. L. Manning's) to varnish sunlight."[1] The point may have been put in an exaggerated fashion, but it contains its element of truth.

It could be urged against the method followed in this study that insufficient attention has been paid to the distinction between what Luke took over from tradition and what he himself has contributed editorially; we must rather distinguish clearly between tradition and redaction, and use the latter as our basic source for Luke's theology. But the virtues of this principle should not blind us to its onesidedness, and the difficulty of carrying it through should not be underestimated. Luke has included in his work what he wanted to include, and therefore traditional items should not be regarded as awkward intrusions into his work but rather as constituting the basis of it. If we confine our attention to what can clearly be identified as redaction, we stand in danger of over-emphasizing a few elements in the total picture and thereby producing a distorted presentation of Luke's theology. Our study has therefore proceeded on the basis that what Luke included was significant for his theology, and our aim has been to see what he did with the traditions which he used. We claim that he has shown himself to be in fundamental harmony with his sources.

Luke, then, is a faithful expositor of the tradition. To this extent his theology is based upon history. Where we have been able to go further and draw lines with some confidence through the tradition to the historical Jesus, this impression has been confirmed. So far as we can tell, the Lucan portrayal of Jesus is historical. This is true in particular of the theme of salvation. By expounding the positive significance of the ministry of Jesus in terms of salvation, Luke was not making a fundamental alteration to its historical significance. The old-fashioned view that Jesus was little more than a prophet of repentance and that the kingdom of God which He proclaimed was little more than an apocalyptic image needs no refutation today.[2] Nor does the old liberal view that Jesus taught timeless truths about the providence of the heavenly Father. On the contrary, Jesus announced the arrival of the era of salvation and summoned men to believe the good news and become His disciples. This central aspect of His ministry is correctly emphasized by Luke. The terminology of salvation fitly expresses the essence of the message of Jesus.

Luke, however, remains a theologian with his own distinctive approach. We have been able to observe his own special vocabulary in which the themes of his theology come to expression. He was not a mere reproducer of tradition, but he has given us his own interpretation of what is significant in it. It is right that he should be regarded as theologian as well as

[1] C. E. B. Cranfield, St Mark, p. 479.
[2] E. Käsemann, Essays on New Testament Themes, pp. 37-45.

historian. This is to be seen in his constructive doctrine of salvation as well as in his doctrine of the nature of witness to that salvation. He does not appear as a profound theologian of the character of Paul, John or the Writer to the Hebrews, but this is partly to be explained in terms of the character of his work. He was not writing theological Epistles, but a Gospel and an account of the early church, works which were closely tied to historical reporting and did not offer opportunities for creative theology in the same kind of way as the Epistles. Moreover, there are some grounds for thinking that there were differences in content between the missionary preaching of the church and the wisdom imparted by a Paul to the "mature" (1 Cor. 2:6), and Luke's material falls into the former class. He should not, therefore, be criticized for failing to do what he did not try to do.

The Place of Luke

Where is Luke to be situated in the early church? The question is not easy to answer. In the first place, our attempts to locate the aims of Luke have suggested that he was largely concerned simply to present salvation to his readers. He wished to confirm the faith of a Theophilus by a fresh account of the historical basis of faith. At the same time his presentation is an effective basis for the evangelism of those who had not yet come to faith. Thus the purpose is primarily evangelistic, although other issues are also important for Luke. If this is the case, it means that in terms of its primary aim Luke's work is to a large extent timeless. It is not written to deal with a particular problem or situation in the church, but rather to help in the church's constant task of evangelism. It could be used anywhere, at any time.[1] This is part of the explanation of the constant appeal of Luke's writings; they are valid for all time.

Consequently, other factors must be taken into consideration. In the course of our investigation we have constantly come across evidence which suggested that the work of Luke was not representative of the "early catholic" situation towards the end of the first century. The emphases which have been loosely grouped under this heading are not Lucan. There is no overt polemic against gnosticism. There is no stress on the church as an institution developing rigid forms of organization and

---

[1] There are some traces of Hellenization of the form of the message, which would suggest that a Gentile or Hellenistic Jewish audience is envisaged. For Luke's debt to Hellenistic Judaism see J. C. O'Neill, *The Theology of Acts in its Historical Setting*, pp. 146–165 (second ed., pp. 139–159).

The situation for which Luke writes would appear to be one in which the Jew–Gentile question was a live issue, and therefore the audience should perhaps be found primarily (but by no means exclusively) among proselytes and "God-fearers"; cf. W. C. van Unnik, Nov. T 4, 1960, p. 59.

taking the place of the Word in the mediation of salvation. There are traces of concern about the situation after the departure of Paul, but there is nothing that could not have arisen towards the end of Paul's own life. Again, we have not found evidence for an attitude to the parousia substantially different from that in the early church. The parousia hope is still present, and the conditions for the coming of the parousia appear to have been partly fulfilled.

The crucial question, therefore, remains that of the relationship of Luke to Paul. There is no disputing that the theologies of Paul and of Luke are two different entities. It has, however, been one of the theses defended throughout this study that the attempt to find fundamental differences and incompatabilities between Luke and Paul has failed. It is not the case that Luke has misrepresented or misunderstood Paul, although he has not developed many significant Pauline motifs. In particular, the case for an existentialist Paul alongside a salvation-historical Luke cannot stand. Pauline theology is rather, as P. Borgen has argued, the presupposition for Lucan theology.[1]

Attempts have been made recently to link the author of Luke-Acts with the Epistle to the Ephesians[2] and with the Pastoral Epistles.[3] Whatever verdict we may come to on the success of these endeavours to prove common authorship, they at least demonstrate how close Luke-Acts stands to Pauline theology. It is true that it has also been claimed that Luke has links with almost every part of the New Testament,[4] but it remains significant that there are such close links with Paul. The conclusion that the author of Luke-Acts stood close to Paul and that he was in fact Luke the physician still remains the most likely historical explanation of the phenomena. Further, there is nothing in the evidence to suggest a date of composition for Luke-Acts much later than the last events recorded in the book. This may be taken to be not so much a conclusion from our study but rather a hypothesis which is confirmed by the evidence which we have adduced and which finds a secure base in wider considerations.

[1] P. Borgen, "From Paul to Luke," CBQ 31, 1969, pp. 168–182; cf. E. E. Ellis, *The Gospel of Luke,* pp. 40–52; F. F. Bruce, "Is the Paul of Acts the real Paul?" BJRL 58, 1975-76, pp. 282–305.
[2] R. P. Martin, "An Epistle in Search of a Life-Setting," Exp. T 79, 1967-68, pp. 296–302; G. Bouwmann, *Das dritte Evangelium,* p. 99 n. 10. The differences between Acts and Ephesians are expressed in E. Käsemann, "Ephesians and Acts," in SLA, pp. 288–297.
[3] C. F. D. Moule, "The Problem of the Pastoral Epistles: A Reappraisal," BJRL 47, 1964–65, pp. 430–452; A. Strobel, "Schreiben des Lukas? Zum sprachlichen Problem der Pastoralbriefe," NTS 15, 1968–69, pp. 191–210.
In view of the great stylistic differences between Ephesians and the Pastorals it is hardly possible to link Luke (or any other single person) closely with both compositions.
[4] H. Conzelmann, "Zur Lukas-Analyse," ZTK 49, 1952, pp. 16–33, especially pp. 16 f.
For the links between Luke and Hebrews see C. P. M. Jones, "The Epistle to the Hebrews and the Lucan Writings," in SG, pp. 113–143. W. C. van Unnik, Nov.T 4, 1960, pp. 46–49, has shown how apt a summary of Acts is provided by Hebrews 2:2–5.

Paul, it is clear, is one of Luke's heroes. Nevertheless, his primary aim was not to write a book about Paul; it is unlikely that his purpose was to rehabilitate Paul at a time when Paul was either forgotten or discredited. Not only Paul would have had to be defended but also his Epistles, and there is no mention of these in Acts. Rather Paul is presented simply as a major witness to the gospel, and he plays his part in the confirmation of the gospel and the spread of the church in the line that leads from Jerusalem to Rome.

What were the circumstances which led Luke to make this presentation of the gospel of salvation? One simple factor which should not be overlooked is his possession of knowledge which up till then had not been published in a coherent account. While Luke had predecessors in the writing of Gospels, we have no evidence for the existence of earlier attempts to write about the early church. To this extent Luke was an innovator, and the impetus for his work lay in his unique position. Much is sometimes made of the fact that he wrote a history of the early church, a hitherto unattempted venture. But the significance may be missed. The precedent of other Gospels and of the Epistles shows that expression of the faith in writing does not need to be accounted for, so far as Luke is concerned. What is significant is his combination of the story of Jesus and the story of the early church in one account. Thereby he testified that the two stories are really one, and that the break between them is not of such decisive importance as that between the period of the law and the prophets and the period in which the gospel of the kingdom is preached. Salvation-history is divided up according to the scheme of preparation and fulfilment, and not into the threefold pattern proposed by H. Conzelmann. For Luke, however, the period of fulfilment is somewhat extended. The pre-requisite for this situation is simply the extension of time since the resurrection which gave a sense of perspective to the observer: looking back Luke was able to see that the first generation of the church formed a continuation of the era of salvation which had begun with Jesus, and that the era was still continuing until the expected return of the Lord. When that would be Luke did not know. It was enough that he should compose this record as a means of evangelism. It is thus timeless in its value, at least as long as time shall last. To this extent it can be said that Luke writes for the long road that faces the church, but this is not because he was motivated by the delay in the parousia but because he was animated by the desire to make the gospel known.

Two centuries ago J. A. Bengel rightly perceived the significance of Luke's work when he concluded his comments on Acts with the words: "Victoria Verbi Dei: Paulus Romae, apex evangelii, Actorum finis. . . . Hierosolymis coepit: Romae desinit. Habes, Ecclesia, formam tuam:

tuum est, servare eam, et depositum custodire."[1] Acts is the record of the progress of the Word of God which brings salvation. The spread of the gospel to the ends of the earth marks the culmination of what Jesus began to do and teach. The pattern of the beginning is definitive for the church in Luke's day, and Bengel's, and ours. Naturally, the work of Luke is not adequate on its own; providentially, it is part of the New Testament, all of which is needed to make men wise unto salvation. This is not surprising, for its purpose is limited, and to no one man is it given to express the fulness of the gospel. But the work of Luke remains the centre of the New Testament, spanning the Gospels and the Epistles and joining them together in one whole. Consequently, our final estimate of Luke is a positive one. He is not the initiator of a decline from the early Christian message of Paul; he is his worthy follower.[2]

[1] J. A. Bengel, *Gnomon Novi Testamenti* (1734), Stuttgart, 1860, p. 522. ("The victory of the Word of God. Paul at Rome, the culmination of the gospel, the conclusion of Acts . . . It began at Jerusalem: it finishes at Rome. Here, O church, you have your pattern. It is your duty to preserve it and to guard it.")

[2] On Luke's purpose see also R. P. Martin, *New Testament Foundations*, Grand Rapids, Exeter, 1975, Vol. 1, pp. 244–250.

LUCAN STUDIES SINCE 1979

S INCE THIS BOOK WAS FIRST PUBLISHED IN 1970 AND REPRINTED WITH some updating of bibliographical information in 1979, the stream of Lucan scholarship has become a torrent. A brief annotated guide may help readers to find their way amid the maze of publications on some major aspects of the work of Luke.[1]

Introductions, Surveys and Commentaries

N. Richardson and D. Juel offer panoramic views of Luke–Acts which can be strongly commended as typical middle-of-the-road introductions to the modern approach.[2] Richardson provides an introduction to Luke–Acts rather than to Lucan scholarship, while Juel is more concerned to commend a particular line of understanding of Luke's theology of Israel and the Gentiles. Probably the best short introduction to contemporary discussion of Luke–Acts is the section on "The Current State of Lucan Studies" in J. A. Fitzmyer's commentary.[3] At greater length R. J. Maddox's book on the purpose of Luke–Acts is valuable among other things for providing a first-rate introduction to the problems currently at issue.[4]

For the scholar the indispensable guide to Lucan scholarship continues to be the comprehensive survey of works on *Luke the Theologian* by F. Bovon who summarizes under appropriate thematic headings research between 1950 and 1975. The recent appearance of an English translation with some updating makes it available to a wider group of readers.[5] Bovon's work is of especial value because it offers a *critical* survey of scholarship. Yet its usefulness is to some extent

---

[1] I am grateful to Mr M. J. Robertson and to Dr. D. Wenham for permission to incorporate here in an altered form material which is to appear in future issues of *The New Testament Student* and *Themelios* respectively.

[2] N. Richardson, *The Panorama of Luke*, 1982. D. Juel, *Luke–Acts*, 1984.

[3] J. A. Fitzmyer, *The Gospel according to Luke I–IX* and *The Gospel according to Luke X–XXIV*, The Anchor Bible. New York, 1981; 1985, I, 3–34.

[4] R. J. Maddox, *The Purpose of Luke–Acts*, Edinburgh, 1982.

[5] F. Bovon, *Luke the Theologian: Thirty-three years of research (1950–1983)*, Allison Park, 1987.

limited by the fact that the author deliberately restricts his attention to Luke as a theologian and does not consider literary and historical questions. This is a justifiable limitation because the exploration of Luke's work as a theologian remains the major preoccupation of contemporary scholarship.[6]

The fruits of recent study of the Gospel are summarized in the invaluable two-volume contribution by J. A. Fitzmyer to *The Anchor Bible*. This is a detailed and comprehensive, but readable and lucid work, and users of it will not need to spend much time on other aids to study. Fitzmyer's own position is a moderately critical one; he gives good coverage to the variety of views on every topic, and his judgments are generally well-founded.[7]

C. H. Talbert draws out the structure and theology of Luke in broad lines and demonstrates abundantly the importance of structure for understanding the whole.[8] The same approach is adopted by D. Gooding in his recent exposition; this is an interesting work which combines a traditional type of evangelical application of the text with a carefully wrought rhetorical analysis that searches for parallels between different incidents and pieces of teaching and shows how Luke develops the impression which he wishes to give of Jesus.[9]

To appreciate the significance of this approach as it is seen by its advocates, we can do no better than summarize Talbert's review of Fitzmyer in which he argues that 1974 constituted a watershed in Lucan studies and that Fitzmyer's work is a throwback to the past: (1). His approach is atomistic, looking at short pericopes rather than larger thought-units; (2). He studies the text by comparing it with its sources instead of reading the text as a finished product using "rhetorical criticism or modern narrative criticism"; (3). He looks for a history of the tradition used in the Gospel instead of looking for the message of the text in its canonical form; (4). He dialogues with H. Conzelmann and his colleagues and has the better of the debate, but he works within the same frame of reference instead of dialoguing with Greco–Roman literature and modern literary criticism. Talbert thus sees Fitzmyer as gathering up the scholarship of a previous generation and

---

6 Other survey-type material is to be found in C. H. Talbert, "Shifting Sands: the Recent Study of the Gospel of Luke", *Interpretation* 30, 1976, 381–95; M. Rese, "Neuere Lukas–Arbeiten', *Theologische Literaturzeitung* 106, 1981, 225–236; E. Grässer, "Die Apostelgeschichte in der Forschung der Gegenwart", Th.R nf 26, 1960, 93–167; "Acta–Forschung seit 1960", *ibid* nf 41, 1976, 141–194, 259–290; 42, 1977, 1–68; E. Plümacher, "Acta–Forschung 1974–1982", *ibid*. nf 48, 1983, 1–56; 49, 1984, 105–169.

7 On an even larger scale R. E. Brown offers what is in effect a commentary on Lk. 1–2 in *The Birth of the Messiah*, 1977.

8 C. H. Talbert, *Reading Luke*, New York, 1982.

9 D. Gooding, *According to Luke*, Leicester, 1987.

himself as representing a "new approach".[10] But it is surely the case that both approaches will continue to be necessary.[11]

As for the Book of Acts, English-speaking readers now have the opportunity to use H. Conzelmann's commentary in translation.[12] More succinct than Haenchen's commentary, it does not have a lot to offer which cannot be found in the earlier work. The two complementary volumes by F. F. Bruce, which represent British conservative scholarship at its best but which were written too soon to take the position of Haenchen and Conzelmann into account, have now been revised.[13] The other major recent commentaries on Acts are in German, and here there is an embarrassment of riches.[14]

Luke as Historian

The question of the historicity of Acts (and, by implication, of the Gospel) has been reopened in the last decade. On general grounds M. Hengel has argued forcibly that "Luke is no less trustworthy than other historians of antiquity."[15]

[10] C. H. Talbert, review in CBQ 48, 1986, 336–8. For Talbert's own work in this direction see his *Literary Patterns, Theological Themes and the Genre of Luke–Acts*, Missoula, 1974. The new approach of "narrative study" is represented by R. C. Tannehill, *The Narrative Unity of Luke–Acts. A Literary Interpretation*, of which *Volume 1: The Gospel according to Luke* has appeared (Philadelphia, 1986). I must confess that I am not sure what Tannehill has to say that is really new compared with practitioners of more traditional approaches.

[11] E. Schweizer's work (*The Good News according to Luke*, 1984) is part of his trilogy on the synoptic Gospels and unfortunately does not give sufficient attention to passages with parallels in Mt. and Mk. I have a considerable affection for Fred Danker's exposition which brings out, as no other work does, the radical call to discipleship in the Gospel (*Jesus and the New Age*, St. Louis, 1972).

Commentaries in German include J. Ernst, *Das Evangelium nach Lukas*, Regensburger Neues Testament. Regensburg, 1977, probably the best and fullest commentary that requires no knowledge of Greek; the somewhat radical work of W. Schmithals, *Das Evangelium nach Lukas*, Zürcher Bibelkommentare. Zürich, 1980; and the two-volume commentary by G. Schneider, *Das Evangelium nach Lukas*, Ökumenischer Taschenbuchkommentar zum NT. Gütersloh/Würzburg, 1977.

[12] H. Conzelmann, *Acts of the Apostles*. Hermeneia. Philadelphia, 1987.

[13] F. F. Bruce, *The Acts of the Apostles*. New International Commentary. Grand Rapids, 1988; *The Acts of the Apostles*, Leicester (forthcoming). D. J. Wiliams gives a very full, detailed exposition presented at a popular level (*Acts*, Good News Commentaries, San Francisco, 1985).

[14] In German G. Schneider offers a massive two-volume work, *Die Apostelgeschichte*, Herders theologischer Kommentar zum NT. Freiburg, 1980; 1982; this is a valuable reference work but fails to bring out the message of Acts. The shorter, but still lengthy two-volume work by A. Weiser, *Die Apostelgeschichte*, Ökumenischer Taschenbuchkommentar. Gütersloh/Würzburg, 1981; 1985, offers a sharply critical study of Acts. J. Roloff, *Die Apostelgeschichte*, Das NT Deutsch. Göttingen, 1981, gives an incisive and stimulating commentary. H.-W. Neudorfer, *Apostelgeschichte* 1. Teil, EDITION C-Bibel-Kommentar. Neuhausern-Stuttgart, 1986 does for German readers what D. J. Williams does for English. Another recent work is R. Pesch, *Die Apostelgeschichte*. Evangelisch-Katholischer Kommentar zum NT. Zürich/Neukirchen. 2 Vols. 1986, which in common with other works in the series emphasizes the theological message of the book and its *Wirkungsgeschichte*.

[15] M. Hengel, *Acts and the History of Earliest Christianity* 1979, 60. See further his *Between Jesus and Paul* 1983.

The brevity of Hengel's remarks have left him rather open to criticism. The case for finding reliable history in Acts needs to be advanced on the basis of more detailed arguments. On the German scene it is significant that Hengel's lead has been followed by G. Lüdemann who criticizes the general lack of interest in the matter and offers a detailed historical commentary on Acts. Two questions must be carefully distinguished at this point. The one is concerned with the reliability of the traditions which underlie Acts, and the other is concerned with the qualities of Luke himself as a historical writer. Lüdemann is concerned with the first of these questions. His method is to separate the redactional work of the author of Acts from the traditions which he has utilized and then to assess the historical value of the latter. He claims to find a remarkable amount of reliable tradition in Acts, but he takes it for granted that the speeches ascribed to the various actors are one and all Lucan compositions; he dismisses accounts of the miraculous with such statements as "People lame from childhood onwards are (regrettably) incurable"; and he advocates a chronology of the early church which is seriously at odds with that of Luke. Despite the sanguine tone of the postscript to his study, Lüdemann's chronology is one which has by no means won the general approval of scholars, and it seems fair to say that, if a different chronology were to be accepted, Luke himself would emerge from the examination with a higher claim to credibility.[16]

The case for regarding Luke himself as a careful and reliable historian has rested mainly with F. F. Bruce and C. J. Hemer. In a series of essays Hemer has produced archaeological backing for the historicity of small details in the narrative. His approach is summed up in his essay on "Luke the Historian", in which he gives the outline of a case for seeing Luke not only as the user of reliable traditions but also as himself a careful historian who stands alongside the best of ancient historians. At the time of his much-lamented early death (June, 1987) Hemer had all but completed a full-scale study of the historical character of Acts.[17] It is not too much to say that the case for

---

[16] G. Lüdemann, *Das frühe Christentum nach den Traditionen der Apostelgeschichte: ein Kommentar,* Göttingen, 1987 (Eng. Tr. *Early Christianity according to the Traditions in Acts,* Forthcoming 1989); *Paul. Apostle to the Gentiles. Studies in Chronology,* 1983.

[17] F. F. Bruce, "The Acts of the Apostles: Historical Record or Theological Reconstruction?", in H. Temporini and W. Haase, *Aufstieg und Niedergang der Römischen Welt* II.25.3, Berlin, 1985, 2569–2603. C. J. Hemer, "Luke the Historian", BJRL 60, 1977–8, 28–51; "Paul at Athens. A Topographical Note", NTS 20, 1973–74, 341–350; "Euraquilo and Melita", JTS n.s. 26, 1975, 100–111; "Alexandria Troas", Tyn.B. 26, 1975, 79–112; "The Adjective 'Phrygia' ", JTS n.s. 27, 1976, 122–6; "Phrygia: A Further Note", JTS n.s. 28, 1977, 99–101; "Observations on Pauline Chronology", in D. A. Hagner and M. J. Harris (ed.), *Pauline Studies,* Exeter, 1980, 3–18. Hemer's MS is currently being prepared for publication.

regarding Acts as a reliable account of the rise of the early church is considerably stronger today than it was in 1970.

Luke as Theologian

The major interest of scholarship remains, as before, in Luke the theologian. J. A. Fitzmyer gives a full-length discussion of Luke's theology with a thematic bibliography in his commentary[18], and there is a briefer but very readable account by R. F. O'Toole.[19] O'Toole rightly identifies the central theme of Luke–Acts as the way in which God continues to bring salvation to his people, and he expounds this topic simply and clearly.

An important basic question is the general character and aim of Luke–Acts. Two important discussions attempt to pinpoint the situation which gave rise to Luke's work.

The first is Robert Maddox's book, *The Purpose of Luke–Acts.*[20] Maddox identifies four main themes in the work. First, Luke is interested in the relation of the church to the Judaism from which it was now separated. He shows a pro-Judaean orientation; he even depicts Paul as a Pharisee, but this is with respect to his Pharisaic eschatology and not in respect of his keeping the law. Yet Luke also shows how the Jewish leaders have rejected the Messiah, and in general the Jewish community shares this attitude and stands under judgment. In this situation Christians must remain loyal towards Jewish traditions, even though the Jews have rejected their gospel. Second, Luke is interested in the figure of Paul, especially in the period of his imprisonment to which he devotes more space than his missionary travels. Luke says little about Paul's theology but depicts him as the greatest Christian missionary and leader. Yet he is not regarded as an apostle. He is distinguished in time and function from the apostles as a "bridge-figure" who has acted blamelessly towards the Jews and Romans, who has endured suffering and (it is implied) martyrdom, and who has remained confident in God. Third, Maddox shows briefly that with regard to the Roman Empire Luke was not writing a political apology but rather was telling Christians to live at peace with the state and not to play the hero. Finally, Maddox tackles Luke's eschatology at some length, and shows convincingly that, while Luke retained the hope of an imminent consummation (within

18 Op. cit., I, 143–270.
19 R. F. O'Toole, *The Unity of Luke's Theology: An Analysis of Luke–Acts*, Wilmington, Delaware, 1984.
20 R. J. Maddox, op. cit., 100–157.

the lifetime of some of Jesus' contemporaries), his emphasis lay on the present fulfilment of eschatology in the ministry of Jesus.

Out of all this Maddox claims that Luke had two main interests, ecclesiology and eschatology. In plain English, Luke wanted to persuade his Christian readers that they really did enjoy salvation, even if the attitude of the Jews might make them feel that they were excluded from salvation; in fact salvation had already come in Jesus and was being experienced within the church as a present fulfilment of God's ancient promises to Israel. Thus Luke aimed to give his readers certainty about the story of those events which had been "fulfilled" in their midst.

Much of the value of Maddox's work lies in its refutation of false and inadequate theories about Luke's purpose, such as that his main motivation was to deal with the crisis caused by the alleged delay in the parousia or that he understood the church in an "early catholic" fashion. He also rightly shows that not everything in Luke–Acts arises from a desire to address the readers directly, so that we must see their situation directly mirrored in every incident—this is the trap into which the next scholar we shall consider tends to fall. Rather, says Maddox, Luke was recounting history, even if lessons were meant to be drawn from it.

In effect Maddox is refining the well-known view of W. C. van Unnik, that Luke is concerned to show how the salvation brought by Jesus is made available after his death and resurrection to people everywhere. But he sharpens this somewhat. "He writes to reassure the Christians of his day that their faith in Jesus is no aberration, but the authentic goal towards which God's ancient dealings with Israel were driving. The full stream of God's saving action in history had not passed them by, but has flowed straight into their community-life, in Jesus and the Holy Spirit. If there are apostates and heretics who have cut themselves off from participation in the Kingdom of God, it is not the Christians to whom such terms apply. It is Jesus, their Lord, in whom the promises of the ancient scriptures are fulfilled; it is Jesus who sends the Holy Spirit, whose powerful influence the Christians actually experience; and it is Jesus alone through whose name salvation occurs".[21]

What Maddox has done is to see the purpose of Luke–Acts in terms of the self-legitimation of Luke's audience, enabling them to hold their heads high despite Jewish claims that they are the true Israel. Yet, on Maddox's view that Luke wrote after AD 70 when the temple and

---

[21] Op. cit., 187. For van Unnik's essay see above, 93.

LUCAN STUDIES SINCE 1979

LUCAN STUDIES SINCE 1979   229

Jerusalem were destroyed, it is difficult to see why the Christians needed so much reassurance on the matter.

This same thought of legitimation inspires the work of P. F. Esler, whose work shows what can be achieved when a barrister turns his attention to the NT using a social-scientific approach.[22] On the basis that Luke–Acts was written c. AD 90 to a very mixed Christian community in a Hellenistic city, Esler argues that its purpose was to help the members to legitimate themselves by a reinterpretation of existing traditions which would provide an appropriate "symbolic universe".

Esler looks at three main areas. First, he depicts the wide gap between rich and poor in the ancient world. Both groups were to be found in Luke's church, but our middle-class bias has prevented us from appreciating how revolutionary was Luke's concern for the poor and his insistence that the rich must work to eliminate injustice and alleviate the needs of the poor. Here Luke's message is exhortatory to the rich as well as legitimatory to the poor.

Second Esler argues—less convincingly—that Luke also writes for Roman Christians in his church. He rejects the idea that Luke is engaged in offering apologetic for the Roman state to the church, although he does argue that Luke presents Roman courts as being fair—despite Pilate, Felix and Festus who represent the *de facto* situation. Rather he wants to show by means of appropriate historical examples that being a Christian is not incompatible with allegiance to Rome.

The third and central topic is the Jew–Gentile problem. This is discussed with relation to table-fellowship, the law and the temple.

The most important issue is the question of table-fellowship. Esler argues that Jews did not eat with Gentiles at this period, but that this practice existed in Luke's church. He legitimated it by a thorough rewriting of early Christian history. Thus the real point of the Cornelius incident for Luke is that Peter ate with Gentiles—contrary to the historical facts. The council in Acts 15 is also to be seen as legitimating table-fellowship by means of the fourfold decree, but once again Luke has presented an unhistorical picture, since in fact it was James and Peter who represented the unchanging attitude of the church in Jerusalem in attacking the growth of the practice of table-fellowship in Antioch and elsewhere.

Luke shows an inconsistent attitude to the law; he wants to show that Christians were faithful to the law, but runs up against the hard

---

[22] P. F. Esler, *Community and Gospel in Luke–Acts. The Social and Political Motivations of Lucan Theology*, Cambridge, 1987.

facts of history. He lands in this situation because he is trying to help Jewish Christians who are attacked by Jews to meet the charge that Christianity and Judaism are incompatible.

Luke's attitude to the temple arises out of the ambivalence within his community. As Esler sees it, the Hellenists (who included some Gentiles) saw the temple as being closed to Gentiles; feeling marginalized from Judaism, they developed an anti-temple theology which was at odds with that of the Hebrews and led to a growing separation between Jerusalem Christians. Luke does his best to cover up this split. But he does claim that the worship of the temple has now been replaced, although he can trade on the affectionate memories of the temple on the part of Jewish Christians to set his Gospel more closely to it and to Jewish ancestral traditions.

Esler's thesis is thus that Luke wrote a work to help the community to legitimate itself over against Judaism. But he did this by taking liberties with the history and rewriting the story of Christian origins to show how the Gentiles were accepted into the church and admitted to table-fellowship, and by showing how Roman Christians need not feel disloyal to the state if they live as Christians.

Esler is aware of the danger of asserting that Luke's main objective was to "legitimate" Christianity to his Christian contemporaries. In fact his thesis is concerned with only some aspects of Luke's theology, and it would be wrong to insist that what is characteristic of Luke is entirely due to his social and political motivations.

Esler is methodologically correct to argue from apparent historical problems to the thesis that Luke was motivated by community concerns rather than to claim that Luke was motivated by the latter and that therefore his historical account must be biased or even falsified. However, his specific arguments for historical falsification are unconvincing.[23]

Neither Maddox nor Esler has provided a completely convincing setting for Luke–Acts. We may not wish, however, to be quite as negative as R. F. O'Toole who asserts: "All attempts to tie Luke–Acts to one community and to its concerns have failed."[24] But there may still be some value in trying to identify a more general situation. In this connection the prologue to Lk. has been particularly studied, since it is obvious that a writer's own statement of his purpose should be the starting point for enquiry. The view expressed there that Luke wrote to provide confirmation for Christians like Theophilus of the truth of the Christian message which they have heard or read should be

23 G. Lüdemann, *Das frühe Christentum*, 130–9.
24 Op. cit., 13.

accepted as the basis for more detailed elaboration. Luke writes to tell again the story of Jesus, based on the accounts of "eyewitnesses and ministers of the word", to substantiate what was taught about Jesus in the preaching and teaching heard by Theophilus; he narrates the story of the foundational period of the early church to show how the mission took place in accordance with prophecy and at the direction of the Lord, and to confirm that the establishment of the church of believers both Jewish and Gentile was part of the divine plan; thus he demonstrates that the gospel really does bring salvation. The story is obviously incomplete in that it is concerned with the church's mission and says next to nothing about the kind of inner-church problems reflected in the Pauline correspondence and other NT writings.[25]

One of the major areas of contemporary discussion is the relative place of the Jews and the Gentiles in Luke's theology. Nobody doubts now that this topic is of central importance in Luke's thought. This has been shown by J. Dupont who has demonstrated very effectively that it is a conscious aim of Luke to show how the conversion of the Gentiles and their incorporation into the people of God is in line with OT prophecy.[26]

But the question whether Luke essentially sees the Gentiles as being brought into an existing Israel which for its part keeps the law or whether he regards the church as the new Israel composed of believing Jews and Gentiles remains a question of debate. J. Jervell denied that Luke thought of a new Israel.[27] S. G. Wilson claimed that Luke had no carefully thought out theology of the Gentiles and held that he took a pragmatic approach to this (and other) problems.[28] In a more recent work Wilson argues that Luke's position on the law is not completely clear or consistent; basically he seems to say that it is natural enough for Jewish Christians to continue to keep the law, but Gentiles do not need to do so although they are in some way bound by Mosaic principles.[29] These conclusions are convincingly challenged by C. L. Blomberg and M. M. B. Turner who see in Acts the slowly developing recognition of the implications of the new covenant.[30]

At the opposite pole from Jervell stands J. T. Sanders who in a

[25] I. H. Marshall, "Luke and his 'Gospel' ", in P. Stuhlmacher, ed., *Das Evangelium und die Evangelien*, Tübingen, 1983, 289–308.

[26] J. Dupont, *The Salvation of the Gentiles: Essays on the Acts of the Apostles*, New York, 1979.

[27] J. Jervell, *Luke and the People of God: A New Look at Luke–Acts*, Minneapolis, 1972.

[28] S. G. Wilson, *The Gentiles and the Gentile Mission in Luke–Acts*, Cambridge, 1973.

[29] S. G. Wilson, *Luke and the Law*, Cambridge, 1983.

[30] C. L. Blomberg, "The Law in Luke–Acts", *Journal for the Study of the New Testament* 22, 1984, 53–80, on which see F. G. Downing, "Freedom from the Law in Luke–Acts", *ibid.* 26, 1986, 49–52; M. M. B. Turner, "The Sabbath, Sunday and the Law in Luke–Acts", in D. A. Carson, ed., *From Sabbath to Lord's Day: A Biblical, Historical and Theological Investigation*, Grand Rapids, 1982, 99–157.

thoroughly researched and meticulously detailed book argues that Luke is guilty of a sustained and bitter polemic against the unbelieving Jews and against Christian Jews for their opposition to the inclusion of Gentiles in the church: "In Luke's opinion, the world will be much better off when 'the Jews' get what they deserve and the world is rid of them."[31] Luke had "a fundamental and systematic hostility" (the word is not too strong!) towards the Jews in general because they crucified Jesus and opposed the church, and he must be regarded as a virulent antisemitist.

Sanders claims that Luke has sharpened the picture of the hostility of the Jewish leaders to Jesus which he found in his sources; in particular, Luke gives the impression that the Jews themselves crucify Jesus and not the Romans (Lk. 23:25 f.). Similarly, in Acts, nearly all hostility to the church comes from the Jews. Jerusalem is uniformly hostile to Jesus, and so God's judgment is declared against it. Sanders' case with regard to the Jewish people rests on a distinction which he makes between the picture of them in the speeches and in the narrative. In the discourse material there is a blanket rejection of "the Jews", but in the narrative there is a development in their attitude to Jesus and the Christians from initial favour to total rejection. Correspondingly, the emphasis is increasingly on the way in which the offer of the gospel is withdrawn from them; it is presented to them only in order that their rejection of it may be registered, until eventually the final rejection of the Jews and the end of any mission to them is signalled in Acts 28.

Luke presents the Pharisees as more friendly to Jesus and the church than do other writers. Yet they are guilty of legalism and hypocrisy. He uses them in the Gospel as a "type" of the Jewish Christians of his own day in the church who were similarly hypocritical in insisting that Gentile Christians should keep the ritual of the law. Luke himself argued that Gentiles should not keep the whole Jewish law but rather only those specific enactments laid down by God for them in Lev. 17–18.

Sanders raises the question of Luke's motives in presenting the story of the Jews and Christianity in such an admittedly tendentious fashion, making full use of what has been called his "gift of invention" ("Luke dislikes the Pharisees enough to slander them"). He denies that there was sufficient actual persecution of Christians by Jews to justify Luke's attacks, and finds the solution in Jewish opposition to Christianity from outside and Jewish–Christian opposition to Gentiles within the church.

31 J. T. Sanders, The Jews in Luke–Acts 1987, 317.

Although Sanders professes to be carrying out a historical enquiry, he does not consider sufficiently how far the attitudes of which he accuses Luke were already prevalent at an earlier date. For example, he cites various Q sayings in Lk. as evidence of the Evangelist's position without taking sufficiently into account that the attitudes he castigates were present in Q and, as I would claim, in Jesus. He is all too ready to regard the picture of the growth of Jewish hostility to Christians as Luke's literary scheme and to ignore the question whether it is not in fact a reliable historical reflection of the situation. Insufficient consideration is given to the development of strongly nationalist and hence anti-Gentile attitudes during the run-up to the Jewish war. In short, Sanders does not take sufficiently seriously the fact that Luke may well be describing the kind of situation that actually existed in the pre-AD 70 period when there was Jewish hostility to the church and Christians lived in fear of it.

The use of strong language was not unknown among other first-century Christians; Paul can say sharp words against the people he regarded as his opponents—and with specific reference to the Jews in 1 Thes. 2:14–16! The question then becomes one (as Sanders would doubtless agree) of the general Christian attitude in the first century. Were Christians justified in lumping together "the Jews" or "the Jewish leaders" or "the Pharisees" and making blanket statements of condemnation against them? Part of the situation is certainly that Christians did believe that rejection of Jesus as the Messiah cut off the Jews from belonging to the people of God (and prevented Gentiles from entry). They, therefore, saw no future for "the Jews" *as God's people* and claimed that they themselves constituted the new Israel. But, as Sanders must agree, the door was never closed to individual Jews to accept the Messiah. One must ask, then, whether Sanders confuses the theological judgment that "the Jews" are no longer the Israel of God with antisemitism. If Luke says that Jews who reject the gospel thereby side with the members of the sanhedrin who condemned Jesus to death, is that "hostility" to the Jews? No doubt too, one should take into account the ways in which the Jewish opposition to Christians was expressed; what we may loosely call "anti-Gentilism" existed, and in that context some kind of Christian response was inevitable, possibly expressed more sharply than would be considered appropriate in the twentieth century.

Older writers drew attention to Luke's concern for the outcasts of society. The current trend is to explore his attitudes to the problems of the poor and politics. J. D. Yoder is responsible for popularizing the hypothesis that in Luke 4:16–30 Jesus was proclaiming a "year of jubilee" with social and economic as well as spiritual consequences.[32] An exegetical foundation for this hypothesis is offered by R. B. Sloan who stresses that the jubilee concept is *primarily* religious; but while the presence of the motif cannot be doubted, my feeling is that it is much less prominent and decisive in Lk. than Sloan suggests.[33] The view that Jesus adopted a revolutionary political stance is developed on a popular level by R. J. Cassidy, but again, while the social concern of Jesus is rightly expounded, it is a far cry from concern to social and political activism aimed at some kind of political revolution.[34] From Luke's emphasis on loving and forgiving one's enemies J. M. Ford draws out implications for nonviolence today, although her argument that Jesus acted contrary to the expectations expressed in Lk. 1–2 and in the preaching of the Baptist is unconvincing.[35]

The specific question of Luke's teaching on poverty and riches has attracted numerous studies. We may mention the work of L. T. Johnson who argues that possessions have a symbolical function in Luke, of W. E. Pilgrim, who offers a well-balanced and readable exposition of the Lucan material and stresses how Luke is warning the wealthy Christians of his day of the danger in which they find themselves, and of D. P. Seccombe who offers a scholarly dissertation on the topic in which he refutes ideas that Luke sees poverty as an ideal or encourages asceticism for its own sake.[36]

Finally, one or two contributions on christology and pneumatology may be noted. The importance of the Old Testament for Luke's christology is the theme of a dissertation by D. L. Bock in which he argues that Luke presents a unified portrait of Jesus as "Messiah–Servant" who is seen, as the story progresses, to be a "more than Messiah" figure in that he is the Lord. This offers a corrective to an over-stress on the prophetic elements in Luke's picture.[37]

The lack of reference in Acts to the death of Jesus as a means of atonement or as a sacrifice for sins has led to the suggestion that Luke does not see it as a saving event in the manner of, say, Paul.[38] The

[32] J. D. Yoder, *The Politics of Jesus*, Grand Rapids, 1972.

[33] R. B. Sloan, Jr., *The Favorable Year of the Lord: A Study of Jubilary Theology in the Gospel of Luke*, Austin, Texas, 1977.

[34] R. J. Cassidy, *Jesus, Politics and Society: A Study of Luke's Gospel*, Maryknoll, New York, 1978. For the continuing discussion see R. J. Cassidy and P. J. Scharper, ed., *Political Issues in Luke–Acts*, Maryknoll, New York, 1983.

[35] J. M. Ford, *My Enemy is my Guest: Jesus and Violence in Luke*, Maryknoll, New York, 1984.

[36] L. T. Johnson, *The Literary Function of Possession in Luke–Acts*, Missoula, 1977; W. E. Pilgrim, *Good News to the Poor*, Minneapolis, 1981; D. P. Seccombe, *Possessions and the Poor in Luke–Acts*, Linz, 1983.

[37] D. L. Bock, *Proclamation from Prophecy and Pattern*, Sheffield, 1987.

[38] W. E. Pilgrim, *The Death of Christ in Lukan Soteriology*, unpublished doctoral dissertation, Princeton, 1971.

discussion of this topic has been conducted mainly in German.[39] But, whatever be the final verdict on this point, C. K. Barrett has rightly shown how Luke has a clear *theologia crucis* as his own practical equivalent to Paul's doctrine of dying with Christ.[40]

Luke's understanding of the Spirit has been taken up by J. D. G. Dunn[41] who stressed the enthusiastic, charismatic nature of the church's beginnings, as presented somewhat onesidedly by Luke, and who argued that the Spirit functions as the sign of the new age in Jesus whose experience is paradigmatic for the church. Various aspects of this thesis have been challenged by M. M. B. Turner who interprets the Spirit in Jesus as the Spirit of prophecy rather than the sign of the new age.[42] Discussion continues on whether Luke understands the Spirit in Acts as the gift of salvation (as in Paul) or as the prophetic equipping of the church for its mission.

Conclusion

It emerges that the twin issues which occupied us in the major part of this book continue to be alive in Lucan study. The question of Luke as a historian has received new life and today there are more voices urging that he was concerned to write history and that by the standards of his time he was successful in doing so, even if there is continuing doubt over the extent to which he was successful. But it is the nature of Luke's theology which continues to claim most attention. Study of the sociological and other situational factors which helped to shape it has proved fascinating and profitable to several scholars. It is clear that there is still room for more work to be done.

---

39 A. Büchele, *Der Tod Jesu im Lukasevangelium: eine redaktions-geschichtliche Untersuchung zu Lk 23*, Frankfurt, 1978, concludes that Luke presents Jesus as the suffering Righteous One and Prophet; his death shows his closeness to the Father and his forgiving love, and under its impact people like the dying thief come to penitence and conversion. R. Glöckner, *Die Verkündigung des Heils beim Evangelisten Lukas*, Mainz, 1975, sees Jesus more as a martyr and example but also as the One in whom the Spirit is active and who acts as the agent of God.

40 C. K. Barrett, "Theologia Crucis—in Acts?", in C. Andresen and G. Klein, *Theologia Crucis—Signum Crucis: Festschrift für Erich Dinkler*, Tübingen, 1979, 73–84.

41 J. D. G. Dunn, *Jesus and the Spirit*, 1975; see also his *Baptism in the Holy Spirit* 1970.

42 M. M. B. Turner, *Luke and the Spirit: Studies in the Significance of Receiving the Spirit in Luke–Acts*, unpublished doctoral dissertation, Cambridge, 1980; "Jesus and the Spirit in Lucan Perspective", Tyn.B 32, 1981, 3–42.

INDEX OF SUBJECTS

INDEX OF AUTHORS

INDEX OF REFERENCES

DATE DUE